The Right and Labor in America

POLITICS AND CULTURE IN MODERN AMERICA

Series Editors: Margot Canaday, Glenda Gilmore, Michael Kazin, and Thomas J. Sugrue

Volumes in the series narrate and analyze political and social change in the broadest dimensions from 1865 to the present, including ideas about the ways people have sought and wielded power in the public sphere and the language and institutions of politics at all levels—local, national, and transnational. The series is motivated by a desire to reverse the fragmentation of modern U.S. history and to encourage synthetic perspectives on social movements and the state, on gender, race, and labor, and on intellectual history and popular culture.

The Right and Labor in America

Politics, Ideology, and Imagination

Edited by
Nelson Lichtenstein
and
Elizabeth Tandy Shermer

UNIVERSITY OF PENNSYLVANIA PRESS

PHILADELPHIA

Published by
University of Pennsylvania Press
Philadelphia, Pennsylvania 19104-4112
www.upenn.edu/pennpress

Printed in the United States of America on acid-free paper
10 9 8 7 6 5 4 3 2 1

Library of Congress Cataloging-in-Publication Data

The right and labor in America : politics, ideology, and
imagination / edited by Nelson Lichtenstein and Elizabeth
Tandy Shermer.—1st ed.
        p.   cm.— (Politics and culture in modern America)
    Includes bibliographical references and index.
    ISBN 978-0-8122-4414-4 (hardcover : alk. paper)
    1. Labor unions—United States—History—20th century.
2. Labor unions—United States—History—21st century.
3. Labor disputes—United States—History—20th century.
4. Labor disputes—United States—History—21st century.
5. Labor policy—United States—History—20th century.
6. Labor policy—United States—History—21st century.
7. Conservatism—United States—History—20th century.
8. Conservatism—United States—History—21st century.
I. Lichtenstein, Nelson.   II. Shermer, Elizabeth Tandy.
III. Series: Politics and culture in modern America.
HD6508.R525   2012
331.880973—dc23   2011049649

Contents

Preface

In the years since the publication of this book, two seemingly contradictory phenomena have framed the way many Americans think about working people and the institutions that once represented their interests. Today, virtually all politicians and pundits, even those decidedly on the right, think income inequality a serious and pressing problem in the United States. Even as economists declared the country in recovery from the Great Recession, family incomes remained stagnant in the face of rising productivity. That alarmed Mortimer Zuckerman, the influential and opinionated conservative who runs a media empire in New York. He editorialized that American workers are finding that the "mismatch between reward and effort makes a mockery of the American dream."[1] Republican Jeb Bush agreed. "If you're born poor today, you're more likely to stay poor," Bush told conservatives at a 2015 meeting of *National Review* staffers and supporters. "While the last eight years have been pretty good ones for top earners," announced his presidential campaign web site, "they've been a lost decade for the rest of America."[2]

As a consequence, the movement to boost the minimum wage, even to $15 an hour, has gained remarkable traction, if not in the Republican-controlled Congress, then certainly outside Capitol Hill. Many big cities on the West Coast, in the upper Midwest, and along the Northeastern corridor have all passed ordinances that roll out incremental minimum-wage increases. Some laws will raise hourly pay by more than 30 percent within just a few years. A handful of cities and states have even sought to intervene within the workplace itself by mandating sick leave for employees and prohibiting managers from scheduling work in an unpredictable fashion.

Some big firms, including Starbucks, Wal-Mart, Home Depot, Whole Foods, and Costco, have followed along. CEOs have publicly pledged at least modest pay raises and more predicable hours of work. Indeed, in a *New York Times* opinion piece, "Capitalists, Arise: We Need to Deal with Income Inequality," former advertising executive Peter Georgescu spoke for at least a slice of the 1 percent when he posed the choice before them: raise wages now, or face either "major social unrest" or the kind of high taxes advocated by the French economist Thomas Piketty, author of the bestseller *Capital in the Twenty-First Century*.[3]

Of course, neither minimum wage campaigns nor corporate hand-wringing have opened the door to a revival of trade unionism in the United States. Depression-era policymakers once emphasized that collective bargaining was the lever by which working-class wages might be pushed higher. But even after 2008, when for a brief moment there was much talk of a new New Deal, the very idea of trade unionism came under unrelenting attack, often along the same well-trod avenues outlined in our book.

For example, hostility to private sector trade unionism remains deeply embedded within the American South's political culture. This anti-unionism dominated headlines in recent years, when "Yankee" trade unionists sought to organize two large industrial facilities, one in South Carolina and the other in Tennessee. In both instances conservative politicians spearheaded the anti-union charge, even more so than the companies themselves.

That hostility surprised the United Automobile Workers. Until the end of 2013, organizers were confident that they could persuade most workers at Volkswagen's new assembly plant in Chattanooga to vote for the union in an NLRB supervised election. Top VW management, in Germany and in the United States, wanted a union in their Tennessee factory because they expected to put in place a "works council," similar to those established in every VW factory in the world, save those in China and Russia. VW managers thought participatory councils enhanced shop productivity. They also knew that IG Metal, the powerful German union, held ten seats on the VW board and strongly advocated for such shop-floor representation.[4]

So, unlike many other European firms with manufacturing operations in the American South, VW did not oppose the UAW organizing effort. Instead, a phalanx of conservative political strategists and politicians declared war on organizers. For example, Grover Norquist's anti-union Americans for Tax Reform bankrolled a faction of plant employees, who demonized the UAW's Detroit roots. Even more important, Republican politicians like Tennessee Governor Bill Haslam and U.S. Senator Bob Corker, the former mayor of Chattanooga, in effect blackmailed VW workers by threatening to cancel or withhold state tax abatements and other incentives designed to help VW expand the plant.[5] Their intense opposition arose out of a GOP fear that a unionized "transplant" would soon transform the political and economic landscape. Corker thought that if VW workers were able to unionize, "Then it's BMW, then it's Mercedes, then it's Nissan."[6]

Amidst all this fear-mongering, the UAW lost the closely contested 2014 NLRB election. However, the potential for unionism at the VW Chattanooga facility has not been entirely vanquished. Deploying an industrial relations structure that in some ways resembles pre–Wagner Act procedures, VW management has agreed to periodically meet and confer with any organized group of workers, including the UAW as well as the anti-union "union" initially pushed forward by right-wing elements within and outside the plant.[7]

In South Carolina, the Republican establishment also took a leading role in preventing organization of a production unit that was part of an otherwise thoroughly unionized private company. When Boeing built a large assembly plant in Charlestown, the Seattle-based aerospace company sought to escape the labor militancy historically associated with the Pacific Northwest. The International Association of Machinists charged that Boeing violated the labor law when the company sought to penalize strikes and aggressive bargaining in Seattle by shifting so much production and employment opportunities—estimated at about 3,000 jobs—to a right-to-work state.

In this fight Boeing had an important and effective ally: South Carolina governor Nikki Haley. *Bloomberg Businessweek* called her "Boeing's strongest weapon in its fight with IAM." She appointed a veteran anti-union lawyer as head of the state's Department of Labor, Licensing, and Regulation to help her "fight the unions." She also appeared in Boeing radio ads encouraging workers to reject the IAM and also devoted part of her 2015 State of the State address to the issue. "We have a reputation internationally for being a state that doesn't want unions, because we don't need unions," she told the legislature. In April of that year the IAM admitted defeat when it withdrew a petition for an NLRB-supervised election at the Dreamliner plant. "It's hard to tell the difference between Boeing and Nikki Haley," said an IAM official. "The implication that people are left with is that if you support collective bargaining rights in South Carolina, you are somehow opposing the official position of South Carolina."[8]

Both Tennessee and South Carolina are "right-to-work" states. It was the 1947 Taft-Hartley Act, which permitted states to ban collective bargaining contracts that require union membership and payment of dues as a condition of employment. For decades, right-to-work states were largely confined to the South, the Great Plains, and the Mountain West. As one might expect, these restrictions weakened unions by providing plenty of opportunity for "free riders" to take advantage of union-bargained wages and benefits without paying their fair share.

In the aftermath of the Republican statehouse victories in the 2010 elections, right-to-work laws have spread throughout the Midwest. Some combination of genuine anti-union sentiment and clever GOP gerrymandering has tilted state legislative bodies well to the right on this issue. Both Indiana and Michigan passed right–to-work statutes in 2012, while in Wisconsin, governor Scott Walker, who four years earlier had waged a tumultuous battle that succeeded in slashing collective bargaining rights for most public sector workers, signed a bill that made his state the twenty-fifth to adopt the right-to-work policy. In early 2016 West Virginia followed suit with a new right-to-work law of its own. Meanwhile, in Ohio and Missouri right-to-work statutes targeting private sector unions came close to passage: in Ohio a right-to-work law was enacted by the legislature and signed by the governor but then overturned in a popular referendum; and in Missouri, only a gubernatorial veto prevented enactment of the anti-labor statute. In Illinois and Kentucky, conservatives sought to bypass such state-level divisiveness by encouraging cities and counties to adopt right-to-work ordinances.[9] Such local initiatives were likely to encounter resistance in the federal courts, but whatever the judicial temperament, right-to-work controversies seem destined to roil for years in a region that once constituted America's blue-collar heartland.

As this book makes clear, such anti-union assaults have taken many forms over the past century and more. Depending on ideological fashion, economic circumstance, and political opportunity, conservative opposition to trade unionism has changed its colors and taken different forms. In the mid-twentieth century, politicians and pundits, no matter how hostile to organizing, never openly denounced the working man and woman. They instead trained their fire on the organizers behind "monopoly unionism," which led to an inflationary spiral and a flood of low-wage imports. But a decade ago, when the Employee Free Choice Act was being debated, the right attacked private sector unionists for their presumptively thuggish and autocratic character. Later, at the depths of the recession that began in 2008, conservatives targeted public employees and their unions for the wages, pensions, and other benefits that cash-strapped cities and states were thought no longer capable of affording. Critics often declared workers selfish and conflated such denunciations with an assumption that government unionism was inherently corrupt, because the supposed political power of unions like the Service Employees International Union meant that in negotiations the government was bargaining with itself.[10]

Conservatives continued to hone their methods of crippling unionism. Right-to-work laws were a tried and true method of depriving locals of dues income by invoking the all-American principle of self-determination. Union income increasingly came under attack from an evolving libertarian logic that posits a conflict between the free speech rights of individual workers and the traditions of solidarity and democratic decision-making that have traditionally legitimized the existence of both public and private sector trade unionism. The Supreme Court's 2014 *Harris v. Quinn* decision, for example, ruled that home health care aides did not have to pay any fees to the unions representing them. These men and women were but "partial public employees" whose "fair share" dues payments constituted a violation of their free speech rights insofar as the union lobbied, negotiated, and mobilized the public on behalf of issues with which the plaintiffs disagreed.

Many in the labor movement feared this ruling's broader ramifications. *Harris v. Quinn* itself was unlikely to have a major impact on public sector trade unionism. But Justice Samuel Alito Jr. led a conservative majority on the Supreme Court, which came close to ruling that since all public sector unionism was inherently political, any "fair share" monies paid to the union by the workers constituted a form of coercion that violated the First Amendment rights of individual employees with contrary views. In this libertarian universe, not only were electioneering and lobbying political activities, but so were contract negotiations and grievance handling. Many unionists feared that the legal discourse sustaining the *Harris v. Quinn* ruling could possibly lead to a national right-to-work regime for all public employees. As the right-wing Center for Individual Rights, which represented the plaintiffs, proclaimed, "We are seeking the end of compulsory union dues across the nation on the basis of the free speech rights guaranteed by the First Amendment."[11]

Like the "liberty of contract" doctrine, which a century before had crippled trade unionism and much progressive governmental regulation during the early twentieth-century Lochner era, judicial conservatives have increasingly equated the expenditure of money by an individual or organization with the free speech rights protected under the First Amendment. Such opinions have distorted and obscured existing inequalities of power, most notably in a 2010 opinion, *Citizens United v. Federal Election Commission.* That Supreme Court ruling lifted virtually all limits on the capacity of the rich to fund political candidates and influence public opinion. Likewise in *Harris v. Quinn* and other judicial cases bearing on the ability of trade unions to financially sustain themselves, conservatives have similarly equated dues payments with free speech itself. Such decisions subvert both the principle of solidarity and the capacity of a trade union to organize on a truly democratic basis. As the AFL-CIO warned, "Business has used the First Amendment as a sword, to argue that regulation, including of their labor relations, interferes with corporate liberty, and as a shield, to protect the ever increasing flow of money into our electoral system."[12]

The last time that most Americans thought extreme social and economic inequality a pressing danger to democracy came during the Great Depression. New Dealers then saw the growth of trade unionism and the practice of collective bargaining as the essential mechanism that could raise working-class living standards, curb corporate power, and democratize the polity. Today, with inequality once again a widely perceived social and political pathology that threatens the stability and democratic character of the republic itself, that 1930s remedy remains under sustained political and ideological assault. The essays in this book help explain why, if only because the very existence of a trade union movement stands athwart the political and economic ambitions of American conservatism.

Notes

1. Mortimer Zuckerman, "Making a Mockery of the American Dream," *U.S. News & World Report*, March 27, 2015.

2. S. V. Date, "Why Jeb Bush Is Talking About Income Inequality," *National Journal*, April 30, 2015.

3. Peter Georgescu, "Capitalists, Arise: We Need to Deal with Income Inequality," *New York Times*, August 9, 2015, SR 6.

4. Lydia DePillis, "The Strange Case of the Anti-union Union at Volkswagen's Plant in Tennessee," *Washington Post*, November 19, 2014.

5. Ibid.

6. Pat Garofalo, "The GOP Gets All Up in Volkswagen's Business," *U.S. News & World Report*, February 13, 2014.

7. Josh Eidelson, "Volkswagen's Sort-of Union in Tennessee," *Bloomberg Businessweek*, February 19, 2015.

8. Josh Eidelson, "Boeing's Best Union Buster Is South Carolina's Governor Nikki Haley," *Bloomberg Businessweek*, April 17, 2015.

9. Monica Davey, "Unions Suffer Latest Defeat in the Midwest," *New York Times*, March 10, 2015, A1.

10. For the latest book-length iteration of this argument see, Daniel DiSalvo, *Government Against Itself: Public Union Power and Its Consequences* (New York: Oxford University Press, 2015).

11. Brian Mahoney, "High Court May Deal Unions Serious Blow," *Politico* online, June 30, 2015.

12. Richard Trumka and Craig Becker, "The Future of Work: Labor Law Must Catch Up," *Pacific Standard* online, August 14, 2015.

Entangled Histories: American Conservatism and the U.S. Labor Movement in the Twentieth and Twenty-First Centuries

Nelson Lichtenstein and Elizabeth Tandy Shermer

This volume explores how American conservatives, in business, law, politics, and academe, have come to understand the labor movement in the United States and sought to contain, defame, and defeat the union idea. Their multidecade effort requires examination for two reasons. First, that conservative project sheds much light on contemporary political controversies that have made the labor movement, indeed the very idea of unionism, a lightning rod for campaign invective and policy contestation. When the administration of Barack Obama took office, a significant reform of American labor law seemed once again on the political and legislative agenda. A liberal, union-friendly senator, a former Chicago community organizer no less, assumed the presidency in an electoral season that also saw large Democratic majorities take control of Congress. Labor-liberal forces pushed forward a newly crafted Employee Free Choice Act (EFCA), which was designed to facilitate union organizing and enhance collective bargaining. Once President Barack Obama and the Democrats had enacted a landmark health care reform, many expected the 110th Congress to pass EFCA as well. A rebirth of unionism, as a potent organizational and social ideal, would surely follow.

But it was not to be. Conflict between labor and corporate management, at the bargaining table or in the halls of Congress, has always generated an overabundance of heated rhetoric. This fight was no exception. Controversy engulfed EFCA as anti-union conservatives mobilized their money, their men (and women too), and some of the most sophisticated telecommunication techniques to damn the legal reform and the labor movement itself as corrupt, coercive, and undemocratic. "This is the demise of a civilization," moaned Bernie Marcus, Home Depot cofounder and its former CEO, during the brief season when it seemed that EFCA would actually be enacted. "This is how a civilization disappears," he predicted if the majority sign-up provisions of the new law, "card check" in the parlance of the time, actually made it possible for unions to organize companies such as his. "It's our number one issue to raise money on," reported Senator John Ensign of Nevada, the chair of the National Republican Senatorial Committee during the run-up to the 2008 election.[1]

The U.S. Chamber of Commerce, which warned that the new law would "Europeanize the American workforce," orchestrated a sophisticated, expensive advertising and lobbying campaign against the new law. Like Marcus, they too thought the legislation a radical assault on American traditions and a blueprint for the unions' "big government agenda": "Workers deprived of a private vote. Work rules and pay dictated by government. Employers stripped of basic legal rights. They aren't relics of the Cold War. They are the goals of the Orwellian 'Employee Free Choice Act' and a radical agenda for the National Labor Relations Board. Now Americans are fighting back."[2]

These claims tapped deeply into long-standing ideological and cultural tropes that remained vibrant even in a moment—at the dawn of the Obama administration—when American liberalism seemed on the verge of a new awakening. But American conservatives clearly saw opposition to virtually any legislative initiative that strengthened the institutional weight of organized labor as a "wedge" issue that could effectively divide the Democrats, energize conservatives, and malign trade-union ideals. This became clear as the American Right regained the ideological and political initiative after the first year of the Obama presidency. Not only did conservatives sideline EFCA, but the aftereffects of the 2008–2009 financial calamity plunged dozens of states into a fiscal crisis that Republican governors—and some Democratic ones—too often blamed on public employee unions and the wage standards and pension benefits they had negotiated during the previous third of a century.

Indeed, the fact that union density in the public sector stood at over 35 percent seemed anomalous in an economy where private-sector unionism had been reduced to a paltry 7 percent or less. This made the public sector unions ready targets even in those northern states, such as New Jersey, Ohio, and Wisconsin, that had long been union strongholds. There, conservative Republican governors accompanied their successful efforts to enact legislation severely curbing public sector collective bargaining rights with a rhetoric that delegitimized the very idea of trade unionism. New Jersey governor Chris Christie labeled the teachers' union "a group of political thugs,"[3] while Wisconsin's Scott Walker, who faced massive and sustained protests against his anti-union initiative, denounced "tone-deaf and out of touch union bosses."[4] He also deployed the argument, burnished by a century of anti-union denunciations, that assumed compulsory union dues were nothing more than an exploitative rent, the abolition of which might well put hundreds of dollars into the pockets of Wisconsin's hard-pressed state employees.[5]

This conservative political vilification of contemporary trade unionism raises a second, larger question: to what extent does such a critique of organized labor explain the rise of the contemporary American Right, now the subject of much inquiry by historians, social scientists, and journalists? The origins and character of American conservatism has never been entirely neglected, but the contemporary explosion of historical studies on this topic began in the late 1980s when it became apparent that the twentieth-century reform moment, which traced a line from the Progressives to New Dealers and on to the partisans of Great Society social innovation, had ended. From the White House on down, conservatives seemed to hold the initiative, which sent American historians and other scholars scurrying into the archives to find the social dimensions, cultural values, and ideological structures that had made conservatism such a potent strand in the American past. As historian Leo Ribuffo put it in the nation's leading historical journal, "Why Is There So Much Conservatism in the United States and Why Do So Few Historians Know Anything About It?"[6]

To remedy the situation, historians proceeded on multiple fronts to flesh out a history of American conservatism with deep and varied social, cultural, and ideological roots. Rather than see right-wing ideology and its advocates as some form of social or psychological pathology, which had been the conceit of an earlier generation of pluralist social scientists who celebrated an American cultural and political consensus, a new generation of biographers and historians began to write respectful, nuanced narratives that put writers and politicians like Whittaker Chambers, Barry Goldwater, George Wallace, William F. Buckley, Ayn Rand, Phyllis Schlafly, Westbrook Pegler, and Father Charles Coughlin in a far more creative and resonant dialogue with mainstream political and social ideas.[7] And with equal energy and archival resourcefulness an even larger group of historians turned their attention to what Michael Kazin called "the grass-roots Right," the social movements and community organizations that seemed to mirror, on the conservative side of the political spectrum, the insurgencies that the New Left and post–New Left generation of social historians had celebrated in their many studies of working-class self-organization, student activism, African American or Latino protest, and the feminist awakening.[8] Such studies of the Right have often been framed in terms of a populist backlash against liberal social policy or a capitalist, if naturalistic, transformation of community social relations. Thus in recent years historians have explored the antimodernist character of the twentieth-century Ku Klux Klan, probed the social basis of suburban anti-Communism, delineated white, working-class resistance to racial integration, both on the job and in the neighborhood, and deconstructed theological and cultural aspects of evangelical Protestantism, especially in terms of those ideas and impulses that resist gender equality, abortion rights, and the welfare state.[9]

As valuable as these studies have proven, they largely overstate the degree to which the rise of the contemporary American Right was either a post–New Deal phenomenon or a set of plebian social movements often labeled "populist." More important, as Kim Phillips-Fein and others have argued, is a definition of the American Right that emphasizes the extent to which it is engaged in a protracted fight to maintain corporate power and legitimize a market economy, even as this agenda is often embraced with a pseudopopulist devotion to conservative cultural and social values.[10] In the second decade of the twenty-first century it is apparent that efforts to reduce taxes, weaken social provision, limit the regulation of business operations, and curtail the power and legitimacy of organized labor stand at the heart of the American conservative worldview.

American conservatives have disdained organized labor not simply because individual companies or whole industries have found union economic demands troublesome but even more so because the labor movement stands for a set of ideas and social impulses that most on the Right find anathema: social solidarity, employment stability, limits on the workplace power of corporate management, plus a defense of the welfare state, progressive taxation, financial regulation, and a government apparatus energetic enough to supervise the health and safety of millions of American workers and consumers. And even when it comes to immigration, race, and gender, American trade unions, despite a highly checkered history well explored by numerous scholars, today stand on the left side of the political divide. Thus the steady decline in union density and social power, from about one-third of the nonfarm workforce in the early 1950s to something approaching 10 percent today, is one of the most startling and consequential social trends imaginable, and even more dramatic when considered in terms of the private sector workplace, where union density is now below 7 percent, a figure not seen since the late nineteenth century, when trade unionism was but a semilegal institution whose ranks were largely confined to skilled workers in workplaces marginal to the great mass production industries emerging in that era.

Post–World War II pundits and professors downplayed the decline in organized labor, and the corporate antagonism that stood behind it, because of their commitment to a body of social analysis whose leading assumption held that in the United States and Western Europe most of the historic conflicts between capital and labor had been resolved. It was not just Daniel Bell's *End of Ideology* (1960) that posited such a social truce but also the work of such academic mandarins as Clark Kerr and John Dunlop, whose *Industrialism and Industrial Man* (1964) marginalized the very concept of capitalism and devalued the idea that classes existed and clashed. This was a world governed by managers, technicians, committees, and academic knowledge producers, a bureaucratic society evoked by John Kenneth Galbraith's *The New Industrial State* (1967), which reconsidered the modern corporation as a planning apparatus in which trade unions functioned as junior partners to top management.[11] Kerr quipped that in contemporary industrial America class conflict was being replaced by a far less deadly "bureaucratic contest" over the distribution of wealth and income in which "memos will flow instead of blood." The liberal columnist Murray Kempton, a veteran of the radical 1930s, now complained that "the AFL-CIO has lived happily in a society which, more lavishly than any in history, has managed the care and feeding of incompetent white people."[12]

Historians of labor, business, and politics took the social prognostications of the *End of Ideology* school with a large grain of salt, but if they held that social conflict still existed in the United States, many social historians thought that the labor movement stood on the reactionary side of that divide. The unions, after all, had purged themselves of Communists, supported both the Cold War and the Vietnam War, and often remained on the sidelines during the great battles over the achievement of full citizenship for African Americans, for white women, and for gays and lesbians. Social and political historians who sought the origins of right-wing politics in America could therefore easily overlook those in corporate America and on the right margins of the Republican Party who were critical of organized labor, if only because the unions seemed to be such retrogressive institutions themselves, or at the very least, to harbor within their ranks the kind of white male workers who composed so many of the new recruits won to the cause of the American Right in the 1970s and 1980s.[13]

Yet none of this forestalled corporate attacks on the trade unions, even during the prosperous, early postwar decades. General Electric proved an unrelenting foe of the newly formed, anti-Communist, International Union of Electrical Workers; likewise, southern textile firms fought to a standstill the efforts by even the most conservative unions that sought to organize their industry; and in the 1970s "hard hat" hostility to the anti–Vietnam War movement and other forms of social liberalism had no bargaining payoff for either the Teamsters or the Building Trades during a decade when deregulation of the trucking industry and management determination to slash construction costs devastated a set of unions whose exposure to cheap-labor international competition had been nil.[14]

Indeed, even when liberalism seemed poised to make a concerted advance, a conservative mobilization that reached well into the Democratic Party inevitably stanched efforts to strengthen labor's institutional capacity to organize or make its weight felt within the political process. This was most apparent during the heyday of 1960s liberalism when significant reforms of the U.S. racial order, of health provision, and of immigration policy were swept into law with but little payoff, in terms either political or ideological, for a labor movement that had been a core component of Great Society reformism.[15] Likewise, if in less dramatic fashion, labor law revisions also failed in 1978 and 1993, as well as 2009 and 2010, when a Democratic administration, in cooperation with a Democratic Congress, seemed to briefly hold open the door to legislative victory. Hence, during the last few decades American social politics seems to have reached the point where a militant and united conservatism has structured the political chessboard so as to effectively divorce the fate of the organized working class from liberalism itself.[16]

But this tale of labor's fall also offers us critical insights into the rise of the Right in American politics and social thought. Historians and social scientists have long recognized that accommodation or hostility to trade unionism by the management of an individual firm, or of an entire industry, was the product of a complex set of social and economic relationships, including the competitiveness of the market, the skill and ethnic composition of the workforce, and the political and organizational power of capital as a whole. Capital-intensive firms that were natural monopolies or which did business in an oligopolistic market were thought to be relatively indifferent to the presence of a trade union. Hence the high rate of organizing in such mid-twentieth-century industries as auto, steel, electrical power, and transport. Conversely, where competition was stiff and the use of labor relatively intensive, management proved fiercely opposed to trade unions. This theory proved true, today and in the past, in the case of textiles, home construction, and retail trade. Much scholarship, both of labor and of management, thus probed the conditions under which particular firms and industries resisted, rejected, or even accommodated union organizational efforts.

Such studies now seem antiquated. Those industries within which labor was the most successful, such as automobiles and consumer durables, are no longer insulated from global competition. They must do business in a market where a multinational scale calibrates labor costs and production standards. A dramatic reduction in working conditions, wage scales, and unionization has therefore characterized manufacturing across the globe. But even more important, as so many of the essays in this volume make clear, a recognition has grown that such an economy-centered mode of analysis can be swamped, so to speak, by the larger ideological and political currents that have made the American Right so potent for so many years. In those economic sectors, which have grown the fastest during the last half century—finance, real estate, retail trade, health care, and other services—an ideological propensity toward minimalist government, weak labor standards, and autocratic management has been a prominent characteristic of corporate governance. Wal-Mart, McDonald's, Marriott, and Goldman Sachs are not merely discrete economic entities, but political and cultural institutions whose influence has grown enormously during recent decades.[17]

These lessons are especially salient as researchers interrogate business activity in the public sphere. While the American Right has many ideological and institutional strands, a commitment to laissez-faire within the labor market, or rather to a regulatory regime that precludes the self-organization of the vast majority of American workers, has been consistent and persistent, far more so than even the racial, cultural, and foreign policy issues that receive so much attention as talismans of contemporary American conservatism. Hostility to trade unionism per se was a crystallizing impulse for the modern American conservative movement, reaching back past the 1970s to the aftermath of the 1886 Haymarket Riot and through the 1920s American Plan, the backlash against Operation Dixie in the 1940s, and the political ascendancy of both Barry Goldwater and Ronald Reagan. Such antagonism has only increased in recent years as unions and their activist members have become a critical pillar of the Democratic Party's campaign operation; indeed, with the decline of the civil rights movement and so many feminist organizations, the labor movement remains one of the few institutions on the broad Left capable of mobilizing its membership for social and political action outside of an electoral context.[18]

All this has restructured party politics. In the years since World War II a series of well-connected lobby groups, law firms, and business associations have policed the Republican Party's anti-union agenda and in crucial instances moved it firmly to the right. Thus, the National Federation of Independent Business and the National Restaurant Association have joined such older, manufacturing-oriented standbys as the National Right-to-Work Committee and the National Association of Manufacturers as key formulators of Republican labor policy. Equally important are the think tanks and policy centers of the Right—the Heritage Foundation, the American Enterprise Institute, the Manhattan Institute, and the Pacific Research Institute, often funded by a set of medium-sized foundations, like the Templeton, Olin, Bradley, and Simon Foundations, many with pedigrees that stretch back to an early-twentieth-century hostility to the New Deal and the new unionism of that era.[19]

In addition to these institutional innovations, conservatives have also reworked the ideological and rhetorical weapons they have deployed against the labor movement. An earlier generation of labor and social historians emphasized the anti-immigrant and anti-Communist nature of this right-wing ideological assault. To conservatives, trade unionism was an epiphenomenon of the first and second immigrant generations, easily prone to an un-American radicalism, a charge that had much resonance in an era when Protestants were a minority of the working class and when anti-Communism convulsed the entire political culture.[20] Echoes of such a critique are with us still, but even in the 1930s and 1940s the attack on organized labor was shifting to another and longer lasting set of rhetorical tropes: the argument that unionism itself oppressed and misrepresented ordinary workers, either those in the unions or those who sought to remain outside. This idea was powerfully reinforced by the high-profile scandals and investigations that revealed undemocratic and self-interested practices among the leaders of the Teamsters, the Laborers, the East Coast Longshoremen, and a variety of other labor organizations.

The multidecade persistence of such a critique transcends those instances in which bossism and theft were uncovered and penalized. The ever-present discussion of union corruption reflects both the continuing illegitimacy of the very idea of unionism among many conservatives, as well as a legal and administrative redefinition of corruption itself. An increasingly large number of heretofore legal and legitimate union activities, especially those designed to advance a sense of collective action and social solidarity, are now labeled unethical and undemocratic. Thus courts and legislators have eroded the right to picket, to strike, to negotiate many aspects of the employment relationship, and to spend union dues on behalf of candidates and causes. To American conservatives, all of this collective activity embodies a coercive effort that thwarts the will of those who seek to escape union power.[21]

Contributors to this volume grapple with many of these ideas. Most tilt away from specific moments of labor-management conflict and instead engage and, in some instances, contest historiographic themes long influential in the writing of American intellectual, cultural, and legal history. The idea of a post–World War II labor-management accord looks quite different when considered in this light, likewise the idea of an American "exceptionalism," a phenomenon more likely found within the ranks of management than in the minds of U.S. workers or their conduct on factory floor or in a high-rise office building. Race, region, and gender have always divided American workers, but such distinctions require a recalibration when measured against the reality of business power and the ideology it commands.[22]

This volume is divided into four parts, each of which offers a distinctive probe into the structure of right-wing thought and praxis on what was once known as the American "labor question." The first set of essays explains why and how the very existence of class-based institutions violated key cultural and ideological structures that had been sustained not only by conservative elites and ideologues but by a steadily increasing slice of the American populace. The second part probes the ways in which region and race have often shaped attitudes toward organized labor in unexpected and divergent fashions. The third part of the book explores how conservatives, most notably those in the National Right to Work Committee, have sought to appropriate the language of civil rights in their multidecade effort to weaken the labor movement and delegitimize the union idea. The final set of essays historicizes the charge that unions are either corrupt, undemocratic, or wield illegitimate power, an understudied set of ideas that has nevertheless been a far more potent and long-standing right-wing indictment against the unions than that of Communism or other forms of political radicalism.

PART I

The Conservative Search
for Social Harmony

The essays in this section focus on the ideas and ideologies put forward by early twentieth-century conservatives, some elite and others middle class, who sought to frame the "labor question" of that era in a fashion that would deradicalize labor, generate loyalty to country and corporation, and insure harmonious class relations. Andrew Cohen begins with a reappraisal of an old controversy that has once again become a flash point between labor and its adversaries. The tariff, a perennial source of heated debate in the nineteenth century, has today reemerged under the rubric of "protectionism," a convenient bludgeon to denounce those trade unions that seek various forms of trade restriction as technologically Luddite and economically retrograde. Cohen demonstrates that the nineteenth-century tariff question was never merely a parochial issue of interest only to U.S. producers and those workers threatened by foreign imports. Rather, the tariff was defended by its supporters as part of a modernizing telos, a defense of an industrially advanced, yet egalitarian society in which continental enterprise and the urban working class were protected against the products of a decadent, class-bound Europe. Free traders, by way of contrast, were identified with the old Confederate slavocracy or with unpatriotic smugglers and corruptionists. This ideological construct linking the interests of employers and their workers could not withstand the very real class conflict of the era, which is why New Deal Democrats proved temporarily successful in constructing a new mid-twentieth-century compact that linked free trade to progressive taxation, direct labor protection, and the regulation of business. This species of liberalism collapsed in the 1970s, leaving American workers with a free-enterprise regime that defines organized labor as little more than a self-interested political obstacle—a market imperfection—at war with the interests of American consumers and global economic progress.

Like nineteenth-century high-tariff advocates, American Legionnaires also championed an ideology of American exceptionalism and cross-class unity. In theory, these middle-class World War I veterans were not anti-union. In practice, they found interwar strikes and picket lines offensive to their conception of a patriotic Americanism, especially when such a high proportion of all labor activists were immigrants, radicals, or both. As Christopher Nehls argues, Legionnaires were not merely reactionaries in cahoots with the nation's business elite, nor were they the first conservative group to blame domestic radicalism on immigrants. But the Legion's investment in a patriotic nationalism that would bridge class divisions intensified a postwar propensity to see strikes and union organizing drives as a revolutionary plot designed to rip apart the fabric of the nation. These veterans thus turned strikebreaking into a patriotic affirmation of what they saw as essential American values. And this widely shared view reflected a broader rejection of class as an organizing principle in American life, which was close to the essence of the trade union idea in the 1920s and 1930s, as well as in later decades.

If the Legion's search for cultural and social harmony put some members on the path toward a violent, xenophobic brand of anti-union militancy, there were other roads toward this same end that seemed far more sophisticated, efficacious, and amenable to corporate elites long after the Legion's methods fell out of favor. Chris Nyland and Kyle Bruce demonstrate why in their discussion of the ideas and influence of the two great management theorists of the early twentieth century: Frederick Taylor and Elton Mayo. While Taylor is well remembered as the father of an authoritarian brand of scientific management, Nyland and Bruce show how his many followers came to see trade unionism and collective bargaining as essential to productivity, democracy, and social progress during the interwar years. However, these Taylor Society progressives were soon eclipsed by Harvard Business School professor Elton Mayo and his many students in academe and high-level management. Mayo promised social harmony in the factory and the society. Instead of crude appeals to an insular American-ism, he deployed the latest psychological and anthropological research to give managers the tools to construct a set of workplace social relations that would legitimize their authority and marginalize an independent, working-class challenge to corporate hegemony. Seemingly modernist and social sci-entific, Mayo's zeitgeist has become embedded within virtually all strains of management ideology and praxis, from progressive, high-tech firms in the Silicon Valley to conservative, labor-intensive companies such as Wal-Mart and Target.

Chapter 1

Unions, Modernity, and the Decline of American Economic Nationalism

Andrew Wender Cohen

For over a century, unions have fought the contention that they obstruct "progress." Their attempt to prove themselves forward looking has been hampered by the reality that unions have, by design, hindered an elite vision of a mechanized workplace, a corporate economy, and a docile workforce. Only gradually between 1900 and 1950 did organized labor convince middle-class voters that unions were an essential component of a modern liberal society, needed to shepherd technology into the factory, democratize industry, prevent inefficient disruptions, and uplift employees.[1]

But labor's identity as an agent of modernization declined in the economically stagnant 1970s, when critics argued that America's future as a global economic power demanded the weakening of unions. To compete with nations like Japan, U.S. manufacturers purportedly needed to shed supposedly inefficient work rules, pay scales, and employment protections.[2] These arguments ironically grew louder during the boom of the 1990s, when commentators began routinely calling unions "dinosaurs," anachronisms in the frictionless economy being imagined by multinational corporations and their breathless publicists. When contractual givebacks failed to stanch manufacturing decline, critics added the charge of protectionism to their arsenal. Having demanded workers abandon their rights for the sake of national competitiveness, commentators said little as corporations moved their facilities abroad anyway, then vilified the remaining union members for opposing treaties like the 1994 North American Free Trade Agreement (NAFTA).[3]

The conflation of modernization with unrestricted global trade represents a major challenge for American manufacturing workers in the twenty-first century. Perhaps no single factor plays a larger role in the decline of industrial unions than offshoring, outsourcing, and competition with unorganized workers in poorer parts of the world. This process is greatly facilitated by conservative rhetoric sanctifying the free market and attacking workers for the crime of using the political process to defend their own interests.

Yet protectionism has been a major force in America's past, and particularly the history of the nation's industrial workers. Its prevalence reflected not only the might of corporate manufacturers but also the intense class resentments endemic to the nineteenth-century United States. In the late twentieth century, reformers, businessmen, and politicians all came to see free trade as the hallmark of modernity, and protectionism went into decline, undermining the Reutherite labor bargain of the post–World War II era. As the labor movement seeks to regain its relevance as a crucial component of (rather than an obstacle to) an emerging global trade system, workers must figure out how to leverage the last vestiges of economic nationalism to create new rights and protections.

Despite intense popular debates within labor about contemporary American trade policy, economic nationalism is not a fashionable research topic among scholars. Aside from David Montgomery and Dana Frank, few labor historians have seriously considered the tariff.[4] The reasons for this are not hard to discern. Some scholars find trade policy sleep inducing. Others see protectionism as an ideological distraction for workers. Historians are uncomfortable with the protectionists' occasional xenophobia, anti-Semitism, and racism. Scholars reject their gendered attacks on consumption, defending the workers' desire for material comfort and celebrating activism unifying consumers and producers. Historians cannot but be influenced by economists, who view tariffs as marginally beneficial to industrial workers, yet extremely costly to consumers.[5] And scholars of labor history are all too aware of the disappointing disjunction between protectionist promises and the workers' pay packets. They know that a high steel tariff, for instance, did not prevent wage cuts at Henry Clay Frick's Homestead Works in 1891, forestall Frick's infamous lockout in 1892, or check the brutal violence that followed.[6]

Nonetheless, American protectionists have long viewed working-class voters as a core constituency for high taxes on imported manufactures. In the nineteenth century, the tariff's staunchest advocates certainly presented the law as a boon to workers. Citing the threat posed by "the pauper labor of Europe," Whig senator Henry Clay endorsed trade laws to "protect" Americans against foreigners lacking the rights of U.S. citizenship.[7] After the Civil War, Radical Republicans like Pennsylvania congressman William "Pig Iron" Kelley justified the high tariff primarily as a guard for workingmen: "It is not for the rich, the comparatively few who have accumulated capital, that we demand protection. We ask it in the name of the millions who live by toil, whose dependence is on their skill and ability to labor, and whose labor creates the wealth of the country."[8]

The fact that employers benefited handsomely from trade barriers did not undermine this faith, for these officials believed that employers would share their profits with operatives. By barring competition with what they saw as the sweatshops of aristocratic Europe, protectionists claimed to eliminate the basis for rancor among producers.[9]

Despite their paeans to economic harmony, protectionists defended import restrictions in stark class terms, as a means of containing the cosmopolitanism of the wealthy. Even before the revolution of 1776, many Americans embraced a republican ideology that defined consumption as a hedonistic, feminine, and antidemocratic pursuit. Those who did accept consumption often fought to secure more balanced trade with England, a relationship where Britain served as a market for American manufactures, not just raw materials and agricultural products. The fact that the early nineteenth-century United States still imported most of its finished goods intensified such concerns. Serving in the Kentucky state assembly in 1809, during the Jeffersonian embargo of British and French manufactures, Henry Clay pushed for the so-called homespun resolution, requiring legislators to wear American-made clothes. Tariffs—raised considerably after the War of 1812—not only aided industrial workers, they restrained Americans from acquiring aristocratic habits.[10]

During the remainder of the nineteenth century, nationalists painted the tariff as the guardian of an egalitarian society endangered by America's growing affluence. In 1849, for instance, the secretary of the Treasury,

Pennsylvania Whig William M. Meredith, noted the importance of having tariffs on "foreign cloths, foreign wines, foreign fruits, foreign jewelry, in short, every minute article of personal luxury," arguing that "republics are governments for the poor, and it is agreeable to their institutions to discourage luxury. The doctrines of free trade are for the benefit of the idle and luxurious, removing the burthens of wealth to the back of poverty and industry."[11] Novelists made this point metaphorically. In George Thompson's scandalous 1849 best-seller *Venus in Boston*, the hero is Corporal Grimsby, a Revenue Cutter commander and Revolutionary War veteran, who saves the poor all-American maiden Fanny Aubrey from the lecherous man of wealth Timothy Tickles.[12]

As the economy expanded, the protectionists' attacks on the wealthy grew more conspicuous. This was evident in the popular discussion of smuggling. Today, we associate smuggling with the trafficking of goods like cocaine. But because virtually no products were unlawful to import before 1900, nineteenth-century Americans smuggled to avoid paying duties that added as much as 100 percent to the cost of many items. Because tariffs were highest on luxury goods like silk, art, and diamonds, hedonistic commodities like tobacco, opium, and sugar, and technologically sophisticated manufactured goods like steel, brass, and glass, the public viewed smuggling as a crime specific to the upper classes. Newspapers routinely chastised tourists for lying to inspectors about their foreign purchases, calling for increased vigilance against the "universal habit of polite smuggling."[13]

But the weight of criticism fell on importers. Indeed, attacks on merchant smugglers date back to the Jeffersonian period, when Democratic-Republicans accused New England Federalists of illicitly trading with the British. Such resentments grew during the Civil War, when critics savaged businessmen who ran the Union blockade of the Confederacy. After the war's end, Radical congressman Benjamin Butler lambasted the "merchant princes" like metal importer William E. Dodge, whom he accused of undervaluing their imports and thus cheating the government out of millions in revenue. Butler charged wealthy smugglers with undermining the Union and promoting the misery of the laboring classes living in his Lowell, Massachusetts, district.[14]

Meanwhile, protectionists made industrial workers themselves the protagonists of their modernization narrative. Manufacturing was once seen as the future of the nation. Dating back to the time of Alexander Hamilton, protectionist rhetoric styled manufacturing an "infant" to be nurtured by trade barriers, not a sick patient, being kept alive by government subsidy. As the name "Whig" suggests, Henry Clay's faction styled itself as the party of progress, positioning the tariff as a spur to America's industrial destiny, necessary for the "full development of the resources of the country." As the Whigs became Republicans, they likewise celebrated workers as the agents of the nation's economic maturity. For instance, in 1859, William David Lewis, a close friend of protectionist economist Henry C. Carey, declared that the tariff could increase wages beyond those of "old manufacturing nations," raising the workers' "intelligence" and spurring the "higher development of mankind." Painting the tariff as fostering America's ability to compete economically with world powers like England, supporters convinced workers that protection was a path to modernity, not a backward-looking alternative to more substantive labor reforms.[15]

Since no public opinion polling exists for the nineteenth century, we cannot know exactly what ordinary workers thought about these arguments. But high tariffs reigned for much of the period 1816 to 1937, and the issue was central to the campaigns of the nineteenth century. Someone must have supported the tariff, and we know it was not elite merchants and shippers in the Northeast, or midwestern farmers or southern planters. It is reasonable to conclude that workers were voting for protectionists. Indeed, the tariff helps explain how the pro-business Whig and Republican Parties managed to win any offices at all. And the GOP's special dominance in the nation's top manufacturing states, Massachusetts and Pennsylvania, suggests that workers embraced protection.

Some early nineteenth-century labor reformers endorsed a universal vision of industrial reform that critiqued tariffs as harmful to workers. As historians like Bruce Laurie have shown, abolitionists like Elizur Wright Jr. attacked the New England Whig elite, rejected protectionism, and promoted a broader notion of labor rights. Antislavery politicians sought to expand the appeal of their parties by advocating reforms like the ten-hour day in addition to limitations on slavery. And these activists made some inroads among the working people of the mill towns of Massachusetts, allowing the Republican Party to dominate the state's politics by the late 1850s.[16]

But not all labor reformers dismissed protectionism or advocated the immediate abolition of slavery. Lowell's Benjamin Butler, the "leader of the ten-hour movement," supported a moderately protective tariff and defended slavery until secession. Early labor organizations clearly favored high tariffs on nonessential imports. New York Typographical Union

Number 6 had supported tariffs on imported books since its founding in 1852. Threatened by competition with a more advanced British metal industry, the iron-puddling Sons of Vulcan (formed in 1858) were "consistent protectionists." Likewise, in 1868, the National Labor Union, established by iron molder William Sylvis, called for an end to duties on "necessities of life," but high tariffs on "articles of luxury" and products that "will develop the resources of the country, increase the number of factories, give employment to more laborers, maintain good compensation, cause the immigration of skilled labor," and "enable us to successfully compete with the manufacturers of Europe in the markets of the world." In 1872, the platform of the National Labor Reform Party endorsed an eight-hour day, public ownership of the railroads, greenbacks, and a protective tariff.[17]

In the main, such protectionism was merely practical, insofar as import duties were the one legally uncontestable form of assistance the federal government offered workers. Through the 1920s the U.S. Supreme Court cited federalism and freedom of contract to kill basic protections guarding the length of the workday, the minimum wages an employer could pay, and the condition of the workplace. Even federal statutes barring the employment of children failed constitutional muster. By contrast, judges sustained the constitutionality of tariffs and subsidies. The contrast naturally channeled working-class politics in protectionist directions.[18]

But it is worth noting that the tariff accommodated the nineteenth-century workers' republican assumptions about contract, manhood, and independence. To the present, American workers have often preferred a state that increased bargaining power to laws making the government the guardian of labor standards. Free-Soilers called for the state to guard free white men from competition with slave labor, while Republican workers favored policies such as homesteading and mass education that did not create the appearance of dependency. The tariff accommodated this sensibility, for it protected America's workers from "unfair" rivals rather than placing them in tutelage, or offering them charity. Just as significantly, protectionist writers like Horace Greeley believed that workers could not gain advances like the shorter workday unless tariffs shielded them from poorly paid foreign workers.[19]

Working-class protectionism walked hand-in-hand with patriotism. Having fought on behalf of the Union, many late-nineteenth-century workers saw the taxing of imports as necessary for funding the federal government, including the occupation of the South. Following the struggle, Henry

Adams observed, "The suspicion of free trade sounded to the ears as terrible a charge as that of having worn a rebel uniform or having been out with the Ku Klux Klan."[20] Protectionists fed this sentiment over the next fifty years, appealing to workers by making them central to a nationalist narrative of American community. Consider this 1922 editorial: "Loyalty to the home producer and manufacturer is the motive back of the Tariff. If we buy goods made in America, we keep American mill wheels going and our money circulating among the Americans. If we buy goods made abroad, we throw our own workers into idleness and send our money abroad. . . . Republican Tariff pushes the idea 'Made in America.' Democratic Free-Trade means 'Buy it Abroad.' Which do you think is the sentiment of the patriotic American?" As the labor movement grew more potent, native and immigrant workers may have clung to such sentiments to defend their patriotism against employers who painted radicalism as foreign and un-American.[21]

Scholars tend to associate this patriotism with racism, nativism, and imperialism, but in the nineteenth century, protectionists were neither more bigoted nor more belligerent than their rivals. During Reconstruction, the most active advocates of the tariff were egalitarians like Congressman Thaddeus Stevens, while the staunchest free traders were former slaveholders. If protectionist literature had a foreign villain, he was by-and-large from England, not China, the Pacific, or the Caribbean. Some tariff supporters indulged in anti-Semitism, but so did many free traders like agrarian editor Mark M. "Brick" Pomeroy and Cornell economist Goldwin Smith. The antitariff Knights of Labor strongly advocated Chinese exclusion, while staunch protectionists like Congressman George Frisbie Hoar derided it. If William McKinley embodied both protection and conquest, then this was a departure from the philosophy of the GOP, which had been populated by anti-imperialists like Hoar, and advocates of economic power like Secretary of State James G. Blaine, who explicitly rejected annexation for fear of undermining the tariff system.[22]

Merchants and farmers attacked this vision of the future, but their arguments did not dominate until the mid-twentieth century. Free traders floundered in the 1870s and 1880s because their broad antipathy to government itself offered workers no replacement for tariff protections. The leading opponents of the tariff were libertarians like William Graham Sumner, David A. Wells, E. L. Godkin, and Joseph S. "The Parsee Merchant" Moore.

Though more sophisticated than tariff advocates in their use of social science, their analysis was firmly rooted in the classical economics of Adam Smith and David Ricardo, who rejected all government intrusions into the market. Surrounded by the corruption of the Gilded Age, free traders had ample reason to view regulation with suspicion. But their approach to government was bound up in their class interests. Predominantly urban importers, educated elites, and southern planters, they venerated President Grover Cleveland, the conservative Democrat who crushed the American Railway Strike of 1894. And insofar as they evinced a faith in antimonopoly, they directed it toward both trusts and labor unions.[23]

Free traders achieved lasting success only when they enunciated a newly modern outlook, which replaced protectionism with worker protective legislation, tariffs with a graduated income tax, and nationalism with globalism. This began with the labor republicans of the 1850s and their successors, the Knights of Labor, who proposed abandoning the tariff for laws limiting the power of wealth and corporate power in the 1880s. "The tariff," Samuel I. Hopkins, a Knight elected to the U.S. Congress from Virginia, argued, established "a moneyed despotism in this country" that "is to be feared and fought against by labor more than any one thing." Labor's advocates took note, and began expanding their horizons. In 1883, Rep. William Kelley toured the factories of England with his daughter, Florence Kelley, later the nation's preeminent industrial reformer. While witnessing the destitution of the workers only affirmed the congressman's belief in protection, it radicalized his daughter, who rejected tariff politics in favor of regulation and even socialism.[24]

During the presidency of Woodrow Wilson, tariff reduction walked hand-in-hand with pro-labor legislation. While American Federation of Labor (AFL) was officially neutral on the tariff, fearing that an overt stance might create divisions within the movement and inspire political backlash, the organization's deepening relationship with the Democratic Party made it part of a coalition favoring tariff reform. In 1913, President Wilson pushed through the Underwood-Simmons Act, which slashed duties to their lowest level since the 1850s and created the federal income tax. Considered a monumental political triumph at the time, it depended on the support, or at least the acquiescence, of labor leaders. When protectionists attempted to marshal workers against the reductions, AFL secretary Frank Morrison, a member of the protectionist International Typographers'

Union, publicly questioned the beneficial effects of tariffs on labor. Maintaining his public neutrality, AFL president Samuel Gompers refused to endorse the bill, but he attacked employers for intimidating their workers into opposing it.[25]

Whether or not there was an explicit deal between Wilson and the AFL, labor's success at lobbying for new legislation tied the federation to the Democratic Party, giving it an incentive to oppose higher tariffs and suppress protectionist sentiments in its ranks. In the year after the Underwood Act, Congress gave workers an impressive range of benefits: an exemption from the antitrust law, an anti-injunction bill, the creation of the Department of Labor, the abolition of involuntary servitude on the seas, a federal child labor law, an eight-hour day for railroad workers, postal workers, and women and children in the District of Columbia, and a ban on piecework and Taylorism in federal facilities. Thus, when Democrats proposed an expert Tariff Commission in 1916 to amend the Underwood Act, the AFL endorsed it specifically to neutralize Republican attempts at capitalizing on worker fears regarding foreign competition.[26]

As this suggests, Republicans continued to view protection as the primary legitimate form of federal assistance to labor into the 1930s. The infamous Hawley-Smoot Tariff Act of 1930, which raised tariff rates to their highest level since the 1890s, was officially entitled "a bill to provide revenue, to regulate commerce with foreign countries, to encourage the industries of the United States," and "to protect American labor."[27] Supreme Court justice George Sutherland, the Utah archreactionary, is remembered for his 1923 decision, *Adkins v. Children's Hospital*, which voided women's minimum wage laws as restrictions of the individual's constitutional right to contract. But contrary to common belief, Sutherland was no simon-pure libertarian. He staunchly supported tariffs, giving President Franklin D. Roosevelt unrestrained power to regulate foreign trade.[28]

Despite Sutherland's best efforts, the tariff-centered view of the state declined in the 1930s. It is no coincidence that the year 1937, which saw the validation of the New Deal, also witnessed the beginning of seventy years of rate reductions. Increasingly concerned about international affairs, Roosevelt encouraged his secretary of state, free-trade Tennessee congressman Cordell Hull, to negotiate bilateral treaties lowering tariffs. Hull subsequently shepherded the 1944 Bretton Woods Agreement, which established unrestricted global trade as a postwar economic goal and a basis for international peace. In 1947, twenty-three nations embraced the creation of a permanent organization dedicated to negotiating lower tariffs, the General Agreement on Tariffs and Trade, an idea proposed at Bretton Woods. Industrial workers accepted their growing exposure to international competition not only because American economic dominance made tariffs less necessary but because Democrats had already given them so many new domestic protections.[29]

Labor's willingness to forgo the most extreme forms of protectionism for graduated progressive taxation, business regulation, and the social safety net laid the foundation for the so-called liberal consensus of the 1950s and early 1960s. Whether this was an explicit deal, or merely a product of labor's inclusion in a Democratic alliance, this bargain resembled gradual exchange of the workers' shop-floor control for union recognition, collective bargaining, and high compensation, reluctantly negotiated by union officials like Walter Reuther in the 1940s. In both cases, labor's legitimacy depended on its ability to defend economic governance as a modern means of promoting technological progress and economic stability. By exchanging tariffs for rights, unions appealed to a traditionally hostile bourgeoisie, favoring industrial efficiency and international cooperation.[30]

Unfortunately for manufacturing workers, both pacts depended politically on America's unsustainable dominance of the international economy. After 1945, U.S. consumers had little interest in the products of war-ravaged England, Germany, and Japan, much less China. During the late 1970s and 1980s, however, declining rates of productivity, expanding global competition, stagflation, and a fierce political backlash undermined the economic and electoral support for the Reutherite pact.[31] And similar forces destabilized the bargain on trade. As the United States shifted from being a net exporter to being a net importer, the business community turned against tariffs, leading the Republican Party to abandon its traditional support for import restriction. Changes in the nation's economic structure meant a smaller percentage of the electorate benefited directly from protectionism. As organized labor shrank, especially in manufacturing, the Democratic Party lost its incentive to maintain the agreement, leading to treaties like NAFTA, which offered workers nothing for their sacrifices.

Meanwhile, competition with other nations seemed only to strengthen the conservative hand, allowing the wealthy to assert that organized labor, protectionism, the regulatory welfare state, and heavy industry itself were vestiges of the past, barriers to competitiveness, and speed bumps on the road to the future. Even after the economy started soaring in the 1990s, unions proved incapable of selling their vision to a nation obsessed with "progress," euphoric over new technology and the pleasures of foreign consumer goods. Though tariffs had fallen to historically minuscule levels, labor found itself under attack from libertarian economic commentators like Robert Samuelson and Sebastian Mallaby. But if censure from this quarter was predictable, criticism from nominally liberal columnists like Thomas Friedman and Joe Klein was more damaging. In 2003, Klein called Democratic attacks on NAFTA "cynical" and "extremist," describing the defense of "international labor and environmental standards" as fruitless and tariffs as economically risky. Even more damaging are Friedman's widely read columns and books, which equate globalization with modernization, calling any attempt to enforce labor standards "Luddite."[32]

Lacking the clout to command economic nationalism through law, labor began begging consumers to "Buy American." Yet such pleas only feed the perception that American industries needed help because they are less technologically sophisticated, efficient, and progressive than their Asian counterparts. At the same time, after reading an author like Thomas Friedman, a thoughtful citizen might conclude that choosing to buy imports is itself a humanitarian gesture, as it encourages industrialization in poorer, rural counties, thus alleviating global poverty. Meanwhile, neoliberals have hijacked popular antiracism to subvert legitimate concerns about trade with unfree nations, suggesting that protectionism is merely a form of bigotry. If blue-collar Americans shop at Wal-Mart out of geographic and financial necessity, their bourgeois counterparts shop at Target partly because they perceive its goods to be the hip products of a forward-looking, color-blind, and beneficent globalization process.[33]

Workers today confront a familiar problem: how to stage protests and advocate policies that align their interests with the public interest, identified as a continually rising standard of living. Twice before, workers have made themselves part of a modernizing *telos*, then seen conservatives cast them as regressive, and then recalibrated their position to reclaim their role as agents of development. While no media campaign can or should convince the American people to restore the 50 percent tariffs of the nineteenth century, labor needs to restore the old compromise. Just as the business community demanded intellectual property protections as the price of open markets, workers could block all new trade deals until Americans receive new labor rights. But in the long run, the challenge is for unions to develop a set of policies that actually ameliorate the effects of globalization on the American worker, without offending the Whiggish assumptions of the middle-class voter. The alternative is to abandon industrial workers to a global market in which their citizenship rights are costly handicaps.

Chapter 2

The American Legion and Striking Workers During the Interwar Period

Christopher Nehls

From the outbreak of the first Red Scare through the organizing struggles of the Great Depression, the veterans organization the American Legion became notorious within the American labor movement for its members' brazen red-baiting and vigilantism. To many of its outspoken critics, like the novelist Sinclair Lewis and Northwestern University education professor William Gellermann, the organization represented a germinating seed of American fascism by the mid-1930s. To others, Legionnaires' anti-union vigilantism revealed them as little more than stooges of the local industrial boss or Chamber of Commerce. Legion members themselves, meanwhile, typically explained criticism of labor and intervention during strikes as nothing to do with fascism or the interests of capital. Instead, they claimed to be acting to defend "law and order" and to protect American freedom and liberty from Communist subversion. How the Legion squared the attack on the very same values its members proclaimed they were defending has confounded its critics ever since.[1]

Part of the problem of understanding what motivated Legion vigi-lantism is that the organization's explanations seem so flimsy. Despite its leadership's protests to the contrary, the organization was not neutral in conflicts between capital and labor. It never found patriotic cause to rally its members to workers' defense. National leadership disciplined posts only when members joined picket lines and never when they broke them. Legionnaires often were in cahoots with the business elite, while corporate titans provided generous financial support to get the organization off the ground.

This record does not mean that historians should dismiss the idealism the American Legion poured into its defense of Americanism—its preferred term for the values and ideals at the heart of national identity. By taking conservative Legionnaires' ideas seriously, this essay provides insight into a critical period in the historical development of the "Labor Question." As former Progressive Era reformers, New Deal politicos, and workers themselves searched for new mechanisms and strategies for bridging class division within the political economy, many of the veterans who joined the American Legion puzzled over the Labor Question's effect on the political culture. Their concern was how to reconcile the problems that faced the working class with the nation's individualist republican traditions.[2] Through some noteworthy internal wrangling, the Legion came to a consensus about the limits of legitimate union activity. These limits, which Legionnaires at times enforced physically, created ideological boundaries within interwar political culture. It was not that the organization rejected unionism in some protofascist attitude: rather, Legionnaires argued that union members were bound by the responsibilities and obligations all citizens owed to be considered part of the national community.

Interestingly, Progressivism significantly influenced how Legion leadership conceived of these civic responsibilities to the nation and the Labor Question more broadly. Although after the war most Progressives seriously began to doubt the American people's capacity for national unity in the name of reform, the Legion took up again its prewar discussion of finding a balance between the interests of capital and labor for the common good. For example, Texas Legion commander and future national commander Alvin Owsley told an Armistice Day crowd in 1920, "we can preserve the harmony of all classes and of the masses and the equilibrium of the Union by giving equal and exact justice to all men—all classes alike—by wiping out from the statue [sic] books every law that oppresses one for the benefit of another, and by frowning down the efforts of politicians to kindle the fires of class hatred."[3] Citizens did their part by deferring the political, social, and economic interests of their class to serve the good of the nation. In the context of the immediate postwar political climate, one North

Dakota Legionnaire complained that "the actions of individuals are governed too much by considerations affecting the particular group to which they belong, whether it be that of wealth, aristocracy, labor, or business." The American Legion, meanwhile, was "striving to have all public questions and controversies judged according to the spirit of a broad Americanism."[4] These Progressive-inspired values became the bedrock of the Legion's civic nationalism. As a result, the Legion's Americanism required working-class citizens to be deliberative, accommodating, and incremental in pursuing their economic and political interests to be considered "American."

But men joined the Legion not to participate in political theory debates but to put the values of Americanism into action. And as examples I draw upon in this essay demonstrate, determining when unionized workers had stepped beyond their right to protect their interests and had begun harming the common good was unclear to many within the organization. Given broad directives to maintain law and order, curtail Communist influence, and preserve the spirit of Americanism, posts differed on when they could rightfully intervene in the name of patriotic service to the nation. Those that intervened during strikes represented the organization's most conservative tendencies. While the interventions of individual posts may have generated debate, the legitimacy of veterans acting to preserve Americanism or compel specific behaviors from other citizens did not.

The international context further encouraged Legionnaires to be suspicious of American labor. Postwar revolutions led many veterans to worry about the future of the nation's exceptional historical development. They saw the rise of Bolshevism as a counterpoint to Americanism. A Legion author wrote in 1919 that "Russia has run in a circle. From the autocracy of the classes it has arrived at the autocracy of the masses."[5] Because of immigration, the nation could not guarantee its insulation from foreign radicalism. Although the Legion was hardly the first to blame domestic radicalism on immigrants, its investment in nationalism to bridge class division intensified many of its members' belief that many strikes were a revolutionary plot designed to rip apart the fabric of the nation. The ascendance of Stalin's Soviet Union, Depression era rise of the Communist Party of the United States, and creation of the Popular Front intensified Legionnaires' association of some unions with a hostile international conspiracy. While the Legion was still unwilling to go so far as to call unions or workers "un-American"—a move that would have pitted it directly against the vision of citizenship within the labor provisions of the New

Deal—its interest in exposing Communist plots within labor took precedence over considering the citizenship rights of American workers in the midst of the Depression.

Concern over the Labor Question was embedded in the American Legion from its creation. Its founders, army officers from prominent political backgrounds who had served in France during World War I, envisioned a mass-membership organization to "carry into the new life that effective teamwork and mutual support" that veterans "had so thoroughly learned in the army."[6] But the labor unrest that returning veterans encountered when they began to arrive home after the war channeled this amorphous desire into a new mission: maintaining "law and order." This well-worn phrase encapsulated the Legion's belief that disloyal behavior could easily unravel the polity. It also proved resonant to returning veterans. During the strike by Boston policemen in September 1919, Legionnaires pledged to Governor Calvin Coolidge that they were ready to act "against sympathetic strikes under the existing circumstances as a radical injury to and the abrogation of civil rights and liberty." That week, over a thousand veterans paid their Legion dues. Soon, so many veterans were signing up that the Massachusetts Department ran out of its supply of membership buttons and by year's end sixty thousand Bay State veterans had joined.[7]

During a coal strike in Kansas in late 1919, Legionnaires went much further than merely volunteering to maintain "law and order"—they crossed picket lines as scabs. In November, members of the United Mine Workers led a strike at fields in the state's southeastern corner. Although the U.S. Fuel Administration allotted a 14 percent raise for coal miners, rampant postwar inflation cut into the purchasing power of those wages. Union members walked out, demanding higher pay.[8] Through an order by the Kansas Supreme Court, Republican governor Henry J. Allen took control of the mines and requested National Guard and U.S. Army protection of work sites. The governor justified state seizure of the mines because nearby communities relied exclusively on the mines for winter fuel. To extract the coal Allen asked for volunteers. A Legion post in Wichita supplied two hundred of the nearly one thousand men who showed up to mine coal. Five brought their steam shovels with them. Department Commander W. A. Phares, whom many working-class Legionnaires believed was anti-union, wired posts across the state for additional support, including doctors to tend to the volunteers. The Kansas Board of Commerce helped coordinate these efforts with Phares and offered to buy Legionnaires mining gear. The strike was broken in weeks, although the unionized workers retained their government-mandated raise.[9]

Such strikebreaking divided Legionnaires. The Earl W. Taylor Post of Seneca praised Allen's efforts in a resolution because it "relieved suffering in Kansas." After pledging their "undivided allegiance in all situations in which [the Legion] seeks to exert its authority for the welfare of the masses wherever such Federal action conflicts with the interests of any one class or classes," members asserted that "we do not regard volunteer workers as strike breakers, at the same time admitting the right of labor to benefit from its condition when such action does not bring suffering and distress to unnumbered multitudes." National Commander Franklin D'Olier endorsed this opinion, praising Kansas Legionnaires' actions because they represented the actions of responsible citizens in an emergency.[10] Posts in coal towns like Pittsburg and Frontenac, meanwhile, were particularly critical of the mining operation. One post commander in Frontenac telegrammed the governor to reject his request for manpower "as such offer would scent of strikebreaking we will not issue call for volunteers to dig coal." Ex-servicemen who were out on strike in Arma issued a public petition asserting that "this strike is not the work of a few Radicals, but by 'Honest American Citizens' like our-selves, that are fighting for wages to keep our Families in food and clothing." The thirty-five veterans who signed the petition, almost all of whom were enlisted men, rejected the strikebreakers as "much worse than 'Consienceous [sic] Objectors'" during the war. Commander Phares traveled to Pittsburg to soothe these posts' ruffled feathers and explain that those Legionnaires who had mined coal had done so as individuals, not representatives of the organization. His explanation swayed few and these posts, among the first to be organized in the Sunflower State, lost half their members. Posts in nearby Kansas City also lost members who belonged to railroad and meatpackers' unions.[11]

Unions and unionized Legionnaires elsewhere in the nation had similar reactions to Legion strikebreaking in 1919 and 1920. A Detroit local in the Automobile, Aircraft, and Vehicle Workers Union fined one member $100 when it discovered he was a member of the American Legion. After the New York County Council of the Legion organized a list of members capable of operating city infrastructure during a strike in the spring of 1920, the Central Federated Union ordered its members to resign from the organization.

Larger unions followed suit. The United Mine Workers, Detroit and Montana State Federations of Labor, and New York Central Trades and Labor Council all ordered their members to quit the Legion in 1920. Unions' reactions to Legion strikebreaking pushed working-class veterans out of the organization in droves. By the end of 1922, it had hemorrhaged more than 120,000 members.[12]

This loss of membership from laboring veterans and union supporters further cemented significant demographic trends that were developing among the American Legion's ranks. From its earliest days, the organization attracted many more middle-class and affluent veterans than those from the working class. Some of this trend was due to American conscription policy during the war, which forbade the service of immigrants from enemy nations and granted deferments to farm and industrial workers, particularly in 1918. Only a handful of delegates to the Legion's first national organizing caucus in St. Louis in 1919 were laborers, mechanics, or craftsmen, while lawyers, bankers, and businessmen dominated the proceedings. The Legion attracted many men who had enlisted in the military as opposed to draftees, which further skewed its membership toward greater affluence. It made little effort to recruit the half million foreign-born veterans (100,000 of whom did not even speak English), while its policy of segregating local posts kept its membership among African American members minuscule. Nearly 100,000 ex-servicemen chose to join Marvin Gates Sperry's Private Soldiers and Sailors' Legion, more commonly referred to as the World War Veterans, which distinguished itself from the American Legion by calling for a large ($500) discharge bonus and requiring new members to sign a pledge not to work as strikebreakers.[13]

Although the Legion trumpeted that its members represented a "cross section" of American society repeatedly through the interwar period, after its first year it increasingly resembled the other middle-class service organizations that were popular during this era. The organization found great success not only among professional men in large cities but also among veterans in the nation's rapidly growing small cities and towns. These trends held especially true in the Midwest and Great Plains states. Thirty-seven thousand Iowans, for example, joined one of the four hundred posts in the state, while a single post in Omaha, Nebraska, grew to more than twenty-five hundred members. Professional men, small business owners, and government employees—men inclined to see themselves as the pillars of community life—were among the Legion's most typical members. In a 1938 membership survey the organization revealed that 64 percent of Legionnaires made over $2,000 annually, when the median family income was about $1,200. Only 13 percent of surveyed members were skilled workers while still fewer were farmers (2 percent) or unskilled workers (4 percent).[14] Because leadership positions at any level of the organization required the kind of time and resources most available to middle-class or wealthy individuals, those charting how the Legion should respond to the Labor Question were well insulated from the struggles of working people.

National officers, however, realized that the organization could ill afford the negative publicity that resulted from members' strikebreaking. They quickly tried to clarify the Legion's official position on labor disputes. National Commander D'Olier, himself the heir to a textile company fortune, demanded posts remain neutral between capital and labor during strikes in their localities. National Headquarters in Indianapolis refused, however, to disallow members to "follow the dictates of their own consciences within the law of the land whether this leads them to participate in an organized strike, or whether, on the other hand, this may prompt them to volunteer their services as individuals . . . to continue the production of the necessities of life temporarily, in order to prevent suffering and alleviate distress."[15] This stance reflected the organization's need to compromise between its desire to retain favorable public opinion and yet allow Legionnaires to perform the necessary patriotic service to their communities that labor disputes might necessitate. Fundamentally, it also reflected a broader rejection of class as an organizing principle in American life and the Legion's hopes that its Americanism could bridge the distance between social classes.

This official position of neutrality would last through the entire interwar period. But implementing it remained subject to individual members' interpretations. The ambiguity of this policy stemmed from the Legion leadership's embrace of vigilantism as a legitimate way to preserve social and political order. During World War I, Americans had used vigilante actions to enforce the loyalty of their fellow citizens. This work was done with the blessing of the Wilson administration, which used volunteerism and encouraged citizen vigilance to make up for its own weakness. This conception of civic obligation did not simply evaporate with the signing of the Armistice. As the model citizens their veteran status granted them, Legionnaires felt obligated to serve the state and nation to thwart disloyalty, disorder, and revolution.[16] Posts' strikebreaking took place in a wider context of such vigilante actions against others like the Industrial Workers of the World, the Socialist Party, and even pacifist activists whom veterans suspected of working to overthrow the political and social order. National leadership saw such efforts as completely justifiable because they protected American democratic institutions and ideals from people Legion cofounder Eric Fisher Wood described as "irresponsible, shiftless, and cowardly groups of men, who seek by direct anarchistic action to overthrow the government . . . in order to seize by violent methods what they have been too lazy, too stupid, or too incompetent to obtain by fair means."[17]

Shifting public opinion against Legion vigilantism and the loss of membership forced the organization to seek additional strategies for dealing with class conflict. In early 1920 the American Legion created a National Americanism Commission (NAC) to better coordinate how posts promoted good citizenship. The NAC was modeled on the wartime Committee on Public Information and was charged with the duty to "realize in the United States the basic idea of this Legion of 100% Americanism through the planning, establishment, and conduct of a continuous, constructive educational system." Such a program would "inculcate the ideals of Americanism in the citizen population, particularly the basic American principle that the interests of all the people are above those of any special interest or any so-called class or section of people," and "spread throughout the people of the nation information as to the real nature and principles of American government."[18] The NAC became the focal point of the organization's antiradical activities. Its members, like those serving on all national-level committees, served at the pleasure of the unelected National Executive Committee and were not subject to organizational elections like those at its annual conference that chose a national commander.

The first commissioners of the NAC embraced a vaguely Progressive vision of the values that bound Americans together, which the Legion described as "Americanism." In one of their earliest meetings, Legionnaires described this creed as "the principle of justice, fair play, the square deal, equality before the law for rich and poor, labor and capitalist, the educated man and the illiterate." But even they believed these principles were only as good as Americans' capacity to be loyal to them. In trying to pin down a precise definition of Americanism—which neither they nor subsequent commissioners ever did—they, too, spoke of the need for the preservation of "law and order" in the face of radical unrest.[19] The NAC, in its attempt to clarify what the Legion stood for, reflected the broad tension throughout the organization between the impulse to celebrate American democratic traditions and the perceived need to enforce a necessary spirit of obligation to them among a corruptible public.

To reinforce its precise position on the legitimacy of the labor movement, the American Legion pursued a strong relationship with the American Federation of Labor (AFL). Ideologically, the two organizations had much in common. The AFL curtailed its use of strikes, particularly to win wage gains in boom times, and sought collective bargaining as a method to rationalize shop politics. It claimed not to be after undue benefits but what AFL officer and Legion vice president George L. Berry claimed was "a square deal" that would allow workers the material comforts they needed to become better citizens. As Samuel Gompers's successor as AFL president, William Green, wrote Legionnaires in the *American Legion Monthly* in 1926, "organized labor is coming to believe that its best interests are promoted through concord rather than conflict. It prefers the conference table to the strike field." The average Legionnaire probably admired the AFL's staunch antiradicalism more than its philosophy of industrial democracy. Legionnaires in Oregon, for example, praised the AFL's ultimatum to the Seattle Central Labor Council to rescind its endorsement of the Soviet government in Russia and praised Gompers's antiradicalism.[20]

Renewed labor activism during the Depression again challenged Legion Americanism. Throughout the organization concern rose that radical insurgents would use the economic crisis to foment revolution soon after the Great Crash on Wall Street. The National Americanism Commission warned the delegates to the 1930 national convention that "the sinister powers within that threaten our very existence, offer a grave challenge to our organization. Americanism demands our best vigilance. With these changing conditions we face the task of perpetuating our American traditions and ideals. No quicker way to our country's downfall could be found than to permit the national character to weaken and its ideals to disintegrate."[21] The resurgence of the American Communist movement in the early and mid-1930s convinced antiradicals in the organization all the more that labor activism was being driven by a subversive conspiracy. As had occurred during the first Red Scare, some Legionnaires responded with vigilante action during strikes. Those led by Communist-penetrated unions of the Congress of Industrial Organizations (CIO) or activists whom posts considered outside agitators were particularly targeted. And once again, such action did not take place without significant debate within the organization.

Legion leadership continued to support more conservative unions' efforts to promote the equality of opportunity for workers during the economic crisis. "Ours is a free representative government under which both the individual and his group are entitled to pursue their own happiness, protected in so doing by the hand of government, but subject always to whatever restraint it is necessary to impose under the law and the Constitution to bring about the greatest good for the greatest number," National Commander Harry Colmery explained to the 1936 national convention of the American Federation of Labor. While American politics did not preclude all class-based initiatives, Colmery asserted that Legionnaires "have the right to be concerned about any minority group which oversteps the bounds of liberty and uses it as a license to violate the rights of others, disturb the peace, or defy constituted authority."[22] Still, the Legion proclaimed neutrality in the conflict between labor and capital. But Legionnaires considered strikes and other political organizing by more radical unions to be illegitimate and un-American. Despite their economic difficulties, working-class Americans had no right to usurp American democratic traditions by asserting a class-based political identity.

The claim of outside agitation not only shielded Legionnaires from the impression of attacking struggling workers directly but also created a powerful symbolic image of local patriots defending Americanism from radical insurgents. Intervention in local strikes represented part of a greater struggle against Communist infiltration of the nation. Department commanders in Rhode Island and South Carolina authorized their posts to serve as peace officers during the great textile strike of 1934, asserting that strikes in their states were caused by outside Communist influences. Often, Legionnaires' actions came with the direct endorsement of local or state government. In 1934, California governor Frank Merriam met directly with Department Commander Homer Chaillaux during the San Francisco longshoremen's strike. Chaillaux promised the governor Legion vigilante support because the strike was led by Australian Harry Bridges, thought to be a Communist. Incited by Hearst papers' claims of pervasive radical dominance in the San Francisco general strike that ensued that July, Legionnaires formed the backbone of the "citizen vigilante" force that brutalized and intimidated picketers.[23]

South Dakota Legionnaires perpetrated one of the most violent responses to radical union organizing efforts in August 1934. That summer, a traveling educative initiative designed by the labor-friendly Commonwealth College of Mena, Arkansas, called the "Farm School on Wheels" arrived in Marshall County, South Dakota. On the road since 1932, the Farm School on Wheels traveled across the country, stopping to stage a four-week-long course designed to politicize those toiling in the depressed agricultural sector. Backed by the local sheriff, Legionnaires broke up a demonstration organized by the local United Workers' League and the Farm School in Britton on August 25. Legionnaires in half a dozen cars then pursued one of the rally's trucks in a rambling forty-mile chase over roads and wheat fields into North Dakota. That evening, Legionnaires attacked a dance held by the Farm School in a barn, firing tear gas into the building to disperse the crowd inside. The mob beat six students of the school, including disabled World War veteran Maynard Sharp. Sharp narrowly missed being shot, took tear gas in his eyes, and suffered several broken ribs. The six students were then taken into the post's Auxiliary's rooms and beaten, as newspapers reported, with belt buckles and clubs to "demonstrate the power of the U.S. Government."[24]

Legion vigilantes' periodic xenophobia was connected to both race and class. Both shaped their response to the Imperial Valley agricultural strike of 1934, where union organizing efforts threatened to upset the social and racial order. Mexican and Filipino immigrants dominated the lower rungs of the labor pool used by lettuce growers in the valley. In October 1933, Mexican field-workers organized themselves into a union and won an agreement from growers for a region-wide wage increase. When some farm owners balked, workers accepted the offer of the Communist-allied Cannery and Agricultural Workers Industrial Union to lead a strike that began in January 1934. Local police and Legion vigilantes responded swiftly; they interdicted a caravan of workers traveling between union communities on the highway and broke up a mass meeting in a community center with tear gas. After the American Civil Liberties Union (ACLU) dispatched attorney A. L. Wirin to El Centro to ensure workers' freedom of assembly rights were respected, Legionnaires and other vigilantes abducted him from his hotel. After beating him and threatening him with a branding iron, the vigilantes took him outside a Legion post. Wirin said that members gathered and shone flashlights on him so they could recognize him if he reappeared in the valley. They then drove him into the desert, ditched his car in a riverbed, and left him to find his way back to the nearest town barefoot. The actions taken against Wirin led the National Labor Board and later the Labor Department to send investigators to the valley to quell local conflict.[25]

California Department Commander Chaillaux, an emerging antiradical firebrand within the organization, did little to restore the notion that Legionnaires had retained their neutrality during the strike. At a department convention in Hanford, Chaillaux challenged Wirin's abduction story as a lie, which prompted Wirin to sue him for slander. A committee appointed by Chaillaux to investigate the kidnapping acknowledged the deputization of Legion members as individuals but denied that the organization itself played any role in the labor conflict. For his part, Chaillaux audaciously denied there had even been a strike by workers since much of the organizing work had been done by outside Communist unionists. In its editorial response to the entire episode, the *California Legionnaire* noted "95 per cent of those involved in the troubles were citizens of a country other than the United States."[26] Chaillaux's defense of his members and his willingness to sling radical charges at his opponents earned him a promotion: when fellow Californian and like-minded antiradical Frank Belgrano became national commander, Chaillaux came with him to Indianapolis to head the NAC. There he remained until his sudden death from a heart attack in 1945, using this permanent position to expand the NAC's antiradical staff considerably. Chaillaux installed an index card file system on suspected radical persons and organizations that he pioneered in California in NAC offices and published his investgators' findings in regular reports.

Legionnaires saw outside influence everywhere. Many in the nation's industrial core considered the CIO organizing drives in automobile and steel plants in 1937 to be Communist-driven plots to take over the American industry. To halt this advance, Steel Belt posts struck up direct relationships with plant management. The Ford Motor Company recruited Legion men to form a private vigilante force to bolster its own factory police. In Flint, Michigan, Legionnaires clamored to form strikebreaking units during the CIO's sit-down strike at General Motors. When Michigan governor Frank Murphy, himself a Legionnaire, refused to deputize Legion men en masse, his department demanded his expulsion.[27] Legion posts garnered national notoriety in Monroe, Michigan, in June when Legionnaires were photographed by the press armed with clubs and tear gas launchers to help

local police suppress a United Auto Workers march that did not material-
ize. When criticism poured into National Headquarters, including from at
least twenty-six Legion posts, Monroe members defended their actions by
claiming they were not against collective bargaining but that the CIO had
in essence invaded their community, provoking their response. National
Commander Colmery responded by forbidding Legionnaires from participating in any more antistrike activity wearing Legion uniforms or insignia.
He also told NAC chairman Chaillaux to stop making grandstanding
appearances at strikes.[28] He did not, however, challenge the fundamental
legitimacy of the Legion's role in policing the loyalty of workers in Legionnaires' communities.

During the CIO-led auto strikes of 1937, Legionnaires assumed a new
role in performing vigilance work by directly presenting the results of their
local surveillance work to federal investigators. Legionnaires tailed suspected Communists and Socialists during the sit-down strikes at General
Motors plants. Several members then testified before congressional investigations into the strikes held by Martin Dies's House Un-American Activities Committee. In his testimony before the Dies Committee in October
1938, Mark Reynolds, the chairman of the Michigan Department Ameri-
canization Committee's subcommittee on subversive activities, provided
the government with the names and addresses of suspected Communists
and the locations of known meeting places of Communist groups. He listed
both public and private spaces, including ethnic fraternal halls, barber-
shops, and private homes. He also provided information to the committee
on what his Legion spies had uncovered while monitoring radical speakers.[29] Reynolds also told the Dies Committee that young black men will
"readily admit that their interest in communism lies in white women," and
that the idea of racial equality preached by the Communist Party "serves as
a potent factor in mustering Communist strength for the planned seizure
of the American form of government." He proceeded to name several interracial married couples in Detroit for the public record.[30]

Some Legion posts remained sympathetic to striking workers during the
Depression. A few posts in San Francisco refused to cooperate with Homer
Chaillaux's vigilante plan during the longshoremen's strike, as did other
posts during a simultaneous strike in Portland, Oregon. An entire San Francisco post united to march in the funeral procession for a union member
and World War veteran who was killed during violence preceding the general strike there. Legion railway workers in Texas protested to National

Headquarters the use of deputized Legionnaires who joined police and National Guard contingents that killed ten workers in the great textile strike of 1934 as a "bloodcurdling outrage." While such violent antistrike activities rarely earned Legionnaires suspensions from the organization, veterans in two Manhattan posts did have their membership suspended in April 1936 for wearing Legion helmets, caps, and uniforms on the picket line at a Brooklyn burlesque theater during a theater workers' strike.[31]

Some liberal Legionnaires also openly criticized their organization's broad disregard for civil liberties during the Depression, of which strike-related vigilantism was only one part. In 1936, the ACLU's Walter Wilson prepared a short pamphlet chronicling Legion abuses entitled *The American Legion and Civil Liberty*. Signed by prominent Legionnaires like W. W. Norton, Bennett Champ Clark, and Merle Curti, the pamphlet aimed "to counteract what are essentially un-American attitudes" within the Legion, "totally unworthy of men who fought for democracy." Rather than critique the choices individual members made in participating in such activities, the sponsors of the pamphlet blamed the organization's national leadership. The average member, they argued, "receives no benefits from strikebreaking and red-baiting. If he joins in such activities it is because he is fooled by his Post or state or national leadership. Not until this rank and file Legionnaire makes his officers feel his own faith in democracy, in the Bill of Rights, in tolerance and fair play, will the American Legion be able to fulfill its avowed purpose of transmitting 'to posterity the principles of justice, freedom and democracy.'"[32] The Willard Strait Post of Manhattan, a longtime liberal nonconformist branch, similarly took conservative Legion leadership to task with its 1936 pamphlet *Americanism: What Is It?* Written by former *Stars and Stripes* editor Cyrus L. Baldridge, it was published as a proposed speech for ceremonies honoring junior high students receiving Americanism awards from Legion posts. Real Americanism, Baldridge asserted, "is expressed in a determined and magnificent human struggle to achieve Democracy, Justice & Liberty," which would ensure an equality of opportunity for all Americans. The pamphlet struck particularly at the idea that Communist influence within the labor movement and elsewhere had to be eradicated. While "many people, recently converted to new and un-Democratic forms of government, are eager to bring about similar changes here in America . . . believing in Freedom of Speech for others as well as for ourselves, we must not attempt to abuse or silence them."[33] Where conservative Legionnaires saw a worrisomely fragile system that could be manipulated to inflame the masses, Baldridge and his allies saw in American democracy something unassailable.

This criticism from the Legion's liberal members reflected the chasm that had widened between its ideological left and right during the interwar period. Legionnaires across the political spectrum still shared in common a faith in the exceptional nature of the American nation and nationalistic meaning of its democratic traditions and institutions. Where they differed significantly was how to preserve this exceptional democratic heritage in light of enormous social and economic issues like the Labor Question and the broader problem of class in American society. For liberals in the American Legion and everywhere, the Depression had demonstrated that the state had to use its power to protect workers' rights as the best way to preserve democracy. Legion conservatives remained wedded to the values of citizen obligation, national community, and class-free political participation. As the pro-labor aspects of the New Deal cemented the partnership between the state and working-class citizens, the supposedly timeless conservative values of most Legionnaires seemed at once more antiquated and vulnerable.

The Legion's hostility to liberals' reenvisioning of "Americanism" explains an aspect of a grassroots conservative resistance to organized labor's ascendance by the end of the interwar period.[34] But as the constant drumbeat against Communism that Legionnaires raised throughout the activities discussed in this essay suggest, it is only part of the story. The Legion perpetuated a conception of disloyalty that was rooted in the experiences of World War I and the first Red Scare. Like many conservatives, Legionnaires worried about how disloyal individuals could exploit American freedoms and rally impressionable masses to their radical and "un-American" cause, destroying the interlocking bonds of obligation between citizens that formed the fabric of American democracy. Legion posts understood their role in labor disputes as a unique kind of police power, which could discipline disloyalty and reestablish the principles central to the nation's identity. For liberals, the presence of suspected (or actual) Communist organizers within a union drive was less important than whether or not the effort redressed a fundamental inequality for the workers affected. Many Legionnaires could make no such allowances. For them, the issues of class division and national identity intertwined in such a way that American exceptionalism faced real peril if radicals were tolerated. Hence, veterans demanded again and again that unionized workers prove not the justice of their cause but their loyalty.

Democracy or Seduction? The Demonization of Scientific Management and the Deification of Human Relations

Chris Nyland and Kyle Bruce

Recent decades have witnessed a mounting challenge to the orthodox understanding of the foundational years of management thought in interwar America. On the one hand, a number of revisionist scholars have questioned the orthodoxy that holds Elton Mayo and his colleagues in the Human Relations "school" he inspired were pioneers in a humanist form of management that involved a softer and kinder approach to employer-employee relations than had previously prevailed within industry. On the other, a small but growing number of scholars have questioned the claim that Frederick Winslow Taylor, the "father" of scientific management, advocated a mechanistic and unsophisticated approach to management that deskilled workers and prioritized the interests of property owners and their agents by pointing to the Taylorists' efforts to democratize management decision making. Collectively, these twin streams of scholarship have revealed that Mayo played an inspirational role in developing innovations that helped ensure management remained an elite activity,[1] while the Taylorists attempted and eventually failed in efforts to democratize the management process.[2]

In this chapter we build on these contributions by contrasting how the Taylorists and Mayoists viewed the notion of industrial democracy and how their respective perspectives shaped their interaction. We begin by indicating why the leaders of the Taylor Society (an epistemic community assembled in 1912 by Taylor's inner circle) supported the notion that workers should participate in *all* areas of management and we then detail the distaste for industrial democracy that informed Mayo and his colleagues. Next we trace the continuing interaction of the Taylorist and human relations traditions to the late 1940s. In undertaking this latter effort, we explain how, with the help of John D. Rockefeller Jr. and other corporate oligarchs, Mayo managed to establish the Human Relations School (HRS) as the foundation on which contemporary organizational behavior and human resource management theory and practice is currently constructed and how it was the Taylorists were driven from the field, thus leaving to their opponents the task of creating what became orthodox management history.

Taylorism and Industrial Democracy

That Mayo was a self-confessed advocate of elitist management systems went understated for many years even by scholars who recognized his antipathy to industrial democracy. However, in two devastating 1999 articles, Ellen O'Connor documented both Mayo's conviction that "therapy" could substitute for workplace democracy and his efforts to promote this message to the "rulers" of society.[3] Central to O'Connor's argument is Mayo's claim that workers do not have the mental capacity to participate in management activity and consequently must be managed by those whose background and training has provided them with the emotional and mental capacities required to address the complexity of management processes. In support of her argument O'Connor cites Mayo's 1919 observation: "[The] suggestion that the workers in any industry should control it after the fashion of 'democratic' politics would not only introduce all the ills of partisan politics into industrial management, but would also place the final power in the hands of the least skilled workers. In many industries this would give the unskilled laborer control over the craftsman properly so-called. And, more generally, the effect would be to determine problems requiring the highest skill by placing the decisions in the hands of those who were unable even to understand the problem."[4] In espousing his conviction that workers need to be "ruled" by an informed and not necessarily humane elite, Mayo situated himself against those who embraced the participatory conception of democracy associated with figures such as Jean-Jacques Rousseau, Jeremy Bentham, John Stuart Mill, or G. D. H. Cole. Democracy for Mayo was a form of government rather than a social condition. In other words, he did not believe that for a democratic polity to exist it is necessary for a participatory society to exist.[5] For Mayo, an argument for such necessity conflated the moral or civic function of the citizen-voter with the technical function of the professional or expert in industry. He took particular exception to Cole's advocacy of industrial democracy on the basis of "Cole's suggestion of quasi-parliamentary control in industry entirely disregards the fact that industries resemble 'professions' in that they are skilled communal functions. In all matters of social skill the widest knowledge and the highest skill should be sovereign rather than the opinion of 'collective mediocrity'. . . . The outstanding failure of democracy is its failure to appreciate the social importance of knowledge and skill."[6] O'Connor rightly observes that the portrayal of workers as individuals with minds that are unsophisticated and motivated primarily by custom and emotion and who consequently need to be managed by elites was very attractive to corporate America. Mayo's message was appealing because he promised a way to alleviate worker dissatisfaction without redistributing power (or increasing the cost of labor), one that, in so doing, would save what those elites deemed to be civilization. In short, the notion that workers were simply incapable of participating effectively in management appealed to corporate conservatives because it justified resistance to all forms of industrial democracy and it appealed to corporate liberals who could accept collective bargaining but wanted this activity to be the outer limit of worker participation in management decision making.

But while acknowledging that O'Connor has made a powerful contribution to the revisionist history of management thought, we do question her assumption that Mayo's ideas were firmly situated within the Taylorist tradition. She links Taylor and Mayo by noting that both men placed great emphasis on the need to found management thought and practice on knowledge and skill rather than on bias and rule of thumb.[7] This is an observation that has some validity, but in a discussion of the struggle surrounding industrial democracy, it does not appreciate key differences between the Taylorists and the Mayoists. Most importantly, it accords inadequate attention to who the two schools believed should control the development and application of knowledge and skill within industry and the wider society.

That O'Connor misses the democratic element within the Taylorist movement is surprising, for the very industrial democrats she deems of particular significance include Ordway Tead, Mary Parker Follett, and Mary Van Kleeck,[8] all of whom were leading members of the Taylor Society. But while her oversight is a little surprising, it is understandable given the strength of the popular belief that Taylorists opposed industrial democracy.[9] Informed by this perspective scholars have found it extremely difficult to accommodate the evidence of Taylorist collaboration with progressive social forces. Indeed, even scholars who are aware of the interwar collaboration between the Taylorists and the trade unions commonly remain propagators of the notion that the scientific managers were opposed to industrial democracy.

But if the association of industrial democracy and Taylorism sits uncomfortably with current orthodoxy, it is very much compatible with Samuel Haber's observation that Taylor's inner circle was firmly grounded within Progressivism.[10] This was a broad movement characterized by a commitment to industrial and social efficiency attained through the application of scientific method, participatory democratic government, and state regulation of business practices where this was deemed to be required to ensure competition and free enterprise.

It is important to note that Taylor and his inner circle were Progressives and consequently were motivated by these beliefs, for it was their commitment to Progressive principles that distinguished them from managers and management theorists who claim heritage from Taylor but have merely embraced his commitment to enterprise efficiency. This appreciation is also necessary to comprehend why Taylor Society members became deeply concerned when they observed that industrialists were repeatedly utilizing their market and political power to ensure that profit accumulation was invariably prioritized over the development and application of scientific method. These men and women accepted that capitalist firms must generate an adequate rate of return if they are to survive. However, they had great difficulty accepting the ease with which property owners were willing to subordinate knowledge that could improve industrial and social life to the profit motive.

This discomfit induced both Taylor and his inner circle to embrace a range of means designed to counter this trend, including a sustained effort to convince the engineering professional associations to accept that knowledge development and application should be prioritized over profit accumulation. As Edwin Layton has documented, in so doing they accorded particular weight to the building of alliances with engineers and non-engineers who they believed would accord knowledge a higher priority than business interests were willing to concede.[11] Who the Taylorists perceived might be effective allies in this quest changed over time. For example, Taylor Society members initially thought company unions could fulfill this role, but gradually they came to accept that only independent unions have the capacity to motivate firms to democratize management and by so doing motivate firms to accord a high priority to knowledge accumulation even if this process did not directly serve the interests of property owners and professional managers.

But while the Taylorists' ideas evolved over time, what remained constant through the late 1940s was their conviction that business power would have to be counter-balanced by actors with interests other than profit accumulation; that is, management would have to be democratized if it was to flourish as a science and not merely be a tool available to those with the power to impose their will.[12] The notion that political and social democracy require the building and sustaining of organizations and forces that can countervail corporate power was popularized by John Kenneth Galbraith in the early 1950s.[13] But this notion was, in fact, developed and popularized at a much earlier period by progressive businessmen such as Henry Dennison, a one-time president of the Taylor Society who hosted Galbraith in his home for several years from 1936 and who played a pivotal role in shifting the young Galbraith away from orthodox, neoclassical economics.[14]

The Taylorists' support for a political and industrial world in which labor would counteract the capacity of corporate interests to stifle the development and application of scientific management goes a long way toward explaining the alliance sustained between the trade unions and the Taylor Society. But a second influence of at least equal importance was the fact that Taylor and his inner circle accepted that workers have the mental and emotional capacity to participate in management decision making. One of us (Nyland) has demonstrated that Taylor himself was wounded by the charge that he believed workers and their unions incapable of participating in workplace decision making and that from 1913 he actively sought to build a rapprochement with the union movement.[15] The extent to which this was a conscious effort on Taylor's part is indicated by a letter he wrote to his friend Louis Brandeis, who had criticized Taylor for not making a greater effort to reconcile unionism and scientific management:

> My dear Mr. Brandeis: The farther I get into the question of the economics of handling labor, with especial regard to the labor union features, the more difficult it seems to me to see my way out. You know my friendly attitude toward the unions. At the same time you realize how incompatible some of their principles are with any scientific method of doing things. I feel as if I should like to read three or four books written by friends of labor, in which the essentials of the labor union movement are developed. It is quite clear to me that we must figure on a world peopled for some years hence with labor unions and those organized along lines that are not absolutely different from those we know today. I want to see how nearly I can come to mapping out my industrial life to help them rather than to hinder. I am quite sure that you must be very familiar with the literature on the subject and I want to ask you to recommend several books for me to read.[16]

In the month following this communication, Taylor had his friend Charles McCarthy convince the Federal Industrial Relations Commission to undertake a study of scientific management and labor, began actively collaborating with trade unions, and participated in a Taylor Society debate on the relationship between organized labor and scientific management.[17] On the last occasion Taylor took care to stress that he was a "union man" and that unions must remain fighting organizations while at the same time insisting it was necessary that workers collaborate with the technician and the manager in the drive to raise productivity and to promote the development and application of science in the workplace: "I never look for the unions to go out. I am heartily in favor of combinations of men. I do not look for a great modification in the principles of unions as they now exist; they are of necessity largely now fighting organizations; I look for educational institutions, for mutual and helpful institutions; I look for great modifications, but never for the abolition of them. I simply look for a change, that the union shall conform itself to this new idea, the idea of a standard that is over all of us, and a set of laws that will be over all sides."[18] That Taylor

accepted that workers have the mental and emotional capacity to comprehend the laws of science and participate in management activity was made
even more explicit in an address he gave to the Taylor Society in 1914. In
what proved to be his last statement to the Society, he urged unionists
to join management in raising industrial efficiency and advised that the
appointment and control of efficiency engineers should be undertaken
jointly by employer and union in order to ensure that knowledge and not
power ruled in the workplace. Having issued this call, he concluded by
advising:

> If the unions will take up the education of their members, it will be
> a step in the right direction. They will have to take this step before
> we can cooperate with them. Instead of preparing for war they must
> try to promote working conditions which render possible higher
> wages. The unions have done an immense amount of good. Unions
> have made better working conditions. They have stopped great
> injustices in the trades and for that they deserve commendation.
> Because a man points out that they are doing a few things that are
> wrong it does not mean that he does not tolerate anything that they
> are doing.[19]

Taylor's inner circle was to build on his outreach to the unions over many
years following his sudden death in 1915. This effort was undertaken both
in their workplace and social practice and in publications that members of
the Taylor Society wrote jointly with trade union leaders. An early example
of these latter works was a 1920 special edition of the *Annals of the American
Academy of Political and Social Science* titled *Labor, Management and Production* edited jointly by Samuel Gompers of the American Federation of
Labor (AFL), Morris Cooke (Taylor's "favorite disciple"), and Fred Miller
of the Taylor Society. In this publication, the three editors called on "organized workers" and the "scientists of industry" to unite in a campaign to
both democratize and increase the efficiency of industry. It is notable that
when issuing this call, Cooke observed that while the editors accepted that
property owners have a right to receive a profit on their investment, they
did not accept that ownership *alone* is a sufficient criterion to justify participation in the management of an industrial enterprise. In short, the three
men viewed management as an activity that should involve only those who

directly participate in production, that is, workers, technicians, and professional managers. Accordingly, no one was invited to contribute to the 1920 text *"simply because he owned something or employed somebody."*[20]

The message that workers have the mental and emotional capacity to participate in the management process was reiterated continuously by Taylor Society leaders through the next quarter century. Most notable of union-Taylorist publications in which this message was promulgated is the 1940 book *Organized Labor and Production*, written by Morris Cooke and Philip Murray of the United Mine Workers of America; Murray was subsequently president of the Congress of Industrial Organizations (CIO). The message made explicit in the Cooke-Murray text has been well summarized by Sanford Jacoby.[21] "Cooke and Murray advocated 'tapping labor's brains' by which they meant making organized labor an active participant in determining production procedures and administrative policies designed to increase the output and distribution of goods and services."

That workers have mental faculties capable of being "tapped" in the manner specified by Jacoby was also stressed much earlier in publications emanating from within the Taylor Society. For example, in a presidential address to the Boston branch of the society in 1917, Harlow Person explained the principles motivating the society's governing body to invite professional managers, workers and social scientists to participate in the organization's internal debates. This was being done, he said, because the society's leaders recognized that the professional manager, the social scientist, and the worker all have the capacity to make a unique contribution both to debate and to the management process:

It is my thesis that no one of these individuals sees the problems of scientific management with an eye which reveals the whole truth; that each is by some economy, manifest in the unconscious organization of persons for the investigation of truth, a functionalized observer of industrial facts and judge of their significance; that each is complementary to and essential to the other; and that no organization which stands as advocate for one of the latest major contributions to industrial development, as does this Society, can accomplish its purpose if it fails to consider every possible approach to the examination and valuation of the particular contribution which it seeks to promote.[22]

Person argued that the ability of professional managers to debate and reach decisions on management issues is underpinned by their training, experience, and consequent capacity to combine resources efficiently. But he insisted this was a contribution that is both warped and limited by managers' class position and function. In class terms they are the servant of the shareholder and hence bound to regard and value all things from the point of view of profit. This is a myopia compounded by the manager's need to strive for the greatest efficiency compatible with the profit motive, and this function drives managers to focus on a narrow range of tasks, to standardize where flexibility and subtlety is required, and to regard all inputs into production as commodities even when a clear "spiritual" factor is in play: "Particularly, he too frequently fails to recognize that labor as a simple physical force cannot be separated from labor as a distinct and original seat of human intellect, feelings, desires and opinions. Labor as a spiritual force is the most subtle and changeable of all the factors which he combines for the purpose of service through production."[23] As with managers, Person accepted that a mix of strengths and weaknesses shaped and limited what workers could contribute to management debate and decision making. By the "worker" Person meant "the individual employee, or any spokesman of organized labor."[24] He accepted that workers' onerous conditions of life and need to struggle to defend their class interests limited their ability to address management issues in a scientific and dispassionate manner and added that he considered workers' lack of education to be a "damning indictment of society." He also acknowledged that many observers who agreed workers should be able to participate in management activity believed this was not possible because workers lack the needed skills and experience. But upon making these concessions he immediately made it clear that he did not accept that worker's inexperience as managers justified a continuation of the existing state of affairs and asserted that this position was being embraced by the growing body of managers, workers, and intellectuals who believed that

> labor is entitled to exercise the right of acting under the principle, whatever the degree of skill he manifests in making judgements; that he will learn to make better judgements on management matters by experience and responsibility; and that society, even at the cost of a temporary period of less fruitful management (conceded for the

sake of argument), should bear the cost of the workman's apprenticeship in managerial responsibility. They assert also that life is more important than industry, happiness more important than profits and that happiness can be secured only by giving every individual opportunity for the exercise of all his interests and the development of all his faculties, one of which is the faculty of managerial and creative activity. They assert further that the increased technical productivity resulting from the exercise of such a function by workmen, together with the increased productivity resulting indirectly as the result of greater co-operation, will more than compensate for the loss resulting from errors in judgement during the period of labor's apprenticeship in managerial responsibility. Finally they assert that in our society and with our form of government, with labor self-conscious, organized and numerically strong as it is, experiments in the participation of labor in management are sure to be made, experiments which management should anticipate, and in which management should fearlessly and honestly co-operate.[25]

Having advanced this perspective, Person immediately went on to argue that even workers who did not have formal education, management experience, or a knowledge of science could make an important and unique contribution to management debate and activity. He insisted, moreover, that this observation was particularly true of trade union leaders and activists. Summing up what he believed existing workers and their leaders could contribute to management activity, he observed:

In discussing the advantages for forming judgements possessed by the manager, I described certain facilities for intuitive judgement developed in him by experience, which because his experience is different from that of anyone else, make him able to perceive certain aspects of truth not visible to others. So it is with workmen in the mass. They also, because of their function in industrial operations have experience which neither managers nor others have, and develop intuitive faculties which neither managers nor others have. They feel the direction of the current of industrial evolution, not because they are carried along in it, but because they are industrial society. Because of this, their intuitive faculties, specialized by their unique experience, sense the immediate and frequently the ultimate influence of the current industrial progress of specific methods and policies. There may not be convincing reasoning behind their objection to a specific proposal, but there may be something more fundamental than reasoning which guides them.[26]

Having discussed what professional managers and workers could contribute to management practice and theory, Person concluded by explaining why it was important to include social scientists in management debate. He conceded that these intellectuals were limited in their capacity to contribute by the fact that their views tend to be highly abstract and informed by influences outside the arena of production. These were characteristics that he believed commonly lead the intellectual to advance ideas that have no immediate practical value and to misjudge what can be achieved in the short term. But, he insisted, these same attributes also enable the intellectual to perceive events and processes in ways that are invisible to workers and managers: "The social scientist is passing judgment on something which he examines from without. That is a good principle of investigation and valuation, according to scientific management. The professional engineer is impatient of that narrow-mindedness which prompts a board of directors to declare that no one outside their directorate can tell them about their business. It is just because the industrial engineer comes in from outside that he can see things in business which they, who are of it, cannot see."[27]

Person's observation that effective management requires a melding of the minds and insights of the manager and the intellectual (though not the worker) was to be echoed by Mayo and the HRS. However, the latter's assessment of the contribution desired from each of these agents differed radically from that advocated by the leaders of the Taylor Society. For a short period this point was not apparent to these individuals. This was not least because the articles Mayo published when he initially arrived in the United States did not reveal the hostility to democracy and trade unionism apparent in the works he had produced while in Australia. This was a practice he continued when in 1923 he presented a paper to the annual conference of the Taylor Society, which couched his argument that psychology had much to bring to the workplace in a manner that appeared empathetic with the views Person had detailed in 1917.[28] However, the Taylorists' enthusiasm for Mayo's work was not long sustained once they came to appreciate the undemocratic thrust that underpinned his ideas.

The essence of Mayo's argument before the Taylor Society was that the mind of the worker is extremely complex, that workers are motivated by multiple influences both within and outside the workplace and their work group, and that psychology can assist the development of practices that can make a positive contribution to their well-being. By 1923 these were ideas well accepted within the society, and they had been explored by its members, not the least active being Whiting Williams.[29] Likewise, the notion that the minds of workers were commonly damaged by the onerous and stultifying nature of industrial work and that the professional manager, informed and trained by the psychologist, has a responsibility to address this situation was accepted.[30] However, for the Taylorists the latter effort had to be part of a multidimensional program, with counseling being a last step taken when efforts to eliminate the conditions that might injure workers had proven ineffective. That this was not Mayo's orientation he did not make clear in his presentation to the Taylor Society. However, society members were given the opportunity to comprehend the dimensions of his perspective when in 1925 he published an article on the role of the industrial psychologist in *Harper's Magazine*. In this work Mayo sought to clarify to the "rulers of society" how the challenge posed by trade unionism and left-wing democratic politics could be addressed in a manner that would leave management as an elite activity. His message was that modern democracies had accorded too much attention to Rousseau and too little to Machiavelli. He noted that Rousseau had hoped social conflict would be resolved by democratic debate and assembly while Machiavelli had advised that what was required was that "administrators set themselves the task of understanding human motives, of cultivating desirable social movements, and checking the undesirable."[31]

Perceiving himself as a modern Machiavelli, Mayo noted that U.S. employers tended to favor the open shop. He had no problem with this position but was highly critical of the fact that employers overwhelmingly strove to attain this goal by embracing "blind unthinking opposition to the growth of trade unionism."[32] The evidence from Australia and Britain, he insisted, had made it clear that this crude response was bound to fail in the long term, for it sought to combat the growth and diffusion of unionization when what was needed was an innovation that would induce workers to conclude unions were unnecessary.[33] This was a goal that he argued required two fundamental steps. First, the rulers of society must reach agreement on what is meant by an "open shop," an issue on which he lamented there existed no consensus among employers. Second, business firms must support studies that could clarify how social conditions affect the workplace and how social influences interact with developments inside the workplace to create an environment conducive to unionism. He was insistent that the resultant awareness could not be achieved via an "industrial council or variant of industrial democracy," for this approach "savors too much of the pious hopes and evasions of Rousseau—Rousseau the *ignis fatuus* that has led democracy into the mire." Rather, employers must grasp Machiavelli's insight that "someone must make it his special business to understand human nature"[34] and he insisted this someone must be the social psychologist and educator who can identify what is troubling the mind of the individual worker and by so doing ensure that the latter is not attracted to trade unionism or industrial and social democracy.

The 1925 *Harper's* presentation made it patently apparent that Mayo's perspective was markedly at odds with the views that prevailed within the Taylor Society. This point was highlighted in the response that was immediately forthcoming from Robert Bruere, a longtime society member and trade unionist. Bruere's reply was published in *Survey* as was a counter-response to Bruere from Mayo, and both contributions were republished in the *Bulletin of the Taylor Society*. Bruere believed industrial psychology could make a major contribution to the well-being of the worker and hence should be developed and applied with both enthusiasm and rigor. However, he was appalled that Mayo had elected to promote the emergent science of industrial psychology as a union avoidance tool. He observed that Taylor had initially sought to render unions redundant and as a consequence had unnecessarily affronted organized labor and by so doing greatly retarded the "indispensible progress" of the science of management. It would be a tragedy, he insisted, if clinical psychologists were to repeat this error and even worse if they were to join the class struggle as active agents of the employers.[35] Class war may be inevitable, he acknowledged,

> but when we have recognized the existence of the problem, the question arises . . . whether we shall spend our energies girding ourselves for battle, or whether we shall subject the problem to intelligent and objective scrutiny, bring the method of science to bear upon it, and seek the basis for a concert of classes . . . grounded in reason, justice and goodwill. This is what the more thoughtful followers of Taylor, members of the society which bears his name, to whom science is

not a catch-word but the breath of life and the hope of peaceful progress, have during recent years, under the leadership of their managing director, Harlow S. Person been attempting to do.[36]

Bruere concluded his commentary by urging Mayo to follow the path taken by the Taylor Society. In his response, however, Mayo made it clear he had no such intention. He replied that he had not meant to give the impression that he was anti-union, for he accepted that organized labor had played a vital role in civilizing capitalism in the nineteenth century and conceded that unions were still needed to ensure workers against the "possible concentration of power in the hands of embittered reaction." But at the same time, he asserted that what he was seeking to do was to make it clear to the nation's rulers that it was "stupidity" to confront the challenge posed by unionism and radical politics with violent suppression when there exists a nonviolent and much more effective means of preserving elite rule both within and outside the workplace. To ensure that his opposition to industrial democracy and commitment to the interests of the "rulers of society" was clear, he concluded by observing, "Machiavelli's sage observations upon Florentine history and the education of princes make an admirable contribution to the study of industrial organization. It does not matter whether one is considering industry under a Russian or an American regime. There must always be skilled executives set more or less in authority over working groups: this is not a political question, it is a necessity of efficient operation."[37]

The Long Struggle

In addition to the notion that the antidemocratic thrust of Mayo's work had its roots in Taylorism, the second of O'Connor's assumptions requiring closer inspection is the idea that the industrial democrats' efforts to democratize management were purely a 1920s phenomenon. This is a claim we have refuted (Nyland, Bruce and Nyland, and Nyland and McLeod).[38] These works have documented the contribution made by Taylor Society members to the democratization of both society and industry through the New Deal years to the late 1940s. But despite the efforts of these revisionists, the notion that in the 1930s the HRS developed a humanist alternative to scientific management continues to prevail within orthodox renditions of labor and management history, and consequently this belief still needs to be addressed. It needs to be supplemented with knowledge of the interaction between the Taylorists and Mayoists through the late 1940s.

Critical to understanding the nature of the struggle between the industrial democrats associated with the Taylor Society and the scholar-activists of the HRS is the fact that Mayo was able to win support for his perspective from corporate magnates.[39] He was able to gain this support because the corporate sector eagerly embraced the notion that labor unrest has less to do with conditions in the workplace and more to do with workers' minds. As corporate enthusiasm for the HRS intensified, Taylor Society progressives became increasingly alienated from the business community, a process that accelerated as the society became ever more uncompromising in opposition to company unionism and began to advocate democratizing not only the management of the workplace but also that of the national economy.

Mayo's ability to attract support from corporate America was helped enormously by the fact that within a short time of arriving in the United States he gained the attention of John D. Rockefeller Jr. The latter subsequently bankrolled Mayo's salary at both the Wharton School and at Harvard, and it is largely because of the support Rockefeller accorded the HRS researchers that he has been labeled (alongside Sidney and Beatrice Webb and John R. Commons) a cofounder of the field of industrial relations.[40] Rockefeller could fund a significant corpus of industrial relations research because he was heir to the world's largest fortune and was willing to commit a portion of this wealth to shaping the social sciences, which he wanted to generate knowledge that could contribute to stability and social control and thus preserve the security of his family and his class. His willingness to support social research was greatly enhanced by the infamy that befell the Rockefeller name as a consequence of the 1914 Ludlow massacre in which six striking miners, two women, and eleven children were killed at the Rockefeller-owned Colorado Fuel and Iron (CFI) Company.[41] As Donald Fisher has documented, in the aftermath of this atrocity Rockefeller engaged the public and industrial relations services of Clarence Hicks and W. L. Mackenzie King, began funding social science researchers whose work would help cement ruling class domination, and established company management practices that would both provide a venue in which management and employees could discuss issues of common concern and present the Rockefellers in a positive light.[42] In reality, the so-called Rockefeller Plan that developed from these efforts was a union avoidance strategy, though one achieved through union substitution, rather than union suppression. Rockefeller, in brief, sought to exclude independent unions from the workplace by improving communication and coordination within the firm and by developing what today would be called a "high-involvement" or "high-performance" Human Resource Management regime.[43]

Rockefeller's support was fundamental for the development of the HRS tradition not only because he funded Mayo's salary at Wharton and Harvard but also because he arranged access to firms for HRS researchers (including the ongoing "experiments" being conducted at the Hawthorne plant of Western Electric) and enabled Mayo to gain access to corporate venues where he could "sell" his alternative to the industrial democrats. Mayo's first applied work in the United States, which involved a study between 1923 and 1925 of labor turnover in Philadelphia textile mills, was bankrolled by Rockefeller from his personal funds. The magnate was induced to make this contribution by Beardsley Ruml, the director of the fellowship program of the Laura Spelman Rockefeller Memorial Fund, who was intrigued by Mayo's claim that workers' interest in trade unionism and socialism was a manifestation of maladjusted minds. Mayo eagerly sought to encourage this interest, writing in 1923 to Joseph Willits, head of the Industrial Research Unit at Wharton and to whom Ruml had recommended Mayo for work, that "socialism is a disassociated reverie in that workers have failed to achieve self-expression and control over their destiny and have substituted for such development a reverie, an imagined social situation, in which the individual worker is free to direct his life work."[44] Building on this effort, Mayo followed up with a 1924 unpublished memo to Ruml in which he argued that "wars and strikes [are] never the product of a sudden and unexpected irrationality but rather are a product of 'unreason' or 'irrationality' induced by the debilitating character of the industrial labor process."[45]

Enthused at these notions, Rockefeller provided Harvard with funds sufficient to convince the business school to host both Mayo and his research program and actively promoted the work of HRS researchers to the special conference committee, the Industrial Relations Counselors (IRC), and subsequently the fledgling Harvard executive education program—the so-called Cabot Weekends. Financed chiefly by Rockefeller, IRC superseded the law firm of Rockefeller's chief in-house counsel, Raymond Fosdick (Curtis, Fosdick and Belknap), and was headed by Arthur H. Young, formerly a Colorado Fuel and Iron manager. It strove to promote diffusion of company unionism and the notion that the form of representation introduced at CFI aimed to "advance the knowledge and practice of human relations in industry, commerce, education, and government." In reality the form of representation advocated was very much a unitarist solution and reflected Rockefeller's distaste for the independent trade unions and free collective bargaining advocated by industrial democrats.[46]

Rockefeller's views regarding unions were ambivalent in that he was willing to support company unionism, which many industrialists were not, but at the same time was determined to exclude independent unions from Rockefeller enterprises. Two confidential memos involving some of his closest legal advisors reveal his views. The first, dated December 15, 1923, was from an industrial relations investigator and addressed to George J. Anderson, the former head of the industrial relations annex of Curtis, Fosdick and Belknap, the organizational precursor of IRC. The memo concerns a survey of employee representation plans in five Rockefeller-owned oil companies and reports that "these companies have *never recognized trade unions as collective groups for bargaining* or making contracts. . . . The spirit and attitude of the leading executives is *anti-union*, and even anti-industrial representation. The policy is strictly individual bargaining. . . . A union man is absolutely persona non grata, and is even discharged after hiring, if his identity becomes known."[47] The memo goes on to note, "these policies raise far-reaching questions. Do the Industrial Representation Plans and other features of the Standard Oil labor program tend to take the place of unionism and resist its encroachment?" The author then provides his own answer: "The labor policies in the Standard Oil companies have unquestionably offset attempts at unionism during the last ten years. Any company which keeps one step ahead of the demands commonly put forward by unions is not so vulnerable to the first line of attack by unions. . . . Therefore, every feature of a labor policy or a labor program which eliminates the more common causes of union organization, weakens the inroads of unionism."[48]

The second memo is from Raymond Fosdick to Rockefeller in 1934 and relates to the latter's continued financing of IRC. He writes:

One of my responsibilities in the 21 years in which I have been associated with you has been to point out possible dangers ahead in connection with your multifarious interests. The country is at the moment witnessing a head-on collision between the labor union and the company union. Your position has always been clear, i.e., that you stood for adequate *representation* no matter whether it was by one method or another. We have always tried to hold the scales evenly as far as the management of IRC was concerned, and we have friends on both sides of the fence. . . . Mr Hicks with entire frankness has pointed out to me that the very nature of the work of IRC implies a sympathy toward the company union which, as an organization, we do not have toward the labor union. If this is true—and I fear it may be—it is possible that the charge might be made that you were financing an organization to fight union labor, and you might thereby be maneuvered into an uncomfortable public position.[49]

Further clarity on Rockefeller's view of independent trade unionism is reflected in correspondence associated with an article he wrote for the *International Labour Review*, which he titled "Cooperation in Industry." In private correspondence to Fosdick he observed that originally the article had been titled "Democracy in Industry," but he added, "I finally adopted as a title COOPERATION IN INDUSTRY. The word 'Cooperation' does not suggest to my mind as it does to yours, a relationship with Profit Sharing. . . . I felt it a safe title to use and really a safer one than DEMOCRACY IN INDUSTRY, which to my mind would more generally be regarded as indicating control rather than cooperation by Labor with Capital."[50] In brief, though Rockefeller wanted to promote a public perception that he and his managers accepted that trade unions had a place in industry, ultimately he could never bring himself to accept unions as the workers' principal bargaining unit. His rejection of even this limited form of industrial democracy, it has been suggested, was largely if not entirely because he was indentured to his father's wishes, and his father was vehemently against the unionization of any of the family businesses.[51]

In October 1927, the IRC director, Arthur Young, arranged for Mayo to explain what his management could offer to a group of industrialists known as "The Lunchers" who met at the Harvard Club in New York. Many of the attendees were from leading American industrial organizations and met periodically to discuss and collude on labor policies. Leading corporations represented included Standard Oil of New Jersey, General Electric, Bethlehem Steel, DuPont, General Motors, U.S. Rubber, Goodyear, Westinghouse, International Harvester, and the Irving Trust. Key to the activities of the group was the need to legitimize management authority without limiting the prerogatives of ownership.

In his address Mayo spoke directly to the concerns of his audience, asserting that his research had revealed how to calm the irrational, agitation-prone mind of the worker and proposing how to develop a curriculum to train managers in the required techniques. He asked members to approach him directly if they wished to discuss the possibility of having the Harvard HRS researchers provide their firms with advice or training.[52] This effort had two important consequences. First, the personnel director of Western Electric invited Mayo to become involved in the Hawthorne studies, thus precipitating the most public and enduring aspect of the diffusion of his knowledge claims concerning human motivation, worker irrationality, and the need for a managerial elite. Second, Mayo was invited to a personal meeting with Rockefeller and subsequently commissioned to research "possible causes of improper functioning of the Industrial Plan and the possible use of forces to bring about a more cooperative relationship between management and employees."[53]

Mayo's subsequent examination of the Rockefeller Plan led to a confrontation with Mary Van Kleeck, who was the first woman to join the Taylor Society and in the 1920s also headed the Department of Industrial Studies at the Russell Sage Foundation. In the latter role she commissioned or undertook a series of studies that focused on "relations between employers and employees . . . looking toward more definite representation of workers . . . through shop committees and trade unions."[54] By 1930 her department had produced four monographs under the generic title "Labor's Participation in Management," and it was this issue that was prominent in a study of the Rockefeller Plan she undertook with Ben Selekman in 1924. In their report the two researchers conceded employee voices had been enhanced by the plan, but insisted Rockefeller management was not democratic because the employer was "not bound to abide by [the workers'] vote on any specific subject" and independent union representation was not permitted.[55] As a result of their extensive interviews with CFI workers, the two industrial democrats added that the employees' apparent lack of interest in voting for representatives or in serving on committees in employee representation plans was due to structural and procedural impediments. More specifically, employee representatives were dependent on the goodwill of foremen and supervisors, and so were unable to reliably represent workers or negotiate such basic issues as wages, working hours, and educational opportunities. It was the workers' inability to negotiate these issues, Selekman and Van Kleeck insisted, and not apathy or lack of intelligence that was limiting employee participation. In brief, as Julie Kimmel observes, Selekman and Van Kleeck's use of interviews allowed them to "construct an image of workers as intelligent, self-aware, and capable of informed participation in decision-making processes—in other words, as fit for democratic participation in the workplace."[56]

The message generated by Van Kleeck and Selekman drew the ire of Rockefeller and other corporate magnates who wished to pose as liberals, and Rockefeller sought to utilize his influence to have both her and her perspective deemed unacceptable to personnel professional bodies.[57] Following his 1928 meeting with Rockefeller, Mayo undertook a study of the Rockefeller Plan for him and in a 1929 letter reported he had found that the Colorado workers had a "morbid preoccupation with personal issues as between worker representatives and local management." Commenting on the Selekman and Van Kleeck report, he added that he was "unable to accept the assumptions of the investigators" because where workers were involved in management decision making they invariably created a disastrous industrial relations environment.[58] In advancing this opinion, he took a barbed thrust at Van Kleeck: "There is another difficulty for me in Miss Van Kleeck's approach to the investigation—she seems to assume that a 'democratic' method of managing industry is necessarily appropriate. . . . If it means that industry is to develop a two-party system and to determine any issues that arise by discussion and compromise then it would seem that such a method would revive and accentuate a situation of class conflict. This is indeed exactly what has happened in Australia—the country that has provided a 'shocking example' of how things should not be done in industry."[59] Two months after completing his Colorado study, Mayo received a retainer from IRC and began an ongoing close collaboration with Young, whom he invited to lecture at the Harvard Business School. Reciprocating, Young invited Mayo to accompany him to Geneva as an "expert industrial relations advisor" when IRC established a branch at the International Labour Organisation and arranged for Mayo's work to be translated into French, German, and Italian. Young in effect became a bridge and broker between Mayo and Rockefeller, drew Mayo into the inner circle of other major corporations, and strove to ensure that those corporations came to appreciate the importance of Mayo's research.[60]

Mayo's and Van Kleeck's divergent analyses of the Rockefeller plan do not appear to have generated open conflict between the industrial democrats and the HRS. Rather, the two groupings largely ignored each other or made passing comment that was not necessarily hostile. In 1930 Ordway Tead, at the time the editor of the *Bulletin of the Taylor Society*, for example, published an article titled "Trends in Industrial Psychology" in which he included Mayo "among those who have made notable contributions" to the psychology of work and applauded the research being undertaken at the Western Electric Company.[61] This was a significant article, for it makes clear the Taylorists' acceptance that there are multiple factors that influence employee work effort and morale, the importance of studying "the whole man . . . in real and typical settings," the difficulties associated with effective staff selection, the importance of training both line workers and executives, the need to provide for the "maladjusted worker," and the psychology of group action. Tead's article is also important in that while it suggests there was not open hostility between the Taylorists and the Mayoists, it does highlight the difference in views; the HRS focused on groups of workers, but Tead conceived of "group psychology" in terms of all the individuals—including executives—who work together to attain corporate objectives and made it clear that leadership must be inclusive and nurtured, for there are few "natural leaders" either in industry or the wider society.

But while the industrial democrats and the members of the HRS would coexist through the prosperous years of the 1920s, their mutual animosity could not be contained in the context of the Great Depression. This was the more so as the crisis deepened and the notion surfaced that management needed to be both a macro and a micro activity. We have observed elsewhere that by the second half of the 1920s, the Taylorists had begun to argue that demand as well as supply would have to be managed scientifically if the growing national product was to be consumed.[62] With the onset of the Depression, awareness that national production and consumption were not in equilibrium became manifestly apparent and within the United States all but a small minority of neoliberal economists came to accept that restoring equilibrium would require that the invisible hand of the market be supplemented by the visible hand of the economic planner.

Although a consensus emerged that conscious planning of the economy was required to return supply and demand to equilibrium, consensus did not develop regarding who should control the process of economic management. Corporate America had little doubt on this score. With few exceptions big business insisted the Depression was a crisis of overproduction and that consequently corporate leaders should be freed from the constraints imposed by the antitrust laws and allowed to collude in ways that would restrict price competition and contain output to a level that would match supply and effective demand. The Taylorists and their union allies, by contrast, insisted that scientific analysis had shown the crisis was a consequence of inadequate purchasing power and that consequently the state had to redistribute the nation's wealth and by so doing ensure there was sufficient demand to clear markets. As part of this process the state would have to build independent trade unions, thus enabling the latter to become instruments of demand management that would pressure employers to distribute productivity gains to workers and by so doing enable workers to be effective consumers. The democratic, pro-union perspective prevailed in the Taylor Society through the first years of the Depression. In April 1931 this stance induced a number of individuals within or close to the society to form Industrial Experimenters Associated, and over the following year, Henry C. Metcalf reports, meetings were held across the country that linked "hundreds of individuals and concerns seeking light on the objectives, policies, principles and procedures of industrial cooperation."[63]

The associated debates reached an important milestone at the society's 1931 national conference, when Harlow Person argued that as market forces had proven incapable of restoring equilibrium the time had come to apply scientific managers' principles and practices to the national economy. This proposal was greeted with approval by those in attendance, Van Kleeck, by now a Marxist, gaining acclaim when she declared that the management of the nation's economy must be democratized because if the corporate sector gained exclusive control of national management, then profit rather than knowledge would determine the policies and programs that governed the lives of the American people.

That the Taylorists' views regarding the management of the economy were a form of proto-Keynesianism has been argued by Galbraith.[64] He observes that well before Keynes advanced his belief that national wealth had to be redistributed in favor of those with a high propensity to consume, this was the prescription urged by the Taylorists.[65] That the Taylorists pioneered many of the policies that were to become orthodoxy with the onset of the Depression has also been argued by Mark Barenberg, who has observed that the Taylor Society was

> a progressive "oasis" in the 1920s for future inner circle New Dealers. . . . Although the appeal of centralized administration and planning was intensified by the economic emergency, Wagner understood it to be a permanent requirement of the industrial state in the era of mass production. The intellectual groundwork for that view was laid during the 1910s and 1920s by such collectivist luminaries as Veblen, Herbert Croly, George Soule, and Stuart Chase, and by the less celebrated progressive engineers, managers, labor officials, and academics associated with the Taylor Society. They transformed scientific management from a theory of unilateral managerial control in the workplace into a vision of centralized administrative planning and decentralized collective bargaining in the larger political economy. Their views culminated in the overblown Veblenism of the Technocracy craze of 1932, but also influenced the planning proposals of inner-circle New Dealers such as Tugwell, Moley, Berle, Lubin, and Wagner.[66]

But if the Taylorists remained consistent advocates of industrial democracy when they turned to considering the need to manage the national economy, Mayo also remained consistent in opposing the extension of democracy. In short, he insisted that the illogicality of workers not only required they be excluded from the management of enterprises but also required that they not be allowed to participate meaningfully in the management of the social and economic life of the nation.

Two volumes published in 1933 indicate the divergence of views between the Taylorists and the Mayoists—a divergence that was in subsequent years to become manifest in overt antagonism. The scientific managers' perspective was detailed in the third edition of Tead and Metcalf's *Personnel Administration*. This work, initially published in 1920, was subjected to major revision in order to address the Depression. The two long-time Taylorists wrote that they believed the following matters required "most urgent attention and constructive thinking." First, it was necessary to provide reasonable security of employment and livelihood for all. Second, there was a need to expand the resources available for training workers in the skills required for effective workmanship and rounded personalities.

Third, there was a need to acknowledge that the principle of representation of the "different interests involved [in] deliberations on policy should be applied in industrial and corporate government." Fourth, there was a need to admit that the support of the rank and file in helping to realize the objectives of corporations can be expected only when these objectives were "broad, sound, and inclusive enough to make it likely that the workers will feel safe and benefited by them." Fifth, there was a need to accept that if industry wants genuine cooperation from workers, "a price must be paid— the price of admitting them as more nearly equal partners in the conduct of the enterprise." They added, "Our aim, in short, is to see the personnel movement for what it really is—a constructive, dynamic, clarifying influence in helping to forward the inevitable urge to make our economic system more truly and completely the servant of all the people, ministering both directly and indirectly to the 'good life' of every citizen."[67]

The second of the 1933 volumes that demonstrates the divide between the industrial democrats and the elitists associated with Mayo was the latter's *The Human Problems.* In this work Mayo began by denying that industrial work was necessarily a source of fatigue or damaging to workers' mental health. The "maladjustment" common among workers was rather alleged to be a consequence of workers' preoccupation with their personal problems, the obsessions and mild neurosis that permeated the whole fabric of civilization, and the group relationships and routines that workers initiate in the workplace. Having absolved employers of any blame for the maladjusted worker, Mayo proceeded to paint a picture of what he deemed the obsessional character: an individual who is alienated, distracted, and unable to attain the emotional satisfaction realized by workers with a more normal temperament and who consequently is prone to step forward when workers conclude they need leaders who can liberate them from their alienated existence. These obsessive persons exist, Mayo wrote, both within the workplace and in the wider political world; having advanced this last observation, he entered the debate on macroeconomic management by asking, "Shall industries be government controlled?"[68]

The message advanced by Mayo and subsequently developed by other members of the HRS drew heavily on scholars who were on the extreme right of the political spectrum, on the Hawthorne studies, and on Bronislaw Malinowski's anthropology. He observed that the notion that the government should take control of industry had become widespread and suggested this was due to the all but universal embrace of Rousseau's notion of rule by the people, the collapse of traditional social codes, and the insecurity that had become a feature of industrial society. In brief, imbued with the belief that in a democracy the people have the right to override property rights, the people had decided this had to be done in order to preserve their security.

Mayo made it clear he was not necessarily opposed to government regulation of the economy but did oppose the notion that control of the national economy should be transferred from the rational manager to the irrational "horde." This rejection of government by the "nonlogical" was fully consistent with his belief that enterprise management must be monopolized by administrative elites. In both cases this was deemed necessary because management requires "a high order of generalizing mind—a mind which can grasp a multitude of complex relations . . . a mind which can, at best only be produced in small quantity and at high cost."[69] He made clear that this is not the mind of the worker, who characteristically is informed by a "social code" rather than rationality. Indeed, he insisted that with the advance of science in industry, workers had lost the "possibility of comprehension, or any element of control." Nor is the mind of the trade union official suitable for the task of macroeconomic management, for these individuals manifest the "very essence of conservative reaction—the resistance of a dying social code to innovation."[70] Having dismissed democracy within and outside the workplace, Mayo returned to his long-established theme that what is required to save societies is an elite body of administrators who have been trained and advised by individuals such as himself. Again the division of labor envisaged is the rational manager in control but advised and trained by the intellectual on how best to nurture and sustain a social code that will ensure workers' minds and activities remain in concert with the wishes of the elite. In summary:

> Mayo consistently rejected the view that workers had any contribution to make to the organization of their work. . . . Workers were able only to adopt a nonlogical relationship to their work and society, accepting unquestioningly the existing social code. Workers who did question that code, who became radicals and "destroyers" did so because they overintellectualized their situation, probably as a result of some personal psychic trauma. . . . A logical understanding of the workplace and society was reserved for only a few—the managers and administrators who would work to ensure that the social code was adapted to scientific and technical change.[71]

While the scientific managers and the HRS advanced very divergent positions, they made few direct references to each other's work before the mid-1930s. In 1935, however, Mayo went on the offensive. The previous year he had begun participating in executive education training workshops organized by Philip Cabot, a Harvard colleague, which focused on the social and human problems of industry.[72] As Fritz Roethlisberger notes, "Cabot at this time must have felt that Mayo's diagnosis of the ills of modern industrial civilization wanted an audience of responsible businessmen. He bought together some of the outstanding business leaders of the time and brought them Mayo in person."[73] Mayo himself notes, in a letter to the head of the Harvard Business School in 1937, "Cabot's original idea was that very considerable social changes are in process; the capacity of society to adjust itself to such changes without serious damage, without loss of order, will be determined by the adequacy and courage of our leaders . . . developed only by experience, knowledge of fact and situation, and intelligent understanding. . . . [Accordingly], Cabot has been driven to make even more use of the services of my immediate colleagues which the group is developing as a result of its investigations."[74] The core of the message that Mayo and his colleagues conveyed at the Cabot meetings was that business executives are the natural leaders of America and that the underlying factor inducing workers to support democratic reforms within and outside the workplace was mental disintegration and delusions of conspiracy and lunacy. This was a story well received by corporate America, which by the time the meetings began was having difficulty differentiating between liberal and Communist industrial democrats. This was a tendency that Mayo encouraged with increasing enthusiasm, observing in so doing that "Human Relations, in the form of skills taught to business leaders and administrators, could ensure social collaboration in the factory and in society at large and win the war against Communism."[75]

In 1935 Mayo carried the message that the industrial democrats were a threat to business interests into a key institution of the Taylorists when he presented a paper to the Sixth International Congress for Scientific Management in London, which he titled "The Blind Spot in Scientific Management." This so-called blind spot was the scientific managers' inability to perceive that the "spontaneous social organization of a group is the chief determinant of individual attitudes." This blindness, he argued, was induced by the scientific managers' conviction that working people are motivated by their economic interest and logic.[76] This was a charge bound to appeal to employers and to those theorists opposed to the industrial democrats, and having advanced his claim, Mayo sought to render his argument even more attractive to these agents by charging that the Taylorists had a simplistic understanding of human motives and were inciting discord in the workplace: "Scientific management has never studied the facts of human organization; it has accepted the nineteenth-century economic dictum that economic interest and logical capacity are the basis of the social order. It would seem possible, therefore, that scientific management has itself done much to provoke that apparent hostility between management and workers which now inconveniently hampers every development towards 'rationalization'."[77] In addition to charging that the industrial democrats were undermining harmony in the workplace, Mayo urged those of his audience who desired an alternative to scientific management to consult his 1933 edition of *Human Problems* and the works of his Harvard colleague T. N. Whitehead. At the time the latter was preparing a book that challenged the Taylorists' understanding of what democracy entails. Titled *Leadership in a Free Society*, this volume was a rambling text that utilized the evidence generated by the Hawthorne experiments to extend Mayo's claim that workers do not have the rationality or insight needed to participate in the management of either the workplace or society. Whitehead was aware that to gain acceptance of this notion from a U.S. audience it was necessary to reconcile his claims with the notion of democracy. He strove to achieve this goal by asserting that while the term *democracy* tends to be interpreted in many ways, it in essence involves the selection of leaders from organizations that the people believe will act in a manner likely to provide the opportunities they need to thrive and prosper. The question then becomes which organizations do people accept to provide their leaders. In the case of Britain, the populace was held to believe that the state is the agency best able to provide competent leadership. But in the United States, the people's trust is placed overwhelmingly not in politicians but in businessmen and businesswomen. Hence the "real leaders of America are not to be found so much in Washington as at the head of business enterprises." Given that this is the case, Whitehead asserted, it is clear that it is the business community and not the elected representatives in Washington who have the duty and the right to lead the American people both in the workplace and in the wider society. The fact that elected politicians were usurping this role, he argued, was a situation that needed urgently to be rectified: "A real solution will only come when society is integrated around its major activity, business. . . . There is ground today for supposing that industrial nations expect their vitalizing organizations as well as their leaders to come from industry. [Currently society] is being organized somewhat inefficiently by other leaders who have no direct responsibility for the industrial activities. . . . Someone must take the lead in integrating social living, if civilization is to continue."[78]

If the members of the HRS group at Harvard hoped that the American people and Taylorists and other industrial and political democrats who rallied to the New Deal would accept a business-dominated concept of democracy, they were quickly disillusioned. When Whitehead's book appeared, President Franklin D. Roosevelt was in the process of winning the greatest electoral landslide in the history of the two-party system in the face of rabid hostility from the business community. In this context, the response to Whitehead was well exemplified by Robert S. Lynd when he observed of Whitehead's contribution to the debate on leadership: "This collection of somewhat miscellaneous papers is chiefly significant for two unintended reasons: as a rationalization of a fascist America to be run by and for businessmen, and as evidence of what can happen to an alert mind bent on the purposes of a modern business school."[79] Lynd, who had a history of conflict with corporate America and with Rockefeller in particular, acknowledged that Whitehead had initially advanced a number of useful observations regarding the social alienation that had been induced by the manner in which the U.S. business community had shaped industrial life, but then wrote, "He goes off the deep end. Business having ruined the girl, he proposes a shot-gun wedding to rehabilitate not the girl but her seducer. Confronted by the confessed need to socialize business or business-ize society, he chooses the latter [and] blandly accepts business as embodying the central purpose of society."[80] The overt hostility that emerged between the industrial democrats and the HRS in the last years of the Depression is further exemplified by Mary Gilson's 1940 review of Roethlisberger and William Dickson's *Management and the Worker*. Gilson was a longtime member of the Taylor Society. She had also been the employment and service manager of Clothcraft, a firm that pioneered the application of Taylor's principles from 1913, and subsequently a professor of economics at the University of Chicago. Following her appointment to Clothcraft, the firm became the first enterprise in the United States to develop psychological tests capable of assessing the capacities of workers at all levels of the enter-prise. With the support of management she also introduced worker partici-pation in management decision making. What this effort entailed has been outlined by C. D. Wrege and R. G. Greenwood:[81] "Employee participation in the decision-making activities at Clothcraft was encouraged by Feiss and Gilson and accomplished through three groups established by Gilson: The Foremen's Meetings, Employee Advisory Council, and Heads of Tables Conferences. All of these groups were empowered to propose changes to management (which could be vetoed by management) and also empowered to vote on changes proposed by management (and veto those changes if they decided to do so)." Consistent with the prevailing perspective within the Taylor Society, Gilson believed in worker education that was directed to both the learning of job techniques and the development of the worker as citizen. She insisted that the Clothcraft program was not based on pater-nalism, for it did not entail condescension to one's "inferiors." Rather, it involved an acceptance that employers have a responsibility "to strengthen the bulwarks of democracy [by taking] the initiative in training workers to assume the responsibilities industrial citizenship requires."[82]

When Gilson reviewed *Management and the Worker* in 1940, she came to the task with twenty-seven years' experience as practitioner and scholar and an abiding commitment to the principles advocated by the Taylor Soci-ety. She began her commentary by noting that the work was the product of extensive funding by the Rockefeller Foundation and that the first few years of the study had focused on measuring the effect of working conditions. Not mincing her words, she proceeded to make clear her disdain for the volume. Her derision was based partly on her conviction that what the HRS researchers claimed they had determined would have been clear at the out-set to any individual with knowledge of the relevant literature or practical experience of the industrial workplace. She noted, for example, that the notion that employees' practices and beliefs at work are influenced by what happens in their wider world she herself had documented as early as 1916. As for the science that allegedly underpinned Roethlisberger and Dickson's contribution, she observed that all the paraphernalia and statistical tools they had utilized had not produced anything as sophisticated as what was already available to any intelligent person who had worked on a factory floor. Accordingly, she asserted that rather than generating information that anyone in the "kindergarten stage of industrial knowledge" knew already, the researchers might have made better use of their time training foremen how to elicit and handle complaints from workers; they should as well have embraced Taylor's advice that before beginning research on workers' practices and beliefs the scholar-practitioner should first do everything possible to improve plant and personnel.

Warming to her message, Gilson noted that in his preface Mayo had asked how humanity's capacity for spontaneous cooperation could be restored. The answer, she wrote, was not to be found in *Management and the Worker* and she suggested that if Mayo really did want an answer to this question he would be wise to look to a book that pointed far more significantly to what should be the way forward: "It is *Organized Labor and Production* by an industrial engineer, Morris Llewellyn Cooke, and a labor organizer, Philip Murray, and it spells out simply and clearly the effects of union-management co-operation. It does not stop with 'two-way communication' from management to worker and worker to management as does this book, but it shows what can be done by management taking labor into its confidence and working shoulder to shoulder on operational processes and industrial policies at every level of production and supervision."[83] In drawing her review to a close, Gilson noted that *Management and the Worker* makes almost no reference to organized labor, an omission justified on the grounds that interviewed workers had made no reference to unions. Why this would be, she pondered, might possibly have something to do with the fact that Western Electric workers were aware the firm was spending tens of thousands of dollars on "espionage," an effort aimed at identifying union sympathizers; she added that the existence of industrial spies might also help explain why in twenty thousand interviews the workers are reported to have "criticized the company in no instance." Finally, Gilson wrote that she was willing to make one concession to the authors, for she fully agreed with one of their observations, and in so doing took a sideswipe at Rockefeller: "Some day a study should be made of 'researches in the Obvious financed by Big Business.' But maybe that too will turn out to be a set of tables and charts and mathematical formulas to prove what we already know. In any case the originator of the Western Electric experiment, Elton Mayo, modestly states that the authors of *Management and the Worker* do not claim that the enlightenment the many collaborators of the scheme got from their researches was 'either very extensive or very profound.' With this I am in complete agreement."[84]

Mayo responded to Gilson's review by telling his collaborators that she was insane. However, the ability of the HRS theorists to dismiss their Taylorist critics in such a cavalier manner was almost immediately undermined when in mid-1940 Roosevelt appointed Sidney Hillman, the leader of the Amalgamated Clothing Workers of America, as commissioner of employment on the Council of National Defense. This was a critical development, for as Steven Fraser has documented, Hillman had maintained a close working relationship with the Taylor Society from before World War I.[85] Roosevelt charged Hillman with the task of building the workforce that was needed to support the allies in Europe and prepare America for possible entry into the war against fascism. To further this objective, Hillman sounded out industrialists and the AFL and CIO and subsequently appointed Channing R. Dooley, a personnel manager with Socony-Vacuum, as director of the Training Within Industry (TWI) organization and appointed Walter Dietz of Western Electric as his assistant. These twin appointments reflected the views of the trade unions and corporate heads respectively. Dooley had the support of the trade unions not least because he was endorsed by the Taylor Society, of which he was a longtime member, while Dietz had the support of corporate liberals who were attracted to the ideas of Mayo and his colleagues at Harvard, with whom he had collaborated when employed at Western Electric.

William J. Breen has provided a detailed study of how Dooley and Dietz interacted through the years they remained with the TWI.[86] He notes that initially the Taylorists dominated the training effort. Aware that there was an acute shortage of skilled craftsmen, these technicians focused on job redesign, expanding the number of tradesmen, who were then prepared for tasks that required long-term training, and removing tasks that were relatively unskilled and could be undertaken by workers with relatively little training. To ensure this did not become an exercise in deskilling, the scientific managers insisted that those employees' unions must actively participate in making all decisions relating to policy and practice. By incorporating the unions into the management process in this manner, the Taylorists were able to achieve a great increase in the quality of the training available to both workers in skilled trades and workers who were formerly unskilled. They were also able to gain union support in this effort (only a very small minority of craftsmen resisted and their resistance was based not on a fear of deskilling but on fear that increasing the number of skilled workers would undermine their bargaining position). Employers, by contrast, found the Taylorist job training program very much to their distaste both because unions were intimately involved in the management of the process and because it involved a great increase in the resources they had to commit to training.

If the training program reflected the dominant influence of the Taylorists within the TWI, Dietz's commitment to the HRS became increasingly influential over time. In the face of suspicion if not hostility of the unions and the Taylorists, those trying to develop an HRS input into the training agenda found progress difficult. This was despite the fact that employers were much more supportive of the notion that foremen should be trained as counselors than they were of enhancing the skills of workers. Important in overcoming the Taylorist-union resistance were the great influx of women with no experience of industrial life into the nation's workplaces, the HRS advocates' robust adherence to the notion that counseling must be developed as a neutral science and not merely as a tool to promote the interests of elite managers, and their willingness to accept unions participation in designing and managing all aspects of the counseling effort. Also of significance was the fact that Roethlisberger began to distance himself from Mayo in 1940.[87] This was a process that involved not least an attempt by Roethlisberger to build a positive relationship with the trade unions and the Taylorists, as is evidenced by a positive, if not enthusiastic, review of Cooke and Murray's *Organized Labor and Production*.[88]

With these developments the advocates of the HRS were able to convince both the scientific managers and the trade unions that the techniques they advocated need not necessarily be mere tools for consolidating elite control of the workforce. This development enabled the two groupings to collaborate in implementing a joint program of personnel training and industrial democracy in over five thousand workplaces.[89]

Jacoby has observed that the program developed by the TWI was the last spasm of the continuing campaign that the industrial democrats had sustained over many years as they strove to build management as a class-neutral science. This effort, he adds, had embodied the best attributes of the "scientific, neutral approach to personnel management [and the] independent profession that Brandeis and the Taylorists had hoped it might prove to be."[90] The war years revealed on a mass scale that "science and the democratic way of life" can flourish within industry and the wider community. Reflecting the appreciation of what was achieved, the scientific managers in 1945 awarded Dooley and Dietz the initial prize given by the Taylor

Society (by now renamed the Society for the Advancement of Management) for their work in promoting human relations in the TWI program. After the Taylorists scaled this pinnacle, however, they were compelled to abandon it in the immediate postwar years once corporate America mobilized to win back the gains won by labor and those who had dared to hope that management might be developed as a science and not merely as a tool available to the rulers to whom Mayo had successfully appealed for support.

The Taylorists' unrelenting efforts to combat business insistence that profit accumulation must be the primary driver in both industry and society made them aware that the war years were extraordinary times and that eventually the corporate rulers of America would seek to restore what they saw as their "right to manage." Similarly, they were aware that when this period of reaction came, the commitment of the industrial psychologist and the personnel administrator to science would be seriously tested. In an effort that harked back to Taylor's attempts to convince the engineering profession that knowledge should trump profit in industry and the wider society, they prepared for the postwar years by urging personnel professionals to embrace a code of conduct that maintained that their field would be ruled by knowledge and not by the desires of the employer. As Tead observed in 1943 when seeking to further this position in an extended discussion on employee counseling, "In a democracy it is peculiarly true that those responsible for the labor and laboring welfare of other self-respecting individuals should gladly hold themselves to standards of dealing which reflect the rights of persons as such along with the recognition of their responsibilities to the organization for which they work."[91] Promotion of this perspective, however, was to be in vain. As with the engineers, corporate America simply refused to allow the industrial psychologist and the personnel administrator the freedom to prioritize knowledge over profit accumulation. The means by which corporate leadership prevented such a development has attracted little attention from management analysts. By contrast, historians of economics have made a significant effort to explain the rapid postwar halt to the critical trend manifest within their discipline during the interwar years. Their efforts have revealed that central to the decline was the patronage that the financiers and managers in academia provided to what they deemed acceptable schools of thought. Notable in this regard is the work of Crauford Goodwin, who revealed how higher education administrators, the government, the business community, and charitable foundations interacted in a successful effort to cleanse universities of critical thought and activism.[92] As a result, he observes, economics was rendered a discipline committed to "scientifically" solving problems, but only those problems deemed worthy of study by business or the state. Goodwin further notes that in the conduct of this cleansing, particular vitriol was heaped on those scholars who had played an active role in the New Deal. The crimes of these individuals were perceived to be particularly heinous because they had been committed "far from the ivory tower": "It was particularly offensive that these dissenting economists chose to express their views not just to scientific colleagues in codes that only the initiated could comprehend but also to external audiences that ran the gamut from the local Rotary Club to the U.S. Congress. . . . If these economists had said the same things only in the classroom or in their departmental common rooms, or had expressed them in matrix algebra, nobody would have cared."[93]

So successful was the campaign to cleanse critical thought and activism from economics that few present-day economists are even aware that in the 1930s their discipline was widely perceived to be a seat of radicalism. This lack of historical knowledge is even more manifest within present-day industrial psychology and management studies, disciplines that by comparison with economics have sustained little interest in their own history. Very few scholars within these fields are aware of even the more outrageous cases of intellectual cleansing that occurred in the immediate postwar years as part of the process of redefining what constitutes a "scientific business education." Indeed, the all-but-total lack of interest enabled the common understanding of the evolution of these disciplines to take an Orwellian twist. In the hands of the victors and their scribes, the Taylorist industrial democrats came to be perceived as mechanistic, anti-union authoritarians, while Mayo was deified, and the elitist tradition he advocated was successfully marketed as a manifestation of corporate humanism. Sadly, this was a development to which many labor historians, blinkered by an "armed camp" approach to employer-employee relations, helped to sustain.

Goodwin has further observed that few scholars needed to be openly persecuted to convince postwar economists that critical thought was no longer on the agenda.[94] Similarly, within management studies, only a small number of critical teachers and consultants had to be branded as radicals and publicly disciplined in order to convince professional bodies and education institutions that a sympathetic view of the corporation was appropriate. This was a process that transformed even the Taylor Society, whose members soon abandoned industrial democracy once old-school Taylorists such as Mary Van Kleeck were branded as Communists and dragged before the House Un-American Activities Committee.

Conclusion

This chapter has drawn on two streams of revisionist history that are currently challenging the orthodox understanding of the early years of scientific management and human relations. By tracing the interaction between these two management traditions, it has added to the mounting body of scholarship that has questioned both the demonized view of Taylorism and the notion that Mayo advanced a humanist response to the alleged inhumanity of scientific management. In so doing, we have highlighted the Taylorists' conviction that management could develop as a science only if business power was countervailed by other actors; that is, if management was democratized. This was a notion rejected by the HRS, which eagerly bought into a complex web of power and influence revolving around Rockefeller and his closest advisors, who found highly attractive Mayo's belief that the business world and indeed the world as a whole should be government by a natural elite, though they did concede that "the Prince'" at times can benefit from the advice offered by the many willing to compete for the well-rewarded role of Machievelli. In this context, Mayo's elitism found strong support from Rockefeller and his conservative allies. Though compelled to pause for breath during World War II, the HRS soon revived its antidemocratic thrust in the postwar years and flourished in the 1950s and 1960s in the guise of humane "high-performance" personnel management. In this way, the business community was able to gain access to a body of intellectual "servants of power" willing to help crush the notion that management activity and theory should be democratized while concomitantly deifying themselves as humanists who should be applauded for expelling the demon of Taylorism from the workplace.

PART II

Region, Race, and Resistance to Organized Labor

Region and race have often shaped attitudes toward organized labor in unexpected and divergent fashions. The next three essays in this book demonstrate how this played out in New York, Mississippi, Arkansas, and the American West. In her study of the removal of a Yonkers, New York, carpet factory to Greenville, Mississippi, Tami Friedman demonstrates how capital mobility became a potent weapon against union strength and labor standards in both the North and the South. The effort to take advantage of cheap labor and weak unions proved a powerfully unifying ideology among corporate executives from both regions, especially when the northerners took up posts in southern industry.

A shift to the anti-union right is also apparent in Michael Pierce's study of Governor Orval Faubus and Arkansas politics. Faubus himself had once been an economic liberal and a racial moderate. In the early 1950s, the state labor movement even considered Arkansas friendly territory. But the rise of militant white resistance to school integration in the mid-1950s subverted New Deal liberalism all across the South and made Arkansas near synonymous with racial segregation and anti-union demagoguery. This reaction was particularly virulent in northwest Arkansas, where the white working class had long supported trade unionism as well as white supremacy. The Little Rock crisis, which Faubus engineered, forced white workers to choose between the two, giving anti-union entrepreneurs like Sam Walton and Don Tyson a decisive boost on their road to competitive success and national political influence.

Much of this resistance to labor and the New Deal was codified in and embodied by the state "right-to-work" laws that proliferated across the South and Southwest during the 1940s and 1950s. As Elizabeth Tandy Shermer points out, avoidance of "union security"—contractual union membership guarantees for workers in an organized company—topped the agenda of local business groups eager to attract industry into areas tied historically to agriculture, mining, and ranching. Local merchants, professionals, and other business elites had a visceral, philosophical opposition to the influence of organized labor, if only because high wages and high taxes on business, which labor often favored, made it more difficult to lure manufacturers out of the northern industrial core, where a union oriented liberalism was the most entrenched. Across the developing Sunbelt, growth-oriented, conservative coalitions favored state restrictions on union power, especially those collective bargaining contract provisions that mandated union membership as a condition of employment. The unions saw such clauses as assurance that their corporate adversaries recognized organized labor's need for institutional "security" while most in management saw such union security provisions as a violation of the individual employee's right to work and as a hindrance to economic progress and technological dynamism. By the end of the 1950s, business groups and conservative politicians had made anti-unionism a pillar of Sunbelt economic growth, thereby solidifying a political discourse that celebrated entrepreneurial autonomy, free enterprise, and hostility to big labor as core governing principles.

Chapter 4

Capital Flight, "States' Rights," and the Anti-Labor Offensive After World War II

Tami J. Friedman

According to many scholars and popular commentators, modern U.S. conservatism came of age during the 1960s and reached the pinnacle of its power in successful Republican electoral campaigns. An examination of capital migration after World War II, however, demonstrates that the Right's ascendancy had strong roots in an earlier era and reached across political party lines. In the late 1940s and 1950s, northern employers deployed a range of strategies, including the relocation of manufacturing operations, in order to counter the growing influence of organized labor. Southern boosters, hoping to attract investment to their region, shared northern businessmen's desire to combat the union threat. Eager to promote competition between communities, states, and regions for the favors of industry, these two groups forged a cross-regional alliance geared toward reducing the power of the federal regulatory state. Their shared interest in promoting "states' rights"—a goal closely linked to their anti-union economic agenda—contributed to the rise of conservatism in the postwar United States.[1]

For northern business leaders, capital migration reinforced the relationship between anti-unionism and conservative political aims. Scholars have

generally identified two main tendencies within the conservative movement, both closely related to postwar anti-Communism: a traditionalist
element concerned with promoting conservative social and cultural norms
and values and a libertarian strain dedicated to "getting government off
our backs." The attack on federal power has carried important economic
implications, for in the guise of championing individual initiative and con-
serving taxpayer dollars, deregulation of the private sector—coupled with
curtailment and privatization of public services—has enabled business
leaders to exert considerable influence over public policy and to profit
handsomely at the public's expense. Unions, even fairly tame ones, have
threatened this project by interfering with employers' control over wages
and working conditions, and by pressing for a class-neutral, if not pro-
labor, state. Quashing collective action by workers, then, has been a key
conservative goal. The popular emphasis on traditionalist concerns, however—particularly by those who see modern conservatism as a reaction
against 1960s-era disruptions of the social order such as racial unrest and
cultural experimentation—has deflected attention from conservatives' economic objectives. Further, the widely held view that until the 1980s most
employers adhered to a postwar "social contract," in which they presumably accepted unionization in exchange for harmonious labor-management
relations, has obscured the powerful link between anti-unionism and the
Right. But as the history of industry relocation shows, many northern executives not only tried to impede organized labor in the early postwar period
but also understood their efforts as part of a larger conservative program
to limit the power of the federal state.[2]

Capital mobility also placed southerners at the forefront in promoting
the conservative cause. Students of the postwar era have correctly characterized southern segregationists as racial conservatives, based on their intense
resistance to civil rights advances in the late 1940s and 1950s as well as their
vicious and often violent attacks on African Americans themselves. Since
most prominent postwar conservatives were affiliated with the Republican
Party, however, few observers have identified white southerners—largely
ensconced in the Democratic camp until the late 1960s—as major players
in shaping the modern Right. In part, this exclusion may have reflected a
tendency to treat the white supremacist South as an anachronistic "Other"
far out of step with the nation's political mainstream. Moreover, many
scholars have attributed the eventual triumph of conservatism nationally to
Republicans' strategic targeting of southern voters rather than to the active

agency of southerners themselves. But as the history of capital flight suggests, southern industrial recruiters, anxious to create a favorable business climate while also preserving segregation, avidly promoted a "states' rights" program that meshed neatly with northern businessmen's efforts to curb unionism through constraints on federal control.[3]

Well before the postwar period, northern business leaders were challenging efforts to enlist federal power on labor's behalf. During the Great Depression, for example, workers fought for federal aid to win union protections, improved wages and working conditions, and relief for the unemployed. The National Association of Manufacturers (NAM) opposed New Deal measures that allowed workers to join unions and bargain collectively. During the debate over the Social Security Act (SSA) of 1935, the Chamber of Commerce of the United States advocated state rather than federal standards for old-age pensions, and sought to exclude farm laborers, domestic servants, and casual workers from the pension and unemployment insurance provisions of the act. Both NAM and the U.S. Chamber opposed the Fair Labor Standards Act (FLSA) of 1938, which established maximum weekly working hours and a phased-in federal minimum wage. Although business leaders readily accepted some forms of federal largesse—such as Reconstruction Finance Corporation loans—they were quick to condemn federal policies that, by freeing workers from near-total dependence on employers for survival, enabled employees to wield greater power as a class. While often unsuccessful, business-minded northern Republicans in Congress did their best, in the tumultuous 1930s, to advance anti-labor views.[4]

During World War II, northern businessmen grew increasingly uneasy about labor's challenges to corporate control. The wartime necessity of labor-management-government cooperation enabled many unions to stabilize memberships and consolidate gains. During the war, U.S. union membership increased from less than nine million to almost fifteen million; by war's end, over two thirds of production workers in manufacturing were covered by union contracts. As unions grew in size and strength, employees sought to protect their interests by, among other actions, pressing claims with the National War Labor Board, on which several national union representatives sat. While unions were certainly the junior partner in the war effort, federal policy gave organized labor greater visibility and legitimacy in the public realm.[5]

The direction of postwar industrial relations intensified employers' concerns. Between August 1945 and August 1946, about five million workers walked off the job in a wave of strikes intended to preserve wartime gains. By the late 1940s, unions in key industries such as steel and auto were winning substantial wage increases, paid holidays, and even pension plans.[6] Alongside these workplace successes, laborites sought greater power in the federal arena. Thanks largely to the efforts of union leaders such as Walter Reuther of the United Automobile Workers (UAW), a Democrat-dominated Congress passed—and President Harry S. Truman signed—the Employment Act of 1946. While watered down substantially by congressional conservatives (the word "Full" was removed from the title, for one thing), the legislation nonetheless suggested that the federal government would play a central role in managing postwar prosperity. In order to further influence federal policy, unionists engaged in fund-raising, political education, and voter mobilization during election campaigns. Many laborites hoped unions would wield power even more directly. In 1946, 23 percent of Congress of Industrial Organizations (CIO) officials and 13 percent of American Federation of Labor (AFL) officials favored a labor party in the next few years—and when asked about building such a party by the mid-1950s, 52 percent of CIO leaders and 23 percent of their AFL counterparts agreed. Among national CIO officers, positive reaction jumped from 8 percent to an astonishing 65 percent.[7]

In response to labor's advances, corporate leaders went on the offensive in the early postwar years. Despite the popular notion of a postwar social contract, many employers were anxious to reassert power both within and beyond the workplace. Among their efforts, they launched or revived programs of welfare capitalism intended to reestablish goodwill in labor-management relations, initiated public relations campaigns to convince Americans of the superiority of "free enterprise," and adopted a tough bargaining stance in order to contain unions' influence on the production floor. The anti-labor program was bound up with a conservative critique of the federal regulatory state. In 1946, NAM president Robert Ross Wason announced that his organization intended to "restor[e] some liberties that had been lost through fourteen years of anti-enterprise sabotage by government"—a task to be achieved by rolling back price controls, excess taxation, and national labor policies that produced important gains for employees. When the Republicans recaptured both houses of Congress in that year's November elections, they implemented much of the business agenda, including reduced wartime excess-profits tax rates and the ability to write off strike-induced losses from wartime gains.[8]

In hopes of escaping or avoiding unionization, many businessmen turned to capital flight. Since the early twentieth century, textile mill owners had been moving from New England to the South in search of lower labor costs. In the wake of Depression-era and wartime union organizing, which proved far more successful among northern than southern workers, executives in a host of industries—including textiles, apparel, automobiles, electrical appliances, and rubber tires—pursued similar goals. As early as 1946, officials with Alexander Smith, a Yonkers, New York-based carpet firm, may have begun considering southern options; by late 1950 they had settled on Greenville, Mississippi (in the Yazoo-Mississippi delta) and were arranging for public assistance from local and state authorities to build a brand-new plant. In the summer of 1954 they announced plans to abandon Yonkers, in the midst of a Textile Workers Union of America (TWUA) strike. Royal Little of Textron, Inc., based in Rhode Island, built a textile empire by shutting down unionized northern facilities and shifting production to the South. Robert E. Wood, former army general and chair of Sears, Roebuck, and Company, was a particularly ardent advocate of migration; having established numerous stores in the South by the late 1930s, he began guaranteeing markets for manufacturers such as Armstrong Rubber that agreed to build southern plants. In 1948, enthused about the arrival of numerous industries along the Gulf Coast, including chemical plants, paper mills, and agricultural processing facilities, he depicted the region as "a throbbing new frontier" where "a fresh, vigorous spirit" prevailed. Wood was also a master at implementing techniques of welfare capitalism and industrial psychology in his mail-order and retail operations in order to keep unionism at bay.[9]

Not surprisingly, corporate leaders who wanted to maximize capital mobility also sought to minimize the role of the federal state. Alongside the desire to wrest power from unions, corporate migrants often articulated larger conservative goals. In the fall of 1945, top Alexander Smith executive William F. C. "Bill" Ewing—remembered by his daughter as the "most liberal" of Republicans—echoed NAM's complaint that federal authorities had been "deliberately unfriendly to business" during the preceding ten or twelve years. In the spring of 1950, Smith's in-house organ, *The News*, distributed to thousands of employees, carried a piece by Frank E. Masland Jr., a Smith board member and owner of a Philadelphia carpet factory, that highlighted the dangers of a too-dominant government role. "There is much talk today," Masland observed, "about a welfare state in which the benevolent government furnishes its people with protection against the rigors of life" through free pensions, free health care, free education, and more. Such an arrangement, he argued, was "part and parcel of the Socialist State." According to Masland, "once proud England"—formerly "a free capitalistic nation" that "ruled the world"—was now a "Socialist State" pleading desperately for U.S. assistance. This could be America's fate, he warned, "if we pursue the path of the welfare state." In 1951 Royal Little, defending against union-inspired attacks on southerners' use of industrial revenue bonds to aid business, complained that high federal taxes on wealth and corporate income were inhibiting private investment and thus stifling industrial growth. Robert Wood, active in numerous right-wing causes and a staunch supporter of Senator Joseph McCarthy at the height of the Red Scare, was a close associate of Clarence Manion, whose weekly radio broadcasts, launched in 1954, railed against the federal state. By 1961 Manion was on the governing council of the John Birch Society, as were Frank Masland and two former presidents of NAM.[10]

When considering new locations, northern-based businessmen worked closely with southern boosters who, despite differences in political party affiliation, had long shared their antipathy toward unions and the federal state. During the early New Deal, southern employers—worried that minimum wage provisions in federal industry codes would undermine both the South's wage advantage vis-à-vis the North and race-based earnings disparities within the South—formed the Southern States Industrial Council to defend their region's lower rates. Unable to kill the provisions, they did manage to preserve North-South wage differentials in about half of the codes, as well as in earnings for federal work relief. They also succeeded in excluding farm labor and domestic service, performed in the South largely by black workers, from coverage under the SSA, the FLSA, and other federal laws. Moreover, southern leaders ensured that control over eligibility criteria and benefit levels for key SSA programs, including unemployment insurance, would rest with the states. Importantly, southern Democrats found support from Republicans on labor issues; both groups, for example, voted against the FLSA (southerners had tried but failed to incorporate regional differentials into the act). Like northern businessmen, southerners embraced federal benefits—such as generous agricultural subsidies—while resisting New Deal measures that undermined control over their labor supply.[11]

Like northern and national business leaders, the southern elite grew more concerned about unions during World War II. On the eve of the war, southern union activity lagged far behind northern organizing: in 1939 the unionization rate among nonagricultural workers in the South was just under 11 percent, compared with nearly 21 percent in the Mid-Atlantic and New England states. However, the wartime decentralization of industry and the rise in federal spending on military production brought new economic opportunities to southern workers and, with them, new possibilities for collective action. In 1938, for example, Ingalls Shipbuilding Corporation was established in Pascagoula on Mississippi's Gulf Coast. After a strike in 1940, more than 83 percent of the shipyard's workers voted for union representation by the metal trades. At the time the labor force stood at just 650, but during the war it skyrocketed, peaking at 11,000. As a result of such developments, southern unionism became far more widespread. Between 1938 and 1948 union membership in the South more than doubled, from less than 500,000 to over one million.[12]

In the early postwar period, southern business and political leaders found unions an increasingly serious threat. In the mid-1930s, Mississippi politicians, desperate to improve economic conditions, had pioneered "Balance Agriculture with Industry" (BAWI), a program allowing municipalities to issue industrial revenue bonds and use the proceeds to build factories for northern firms. Other southern states adopted similar plans. While wartime economic growth diminished the importance of these efforts, after the war southern leaders avidly pursued northern investment in hopes of reversing population losses and reviving their region's economic base. They knew that the South's attractiveness to potential corporate migrants rested, to a great extent, on its low wages and relative lack of union strength. As northern manufacturers turned their gaze southward, however, union leaders prepared to follow suit. In the spring of 1946 the AFL and the CIO targeted the South with major organizing drives, each vowing to bring at least a million southern members into the union fold. If the campaigns proved successful, many more southern workers could be expected to contest employers' power and enjoy expanded protection under federal labor laws. By narrowing the North-South differential in wages and working conditions, moreover, high levels of unionization would likely reduce the South's competitiveness and diminish its appeal as an alternative investment site.[13]

Southern leaders' concerns about the prospect of unionization were closely linked to their fears about challenges to Jim Crow. Within the South, elite support for industrialization depended on boosters' assurances that the arrival of northern manufacturing would not interfere with the region's racial status quo. Before and during the war, however, civil rights advocates and their allies had fought hard for federal policies promoting equal employment opportunity in military industry, and at war's end they continued to press for a permanent Fair Employment Practices Commission (FEPC). In early 1948 President Truman openly endorsed a series of recommendations for countering racial discrimination, and several months later the national Democratic Party did the same. These efforts, which reflected African American voters' growing influence inside the party—a political home shared uneasily with white southerners—threatened to interfere with southerners' ability to preserve labor-market segmentation along racial lines. The CIO in particular aligned itself with the civil rights program, supporting the FEPC and, through its political action committee, targeting racist, anti-labor southern politicians for removal from their congressional seats. In launching the CIO's southern drive, President Philip Murray promised to "deliver to [southern workers] their political and economic emancipation." The campaign would be "only 50 per cent effective," according to TWUA president Emil Rieve, "unless we purge the Congress of its labor haters and . . . its rank conservatives." Union leaders understood—as did their southern adversaries—that successful organizing in the workplace, provisions for equal employment opportunity, and the expulsion of labor's enemies from positions of power in the federal government went hand in hand.[14]

Like the northern employers whom they hoped to lure southward, southern boosters understood that labor's access to federal power threatened their region's business appeal. In July 1948 a number of prominent business and agricultural leaders met in Greenville, Mississippi, to discuss forming an organization that would represent diverse economic interests across the state. The group, the Mississippi Economic Council (MEC), was founded later that year. The July meeting, held under the auspices of the Delta Council—which represented the delta region's planters—was initiated by Greenville's most avid industrial promoters. Their goal, according to Greenville wholesaler Edmund Taylor, was to "protect . . . against laws or minority groups which might keep the state from progressing as it should." United action was needed in both the economic and political arenas, Taylor asserted, because "we've gotten to where everything is either run out of Washington or an attempt is made to control it out of Washington." Greenville attorney and cotton planter W. T. "Billy" Wynn—in terms that neatly mirrored Frank Masland's pronouncements—underscored the need for mobilization by describing conditions since the war: "We saw England overnight become socialized . . . ; the one country in the world which we felt would be a democracy forever. We saw France nationalized overnight." Conditions at home were no better, Wynn contended, for "the businessmen of America have been mealy-mouthed for all these days. In the meantime the organized labor people of America, subsidized by the government, ran the country. You businessmen have sat down, unorganized, and let them take it away from you." In 1950 Walter Sillers Jr.—a delta planter and speaker of the Mississippi House of Representatives—expressed similar views. While claiming to "have no quarrel with labor or labor unions as such," Sillers backed state legislation to limit union activity and attacked the CIO's political objectives, "especially their plan to defeat our Mississippi-United States Senators and Representatives and take over the political affairs of our country."[15]

Capital migration offered northern businessmen and southern boosters—already committed to impeding labor's progress—new opportunities to counter the union threat. In 1950, for example, Alexander Smith executives engaged the Fantus Factory Locating Service to find a new plant site. After examining numerous possibilities in several regions, the consultants touted Greenville as the most attractive choice. "Mississippi is one of the few non-union strongholds of the United States," Leonard C. Yaseen of Fantus told Smith's Bill Ewing. "There is every indication that with proper management you could operate a non-union plant. . . . Probably nowhere else in the states under consideration can such outstanding community cooperation be obtained." Because of "fewer restrictions imposed as the result of non-union operating conditions," Smith could simplify personnel policies as well as reduce shift premiums and training costs. Hourly wages would likely average 40 cents below those in Yonkers ($1.10 compared to $1.50)—particularly important since wages and salaries accounted for nearly 36 percent of Smith's operating expenses—and "prevailing custom in the area does not require the many fringe benefits called for" in Smith's contract with the TWUA. Greenville's business and civic leaders confirmed that wages in the area's few industries were low and that unions, where they existed, were very weak. According to state employment officials, Smith would have no trouble attracting an ample labor supply in the delta because mechanization of farming and federal cutbacks in cotton acreage "have thrown a great many people out of work." Indeed, local boosters showed Fantus the results of a "Survey of White Labor" demonstrating the presence of a substantial labor surplus; of 2,719 white men and women interested in industrial labor, more than 47 percent were unemployed. The Smith case was hardly unusual; alongside such factors as proximity to markets and access to raw materials, labor costs and conditions were among the key variables inducing industrialists to move southward in the postwar years.[16]

Once such deals were consummated, northern employers and their southern advocates collaborated to ensure that southern communities remained inhospitable to the union cause. In the Smith case, Herbert J. "Jack" Potts, who relocated from Yonkers to become Greenville Mills' first plant manager, pursued a range of anti-union techniques. Wary of TWUA organizers who might head southward, especially after Smith's 1954 decision to leave Yonkers, Potts met regularly with new employees to warn them, "very frankly: 'We don't want a union in this plant.'" He also used less coercive methods such as sponsoring company sports teams and hosting Fourth of July picnics and Christmas parties for workers and their families—tactics that had worked to the firm's advantage in its pre-union days up north. Such activities were not carried out entirely independently, however. While Smith wanted to offer wages high enough to recruit quality workers, management was careful to consult with major employers in the area in order to avoid upsetting prevailing wage scales—which could lead workers to abandon other firms in favor of the carpet mill. "You start a bidding war, you make enemies, so we want to tie in exactly with those companies," Potts explained. In turn, area businessmen helped ensure a compliant workforce; according to John W. "Jack" Baskin, the mill's first personnel manager, Smith sought recommendations from local shopkeepers, such as corner grocers and gas station owners, who would be well placed to influence employees in the event of a union campaign. If a union threat did arise, leading citizens were quick to defend new industry; by the late 1950s, communities throughout the South were passing ordinances requiring registration and licensing of union organizers—complete with fines and jail terms for noncompliance—as part of the campaign to attract outside firms. Newcomers to the region also benefited from the expertise of colleagues already familiar with southern operations; the personnel manager at James Lees and Sons, a Philadelphia-based carpet company with a long-running Virginia facility, was an old friend of Jack Potts who offered suggestions for preserving industrial harmony in the new location, such as hiring rural workers with no factory experience and learning to greet employees by name.[17]

Such cooperation was facilitated by the establishment of personal and professional ties between newly arriving executives and the local elite. Soon after arriving in Greenville, Jack Potts was elected to the county Chamber of Commerce board and became active in the MEC's Labor-Management Relations Committee. Since membership in service organizations was an important networking tool, Potts joined the Rotary Club and ensured that colleagues joined the Lions and Kiwanis clubs. Potts and his family, along with other top plant officials, soon became fixtures at Greenville's country club. In turn, southerners who had helped lure northern industry were often rewarded with managerial jobs. In 1949, Baxter Laboratories, a pharmaceuticals company that had moved to the delta town of Cleveland, named a representative of the Mississippi Power and Light Company (MP&L)—a key player in the region's industrial development program—to a management post. Smith officials appointed to the Greenville Mills board of directors a local real estate agent and city councilor, Rhodes Wasson, who had proved pivotal in recruiting the firm. Jack Baskin was the son-in-law of prominent delta planter John S. Kirk, who also served on the Greenville City Council. Such developments reinforced the mutuality of interests across regions by blurring the distinction between northern-based employers and their southern friends.[18]

Capital flight stimulated joint anti-labor action not only in local communities but at the state level as well. Eager to attract northern industry, southern governors and legislators offered a host of benefits to business, ranging from bond financing and tax abatements to intervention in labor disputes. In 1952, for example, the Amalgamated Clothing Workers of America won a union election at Rice-Stix Corporation, a garment factory established in 1945 at Water Valley through Mississippi's BAWI plan. When workers struck over extension of their union contract to other facilities, a judge enjoined them from picketing and Democratic governor Hugh L. White (who had launched BAWI during an earlier stint in the state's highest office) sent in the National Guard. That same year White signed legislation authorizing five-year local tax exemptions for out-of-state businesses, which was passed on an emergency basis to assist Westinghouse Electrical Corporation in establishing a Vicksburg plant.[19]

All of these efforts were made possible by the relative absence of federal authority to shape economic conditions in municipalities, counties, and states. The appeal of places such as Greenville as investment climates reflected, to a great extent, the reality that regional distinctions enabled many southern communities to compete more effectively for industry than could their counterparts in the North. In some cases the differentials resulted from federal mandates, as with the regional wage variations that southerners enshrined in many Depression-era industry codes. More often, however, they flowed from a hands-off approach in Washington that gave local and state authorities a freer hand in hammering out policy details. In the case of unemployment insurance, for example, Fantus staff—when assessing Alexander Smith's options for a new plant site—found wide disparities between states. In New York State, jobless benefits ranged from $10 to $26 per week and lasted for twenty-six weeks. In Mississippi, by contrast, weekly benefits ranged from just $3 to $20 and were distributed for only sixteen weeks. As a result, Fantus personnel reported, turnover rates were low in Mississippi because "workers [there] tend to stay on the job." Workers' compensation insurance rates, also set at the state level, were nearly three times higher in New York than in the Magnolia State. Employers considering relocation also compared differentials not directly related to labor, such as tax rates and utility costs. Public subsidies could prove significant; indeed, Smith executives were drawn by Mississippi's BAWI program and by Greenville officials' willingness to issue $4.75 million in bonds to build a new plant. Not all southern sites were equally appealing; when evaluating a small Virginia town for a possible Smith operation, Fantus consultants expressed concern about, among other limitations, stringent enforcement of state laws governing industrial waste disposal. But it was easy enough, in such cases, to find more lenient locations; in Greenville, no treatment was required for industrial material discharged into the Mississippi River—except in the case of "poisonous wastes."[20]

To preserve these competitive conditions, northern businessmen and southern boosters were compelled to carry their anti-labor program into the federal realm. In 1947 Congress approved the Taft-Hartley Act, cosponsored by two conservative Republicans, Senator Robert A. Taft of Ohio and Representative Fred Hartley of New Jersey. Avidly promoted by NAM and the U.S. Chamber, the act imposed a host of restrictions on organized labor. Among its provisions was a right-to-work clause allowing individual states to outlaw union membership as a condition of work (the "union shop").

Taft-Hartley—decried by unionists across the country as a "slave labor act"—was passed overwhelmingly by a Republican-dominated Congress elected in the wake of the postwar strike wave. The measure received strong support from southerners, however, nearly all of whom were Democrats: more than 80 percent of southerners in each house backed the legislation, and after President Truman vetoed the measure, 90 percent of southern house members and more than 78 percent of southern senators supported the successful override. Their actions enraged delegates to the 1947 Mississippi Federation of Labor (AFL) convention in Jackson, where union officers called on attendees to overthrow the "Republican slave bill" by electing Democrats who would carry out their party's platform. Indeed, the attendees resolved to "give, bequeath, and deed in fee simple" Democratic senator James O. "Jim" Eastland Jr.—a prominent delta planter whom they lambasted as an abject NAM loyalist—to Senator Taft and the GOP. It was perhaps not surprising that Mississippi unionists, lacking any alternative to the Democratic Party, depicted their own political representatives as captives of the Republican Party. The portrayal unwittingly underscored, however, that in the area of labor policy, northern Republicans and southern Democrats shared a good deal of common ground.[21]

Northern employers and their southern allies found right to work a great boon to capital flight. For decades before Taft-Hartley, business leaders had been fighting to preserve open-shop conditions; between 1944 and 1946, they achieved victory in five southern and western states. Buoyed by Taft-Hartley's promise to preserve "states' rights" on the union-shop question, right-to-work advocates threw themselves into new campaigns. Their efforts proved effective in both Republican and southern Democratic strongholds, and by the end of 1947 they had triumphed in fourteen states. In championing right to work, southern leaders often insisted that it would make their states more competitive in the fight for northern firms. The Delta Council and the MEC took up the cause in Mississippi and won passage in 1954. (Several earlier efforts had failed, probably because many saw right to work as unnecessary in a largely agricultural state.) The legislation quickly became a powerful new weapon in Mississippi's industry-luring arsenal; in updating their promotional materials, Greenville boosters added a news release highlighting the large margin of victory, along with the full text of the law. Northern businessmen paid close attention to these efforts; Chicago-area screw manufacturer William A. Mosow, for example, who found Greenville a welcome respite from the UAW in the late 1950s, asserted that his top priority for a new location was a right-to-work state. Migratory manufacturers themselves played a key role in promoting the measures, as when in the late 1950s, Ralph J. Cordiner—chair of the General Electric Company (GE) and chief architect of a plant decentralization program that moved a significant share of production out of the North— stumped for right to work in several states. Such legislation, Cordiner noted, was "very definitely . . . a factor in deciding where General Electric plants are built."[22]

On the heels of Taft-Hartley, northern industrialists and southern boosters pursued additional strategies for freeing local and state labor policy from federal control. Since the advent of the FLSA, which mandated a national minimum wage reaching 40 cents per hour by 1945, unionists had been trying to raise the rate. In 1949 the act was amended to allow an increase to 75 cents the following year. In 1955 President Dwight D. Eisenhower, a moderate Republican, recommended a hike to 90 cents. While NAM, the U.S. Chamber, and numerous industry associations opposed any increase, laborites—closely allied with politicians whose regions were losing industry—lobbied for $1.25. While eager to boost workers' earnings nationally, pro-labor advocates also hoped that a higher federal standard would help narrow regional wage disparities that encouraged capital flight. New York governor Averell Harriman, for example, hoped the higher rate would protect his state's economy "from unfair competition by low-wage areas of the country." Harriman argued that "it is the Federal Government's responsibility to put a stop to that kind of competition." Harriman's sentiments were echoed not only by unionists but also by some business representatives, such as men's apparel manufacturers, who wanted to stay in New York State. Although Republicans and southern Democrats could not stop an increase altogether, they managed to cap the minimum at just $1. During the 1957–1958 recession, when Eisenhower proposed a temporary extension of unemployment insurance benefits, a similar balance of forces emerged. Republicans and southern Democrats called for individual states' voluntary participation, arguing that local leaders were best equipped to address local problems; indeed, one Georgia official insisted that a mandatory program would interfere with "states' rights." This approach riled adversaries such as Harriman, who argued (unsuccessfully) that requiring all states to follow "a uniform set of national minimum standards" would remove unemployment insurance costs as a factor in the interstate competition for industrial firms.[23]

Northern manufacturers and their southern supporters also banded together to protect federal policies that facilitated capital flight. By exploiting federal tax and other loopholes, for example, Royal Little's Textron empire profited from acquiring and then liquidating northern mills. Textron also benefited from southern subsidies—in the form of industrial revenue bonds whose interest was exempt from federal taxation—that helped the firm establish southern plants. In late 1951, during the Korean War, the TWUA urged federal authorities to deny Textron approval for new southern facilities, two of them apparently slated for South Carolina; in response, that state's governor, James F. "Jimmy" Byrnes, denounced the union for trying to preserve inefficient northern mills. Also during the war, Charles E. Wilson—Ralph Cordiner's predecessor and mentor at GE—oversaw a federal program to promote industrial dispersal as a form of protection against atomic attack. The plan unleashed controversy over whether high-unemployment areas should receive preferential consideration for military contracts—a proposal warmly embraced by congressional representatives from New England, which was rapidly losing textile and other labor-intensive industry, but fiercely resisted by southern politicians who stood to gain from procurement policies that privileged southern locales. When southern inducements came under fire, northern businessmen rose to their defense. In mid-1953, after the Federal Deposit Insurance Corporation deemed BAWI bonds too risky for some Mississippi municipalities, representatives of northern companies that had relocated to the state—including Smith and Baxter Labs—traveled to Washington to testify on the subsidy program's behalf.[24]

As northern and southern leaders worked together to promote shared economic interests, they moved toward greater political unity as well. At the July 1948 meeting that helped create the MEC, Greenville's Edmund Taylor urged business leaders to "fight for states' rights for economic reasons just as we're fighting for states' rights for political reasons." His remarks came barely a week before the Democratic National Convention, from which some southern delegates angrily withdrew in order to form the States' Rights Democratic (Dixiecrat) Party, dedicated to preventing federal interference with racial segregation in the South. In November the Dixiecrats carried Alabama, Louisiana, Mississippi, and South Carolina. The party's leadership included some of the region's most avid industrial recruiters, including its presidential and vice-presidential candidates—South Carolina governor Strom Thurmond and Mississippi governor Fielding Wright,

respectively—as well as Mississippians Walter Sillers and Hugh White.
MP&L officials reportedly donated a substantial sum to the new party, and
key figures in southern business organizations, such as the Arkansas Free
Enterprise Association (which had spearheaded its state's successful right-
to-work effort) and Associated Industries of Florida, backed the movement
as well. Many Dixiecrats had no intention of abandoning the Democratic
Party; rather, they hoped to compel the party to abandon its growing commitment to civil rights. Some, however, acknowledged a greater affinity
with Republicans and saw the Dixiecrat revolt as, in historian Kari Frederickson's words, "a means to creating a more viable two-party system in the
south."[25]

During the 1950s, the shared commitment to a "states' rights" agenda
further narrowed the political distance between northern industrialists and
their southern allies. In 1956 Pulitzer Prize-winning journalist and Greenville booster Hodding Carter Jr. recorded the many changes his city had
undergone since Alexander Smith arrived. "The civic clubs gained new
members, the country club got some exceptional golfers, and Greenville's
voting rolls acquired some Republicans," he wrote. "We have profited in
many ways from these new neighbors whose backgrounds, experience and
thinking are often so different from our own." But was the newcomers'
thinking so different from that of their southern hosts? In 1952 many former Dixiecrats—including pro-industry boosters Billy Wynn of Greenville
and Governor Jimmy Byrnes of South Carolina—swung their support to
the Republican presidential candidate in a "Democrats for Eisenhower"
campaign. Eisenhower not only carried four southern states (Florida, Tennessee, Texas, and Virginia) but also received support ranging from about
35 percent to nearly 50 percent of the vote in the four states that had gone
Dixiecrat in 1948. In the wake of the 1954 *Brown v. Board of Education*
decision, southern segregationists launched a virulent campaign of "massive resistance" against racial integration and federal power; Mississippi's
Jim Eastland led the way in calling for "a people's organization" that would,
among other actions, "return the control of our government to the people,"
protect "free enterprise," and fight the CIO and the U.S. Supreme Court as
well as the National Association for the Advancement of Colored People.
In the 1956 presidential race, Eisenhower, who had sought to dissociate
himself from *Brown*, picked up two more southern states (Kentucky and
Louisiana). By 1958 southern Democrats had formed an alliance with
northern Republicans, NAM, the U.S. Chamber, and others opposed to

judicial activism as a means of federal control. As these developments suggested, white southerners' brand of political conservatism seemed increasingly in sync with that of the GOP.[26]

The 1964 presidential race further solidified the political bonds between corporate migrants and their southern friends. Arizona senator Barry Goldwater, angling for the Republican nomination, embodied precisely the combination of anti-unionism and opposition to federal regulation that conservatives—whether northern or southern—held dear. Leading proponents of capital flight, including Robert Wood and Ralph Cordiner, were among his staunchest supporters, with Cordiner serving as the Republican National Committee's finance chair during the campaign. Goldwater also attracted the enthusiastic backing of southern boosters. In the fall of 1963, Greenville Chamber of Commerce president Robert O. May invited the candidate to address the group's annual meeting the following year. Greenville, Mississippi, according to May, was a "good Republican community" where Goldwater—not yet chosen as his party's standard-bearer—enjoyed a "strong following"; the county had just voted for the state's Republican gubernatorial candidate by a two-to-one margin and, May suggested, "could be the beach-head for the Republican Party in this part of the Mid-South." Had Goldwater accepted, Jim Eastland—still a Democrat—would have delivered the introductory remarks. In addition to Arizona and Georgia, the Republicans carried the same states where the Dixiecrats had triumphed; indeed, Goldwater received higher shares of the vote totals in his southern strongholds (ranging from 54 percent in Georgia to 87 percent in Mississippi) than in his own home state (just over 50 percent).[27]

As the conservative cross-regional alliance grew stronger, laborites found it increasingly difficult to hamper industry's freedom of movement and lessen competition between the states. Capital mobility undermined unionism not only in southern communities but also in northern locales. As corporate leaders reduced their reliance on older locations, they disposed of obsolete facilities, removed equipment, and discharged redundant employees. These actions, by diminishing the size and strength of unions, hindered organized labor's ability to defend workers' interests. When employers tried to maximize leverage by threatening to abandon northern operations in favor of more hospitable climates, northern workers—made especially vulnerable to such pressures by a series of recessions between the late 1940s and the early 1960s—often felt compelled to accept concessions and temper their own demands.[28]

The weakening of union power in the workplace was accompanied by diminished political returns. In 1949 the Truman administration rebuffed a union-led effort to repeal Taft-Hartley, and a coalition of Republicans and southern Democrats succeeded in blocking labor's move. Overturning the right-to-work provision remained high on the union agenda, and even the national Democratic Party, in its 1960 and 1964 platforms, appeared to share labor's view. President John F. Kennedy, however, feared alienating the southern wing of his party and took no action to further labor's goal. A new opportunity arose in 1965 when President Lyndon B. Johnson, pushed by union leaders, publicly declared his support for repealing right to work. The nation's unions launched an intensive lobbying campaign and mobilized union members and allies on a massive scale. Right to work, they argued forcefully, encouraged firms to relocate to low-wage southern settings; indeed, according to the UAW's Walter Reuther, it represented "a cynical states' rights surrender of human rights and federal power over national labor relations." NAM, the U.S. Chamber, and other business groups bitterly resisted the union campaign. Although a House majority agreed to scrap the right-to-work provision, Senate Republicans and southern Democrats—some of whom, including Strom Thurmond, had joined the GOP—successfully filibustered to preserve the clause. Johnson proved unwilling to bring the full weight of his power to bear on behalf of the unions, suggesting that even labor's allies could not be counted upon to impede capital mobility or oppose "states' rights" in the economic realm.[29]

By the late 1960s, corporate migrants and their southern advocates had made considerable progress in maximizing the advantages of capital flight. In coalescing around a "states' rights" program that privileged local, state, and regional initiative over federal power, pro-business northerners and southerners helped weaken unionism while expanding conservative influence in national economic and political affairs. Their efforts laid the basis for the intensified competition for industrial and, increasingly, commercial investment that in recent decades has become commonplace among desperate communities, states, and regions throughout the United States. Moreover, their successes foreshadowed "neoliberal" international development strategies—premised on suppression of workers' rights and curtailment of government regulation—that U.S. policymakers and their overseas allies have touted as the key to economic progress around the globe.

These developments suggest the need to reexamine the popular notion of a postwar "social contract," in which U.S. business leaders presumably offered economic security and stability to employees in return for industrial peace. As the study of capital migration makes clear, many northern-based employers moved aggressively against organized labor in the postwar period. Working closely with southern segregationists, they attacked workers' well-being not only by shifting production to new locations but also by undermining union campaigns to harness federal power on labor's behalf. Through their actions, they helped unleash a cross-regional conservative movement in which anti-unionism played, and continues to play, a pivotal role.

Chapter 5

Orval Faubus and the Rise of Anti-Labor Populism in Northwestern Arkansas

Michael Pierce

In March 1914, the Bache-Denman Coal Company abrogated its contract with the United Mine Workers of America (UMWA), announced that its seven mines in Sebastian County, Arkansas, would operate on a nonunion basis, evicted union families from company housing, and began bringing in scab miners from Tennessee and heavily armed thugs of the Burns Detective Agency. These actions provoked a confrontation in which union members and local residents routed the guards and took over Prairie Creek Mine No. 4. The miners promptly flooded the shaft and strung a banner from the tipple declaring, "THIS IS A UNION MAN'S COUNTRY." Through the summer, armed union members alongside deputy sheriffs and local constables battled company guards and federal marshals. Writing about these events eight years later, U.S. Supreme Court chief justice William Howard Taft, who had adjudicated some of the nation's most vicious labor disputes, expressed dismay: "The vicinage was so permeated with union feeling that the public officers did not hesitate to manifest their enmity toward the non-union men." Southern Sebastian County did not witness a civil war in the spring and summer of 1914 but rather a united community rising in defense of a trade union and its members.[1]

During the first half of the twentieth century, this type of labor and anticorporate radicalism was endemic in hills and valleys of northwestern Arkansas, home to what historian James Green describes as "grass-roots socialism." Clergymen, such as Thomas Hagerty Jr. and Claude Williams, used their pulpits to enunciate visions of Christianity that they insisted were compatible with the teachings of Karl Marx—Williams would become a Communist while in a Sebastian County jail in the 1930s, and Father Hagerty would leave his Van Buren parish to become the ideological father of the Industrial Workers of the World. Socialist orators—Mother Jones, Oscar Ameringer, Eugene Debs—crisscrossed the region, holding encampments and spreading an anticapitalist gospel, and Debsian socialists established Commonwealth College in Polk County for those wanting more formal education.[2]

Socialists, though, were not the only Arkansans to enunciate pro-union or anticorporate ideals. The region's mainstream Democrats drank heavily at the same trough. Critics derided the era's most successful politician, three-term governor and twice-elected U.S. senator Jeff Davis, as the "Karl Marx of the Hillbillies" for his willingness to take on the corporations that he saw as threatening Arkansans. Davis warned, "The war is on . . . knife to knife, hilt to hilt, foot to foot, knee to knee between the corporations of Arkansas and the people. . . . If I win this race I have got to win it from every railroad, every bank, and two-thirds of the lawyers." Less flamboyantly, Congressman John C. Floyd, a Bentonville native, coauthored the Clayton Act to prevent the formation of powerful corporations and protect trade unions from antitrust regulations.[3]

By the end of the twentieth century, though, labor and anticorporate radicalism had nearly vanished from northwestern Arkansas, the region becoming home to anti-union behemoths Wal-Mart, Tyson Foods, and J. B. Hunt Trucking.[4] No one personified this transformation as much as Governor Orval Eugene Faubus, who was born into an Ozark socialist family in the early twentieth century. First elected governor with the support of a biracial coalition put together by the Arkansas labor movement, he later enunciated an anti-labor populism that resonated throughout northwest Arkansas. Much like Sam Walton and Don Tyson would, Faubus cast himself as the defender of Arkansas's white working class, protecting it from a labor movement dominated by outsiders and intent on undermining traditional values. The transformation of northwest Arkansas has many causes, but the Faubus-led white backlash against integration at Little Rock's Central High helped remake the region into an anti-union stronghold.

A line running from its northeastern corner to its southwestern one divides Arkansas. To the north and west are the rugged Ouachita and Ozark Mountains with the Arkansas River valley running between them. To the south and the east are the Arkansas delta and southern gulf plains. This geography gave way to different types of economic development and settlement patterns. In the east and the south, plantation agriculture, especially cotton production, took hold, and the region resembled other Deep South areas in terms of slavery, paternalistic politics, and economic stratification. The Arkansas highlands, on the other hand, were settled mostly by small-scale and subsistence farmers with neither the capital nor the need for slaves. In fact, by 1860 many in the region had come to see slavery as a threat to their republican ideals. An antebellum miner in Sebastian County later recalled that his neighbors were "too poor to own slaves and hated the system as heartily as either Horace Greeley or Wendell Phillips." This hatred did not suggest sympathy for those enslaved but rather resentment at the political and economic power that slavery afforded the planter class. Not surprisingly, the Arkansas highlands became a Unionist stronghold during the Civil War, sending thousands of men into the Union ranks.[5]

In the late 1880s, a deepening agricultural crisis, mostly blamed on railroads and banks, and resentment at the merchants and planters who dominated the Democratic Party pushed many of Arkansas's poor farmers and workers into a biracial political alliance. The Union Labor Party—mostly white farmers and Knights of Labor—and the Republican Party—largely African American—fused in 1888 and 1890, challenging the Democrats who had redeemed the state in 1874. To combat this biracial challenge, the Democrats first resorted to fraud, violence, and assassination. But in the early 1890s, when those methods invited unwanted congressional attention, Democrats invoked Jim Crow to keep the working classes divided by race and enacted a poll tax and other ballot reforms to limit nonelite voting.[6]

The rise of Jim Crow transformed northwestern Arkansas. The region became home to an especially virulent form of Negrophobia. After 1900, towns witnessed pogroms intent on driving the small African American population from the region. Most communities became "sundown towns," that is places where African Americans were not tolerated after nightfall. Only three Ozark towns—Fayetteville, Bentonville, and Eureka Springs—

and a few more along the Arkansas River would allow African Americans to reside within their limits.[7]

Some of the increased racial hostility can be traced to the poll tax. By the early twentieth century, eastern Arkansas planters had begun manipulating poll tax receipts in ways that allowed them to vote on behalf of their mostly black tenants and sharecroppers. This prompted many of those from the northwestern part of the state to see African American voting as corrupting the political process and threatening the prospects of white hill farmers and workers. Ironically, when politicians from the highlands pushed to disfranchise African Americans more completely, the state's urban blacks found allies among the planter class who feared the end of poll tax manipulation. These strange bedfellows prevented the complete disfranchisement of African Americans, much to the anger of many whites in northwestern Arkansas.[8]

With few exceptions, the region's anticorporate/pro-union radicals embraced this racism. Trade unions, including the UMWA, insisted on keeping "white" jobs beyond the reach of black competitors. No one articulated the region's blend of economic radicalism and virulent racism as forcefully or as crudely as the Karl Marx of the hillbillies. "The Negroes ought to be disfranchised," Jeff Davis told one crowd, "because you can't educate a nigger. I would be glad to see the United States deport them. They look like apes." Even the radicals at Commonwealth College refused to accept African American students, insisting somewhat disingenuously that they did not want to offend local customs.[9]

Orval Eugene Faubus was the product this environment, born into a Socialist and fiercely pro-union family in Madison County in 1910. The county's handful of African Americans made up just 0.28 percent of the population that year, and Faubus grew up without any meaningful contact with blacks. The origin of Faubus's first name is unknown, but his father, Sam, selected the middle name to honor Eugene Debs. Of the ten charter members of the Mill Creek Local of the Socialist Party, four were named Faubus, and the beginning of World War I pushed the family to greater activism, prompting the arrest of Sam Faubus for "distributing seditious literature and uttering numerous disloyal remarks concerning the conduct of the war." After the war, the charges disappeared, but Sam, who supplemented his farm income by working as a migratory lumberman and joined the Industrial Workers of the World, continued to espouse Socialism. By the 1930s, Orval appeared to be following in Sam's footsteps, defending Socialism in public debates and attending Commonwealth College.[10]

The Great Depression and the New Deal spurred efforts to build another biracial political coalition of Arkansas's working people. At the center of this effort was the Southern Tenant Farmers' Union (STFU), established in eastern Arkansas in 1934 by black and white sharecroppers and tenant farmers angered at New Deal farm policy. Ties developed between the STFU and western Arkansas radicals, especially those at Commonwealth College or associated with the UMWA.[11] Although the STFU foundered, World War II–fueled industrialization and the arrival of the Congress of Industrial Organizations (CIO) only increased the prospects of both African American unionization and some sort of biracial labor alliance to challenge the prerogatives of Arkansas's elite. The CIO so frightened the planters, utility magnates, and bankers who controlled much of Arkansas politics that they pushed through the legislature a draconian "anti-labor violence" measure in 1943 and convinced voters to approve the nation's first "right-to-work" law a year later, despite the opposition of most of those in the northwestern part of the state.[12]

The passage of such laws made it more difficult for unions to organize, but it also convinced Arkansas's labor leaders of the need for a political alliance of trade unionists, other working-class whites, small farmers, and African Americans. Only through the mobilization of these forces did the labor movement have any chance of repealing the right-to-work law and the anti-labor violence statute, curtailing the power of planters and businessmen, and expanding the New Deal.[13] Arkansas labor leaders were not necessarily racial egalitarians or advocates for African American rights (though some were), but they realized that the working classes of both races shared common economic concerns.

After World War II, the Arkansas labor movement found an ally in Sidney S. McMath, the ambitious prosecuting attorney and decorated veteran who had defeated the political machine that protected illegal gambling in Hot Springs, a Ouachita Mountain spa town. From 1947 through the mid-1960s, McMath and the state's labor movement led efforts to build a biracial working-class political coalition.[14] Bringing together lower and working-class whites, especially those in northwestern Arkansas with a long history of Negrophobia, and African Americans, long suspicious of most white-led endeavors, required a deft touch, and for a while it looked as though McMath and the labor movement might succeed.

McMath won the first of his two terms as governor in 1948, successfully navigating the controversies surrounding Truman's civil rights proposals and the Dixiecrat revolt. McMath never openly embraced Truman's program for fear of alienating working-class whites, but he appealed to black voters by calling for increased political and economic opportunities for all Arkansans, castigating politicians who stirred up racial animosity, and battling those who wanted the state's Democratic Party to endorse the Dixiecrats. As Arkansas's NAACP president Daisy Bates later wrote, McMath won by doing well in those areas where "labor and Negro votes were strong."[15]

During his 1948 run for governor, McMath met Orval Faubus, who entered politics after returning from the service. The ambitious, charming, and gregarious Faubus campaigned hard for McMath, speaking throughout the Ozarks. Faubus then joined McMath's administration, first as highway commissioner and later as the governor's administrative secretary. Faubus emerged as the most liberal voice in an administration that increased aid for African American schools, brought blacks into the Democratic Party, continued to integrate the state's universities, pardoned those prosecuted under the state's draconian anti–labor violence statute, extended the reach of rural electrical cooperatives, and fought the state's powerful Dixiecrat element. Although Arkansas did not repeal its right-to-work law or anti–labor violence statute, McMath's two terms as governor convinced the state's union leaders that biracial working-class politics offered the only hope of increasing aid to education, expanding the welfare state, and ending the paternalistic politics that still characterized much of Arkansas.

After being turned out of office in 1952, McMath decided to challenge Senator John L. McClellan, who was up for reelection in 1954 and had a long anti-labor record. According to the Arkansas CIO, McClellan had voted "against the right to strike, for the use of injunctions in labor disputes, to prohibit company-wide collective bargaining, for Taft-Hartley, to weaken wage and hour [laws], reduce the minimum wage, [and] against union shops."[16] To provide McMath and his chief political strategist, Henry Woods, with income to support their families, the Arkansas State Federation of Labor employed the pair as legal counsel, and the state's CIO federation and dozens of local and international unions put McMath and Woods on retainer. These unions expected to receive legal services but were more interested in sustaining McMath's political career and defeating McClellan.

The ambitious Faubus, though, went back to the Ozarks to plan his political future, one that would put him into the governor's office in 1954.[17]

Faubus owed his election that year to organized labor's efforts to defeat McClellan. The first phase of the labor campaign began in March 1953 when McMath met with CIO political director Jack Kroll, CIO president Walter Reuther, AFL president George Meany, and the leaders of the railroad brotherhoods. McMath told the labor leaders that the key to defeating McClellan was to get as many African Americans, trade unionists, and members of the Farmers' Union and rural electrical cooperatives as possible to pay their poll taxes before the October 1, 1953, deadline to vote in 1954. The labor chieftains agreed, bankrolling a massive program to help these constituencies to pay their poll taxes.[18]

On May 18 and 19, 1953, McMath, Woods, Arkansas Industrial Union Council (CIO) officials, Arkansas State Federation of Labor (AFL) leaders, and African American activists met to plan the poll tax campaign. Both federations launched high-profile efforts to convince working-class whites to become eligible to vote. To help with the campaign among blacks, the CIO's Political Action Committee dispatched Philip Weightman, its chief African American organizer, to Arkansas. Working behind the scenes, Weightman brought rival and often-antagonistic African American leaders together in the Citizens' Committee. Weightman oversaw much of the committee's activity, devising its structure, showing activists the canvassing methods the CIO had developed in the urban North, providing fliers and other registration materials, and bringing in Chicago congressman William Dawson for what some considered to be Arkansas's largest African American political rally since the 1890s. The Citizens' Committee fell short of its goal of making one hundred thousand blacks eligible to vote, but Weightman and state labor leaders thought that the number of poor and working-class voters had increased enough to give McMath and other liberal candidates fighting chances.[19]

One of those liberals was Faubus, who decided to challenge Governor Francis Cherry, the man who had defeated McMath two years earlier. Although discouraged from running by Woods and McMath, who feared his presence would mobilize additional Cherry supporters who would also vote for McClellan, Faubus was close enough to the McMath organization to know that labor and black groups had already made record numbers eligible to vote. But Faubus was more than just riding McMath's coattails; he was a formidable candidate in his own right. Labor journalist Victor Ray later explained that Faubus delivered a populist message that "assuaged a hunger in Arkansas labor as definite as its hunger for the cornbread and beans that so many of its members had grown up on."[20]

McClellan narrowly defeated McMath in the Democratic primary, a contest that witnessed the widespread manipulation of poll tax receipts in the plantation counties of eastern Arkansas. Henry Woods asserted, "I can show you township after township in this state where a plantation owner goes down and buys [600] or 700 poll taxes and those [600] or 700 are voted on election day and there is not a dozen people that show up at the polls." He concluded, "You know that they used that very system to steal the senate election from us."[21]

Faubus, though, forced Cherry into a runoff, and McMath, Woods, the Arkansas labor movement, and their African American allies swung behind his candidacy. During the runoff, Cherry charged that Faubus was unfit to be governor, citing his time at Commonwealth College and his radical past. Faubus, caught off guard, turned to Woods, who, working with other McMath supporters, devised a response: Faubus attacked Cherry for McCarthy-style red-baiting and disingenuously claimed that he had briefly attended Commonwealth because he was too poor to go elsewhere. The response righted Faubus's campaign, allowing him to eke out a narrow victory. Daisy Bates later attributed Faubus's election to "labor, Negroes, and liberals in the cities" who "assumed he had liberal inclinations because of his association with the McMath machine."[22]

Faubus's gubernatorial victory, the election of a Teamster lawyer in the attorney general race, labor's alliance with African Americans, and several successful organizing campaigns convinced one CIO official that organized labor had a brighter future in Arkansas than any other southern state. He told the political staff of the recently merged AFL-CIO, "[T]he program there will make some important history there in the next few years. . . . Keep an eye on Arkansas."[23] Also eyeing Arkansas was conservative columnist Westbrook Pegler, who warned of labor's growing influence in Arkansas. He claimed that Faubus and McMath were more dangerous than Harry Bridges or Alger Hiss.[24]

McMath's defeat, though, angered Arkansas labor leaders. The state's two federations concluded that the poll tax was hindering efforts to remake Arkansas along liberal lines. Not only did the poll tax discourage the voting of working-class blacks and whites, it had facilitated the fraudulent voting that had caused McMath's defeat. In the summer of 1954, the two federations formed Labor's Joint Educational Committee (LJEC) to convince the legislature to place a constitutional amendment repealing the poll tax on the ballot. If the legislature failed to act when it met in early 1955, the LJEC would then use the initiative process to put the amendment before voters. For the rest of 1954, Governor-elect Faubus met regularly with LJEC, helping coordinate the effort.[25]

On January 15, 1955, four days after his inauguration, Faubus appeared before the Arkansas Industrial Union Council's annual convention. He publicly credited the state's labor movement for his defeat of Francis Cherry the previous year. "You made the difference in my victory," he told the integrated audience in Little Rock. The governor promised to repay the labor movement by working for the elimination of the poll tax and the creation of a simple registration system. Faubus admitted that the one-dollar poll tax was not a financial burden but told the audience that he opposed the tax on principle. No one, he insisted, should have to pay for the right to vote.[26]

Making no headway with the 1955 general assembly, LJEC began preparing to repeal the poll tax through an initiated act on the November 1956 ballot. This process began in March 1955 when Faubus, McMath, Woods, and LJEC chairman Odell Smith met with CIO PAC director Jack Kroll to ask that Phil Weightman be sent to the state for another poll tax campaign among African Americans. Increasing the number of blacks eligible to vote in 1956 would not only help repeal the poll tax but would also increase Faubus's reelection chances.[27] Weightman returned to Arkansas that summer, helping black civic groups with their poll tax drives, while the state's two labor federations launched campaigns to convince members to become eligible to vote.[28]

Having worked together during the McMath campaign and to repeal the poll tax, Arkansas's two labor federations merged in March 1956, becoming the first state federation to do so. Faubus attended the merger convention to again pledge his support for the abolition of the poll tax. The governor declared that he had opposed the tax for over twenty-five years and recalled "people back home [who] were so poor that they did not have the money at the right time to pay their poll tax and were left disfranchised."[29]

Just as labor's effort to repeal Arkansas's poll tax was picking up steam, massive resistance hit the state. In the sixteen months after the *Brown* decision, several school districts in northwestern Arkansas, where the small number of black students made the maintenance of segregation very expensive, had integrated with little public disturbance or protest. An NAACP official even called Arkansas "the bright spot of the South" in 1955, and the *Chicago Defender* asked, "Has Arkansas Gone Liberal?"[30] But this quiet ended in the late summer of 1955 as segregationist forces mobilized to stop the integration of schools in Hoxie, a railroad town on the edge of the Arkansas delta about seventy miles northwest of Memphis. Led by Little Rock attorney Amis Guthridge and Jim Johnson, an ambitious former state senator from south Arkansas, segregationists quickly tapped into widespread opposition to school integration. Much of the segregationist agitation came from the lower and working-class whites that the labor movement had worked hard to bring into a political coalition with blacks. Johnson hoped to use the groundswell of support for segregation to defeat Faubus in the following year's gubernatorial election. To help his campaign, Johnson's supporters placed a measure on the November 1956 ballot that would allow the state to nullify any federal law or court ruling that it found to be unconstitutional.[31]

Arkansas labor leaders misunderstood the nature of the segregationist movement, insisting that it had little grassroots support and was simply a "Trojan horse" designed to destroy the labor movement by disrupting the emerging political alliance between poor and working class blacks and whites, much the same way that Jim Crow and disfranchisement destroyed the efforts to unite blacks and whites during the Populist era. The leaders of the Arkansas AFL-CIO insisted that the true intent of Johnson's nullification amendment was to allow the state to block application of the National Labor Relations Act and Fair Labor Standards Act. The labor movement's strategy was to attack segregationist leaders as bent on destroying the labor movement.[32]

The rise of massive resistance served as the opening wedge between Faubus and the labor movement. Faubus had been pretty liberal on civil rights during his first term, bringing African Americans onto the state Democratic Central Committee, integrating the state's undergraduate institutions, and encouraging the removal of segregation in public transit. He had also refused to come to the aid of those resisting local desegregation efforts, insisting that school matters were purely local concerns. But the politically ambitious Faubus understood something that the leaders of the Arkansas labor movement did not—massive resistance was not imposed on the white working class by business forces or conservative politicians; it was a grassroots movement with widespread appeal.[33]

Faubus responded to Jim Johnson's challenge in 1956 and the groundswell of opposition to integration by portraying himself as a less rabid segregationist. To help his campaign, Faubus placed two more mild segregationist measures for the fall ballot: a pupil assignment plan and a resolution on interposition. When Faubus made statements in favor of school segregation, labor leaders were not happy but saw it as an election gambit and assumed that once the nomination was secured he would revert to form. Of course, the Arkansas AFL-CIO backed Faubus with all of its resources, as did many of the state's black leaders.[34]

Although Faubus beat Johnson in the July primary, the three segregationist measures remained on the November ballot alongside labor's initiative to repeal the poll tax. The Arkansas AFL-CIO's Executive Committee called for voters to defeat the three segregationist measures. The labor leaders were especially troubled by the interposition and nullification proposals, warning if the measures passed "labor could lose all of the great gains it has made under . . . federal legislation," and they looked to Faubus for help with the poll tax repeal.[35]

Arkansas AFL-CIO president Odell Smith had received assurances that Faubus, having safely made it through the party's primary, would come out forcefully for the repeal of the poll tax. The governor's chief of staff had promised that Faubus's Labor Day address would contain such an endorsement. But Faubus's speech made no mention of the poll tax. Ten days later, the Faubus-controlled state Democratic convention refused to endorse the repeal of the poll tax, effectively ending any hope of the measure's passage. Faubus never explained his decision, but Arkansas AFL-CIO leaders assumed that the governor did not want to be publicly associated with any measure that might be seen as beneficial to blacks. Arkansas labor felt betrayed—Faubus had sided with the segregationists, supporting the resolution on interposition but not lifting a finger to repeal the poll tax. The prospects of maintaining the biracial coalition that labor had worked so hard to forge were starting to dim. Faubus and Arkansas labor leaders began to part ways, the governor throwing in with the segregationist movement and the labor movement continuing efforts to build a biracial political coalition to make the state more conducive to trade unionism and liberalism.[36]

The rift between Faubus and the labor movement became a chasm in September 1957. During the summer of 1957, Faubus confided to Arkansas labor leaders that he was going to prevent the integration of Little Rock's Central High. Arkansas AFL-CIO executive secretary Wayne Glenn spent five hours at the governor's mansion trying to convince Faubus to allow the Little Rock school board to proceed with its limited integration plan, but he got nowhere with the governor.[37] On the eve of the 1957 school year, Arkansas AFL-CIO president Odell Smith issued a statement supporting the peaceful integration of Central High, and Orval Faubus called out the Arkansas National Guard to block the arrival of the Little Rock Nine.[38] Faubus's actions that fall and winter won widespread approval around the state, the governor becoming a hero to many of Arkansas's working-class whites.

The leaders of Arkansas's labor movement made their displeasure with the governor's action known during Faubus's 1958 bid for a third term. The Arkansas AFL-CIO came forward as the only major white-led civic organization in the state to oppose the governor's reelection. When representatives of some thirty thousand trade unionists met in May 1958 for the biannual meeting of Arkansas AFL-CIO's Committee on Political Education, Odell Smith, Wayne Glenn, and federation leaders convinced delegates—by a vote of ninety-seven to twenty-nine—to censure Faubus for failing to honor his commitments to the labor movement and betraying the interests of the state's workers. Delegates did this even though they knew the enormously popular Faubus would easily win reelection. The resolution of censure focused mostly on economic issues, carefully avoiding mention of the Little Rock crisis or integration.[39]

But the wording of the censure resolution fooled no one. An *Arkansas Gazette* editorial asserted that labor leaders were angry with Faubus "for using the segregation issue as a device for diverting the Southern working man's attention from what they regard as his proper goals and thereby weakening the entire labor movement."[40] Faubus himself insisted that the labor leaders opposed him "because I would not put my National Guard out at Central High School and bludgeon my own people [i.e., white segregationists]."[41] A segregationist probably got it right when she argued that "the labor bosses aren't pleased at all that integration of the races in the South has struck a snag in the governor's stand for States' Rights. . . . This is their dogma: 'Only when racial segregation in the South is ended can labor find the strength to forced closed shops.'"[42]

Facing no serious opposition in his reelection bid, Faubus responded to labor's censure with a vengeance. He centered his reelection campaign around vicious attacks on the labor movement, turning his populist rhetoric against Arkansas AFL-CIO officials in hopes of removing his last rivals for the allegiance of the state's white working class. Knowing that his support among whites in eastern and southern Arkansas, areas with large African American populations, was secure, Faubus spent most of his campaign in northwest Arkansas, where the small black population made the prospects of school integration less threatening.[43] Faubus did not condemn trade unionism per se, but he cast himself as the defender of southern white working-class values against the encroachments of a liberal elite led by Smith, McMath, and Woods.

Faubus formally kicked off his reelection campaign in Springdale, a poultry center in Washington County, on July 1, 1958. There, in the company of chicken magnate John Tyson and his son Don, the governor charged that "outsiders" doing the bidding of national AFL-CIO president George Meany were interfering in the Arkansas gubernatorial campaign, directing local trade unionists to oppose Faubus and threatening to revoke the charters of those local federations that refused.[44]

Faubus followed up these charges two days later, providing more details to an audience in Mountain Home. There he asserted that "self-appointed and outside-anointed king makers," led by Smith, McMath, and Woods and directed by labor officials in "Washington, New York, and Detroit," had forced the measure censuring him through the Arkansas AFL-CIO meeting despite the opposition of most delegates. Faubus concluded that the ultimate purpose of labor's effort was to install Daisy Bates—the state's NAACP director and mentor to the Little Rock nine—as "Colonial Governor of our State." With these charges, Faubus suggested that the labor movement would force upon white Arkansans those things they feared most—a black ruling over whites, a woman with authority over men, interference by elites, the end of self-governance, and, ultimately, white male impotence.[45]

Faubus ended his first campaign swing in Piggot, where he told the eight thousand to ten thousand assembled for a Fourth of July picnic that "high labor moguls" in Washington and Detroit were organizing "teams of two, three, and four" to go into every county in the state to defeat his reelection bid. Faubus suggested that these labor moguls were coordinating their effort with the NAACP. Faubus concluded by warning that, if the flying squadrons sent by labor and the NAACP were successful in defeating him and forcing school integration upon the people of Arkansas, "the trouble at Little Rock [Central High] will look like a Sunday School picnic."[46]

Faubus's anti-labor populism represented a new type of political discourse for Arkansas. The state had its fair share of anti-labor politicians, men like John McClellan and former governor Ben Laney. But these men paid lip service to the importance of trade unions and the labor movement, speaking of the need to balance the interests of business with the legitimate concerns of labor, while simultaneously working hard to undermine the labor movement. Faubus, though, did something that the lavender Cadillac–driving, white linen suit–wearing McClellan could never have gotten away with—he directly attacked Arkansas's labor movement.[47] Faubus appealed directly to the white working class, praising them and extolling their virtues, reminding them that he was one of them, that he was their defender, their champion. Faubus acted like them, talked like them, and warned them that the state's labor leaders were threatening to undermine their culture and values. Faubus's discourse also played on the hill people of northwest Arkansas's long-established fear of outsiders, redirecting it from corporations to trade unions.

The sparring between the Arkansas AFL-CIO and Faubus continued until the end of the campaign. Faubus continued to insist that Meany had sent teams of labor organizers into the state to work against his reelection and to install Daisy Bates as "Colonial Governor." Not only did the labor movement refute Faubus's charges, it also accused the governor of using the state labor department to pressure trade unionists and those receiving unemployment compensation to vote for Faubus. The trade unionists also criticized Faubus for refusing to support increasing the minimum wage and breaking a series of promises he had made to the Arkansas AFL-CIO.[48] In the end, though, labor's efforts were for naught as Faubus won by a landslide, becoming the first Arkansas governor since Jeff Davis to win a third term.

After the election, the leaders of the Arkansas AFL-CIO and Faubus continued to vie for the allegiance of the state's working-class whites, with Faubus running a slate of candidates at the federation's 1958 convention. The AFL-CIO's expulsion of the Teamsters forced Smith, head of Teamsters Local 878, to step down as president of the Arkansas federation. The contest for his replacement pitted Faubus's candidate, Harold Veazey, head of the state's building trades federation, against Wayne Glenn, a Faubus critic nominated by Smith. The contest became a referendum on segregation and the federation's censure of Faubus. Tradition dictated that the sitting governor be invited to address the convention, and Faubus took the opportunity to liken integrationists—a veiled reference to Smith and Glenn—to Nazis and the Communists. Faubus aide Claude Carpenter worked behind the scenes, supplying delegates with booze and promises of jobs and other benefits. But the delegates elected by their local unions chose Glenn by a three-to-two margin, a vote that the *Arkansas Gazette* characterized as a "snub of Governor Faubus."[49]

The battle between Faubus and the state's labor movement for the allegiance of Arkansas's white working class continued through the mid-1960s, centering almost exclusively on matters of race and civil rights. The Arkansas AFL-CIO remained committed to building a biracial alliance of the state's poor and working classes, while Faubus continued exploiting racial fears for political gain. When Faubus ran for a fourth term in 1960, the Arkansas AFL-CIO endorsed his rival, and, when McMath challenged Faubus in 1962, the federation passed another resolution censuring the governor for betraying the interests of labor. Something of a truce finally emerged in 1964 when Faubus supported an Arkansas AFL-CIO-authored measure repealing the state's poll tax and creating a simple voter registration system.[50]

Faubus's attacks on Arkansas's labor movement and the Arkansas AFL-CIO's unpopular stand against segregation took their toll, alienating a large segment of the state's white working class from the trade union movement. Between 1956 and 1960, the number of trade unionists affiliated with the Arkansas AFL-CIO dropped by more than 25 percent, from over thirty thousand to twenty-two thousand. The decline was most pronounced in the building trades. In 1955, twenty-six carpenter locals belonged to the state federation of labor; in 1960 only five belonged to the Arkansas AFL-CIO. In 1955, five plumbing locals belonged; in 1960 there was only one. Subscriptions to the labor movement's newspaper tell a similar story. Between 1956 and 1959, forty-five hundred of the paper's ten thousand subscribers cancelled their subscriptions, most of them in response to editorials calling for Faubus to reopen Little Rock's public high schools.[51]

Arkansas's labor movement never recovered, especially in the hills of western Arkansas, where Faubus's popularity continues unabated. The region's white working class had long supported trade unionism as well as racial segregation, and the Little Rock crisis forced them to choose between the two. Significant numbers remained loyal to the labor movement, but large numbers chose to follow Faubus. Many came to agree with Faubus that the labor movement was too closely associated with the civil rights movement, outside agitators, and an eastern elite, and they began looking not to the labor movement but to people like Faubus for guidance and political leadership. In the 1960s, business leaders responded to union organizing drives and political campaigns by, among other things, distributing photographs of Arkansas AFL-CIO president J. Bill Becker alongside the state's white Student Nonviolent Coordinating Committee director and his African American wife.[52]

Faubus and the civil rights movement separated much of the white working class of western Arkansas from labor unions, but he did not make them like or accept large corporations. That would be done by the likes of Sam Walton and John and Don Tyson. In the 1960s and 1970s, these men forged patriarchal corporate cultures that appealed directly to the members of the white working class, praising them, extolling their virtues, and warning them of the encroachments of outside forces, especially trade unions.[53] These men would not have had as much success if Faubus and his anti-labor populism hadn't helped erode the region's pro-labor culture.

Chapter 6

"Is Freedom of the Individual Un-American?" Right-to-Work Campaigns and Anti-Union Conservatism, 1943–1958

Elizabeth Tandy Shermer

Historians of the U.S. Right have largely ignored right-to-work campaigns. The "right-to-work" issue is a technical legal question involving organized labor's institutional security. State right-to-work statutes prohibit unions from making membership a requirement for work in an organized shop, although this legal language was often simplified as a ban on union or closed shops in elections. Some scholars assert that, prior to 1955, when the American Federation of Labor (AFL) and Congress of Industrial Organizations (CIO) merged and the National Right to Work Committee formed, "there was little national debate over the issue." Yet labor specialists have long debated whether these restrictions have had a debilitating impact on postwar trade unions' economic power. Most agree the controversy served as an ideological marker for labor's legitimacy. Researchers have also considered how the mid-1950s referenda illuminated business's growing power and potency, especially the 1958 off-year initiatives in six states.[1]

Postwar right-to-work campaigns show a deep connection between anti-unionism and modern conservatism. These referenda highlight pockets of uncertainty and resistance that illustrate how anti-union, pro-business discourse helped to delegitimize postwar liberalism and aided in the conservative Sunbelt's formation. The earliest right-to-work referenda were in the South and Southwest. The anti-union movement had different characteristics in each region, which illuminates the coast-to-coast phenomenon's hetereogeneity. Racism defined both regions' histories but the biracial framework used to assess southern constructions of whiteness prior to the 1970s cannot apply to the multiracial West. Historian Bruce Schulman and economist Gavin Wright argued that the postwar South's pro-growth, racially moderate anti-unionism was, in Wright's words, "quite a different phenomenon from the prewar recipe of tradition, racism, and brute-force isolationism." The southern right-to-work referenda in the immediate postwar years were a part of this older tradition. The fights over the union shop were not solely for industrial location and economic dynamism but for preservation of the political power of the agricultural elite and the Jim Crow order. The most recent scholarship shows that only in the early 1960s did urban business elites, open-school advocates, and middle-class suburbanites manage to marginalize the old rural elite and make industrial recruitment and modernization through racial moderation a cornerstone of southern economic planning.[2]

Early right-to-work campaigns in the western half of the Sunbelt were markedly different. Arizona, Colorado, Nevada, New Mexico, Utah, and California proponents came out of the area's traditional economic pillars, mining and agriculture, and also the most dynamic and entrepreneurial sectors of the economy, including tourism, retail, and gambling. Conservative politicians and business leaders spearheaded these compulsory open-shop campaigns in the Southwest. They rebelled against the New Deal regulatory state and envisioned a prosperity based on entrepreneurial freedom and laissez-faire growth that would modernize the region, making it a magnet for high-value manufacturing and efficient distribution. Right-to-work supporters struck at one of the New Deal's key supports, a politically legitimate and economically stable trade unionism, in order to remake the arid West into an oasis for business. Advocates painted these laws as crucial to upholding freedom, democracy, and economic growth. Not every proposition or bill passed, yet this argument won over many voters, including those from the middle and working classes worried over labor's rapid growth and newfound power. The regional support for curbing organized labor's power therefore suggests that a pro-development anti-unionism was a pillar of western-Sunbelt conservatism.

Labor's Hour in the Southwest

This reaction against liberalism had its roots in the region's spectacular midcentury growth. The Great Depression, World War II, and the Cold War had helped transform the West from a supplier of raw materials that eastern businesses needed into a manufacturing power and also a center-piece of the Cold War military-industrial complex. Westerners had always depended on federal dollars but New Dealers sought to decentralize indus-try, which caused the arid and sparsely populated Southwest to become a prime location for government projects. Economic and geopolitical upheavals ensured a steady stream of support that not only provided jobs but also government contracts that would transform some regional busi-nesses, such as W. A. Bechtel Company, Bank of America, and Kaiser Industries, into powerful national corporations.[3]

The proto-Sunbelt labor movement flourished in the 1940s. During World War II, the National War Labor Board (NWLB) strengthened labor's place in an emerging system of tripartite corporatism, balancing the power of business with the strength of a secure labor movement and an involved liberal government. Increased power gave unions that pledged not to strike "maintenance of membership" contract clauses. These provisions gave newly organized employees, or those organized under an older contract, fifteen days to withdraw from the union, although few took advantage of this escape clause. Unionists had to remain members in good standing after this inaugural period. Failure to pay dues or abide by union rules meant expulsion from the union and termination of employment. The no-strikes bargain pleased labor leaders, who had agitated for such security for years, and rank and filers held the protection these clauses provided to be virtually sacrosanct. Such agreements signaled a union's permanency and strength. Complete organization, or close to it, not only forced management to the bargaining table but also gave the local more power. "As factories and mills expanded," historian Nelson Lichtenstein asserted, "new workers were automatically enrolled, increasing the steady flow of dues. With a rising wartime income large industrial unions had the financial resources to orga-nize the new defense plants being built in Texas, Southern California, and other areas far removed from the traditional centers of union strength."[4]

The Depression and World War II changed the proto-Sunbelt's econ-omy. The copper industry collapsed in the 1930s, which created a ripple effect. In Arizona, business dried up for the railroads that employed almost eight thousand workers and connected small towns to markets in and outside the state. Increased mechanization enabled corporations to extract minerals with fewer workers. In Nevada, the percentage of those working in the mining trades dropped from 15 to less than 3 percent of all employed workers between 1940 and 1958. Postwar surges in the tourism, retail, service, and manufacturing sectors, plus an increase in federal jobs, marginalized mining and agriculture, the old mainstays of the region's economy.[5]

Labor adapted to these economic shifts. Union membership grew tremendously in the region. In 1939, union density (the percentage of union members among workers) had ranged from 11.7 percent in New Mexico to 24.8 percent in California. By 1953, New Mexico still lagged behind with just 14.4 percent of the work force organized, but union density in other proto-Sunbelt states ranged between 26.8 and 37 percent. In the 1940s, organized labor won conditions almost tantamount to a closed shop in Nevada. New Mexico labor expanded its base beyond construction sites and mine shafts, moving into sawmills, logging camps, and newspaper offices. Arizona activists targeted construction workers, city employees, and miners. The American Federation of State, County, and Municipal Employees and the United Public Workers had tremendous success organizing Phoenix city employees, including police officers and firefighters. Both of these locals won large wage increases after World War II. The building trades were also well organized. Phoenix locals negotiated closed shop clauses in their contracts, which ensured that only unionized workers would handle all immediate postwar construction.[6]

Growth brought spectacular displays of labor's new strength. The International Brotherhood of Teamsters made impressive gains in the entire region. Denver laborites staged massive boycotts and gained a western foothold, which enabled Teamsters to win contracts across the West. Unions succeeded in manufacturing firms as well. In 1936, General Motors opened a plant in South Gate, California, a white working-class suburb of Los Angeles, because of the West Coast market for automobiles and the open-shop conditions in the city. In less than a year, militant organizers overcame antipathy among workers and the community as well as managerial hostility to unionization. This victory was among the first that transformed Los Angeles from a company town, renowned for its hostility to labor, into a city where organized labor had at least a foothold in almost all of the metropolis's major industries. There were also union beachheads in the southwestern service sector. After owners of Hastings and Kahn's department stores brokered a deal with city leaders to have the police remove striking retail clerks and protect delivery trucks while drivers crossed the picket lines, more than one hundred thousand AFL unionists went on strike in solidarity with store employees. The 1946 "work holiday," later called the Oakland General Strike, shut down the city, only ending when city officials agreed not to use the police to protect replacement workers. Labor also moved into the tourism sector. Unionized culinary workers and bartenders went on strike during 1949 contract negotiations for better wages and benefits, timing the work stoppage with the all-important Fourth of July celebrations. Labor also increased its numbers in mining, a traditional stronghold in the region. Local 890 of the International Union of Mine, Mill, and Smelter Workers (or Mine-Mill) called a famous strike against the Empire Zinc Corporation. In the early 1950s, Anglo and Mexican American miners and their families held out for over a year in Hanover, New Mexico, a demonstration depicted in the famous left-wing film *Salt of the Earth* (1954).[7]

"Labor Has Gone Altogether Too Far"

The threat of a labor-liberal ascendancy spurred conservatives to action. Many southwestern business leaders benefited from federal money but did not support the New Deal's economic prescriptions. The specter of "Big Labor" and "Big Government" united corporate titans and southwestern business owners. Business leaders masterminded right-to-work campaigns that weakened the protections provided by the Wagner Act and the "maintenance of membership" bargain. This fight against the New Deal took place in state legislatures and municipal governments. Phoenix voters elected a group of pro-business candidates, who called themselves the Charter Government Committee, to the city council in 1949. This group campaigned to remove partisanship from local governance but really endeavored to refashion Phoenix into a modern, corporate metropolis. Retailer and future Arizona senator Barry Goldwater used his city- and statewide fame to spread a conservative, anti–New Deal message. His Depression-era editorials for the *Phoenix Gazette* accused President Franklin Roosevelt of "turn[ing] over to the racketeering practices of ill-organized unions the future of the working man. Witness the chaos they are creating in the eastern cities. Witness the men thrown out of work, the riots, the bloodshed, and the ill feeling between labor and capitol [*sic*] and then decide for yourself if that plan worked." Such statements were a rallying cry for local businessmen, one of whom declared, "Compared with the average citizen . . . you are a goliath and I say to you openly and fearlessly . . . I hold the masses in contempt and their leaders and masters." Goldwater and his compatriots soon harnessed this outrage to create a political machine that dominated Phoenix politics for a generation.[8]

Constraining labor was a central part of reorganizing the West on the Right's terms. Opposition to union security clauses, requiring workers to remain members in good standing with the local representing them, was constant throughout the first half of the twentieth century. Right-to-work supporters capitalized on the threat to individual liberty that they thought unionism represented, turning the issue into a moral and economic dilemma. One of the earliest drives began in 1901, a campaign that the National Association of Manufacturers and the National Metal Trades Association claimed to be essential for American industry. A year later muckraker Ray Stannard Baker published an article entitled "The Right to Work," one of the earliest known appearances of the phrase. The journalist preyed on *McClure's* middle-class readership's fears that labor was too powerful by describing the attacks on coal miners who crossed picket lines in the 1902 anthracite coal strike. World War I transformed the open-shop issue into a symbol of patriotism and freedom. Employer hostility to union- and closed-shop clauses continued throughout the 1920s under the "American Plan," which led to a drastic drop in union membership.[9]

Labor's growth and increasing legitimacy during the 1930s and 1940s pushed many conservatives to target labor's right to organize. The crusade intensified in all sectors of the economy after the NWLB enraged business moguls by forcing acquiescence to maintenance of membership clauses in industries at the heart of the wartime economy. Even before the well-funded, energetic National Right to Work Committee formed in 1955, major business and political groups, including the American Farm Bureau Federation, National Association of Manufacturers, U.S. Chamber of Commerce, National Labor-Management Foundation, DeMille Political Freedom Foundation, and Christian American Association, poured resources into ending what they called "compulsory unionism." These national groups provided funds for chapters across the country or worked in concert with local groups to fight the trade union movement. The Houston-based

Christian American Association offered a broad attack against unionism in the southern states. Leaders supported open-shop legislation but also backed any laws and funded any drives against the CIO that would "keep the color line drawn in our social affairs."[10]

Such hostility was embedded within the numerous bills that representatives drafted during this period. Even before the Taft-Hartley Act (1947) legalized a state's right to pass right-to-work laws, legislatures had been actively creating and implementing policies that curbed union security, even though the Wagner Act did not devolve these powers onto the states. Wisconsin's Employment Peace Act (1939), for example, placed limits on union tactics and also strengthened protections for employers, not unions, during organizing drives. This law served as a model for other state assemblies as well as the drafters of the Taft-Hartley Act. In 1943 six states passed similar acts: Arkansas, Colorado, South Dakota, Idaho, Texas, and Kansas. The Colorado "Labor Peace Act," like the Wisconsin law, restricted the union shop. A three-fourths majority "of all eligible employees" had to agree on any union-shop membership clause under a separate election, which the Colorado Industrial Commission then oversaw. The act also forbade wildcat and sympathy strikes, mass picketing, automatic deduction of union dues from the membership's paychecks, and political donations.[11]

So-called right-to-work referenda first appeared in 1944 California, Arkansas, and Florida elections. Passage of these propositions mandated, in effect, that all unions in the state would operate under an open-shop policy, whereby owners of unionized businesses could hire anyone, without a commitment that employees would eventually join a union or be required to already belong to a union. These ballot measures, like the Wisconsin law, relied on appeals to liberty and freedom, typically arguing that a "person has the right to work, and to seek, obtain, and hold employment without interference with or impairment or abridgement of said right because he does or does not belong to or pay money to a labor organization."[12]

State governments across the country used this same language when drafting later bills but southern right-to-work referenda had a region-specific purpose not reflected in the text: to uphold Jim Crow, thereby preserving the agricultural elite's political and economic power. The southern aristocracy's antipathy was rooted in new postwar challenges: a growing industrial class formed out of wartime mobilization, a burgeoning trade union movement, and a new push for racial equality both from African Americans and militant CIO organizers, who believed that the only way to organize was fundamentally to attack the system of white supremacy that structured the South's politics, economy, and society. One reporter noted that, in Mississippi, planters seemed to hate unionists as much as integrationists: "whenever the talk turned to labor unions, the conversation was violent and burdened with hate and fear." These farming elites found common cause with southern industrialists who benefited from the Jim Crow order the planters had created because sharecropping and tenant farming ensured a reservoir of desperate workers who were willing to accept low wages and poor working conditions in southern mills and factories. Southern industrialists also maintained that keeping unions out of the South would provide a competitive advantage in industrializing the region and attracting branch plants.[13]

Still the central message in the southern right-to-work campaigns was preserving the Old South's racial order. Open-shop proponents claimed that "outside influence is just a bunch of pot-bellied Yankees with big cigars in their mouths and the dues they collect will just go up North. . . . If they come in you will share the same restroom with Negroes and work side by side with them. It comes right out of Russia and is pure communism and nothing else." Mississippi planters worried that strengthening the Farm Bureau's membership would "counter the adverse activities to our interests of the communist-inspired labor unions and communist organizations." In the 1944 Florida election, the *Miami Citizen* noted that the principal backers of the bill "come entirely from the backward, low-wage sections of the state, where the lumber and turpentine interests rule their workers like barons of old, and laborers receive little or nothing in groves and on the farms." Support for the Florida and Arkansas statutes came overwhelmingly from the state's rural areas, while the only counties that opposed the measure were those areas that had developed industry during the war.[14]

The entire Louisiana business community supported outlawing the union shop, but the planters were the backbone of early efforts. Organized labor's activities in the state's agricultural sector spurred the rural elite to act. In the 1950s the AFL's National Agricultural Workers Union began to organize cane field workers, and by 1953 Local 317 represented over one thousand cane field workers, 80 percent of whom were African American. Field hands struck that year, leading to a district court injunction that crippled the bargaining unit; organizers could not hold union meetings, distribute strike funds, or meet with legal counsel. In the wake of this conflict, the legislature passed a right-to-work law in 1954. Labor struck a Faustian bargain with the sugar planters in 1956, when the trade union movement threatened more strikes if the planters did not back an initiative to replace the statute with a law that prevented only farmworkers and those who worked in agricultural processing plants from having union-shop conditions. African Americans were the majority of this segment of the workforce. Hence labor's proposal divided the Louisiana business community but still satisfied its most powerful members, the agricultural elite. In effect, the new law allowed labor to protect the workers in Louisiana's ports and industrial sectors but also barred the trade union movement from protecting those in the state's rural areas.[15]

The nature of the right-to-work conflict was radically different in the Southwest. Racism marked the multiracial Southwest as much as the South, but preserving Jim Crow and an agricultural elite was not at the core of the arguments for southwestern right-to-work laws. Western wages were higher, and the labor market was integrated into the national economy. As a result, local boosters did not face the same kind of opposition to industry as their southern brethren. In the postwar right-to-work elections in California, Arizona, New Mexico, Nevada, and Utah, the character of the anti-union rhetoric remained remarkably consistent. These top-down, business-led campaigns capitalized on fears of labor's strength in the industrial Northeast and on Capitol Hill and conflated them with local labor-management conflicts. Proponents stressed that the Wagner Act was a dangerous law that fostered class conflict and allowed labor to grind industry to a halt. The villains were the labor "racketeers," whom New Deal policies had empowered and now protected. For many, curbing union security was an endorsement that the labor movement should not have the power to "check" business's growth, lobby for better wages and hours, and interfere with managerial decisions on the shop floor.

Local business groups in the retail, tourism, service, agricultural, and extractive sectors led these battles against the New Deal. In all of these sectors, save agriculture, unions had been successful in organizing either in the West or elsewhere in the United States because of the Wagner Act's protections. For all businesses in the region, support for right to work represented a stopgap against earlier encroachments, a preemptive strike against unionization efforts before they began, or ideological opposition to any owner's loss of control over the shop floor. In Arizona, the Prescott Chamber of Commerce lauded the "increasing opposition to monopolistic practices of labor organizations." Chief among the retailing militants agitating for union insecurity was Goldwater, who was known throughout his home state for his family's store, Goldwater's. The future senator championed the good employee relations he enjoyed. Goldwater's offered workers a medical and pension plan, which gave the Arizonan the image of a compassionate capitalist and made him an important spokesman. He was especially useful in reaching out to other merchants to make sure they supported the 1946 bill. Nevada casino operators, struggling to control organizing drives in the growing tourist and retail industries, forged ties with other open-shop supporters. They banded together in the Nevada Citizens Committee, which had swelled to two thousand members in both the northern and southern chapters by November 1950. Many of these Nevadans also saw the proposition as a supplement to the "free-port" legislation designed to bolster Nevada's economy. Representatives from the old western economies also lobbied for the anti-union bills. Those in farming, who had escaped government-enforced union recognition procedures, stood with mine owners facing union drives on ideological grounds. Both agriculturalists and mine operators argued that outlawing "compulsory unionism" was necessary because unions were becoming too strong.[16]

The concept of opposing "monopoly unionism" attracted and energized business. The surge in union density and activity constrained managerial control of employees and labor costs. An Arizona branch manager for the Phelps Dodge Corporation in Arizona feared labor's strength because, "with industry-wide contracts, all a labor leader has to do is call a strike, make exorbitant demands, and sit tight until the Government takes over. . . . Therefore, by a repetition of these tactics, an industry can be reduced to such helplessness that full ownership and operation must be taken over by the Government. . . . Unless some change in the approach to this problem is made, our Country faces serious threats from many pressure groups, shielded by the terminology of present laws, any one of which can achieve power sufficient to enable them to challenge the Government itself."[17]

Implicit in these fears was an argument that labor could not help craft responsible economic policy. Robert Valdez of the Western Freight Lines in Santa Fe described the Teamsters, with whom he had negotiated, as "unreasonable, unfair[,] and so stupid they lack knowledge of the intricate problems of the trucking industry." Another New Mexican argued, "Any organization that puts their pocketbook before their nation's welfare does not deserve to exist in America." Anna Gemmell of Tuscon, Arizona asserted that "times are too strenuous to let John L. Lewis, Phil Murray, Walter Reuther, or William Green wreck our economy." W. A. Pray, a mineral surveyor in Fernley, Nevada, supported restrictions because "unions have an unbroken record of selfishness and a desire to look out for themselves only. . . . Unlike men who have figured out ways to produce more, faster[,] and better, (for example, Henry Ford, Cyrus McCormick, Harvey Firestone, Thomas Edison, etc. etc.) the labor unions have always to do less to get more."[18]

Such accusations insinuated that an empowered labor movement created industrial conflict and endangered postwar affluence. Utah Republican Party leaders, for example, highlighted "free enterprise principles as the best means of preserving incentives for business and industrial growth." They advocated a labor policy that "does not foster class warfare, does not seek advantage by emotional appeals to group prejudice but instead encourages free industrial growth in our great American economy." A homemaker from Carlsbad, New Mexico, also blamed "members of the labor party" for "stoppages of work that have brought our economy to the grave pass of things today." Union security, in her opinion, prevented, not promoted, industrial peace. Curbing union power was the only solution for many hostile to organized labor. E. V. Silverthorne of Gilbert, Arizona claimed "the wagner [sic] Act was the most onesided and weakest Law [sic] ever ground out by any Congress," and reasoned, "I can see no reason why Labor should not have the same restrictions that are placed on Management." The Colorado and New Mexico Coal Operators Association also considered the restrictions the Taft-Hartley Act imposed "mandatory for the health and welfare of the Western coal industry."[19]

This conflation of national issues with local conflicts was a key component of the postwar right-to-work elections. In Arizona, pressure to limit union power promoted representatives to introduce many bills in both the House and Senate in 1945. Most died in committee, but Arizona open-shop advocates found a cause célèbre to force a statewide referendum. Highly decorated serviceman Herbert M. Williams started a welding business with five nonunion employees, who had also just returned from the war. When Williams's company lost a construction job in Phoenix, he blamed the builders' unions and their closed-shop clauses. He subsequently helped found the Veterans' Right to Work Committee in 1945. Because his employees were servicemen, proponents were able to describe the Arizona referendum as a crusade against unions that refused to welcome veterans. The right-to-work literature played up the war angle with advertising that preyed on voters' fears, charging: "It's almost as if we were living in pre-war Germany. We just can't let that happen here! These despotic little labor racketeers, the would-be Hitlers, must be crushed now—once and for all—before it's too late." The Williams case became a powerful symbol. Any policy that deprived soldiers of work, the veterans group claimed, was ipso facto corrupt and needed to be repealed immediately.[20]

Ties between the trade union movement and organized crime were also a constant theme in these early right-to-work campaigns. This association was rooted in a national conversation on racketeering, malfeasance, and unionism. In the early 1940s, syndicated columnist Westbrook Pegler had won a large audience and received the Pulitzer Prize for his reports on corruption in two AFL locals. "I could name a hundred thieves and gang-sters, embezzlers and terrorists," he declared. "They infest the A.F. of L. to such a degree that the organization has negligently lost its right to public respect as a labor movement and has become the front for a privileged terror obviously comparable to the Mafia of Sicily." Pegler did not exploit American anti-Communism but made the case throughout his work that since labor could not reform itself, the government had to right the situa-tion. He and his conservative employer, newspaperman Roy Howard, used this argument to question the Wagner Act's protections and to attack the New Deal.[21]

These arguments that legal, normal trade union activities exemplified corruption and racketeering were commonly deployed to weaken labor's capacity to "meddle" in politics or economic life in western right-to-work campaigns. New Mexico Democratic congresswoman Georgia Lusk favored restricting the unions' power in order to "protect working men within the union from the arbitrary action of their leaders." Others celebrated these new punishments for "fly-by-night radicals," which helped "the working-man [who] has very little respect for them." "Labor has gone altogether too far," a Nevadan expounded, "it is about time that these unions were put on the carpet."[22]

Communism was not a prominent issue in referenda on union power. Although Nevada was home to one of the most outspoken anti-Communists, Democratic senator Patrick McCarran, the theme of Soviet subversion did not play an overt role. Without specifically evoking the spec-ter of Communism, right-to-work campaign material focused on how the union shop was un-American. For example, in one ad, the Nevada Citizens Committee underscored "Big Labor's" threat by arguing, "He [the labor boss] tries to tell you that Nevada's Right to Work Law is Un-American. IS FREEDOM OF THE INDIVIDUAL UN-AMERICAN? Is his idea of forcing you against your will to join a union—American? That's what he wants—that's all he wants—complete power! He would be glad to take over—DO YOU WANT HIM TO?"[23]

Those who feared "compulsory unionism" capitalized more on the image of the nefarious labor "racketeer" than on the dangerous Communist. Nevada right-to-work supporters took out a half-page ad showing an angry, fat, ruddy-faced labor "boss" chewing on a cigar, furrowing his brow, and wearing a broad-brimmed hat and a pricey suit, both popularly associated with gangsters at the time. The copy asked readers to consider why organized labor opposed the "right to work": "under the provisions of the Right to Work Law[,] the union labor boss' power is curbed! He even condescends to say 'goodmorning [sic]' in the hiring hall now! He didn't use to!"[24] The "gangster's" appearance encapsulated all of these charges and those made by labor's critics across the country. Accusations of coercion and graft contradicted the internal union democracy the CIO had championed, helping anti-union activists subvert union solidarity. But while authors aimed this particular propaganda at workers, the cartoon in the ad also represented the fears of all those who fought for the open shop: this man was not just a threat to working-class westerners but to the entire country. He seemed poised to grind industry, and ultimately prosperity, to a halt.

Arguments for these restrictions spoke to some in the rank and file wary of labor's increasing power and bureaucratization. Many of the unionists who publicly supported the propositions tended to focus their anger on "Big Labor" and its "bosses," men who represented the evils of an increasingly bureaucratized labor movement. A member of the United Mine Workers, Luther Wofford, was "100% for unionism but I want to tell you and I would like to go on record that I am absolutely against the labor racketeer." E. W. Duhame asserted, "During my career as a member of organized labor, as well as an employer of a lot of men, I have seen good and bad on both sides, but I find that there is less dissension and much less 'boss-ism' under the open shop method than there is where closed shop may reign." William Coxon also believed there were "infamous people who sometimes head our organizations who ought to be cast out of them for the good of the rank and file." "Stand with the working man," Phoenix unionist Dove Riggins begged to the governor, "We depend on you to make that Work to Right [*sic*] Bill a law . . . to cut their scheming out."[25]

"A Return of Un-American Low Wages and Living Standards"

The trade union movement had difficulty uniting against the right-to-work threat. The southwestern labor movement, far removed from eastern strongholds, was fragmented and disorganized. Unlike their brethren in the Northeast, southwestern locals struggled, in the words of CIO officials, to get labor "all going in the same direction." In addition to rank-and-file fears of the increasingly bureaucratic nature of the labor movement, anti-Communism proved an obstacle to union solidarity. The 1947 amendments to the Wagner Act, popularly referred to as Taft-Hartley, weakened and splintered the labor movement. In the West, Mine-Mill locals abandoned the union "on grounds, that the International is dominated by Communists." Rivalry between AFL and CIO locals was also a problem. In Nevada, attempts to unify state labor organizations for political campaigns or legislative action seriously began only in 1945. Yet the various unions and organizing bodies would not unite politically until 1956. In Arizona, AFL leaders lamented that the state's branch of the AFL's political organization, Labor's League for Political Education, failed to endorse, let alone publish a list of, pro-union candidates.[26]

The argument against right-to-work statutes centered on explaining the economic necessity of trade unions. For example, the Reno Central Trades and Labor Council issued a small booklet that predicted that the proposition would "bring a return of un-American low wages and low living standards of a decade ago." Labor leaders also conflated the union-shop issue with an organized and secure working class that could protect the regional economy. Albuquerque's Central Labor Council opposed New Mexico's bill unequivocally, since it would "deprive the working people of New Mexico [of] a living wage and a chance to protect their rights as an employee." In New Mexico, the president of the Santa Rita Lodge 323 of the Brotherhood of Railway Trainmen believed that such anti-union legislation would "destroy for generations the power of the American people to petition for redress, for better wages and better working conditions."[27]

Images of unchecked corporate greed and pre–New Deal working conditions galvanized support for labor's security. Nevada unionists identified the state's Citizens Committee as "the same forces that have fought so bitterly against labor's progress," who still wanted "to hamstring free unions and collective bargaining through punitive laws such as the 'right to work' proposition." New Mexico labor leaders went so far as to describe any incursions on union security as returning "the money changers to the temple." The idea that business needed protection from labor outraged one Las Cruces carpenter: "I listened to Alfred Sloan, Chairman of General Motors, on the radio when he stated that we will have to pass a law to break the big Unions because they are too powerful. He did not mention the National Association of Manufacturers—only Labor Unions." "I have built some mighty fine homes in some big cities," the carpenter fumed, "but could I live in them? No!"[28]

In New Mexico and California, the right-to-work issue was connected to other pressing moral and social causes. Fears of work stoppages in the wake of passage galvanized opposition to the 1944 California proposition. Republican governor Earl Warren opposed the bill because "a campaign on a measure of this kind would be a bitter one that [will] cause disruption rather than unity . . . during this war period." This argument kept even the California Chamber of Commerce from endorsing the initiative. Its president declared that, even though the organization opposed "compulsory unionism," members also disapproved of the open-shop proposition: "Our position is that in the interest of national unity, the uninterrupted prosecution of the war and maintenance of our vital production scheduled at this time of crisis, and because we feel that the proposed amendment if adopted will cause rather than allay confusion and controversy, we are opposed to the initiative proposal entitled 'right to employment.'"[29]

A shared sense of purpose with the Mexican American civil rights movement drove much of the 1948 anti-right-to-work campaign in New Mexico. Unionists did not just reach beyond membership rolls; they saw the struggle for the union shop as a battle for social, economic, and political justice. Mine-Mill locals in particular had strong ties to Mexican American civil rights groups eager to help fight the open-shop referendum. These connections made the trade union movement in the state part of a broader push for equality. An important organization was the Asociación Nacional México-Americana (ANMA), which included members from major independent unions such as the Longshoremen's Union and Mine-Mill. Labor activist Bert Corona described ANMA as "tackling issues directly and without any opportunism. ANMA's members were *mexicanos* who were very deeply committed to their communities and to achieving full rights and better conditions for the Spanish-speaking, primarily workers." Such arguments about union security's larger meaning spoke to a homemaker in Carlsbad, New Mexico, who "considered the bill very dangerous to not only the living standards and the rights of the working man . . . but to the civil rights of the workers to band themselves together in order to sponsor those who would best represent them in their government."[30]

This blending of union and civil rights was not just a political tool. Unionists were part of a unique and powerful movement culture in New Mexico. Mine-Mill's Local 890 prided itself on having "one of the strongest rank-and-file Mexican American memberships in our International." While isolation, persecution, and censorship describe part of Local 890's history, the community's struggles harked back to a more militant, radical, and community-oriented unionism. Clinton Jencks, president of Local 890, described the organization as immersed in a "long struggle for better wages and working conditions, in our struggle for unity between Mexican-American and Anglo-American workers, for equality and against discrimination, [in which] we have been working in the very highest and best democratic traditions of the United States." These same militants also hoped that the cinematic depiction of the strike against Empire Zinc in *Salt of the Earth* would bring their vision to audiences well beyond Hanover, New Mexico.[31]

Local Catholic clergy also took part in this anti-right-to-work coalition. New Mexico's Catholic hierarchy overcame its initial hostility to the CIO and became increasingly pro-labor, especially after Monsignor Edwin Vincent Byrne became the archbishop of Santa Fe in 1942. Byrne, who had spent the 1920s and 1930s in poverty-stricken Puerto Rico, campaigned against the right-to-work referendum openly because he believed the law would cripple organized labor in New Mexico. Reflecting the Church's growing alliance with organized labor, Byrne's successors justified their continued opposition to right-to-work measures because as a "Church we certainly defend the individual's right to employment but this right also implies a just and equitable salary which cannot be obtained unless the individual has the right to collective bargaining."[32]

Right-to-work propositions failed in California in 1944 and New Mexico in 1948, by almost 60 percent of the vote in each race, but anti-union

activists had impressive victories everywhere else. Arizona voters were the
first to restrict labor's strength. The 1946 proposition passed in every
county. Across the state, fewer than fifty thousand voted against it, with
over sixty-one thousand for (44 percent "no" to 56 percent "yes"). Nevada
voters followed suit in 1952, but there the measure passed with just 51
percent of voters. Nevada and Arizona unionists continued to place anti-
right-to-work initiatives on the ballot only to lose by greater margins each
time. In response, Nevada open-shop supporters lobbied successfully for a
law that made the requirements for public referenda practically impossible.[33] The easiest victory came in Utah. In 1955 assembly members did not
bother to turn the measure into a ballot proposition. The final tally split
across party lines, with all Democrats in the legislature (six in the Senate
and twenty-seven in the House) opposing the measure and all Republicans
supporting the new statute (thirteen in the Senate and thirty-three in the
House).[34]

National Entrenchment

Passage of the Utah statute coincided with a crucial year in the history of
right-to-work referenda. The AFL and CIO merged, ending years of rivalry.
Labor's voice was now more unified and its political activities far better
funded. The year 1955, however, was also a moment for the consolidation
of potent anti-union operations. The cohort of business and political organizations that had funded statewide anti-union shop campaigns now
formed the National Right to Work Committee (NRTWC), which soon
coordinated a series of well-crafted political and legal challenges to trade
union power. Some historians have interpreted this organization's founding, as well as the National Association of Manufacturers' and the U.S.
Chamber of Commerce's increased political activism, as evidence that only
in the mid-1950s did business make "shap[ing] the debate over right-to-
work a priority." Such arguments insinuate that when the NRTWC formed
in 1955, it brought a shift in right-to-work rhetoric and galvanized national
businesses to fund local campaigns.[35]

  Yet events in 1955 did not mark a rhetorical revolution in the postwar
debate over the status and legitimacy of the trade union movement. The
discourses found in the early southwestern campaigns, not those discussions focused on preserving Jim Crow and protecting southern agriculture, dominated the national dialogue on the union security controversy.

With both the AFL-CIO and NRTWC headquartered in Washington, D.C., the campaign literature and talking points for speeches in the later referenda became tightly controlled. Materials and strategies now came from the national offices. Neither business nor labor shifted its polemical discourse or underlying ideology, only now the battle was engaged on a national scale and with organizational weapons of far greater reach.

Both sides hoped that pooling resources would strengthen their respective causes and advance their political outreach. AFL-CIO leaders sought to protect labor's rights from the Republican counteroffensive. Fighting right-to-work laws was a major priority. An AFL-CIO subcommittee earmarked over $1 million dollars for the 1958 right-to-work campaigns, funds pooled from affiliated unions and state federations as well as various trades' departments within the AFL-CIO. The NRTWC simultaneously incorporated members of the various groups that had been opposing "compulsory unionism" for years. In their constitution and by-laws, NRTWC members described themselves as having the "conviction that the growing tendency toward requiring people, against their will, to join labor Unions in order to work is contrary to the fundamentals of freedom. We believe that such compulsion is an unjustifiable denial of individual liberty and free choice." The group's newsletters harped on the necessity of their fight continually, since "forced membership in a union is economic slavery and the abrogation of the right of choice of free Americans . . . is the first stage of dictatorship."[36]

Opposing visions for economic growth dominated the right-to-work debate. Pro-union materials deemed union insecurity bad for the economy because "most of the states that have 'right-to-work' laws have comparatively little industry . . . . In Mississippi . . . the average personal income of every man, woman[,] and child—in that 'right-to-work' state was only $946.00 a year, the lowest in the nation." The NRTWC had its own statistics: according to its literature, employment opportunities increased by almost 10 percent in open-shop states but less than 1 percent elsewhere, while wages increased by 25 percent, as opposed to just 21.5 percent in non-right-to-work states.[37]

Southwestern arguments against compulsory unionism began to dominate southern debates. Southern industrialists had argued since the 1940s that the mandatory open shop would bring more economic prosperity to the region but these business leaders had not controlled the South's politics.

As industry supplanted agriculture as the area's economic base, the "progressive business-friendly environment" arguments began to dominate southern right-to-work discourses. Historian James Cobb has argued that by the end of the 1970s, "antiunionism had supplanted racism as the South's most respectable prejudice." One labor organizer noted that Senator Strom Thurmond of South Carolina, a former segregationist, would "acknowledge blacks now, but you still don't see Strom shaking hands with union people." In Louisiana, a new right-to-work effort began in the 1970s because of the growing influence of Kaiser Industries, Cities Service, Dow Chemical, General Electric, Crown Zellerbach, and Brown and Root in the state's economy. Now united under the name Louisiana Association of Business and Industry, the state's business leaders feared the high price of labor in the nonagricultural sectors and set out to take control of the legislature, which resulted in the passage of a right-to-work bill that covered all of the state's workers in 1976.[38]

The mid-1950s, then, heralded a period of entrenchment. Battle lines were clearly drawn, and spokespersons were deep in their foxholes. Open-shop literature emphasized the NRTWC's rank-and-file members. Newsletters often contained stories of workers fighting against closed- or union-shop provisions. Publishers, for example, celebrated the banding together of fifty-two independent contractors in Phoenix to ensure that the state government enforced both the Taft-Hartley Act and Arizona's right-to-work and anti-picketing laws. Testimonials from rank and filers were especially important to counter labor's arguments. Praise from unionists that a "Right-to-Work law is a protection against laborism—the blind concentration of power in the hands of a few irresponsible and self-perpetuating union bosses" underscored the committee's contention that they were working with and for ordinary workers.[39]

The reunited labor movement recruited a phalanx of prominent liberals to counter the NRTWC's rank-and-file supporters. The AFL-CIO's most prominent recruits were Eleanor Roosevelt and former New York senator Herbert H. Lehman, who formed the National Council for Industrial Peace in 1958. The organization aimed to protect the manufacturing armistice envisioned in the Wagner Act's preamble by promoting "good relations between labor and management in the public interest, avoiding industrial strife." A joint statement called for "all right-thinking citizens, from all walks of life, to join in protecting the nation's economy and the working man's union security from the predatory and misleading campaigns now

being waged by the U.S. Chamber of Commerce and the National Association of Manufacturers."[40]

The AFL-CIO also sought endorsements from liberal business giants, a
strategy that downplayed class conflict. Both Dan A. Kimball, president of
Aerojet Corporation, and billionaire John Paul Getty penned testimonials
for anti-right-to-work pamphlets. "While I believe there have been some
abuses by a few labor leaders and some racketeers who have worked their
way into some unions," Kimball wrote, "I don't think we should condemn
unions because of that. The union shop makes for a fair balance in labor
management relations and any union that is properly run is democratic."
Getty was unabashed in his support for labor: "Free and honest—and I
emphasize those words, 'free and honest'—labor unions not only help us
create this way of life, but they are among its strongest, most reliable
bulwarks."[41]

The central theme in much of the labor movement's literature was protecting "free and honest" locals as well as "industrial peace," a message that
inadvertently sabotaged their cause because it ceded ground to business's
long-established rationale for opposing union security. Unionists, labor
leaders, politicians, businesspersons, and clergy acknowledged problems in
the labor movement. Their support for union security often hinged more
on supporting worthy unions without really tackling misrepresentations of
labor's power or its leaders. This election material also did not paint big
business as a serious threat. Labor's reliance on corporate leaders was an
attempt to bridge class lines, but ended up enforcing the opposition's contention that union security was unnecessary. These tactics played right into
the hands of right-to-work advocates, who claimed that unions caused dis-
ruptive industrial conflict and hindered economic growth, insinuating that
there were serious problems within the house of labor, not inside corporate
boardrooms.[42]

Stalemate

The 1958 off-year elections proved a national referendum on the right-to-
work issue.[43] The union shop was on the line in six states, two in the proto-
Sunbelt: Washington, Ohio, Kansas, Idaho, Colorado, and California. Both
sides relied on long-standing rhetoric surrounding the right-to-work issue

and their opposing visions for growth, but the financial benefits from consolidating the labor movement made a significant difference in the character of these campaigns. Western labor had caught up to their politically mobilized brothers and sisters in the Steelbelt. Affiliation with the AFL-CIO gave Colorado labor leaders more funds and resources, $11,000 by the start of October 1958. This figure did not include money the national offices spent on films, pamphlets, campaign writers, and advertisements. The AFL-CIO poured over $600,000 into the six referenda by October. National figures in the labor movement came to state labor rallies "to help fire our people up." Locals also formed political committees. For example, the Durango Carpenters Local 2243 chose five unionists to ensure every member was registered to vote.[44]

National AFL-CIO officials also pushed the state federations to reach outside membership rolls to rally voters around the fiscal promises of a well-organized and secure working class. To convince voters to protect the New Deal order, California AFL-CIO leaders crafted arguments that united the labor and civil rights movements. They quoted Martin Luther King Jr.'s assertion that it was "significant that these 'right-to-work' laws are backed by the same reactionary forces which flout the Supreme Court decision on school desegregation." The National Association for the Advancement of Colored People joined the cause in California, distributing a pamphlet titled "Keep Mississippi Out of California," the cover of which depicted a white manager whipping a California worker with a "Right-to-Work" lash, which had a swastika on one of its tips.[45]

Organizers also endeavored to mobilize the Mexican American population. The Colorado Labor Council's president assigned unionist Joseph Zamora to make Spanish-language radio advertisements designed to persuade Mexican Americans to vote against the right-to-work amendment. Zamora reported resistance because, before this political drive, the Colorado labor movement had not really advocated for these workers. "I found some had been dealt with unfairly by some union officials," Zamora noted. Such treatment meant that "the Mexican pople [*sic*] are poorly organized, and are, in fact, disorganized and submissive. They can be easily used to scab. In fact they were so used in a laundry strike two years ago."[46]

Colorado right-to-work opponents, like federation officials, offered unionists a limited vision. Much of the Colorado unionists' arguments were designed just to win the election without considering that the 1943 Labor Peace Act imposed serious restrictions on union security. In a packet of sample speeches for study groups and meetings, the Colorado Labor Council focused its appeal on sustaining a truce between management and labor. Labor's supporters highlighted this industrial peace idea in their economic argument against the open shop, asserting, "Everybody wants orderly marketing conditions without disruption from industrial unrest." Ads and literature went so far as to proclaim an era of industrial peace in Colorado, concluding, "This misnamed piece of legislation would be a death-blow to the excellent labor-management relationship we in Colorado have enjoyed for so many years."[47]

The sheer political muscle of the anti-right-to-work vote was impressive in Colorado and California. The Colorado initiative failed with 61 percent of the vote, 318,480 against and 200,319 for the right-to-work proposal. In Mesa County, in which Zamora organized, the amendment failed, 10,118 to 7,044. In California, 60 percent voted against the measure. Voters in only six Golden State counties (Alpine, Imperial, Lake, Mono, Sutter, and Orange) approved the proposition. The year 1958 also marked a major victory for Democrats in California. Conservative William Knowland lost the governor's mansion to famed liberal politician Edmund G. "Pat" Brown. Support of right to work had been the cornerstone of the Republican's campaign, an effort that ended in an embarrassing GOP shutout and Democratic control of the California legislature.[48]

Labor won the battle but not the war. The NRTWC's losses in the proto-Sunbelt and three other states in 1958 did not signal the defeat of organized labor's enemy or its free-market vision for economic growth. Coloradans accepted the Labor Peace Act in order to stop the compulsory open-shop measure, a Faustian bargain that undercut labor's claims that union security was vital for prosperity. This tactic left Colorado labor much less secure than the trade union movements in New Mexico and California. Failed open-shop efforts in and of themselves should also not be seen as a total failure. Lisa McGirr has traced the impressive California conservative grassroots efforts for Goldwater's 1964 presidential run to the anti-union campaigns, crediting them with being training sessions for her suburban warriors.[49]

Five years after the Goldwater defeat, Kevin Phillips described in *The Emerging Republican Majority* what had become the spirit of the Sunbelt, an economic dynamism built on industrial relocation and entrepreneurial freedom. Anti-unionism dominated both halves of the Sunbelt, but it would have a distinctly western flavor, emphasizing not the maintenance of a rural elite and Jim Crow, but instead preying on fears of coercion and racketeering, while promising a future of freedom, regional development, and high employment.

This discourse in the early postwar right-to-work elections in the proto-Sunbelt proved crucial to the Right's ideological and electoral victories. Passage of these statutes helped unravel New Deal ideas that held that workers and unions formed a legitimate part of the tripartite body politic. Labor leaders were thus on the defensive from disaffected unionists, middle-class citizens, and business owners mobilizing against a supposedly corrupt cohort of racketeers. The crux of this cross-class agreement was that more and more voters accepted the argument that prosperity depended on overturning New Deal regulatory checks against business. Union insecurity undercut liberal plans for regional growth and modernization, weakened corporatist power-sharing schemes, and devalued liberal Keynesianism before the mid-1950s. Even if all right-to-work supporters were not ready to denounce the entire New Deal state, many rejected the Wagner Act as a crucial pillar of the West's future and the liberal-regulatory order, embracing the laissez-faire anti-unionism that became part of the foundation of Sunbelt conservatism and the modern Right.

PART III

Appropriating the Language
of Civil Rights

Civil rights law and its relationship to employment rights stand at the center of the next three essays. As we have seen, the right-to-work issue always had a powerful racial component, deployed both by supporters and opponents of organized labor. In his study of conservative efforts to pass a California "right-to-work" law in 1958, Reuel Schiller demonstrates that conservative Republicans largely failed to convince African Americans that such a ban on the union shop was in their interest as workers and citizens, even though many trade unions did in fact discriminate against racial minorities. Labor argued, more successfully, that the proposition would weaken unions, lower wages, and turn California into a state whose standard of living resembled that of Jim Crow Mississippi. But the campaign against the California right-to-work proposition was a problematic labor-liberal victory. For Schiller argues that if the rhetoric of racial division used to attack unions and entice minority voters failed at the polls in 1958, it exacerbated tensions in the alliance between labor and the civil rights community, with deleterious consequences in the next decade and after.

One of the most powerful groups to exploit this divide was the National Right to Work Legal Defense Foundation, which grew out of the National Right to Work Committee, founded in 1955. The committee funded numerous right-to-work initiatives during the next decade, but in the 1960s and 1970s, as Sophia Lee points out, the right-to-work forces moved forward with a litigation strategy that mimicked the discourse of the civil rights movement. Legal Defense Foundation attorneys tried to redeploy the civil rights movement's constitutional claims and adopt its political mantle. Instead of attacking unions in the name of enterprise autonomy or managerial rights, right-to-work lawyers won legitimacy, thwarted liberal attacks, and exacerbated divisions within the Democratic Party by putting forward minority plaintiffs seeking redress against big labor. This was a pioneering strategy for the Right, which would soon be adopted by libertarians and free-market advocates in other fields to delegitimize the entire regulatory state and the liberal institutions that sustained it.

The imbricated relationship between the labor law and its civil rights cousin is manifest in Alexander Gourse's study of why and how Illinois employers resisted and reshaped state-level fair employment legislation in the years after World War II. Some were outright racists or anti-Communists who saw the advancement of African Americans as a subversion of the social order. Most employers based their opposition to an effective, executive branch Fair Employment Practice Commission on a fear that the administrative state was inherently biased in favor of organized labor. Led by the Illinois Manufacturers Association, business leaders demanded judicial protection of their rights against executive power, arguing that their "right to manage" constituted a civil right worthy of heightened standards of procedural due process. This strategy had profound implications for national labor and civil rights law. Illinois Republican senator Everett Dirksen, a key figure in shaping the 1964 Civil Rights Act, made sure that the courts would play a large role in defining the powers and reviewing the decisions of the new, federal Equal Employment Opportunity Commission. Judges with little background in labor-management relations, Gourse points out, often expanded civil rights law at the expense of labor law, while the adversarial, winner-take-all outcomes of discrimination lawsuits often alienated workers, both minority and white, from their unions.

Singing "The Right-to-Work Blues": The Politics of Race in the Campaign for "Voluntary Unionism" in Postwar California

Reuel Schiller

During the early fall of 1958, Lester Bailey, a labor organizer and field representative of the Citizens Committee Against Proposition 18, found himself engaged in an unusual activity as he sat in the committee's offices on Sutter Street in San Francisco. He was writing a song: "The Right to Work Blues."[1] "I'd hate to see / My weekly pay go down," Bailey wrote.

> I'd hate to see
> That Right to Work Made law!
> Because the day it is
> They'll pay me like they paid my Paw!
>
> Mississippi has it
> Georgia, Texas do!
> If it comes to California
> I'll have to leave here too!
> Oh I'd hate to see
> That Right to Work made law

Cause I can't live on
What they paid my Paw!

Got the Right to Work Blues
Scared as I can be!
I'm goin' to vote NO! on 18
And keep California *free*!

By choosing an African American musical idiom—the song was to be sung to the tune of W. C. Handy's immensely popular "St. Louis Blues"—Bailey hinted at the identity of his intended audience. The substance of his lyrics also suggested that it was the black voters of California whom he wished to convince to oppose Proposition 18, the right-to-work proposition that would be on the November ballot. African American workers had left the South to come to California in search of the prosperity that had been denied to their parents. Yet the passage of Proposition 18 would bring the South to them, Bailey argued. It would undermine their prosperity and force them to move on once again to preserve both their material comfort and their freedom.

Les Bailey was not the only trade unionist reaching out to the African American community during the 1958 campaign. Indeed, he was part of a concerted effort to ensure that black voters would reject Proposition 18. This effort came into being because the proponents of the proposition had targeted the African American community. They believed that black workers, many of whom had suffered discrimination at the hands of labor unions, could be convinced to vote for a ballot measure that would weaken organized labor in the state. By breaking the "union monopoly" in California, they argued, Proposition 18 would strike a blow for fair employment practices. If it passed, racist unions could not keep African Americans out of jobs, and could not extort money from black union members to further racist policies.

The right-to-work effort to capture the votes of African Americans was ultimately unsuccessful. Proposition 18 was soundly defeated in 1958, and black voters opposed it in even greater numbers than white voters. However, the fact that African Americans voted overwhelmingly against Proposition 18 did not mean that they were entirely comfortable with the alliance that they had struck with California unions. Indeed, the fight over the proposition revealed significant divisions within the black community and profound tensions between African Americans and their allies in the labor movement. Unions seemed to be taking black votes for granted, many African Americans believed. While the rhetoric of racial division that Proposition 18's proponents used to attack unions and entice black voters may have failed in its intended purpose in 1958, it exacerbated tensions in the alliance between labor and the African American community. Over the next decade, these tensions would place limits on the political power of reform elements within the labor movement, the African American community, and the Democratic Party in California.

Proposition 18 and the deep fear and hostility it generated within the labor movement was rooted in the state of midcentury labor law. The National Labor Relations Act (NLRA) required an employer to recognize and bargain with a union that had the support of more than half the workers in a given bargaining unit.[2] The NLRA also dictated that such a union be the exclusive representative of all the workers in that unit. Accordingly, the union had to provide services (contract negotiation and grievance arbitration, for example) for every member of the bargaining unit, even if some of those workers were not union members. This obligation created a problem for unions because it acted as a disincentive for workers to join the union. If the union was required to negotiate the collective bargaining agreement and process grievances on behalf of nonmembers, why should they join the union and pay dues? This so-called free-riding problem was a serious one for unions, since it could create the untenable situation in which a union was spending resources on a group of people far larger than those from whom it was collecting dues. Unions would be bankrupted if too many workers enjoyed the benefits of unionization without paying for them.

Fortunately for unions, the NLRA provided a solution to the problem of free riders. The act allowed a union to enter into collective bargaining agreements that required an employer to dismiss a worker who had not joined the union within thirty days of starting his job. This type of agreement (known as a "union security agreement" or "compulsory unionism" depending on your ideological proclivities) eliminated free riders. If a worker refused to join the union and pay dues for the benefits he received, the union could have him fired. Thus, the collective bargaining agreement could create a "union shop"—a bargaining unit in which every worker was a member of the union, even if he had not voted for the union in the first place, and even if he did not wish to join.

The union shop, however, was not allowed in every state. The 1947 amendments to the NLRA, known as the Taft-Hartley Act, allowed individual states to prohibit union security agreements. This is what Proposition 18 proposed to do. "No person shall be required by an employer to become or remain a member of any labor organization as a condition of employment or continuation of employment."[3] Such prohibitions were known as "right-to-work" measures, in that, according to their proponents, they preserved an individual's right to work for a particular employer regardless of whether he belonged to the union that represented that employer's workers. Unions, obviously, viewed these measures differently. They were "right-to-wreck" measures, laws that would deprive unions of the dues they needed to carry out the obligations imposed on them by the NLRA.

In the decade after Taft-Hartley was passed, national business organizations such as the National Association of Manufacturers and the United States Chamber of Commerce sought to weaken labor unions by funding right-to-work campaigns in a number of states.[4] This movement achieved early victories in the South and Southwest, and by the middle of the 1950s had turned its attention to more industrialized states with higher union densities. After an emboldening victory in Indiana in 1957, right-to-work forces made an enormous push in 1958, launching campaigns in five states, three of which, Washington, Ohio, and California, had large numbers of union members.

The impetus for Proposition 18 came from a cast of characters and organizations familiar to anyone who followed conservative California politics in the years after World War II: Charles Jones, the head of the Richfield Oil Company; Walter Knott of Knott's Berry Farm; Cecil Kenyon of Southern California Edison; the *Los Angeles Times'* Chandler family; Cecil B. De-Mille's Political Freedom Foundation; the California Association of Employers; the Los Angeles Merchants and Manufacturer's Association.[5] The proposition's highest profile supporter, however, was the Republican Party's candidate for governor, U.S. Senate minority leader William Knowland, whose comically inept, catastrophically self-destructive 1958 campaign provided the background against which Proposition 18's supporters and opponents battled for the votes of African Americans.[6]

In early 1957, Knowland, one of the most powerful Republicans in the Senate, stunned political observers by announcing that he would not run for reelection in 1958. Though he gave personal reasons for the decision (his wife, it was said, missed California), the barely hidden motivation was a desire to become governor, the ideal launching pad, in his view, for a campaign for the White House. The fact that the incumbent governor, Goodwin Knight, was a Republican, did not trouble Knowland. Indeed, he seemed to believe that his inevitable victory in a bruising primary battle with Knight would demonstrate what a powerful presidential candidate he would be. Knight was vulnerable, Knowland thought, because of his close ties to California labor unions, connections that alienated Knight from powerful right-wing elements within the Republican Party. Accordingly, Knowland explicitly and forcefully hitched his campaign to efforts to pass Proposition 18. Early polling had showed that the proposition had a commanding lead, so by linking himself to it, Knowland believed that he would not only secure the Republican nomination but also split the votes of labor union members, thereby winning the general election.

Knowland may have been the only Republican in California who thought this strategy was a good one. Everyone else, in the words of one historian, "saw in it the schismatic makings of a disaster."[7] Indeed, throughout the 1940s and 1950s the California Republican Party depended on moderates like Earl Warren, Knight, and the state's junior senator, Thomas Kuchel, to win statewide elections in a state where registered Democrats outnumbered Republicans by over 750,000. They did this by embracing the mantle of nonpartisan politics and committing themselves to positions on issues such as old-age pensions, public health insurance, and government spending on infrastructure that were in line with the preferences of many Democratic voters. Similarly, these moderate Republicans tried, with considerable success, to ensure that labor unions did not become an adjunct to the state's Democratic Party. Indeed, Knight earned the reputation as one of the most pro-labor governors in California's history.[8] Thus, Knowland's strategy seemed designed not only to divide the Republican Party but also to alienate the Democratic voters, many of them union members, upon whom Republicans had depended to dominate statewide politics for more than a decade.

Trying to minimize the damage that Knowland's strategy seemed destined to inflict, the powers that be in the California Republican Party—vice president Richard Nixon, *Los Angeles Times* political editor and kingmaker Kyle Palmer, political consultants Clem Whittaker and Leone Baxter, deep-pocketed banker Howard Ahmandson—denied Knowland the primary fight he was itching for. Threatening to withhold endorsements and campaign contributions, they forced Knight out of the race and engineered "the big switcheroo" in which Knight instead ran for Knowland's vacated Senate seat. ("The booby prize," quipped the presumably ecstatic Democratic gubernatorial nominee, Edmund "Pat" Brown.) That Knight refused to endorse Knowland surprised no one, but it boded poorly for any hopes of Republican unity in the general election.

Knowland's right-to-work strategy also turned out to be a disaster. Far from splitting the labor vote, it unified and inspired it. Furthermore, Knowland had profoundly miscalculated the appeal of the right-to-work issue in the Republican Party. Knowland, it turned out, was several years too early to challenge the hegemony of the moderates within the party. Even Kyle Palmer, himself an ardent supporter of Proposition 18, thought it foolish to link a gubernatorial campaign to an issue that was bound to be controversial. Indeed, Knowland turned out to be one of the very few Republican candidates to endorse it, let alone center a campaign on it. Most Republicans opposed it and the state party, as well as Nixon, remained neutral.

The Republicans' slow-motion hara-kiri ended on election day. Knowland was shellacked. Pat Brown beat him by more than a million votes of the 5.2 million that were cast.[9] Proposition 18 was also decisively beaten, getting even fewer votes than Knowland and losing by 20 percentage points.[10] Knight lost, as did every other Republican running for statewide office, save one. The Democrats seized control of both the State Senate and the Assembly, as well as the state's congressional delegation. The Republican Party, Knight declared, was in "its worst shape in a century."[11] The *San Francisco Chronicle*, which had refused to endorse Knowland despite its consistently Republican editorial preferences, performed the autopsy: "An extreme group in the California Republican Party decided . . . to take California back into the 19th century, away from the 'moderate Republicanism' that the members of the group so heartily loath; away from the Progressive tradition of the great Republican governorships of Hiram Johnson . . . and Earl Warren; away from Goodwin Knight, whom they hold in contempt for the odd notion that the way for Republican candidates to win is to try to gain support from all the elements of the public, including labor."[12]

In retrospect, the *Chronicle*'s description of what happened was correct, but its analysis was profoundly flawed. Knowland's hard right, anti-labor tactics may have represented the Republican Party's nineteenth-century past, but they also presaged its twentieth-century future. As Kurt Schuparra and Lisa McGirr have demonstrated, the California Republican Party's self-immolations of the late 1950s and the early 1960s were a refiner's fire out of which emerged a new, potent conservative movement that would come to dominate the party.[13] Indeed, a closer examination of the battle over Proposition 18 reveals many themes that would become central to this new brand of Republicanism. It also shows how the politics of racial division would become a potent weapon in the arsenal of a reborn Republican Party.

In California, the battle between the pro- and anti-Proposition 18 forces centered around three interlocking arguments. The first was the age-old philosophical dispute over the inherent conflict between majoritarianism and the rights of the individual: should labor law be structured to further the will of the majority or protect the rights of dissenting individuals? Since neither side believed that the other was actually interested in advancing such noble values, each side frequently turned to a second argument: what were the actual motivations of the forces on either side of the proposition? Was it corrupt and subversive labor "bosses" trying to protect their fiefdoms, or greedy industrialists intent on destroying unions and driving down wages? This discussion of wages led to the final argument that was frequently deployed during the campaign: what would the economic effect of Proposition 18 be? Would it destroy California's economy by driving down wages and reducing consumer spending? Or would it create a more vibrant California economy through the creation of a more hospitable business climate, devoid of corrupt and subversive unions?

In the first of these arguments—by far the most high minded—each side tried to lay hold of the traditional values of American political culture. As far as Proposition 18's opponents were concerned, the right-to-work movement was intent on undermining one of the most basic principles of American society: "Our American government is based on the principle of majority rule. That is the American Way."[14] In a democratic society, there would always be people on the losing side of a vote. That fact did not entitle them to "shirk" their responsibilities to that society.[15] Furthermore, the "right to work" was not one that was found in the Constitution, so even if a person believed certain rights should be protected against the will of the majority, the right to be represented by a union without paying for it was not one of them.[16]

To Proposition 18's supporters, these arguments mischaracterized American political values. In American political culture, the protection of individual rights—particularly the right to dissent—was at least as important as furthering the will of the majority. In its editorial supporting Proposition 18, the *Los Angeles Times* stated this argument most forcefully.[17] The free-rider argument, that majorities should be able to force dissenters to join the union, was "an offensive argument." Indeed, it was "a horrifying argument" that rejected "a basic principle of the Constitution of the United States: that men have rights which majorities may not nullify." The protection of the rights of dissenting individuals was one of the most basic attributes of American society: "If a majority in Congress may not deprive a man of his property with a bill of attainder, why may a majority of workmen in a shop deprive a man of his job, which is often one of his most precious properties, because he is a dissenter?" Thus, a vote for Proposition 18 was a patriotic act that would "put California in tune with the spirit of the Founding Fathers." Indeed, anyone who would oppose such a self-evidently and uniquely American right must have corrupt or unpatriotic motives: "It is curious—we could use a more invidious adjective—that so many of the champions of social rights, civil rights, human rights, even economic rights, dance blindfolded around this most conspicuous of latter-day rights."

This argument—that right-to-work's opponents had ulterior motives—sat at the center of the campaign for Proposition 18. The proposition's supporters argued that right-to-work legislation would allow workers to drive corrupt or subversive union leaders out of power. Indeed, in the context of the Senate hearings on corruption in organized labor (known as the McClellan Committee hearings), which were taking place throughout the 1958 election season, the strategy was an obvious one.[18] An ad that the pro-18 forces ran frequently in California's major newspapers focused on this theme: "WHY ARE THE UNION BOSSES SO AFRAID OF PROPOSITION #18? . . . Are they afraid that Voluntary Unionism will put a curb on corruption, rigged elections, racketeering, violence, and 'taxation without representation?' . . . Are they afraid that Voluntary Unionism will make it possible for the captive membership of a corrupt or Communistic union to walk out in a body and join an honest, patriotic union?"[19] Political cartoons illustrating this theme were a mainstay of the pro-18 campaign. "Get Hoffa, Off'a" read a caption of a caricature of the notoriously corrupt Teamsters leader, James "Jimmy" Hoffa, pockets bulging with cash, riding on the back of a bridled and blindered union member.[20] Another cartoon showed a "compulsory union machine" sucking in the dollars of scowling union members and spewing cars, houses, and yachts ("benefits to corrupt union bosses") into the arms of a fat, smiling union leader.[21]

While campaigning, Knowland repeatedly linked Proposition 18 to the work of the McClellan Committee and touted it as an antidote to a labor movement dominated by corruption and radicalism.[22] This theme was stated most piquantly by Knowland's wife, Helen, a frequent campaign surrogate, in an article for the right-wing magazine *Human Events* that the Proposition 18 forces circulated to voters.[23] Without a right-to-work law, workers were forced "to submit to the rule of such bosses as Walter Reuther and Jimmy Hoffa." Of course, Hoffa and Dave Beck thrived on the spoils of their corruption, exploiting "the 1.7 million innocent captive members" of the Teamsters. But Reuther was "infinitely more dangerous" because of what Knowland saw as his commitment to Marxism: "In order for Reuther to put his Marxian creed into effect, he must control the governmental machinery of our country." He was in the process of achieving this by turning the labor movement into "the piggy-back monster which has latched on to the Democratic party."

In the end, red-baiting proved far less potent than the charges of union corruption that Proposition 18 opponents sought to shake. They pointed out that there was nothing in the proposition that directly addressed the racketeering issues so prominently raised in the McClellan Committee hearings.[24] They also argued that the AFL-CIO was leading the fight against corrupt unions and that the proposition would hinder that fight "by destroying sound, honest unions, [and] responsible collective bargaining agreements between employers and employees." Instead, "Proposition 18 would aid the dishonest extremist elements in both management and labor."[25] Labor's main tactic, however, was to change the focus of the debate from the motives of the proposition's detractors to those of its proponents.

"Look Who's Coming to the Rescue! . . . of the poor downtrodden working men and women of California!" one ad sarcastically chortled, listing the National Association of Manufacturers, the U.S. Chamber of Commerce, and other "protectors of the people, rushing nobly and without thought of personal gain (?) to save us from evil."[26] "WHO ARE THEY?" another ad asked. "Meet 'Mr. Divide' and 'Mr. Conquer,'" who were not honest businessmen but "financial manipulators . . . who want cheap 'auction block' wages, the better to swell the pockets of their financial and dictator [*sic*] empires."[27] In several pamphlets, the anti-18 forces described the web of "Big Boys with Billions," both in and out of California, who were bankrolling the right-to-work initiative.[28] Far from having the best interests of Californians at heart, their greedy desire for low wages and total managerial autonomy would wreck California's "prosperity and waste fifty years of hard-won economic and social improvement."[29]

Indeed, if linking unions to corruption and subversion was the main tactic of the right-to-work forces, arguing that Proposition 18 would destroy California's economy was where its detractors placed most of their emphasis.[30] Polling done by the California Labor Federation suggested that the best way to convince voters to reject the proposition was not to focus on how it was bad for unions and union members, but instead to emphasize how it would harm people who were not in unions.[31] "PROP 18 THREATENS CALIFORNIA PROSPERITY!" screamed the headline on a fake newspaper put out by the Central Labor Council of Alameda County. "'RIGHT TO WORK' IS 'RIGHT TO WRECK.'"[32] California workers earned higher wages than workers in right-to-work states, and these wages translated into economic prosperity for all. This argument featured prominently in the anti-18 statements placed in California's official voter guide: "If California income were based on the average income in the 'right to work' states, our 14 ½ million people would have $13 billion dollars a year less in buying power. This would mean lower income and profits for merchants, manufacturers and professional persons whose economic existence rests on the buying power of the consumer public."[33] To emphasize this point even more forcefully, California unions provided their members with small slips of paper reading "paid with union wages, vote no on Prop. 18" that they were to give to merchants when they made purchases and to include with their checks when they paid their bills by mail.[34]

Opponents of Proposition 18 celebrated "the maturity in collective bargaining which enlightened labor and management have developed in California."[35] The state's "prosperity is based on industrial peace," they argued. Right-to-work laws, on the other hand, generated violence, strikes, and low wages: "By destroying our stable labor relationships, [Proposition 18] would create industrial chaos." That, in turn, would drive businesses out of California. Proposition 18 was thus portrayed as an attempt to kill the goose that had laid the golden egg of California's postwar boom.

The pro-18 forces, of course, had a completely different set of statistics. In the decade following the passage of Taft-Hartley, states with "voluntary unionism" had seen larger increases in wages, in union membership, and in the number of jobs created than had states with "compulsory union-ism."[36] The reason for this contrast was obvious, the right-to-work forces argued. The "industrial climate" of states without right-to-work laws "has become so unhealthy that industry . . . finds it unwise to risk new capital there . . . [because] it is well-nigh impossible to bargain with monopolistic labor trusts."[37] Thus, far from wrecking California's economy, Proposition 18 would save it by "assur[ing] an economic and labor climate which will attract new industrial and business risk capital to our shore."[38]

These arguments, both pro and con, were typical of battles over right-to-work legislation in the years after the passage of Taft-Hartley.[39] However, in the fall of 1958, Proposition 18's proponents unveiled a new strategy. On September 10, Les Bailey wrote an "Urgent & Confidential" memoran-dum to his bosses at the Citizens Committee Against Proposition 18: "It has come to my attention that the proponents of Proposition 18 are flood-ing Negro communities throughout California with the rumor that the so-called Right to Work issue, if passed, will guarantee Negroes and other minorities Fair Employment Practices (FEP). The Proposition's promoters are planting people in meetings and spreading this fraud by word of mouth to the degree that immediate action must be taken to offset this vicious rumor."[40] To combat this tactic, Bailey wrote, it was imperative to solicit anti-Proposition 18 statements from African American leaders and publi-cize these statements within the black community.

Prior to 1958, right-to-work supporters in California had not associated themselves with the fight against racial discrimination in employment. Indeed, most of the organizations behind the proposition had opposed state and federal fair employment practices law in the past.[41] Their primary goal, after all, was to promote employer autonomy. The DeMille Foundation was explicit about this. A fact sheet that accompanied its model right-to-work statute responded to the possible objection that "this talk about the right to work opens the door to FEP legislation" with a blunt denial: "Nothing of the kind. The right to work does not mean the right of a particular individual to a particular job. The job is created by the employer, and the right to hire should remain in his hands."[42]

Nevertheless, as Election Day approached, Proposition 18's proponents began to target African American communities, telling black voters that the proposition could be a potent weapon for fighting racially discriminatory practices by unions. In mid-October a pamphlet entitled "The Negro and

His Right to Work" began appearing in the mailboxes of the residents of "predominately Negro neighborhoods" in California.[43] The pamphlet, which was written by the conservative African American public relations specialist Joseph V. Baker, began by recounting the history of African Americans' migration out of the South in search of employment. In the years following World War I, "the Negro . . . knocked on whatever door he could find offering to do whatever a strong man could. Across his path, however, stood the king pins of labor, barring his passage to almost everything of skill."[44] The same thing happened after World War II. In San Francisco he was "shut out of the skilled trades by an airtight labor front." In Los Angeles, the Teamsters treated blacks like "wild animals on the loose" and kept them out of the trucking industry. At best, African Americans were forced into "Jim Crow locals."[45] Such problems continued in the present, Baker asserted. Even while the AFL-CIO throws "the sop of a resolution against discrimination to its truly distinguished leader, A. Philip Randolph, head of the Brotherhood of Sleeping Car Porters . . . its locals have gone blithely leaving the clauses which bar Negroes on sight."[46]

For Baker the solution was clear: passage of the right-to-work propositions in California and Ohio. "Under these provisions," he argued, no union "could tell a Negro in Los Angeles that he may not drive a beer truck if the company's management wanted to show its appreciation of Negro patronage by hiring him. . . . If a Negro qualified as a boilermaker, or a steamfitter, or a plumber, in one of the hundreds of major industries in which these are privileged jobs, kept airtight by union ritual, *no union could tell a Negro that he may not ascend. . . . No union could tell management that it may not promote him because his face is black. And that situation does now prevail!!*"[47] Baker firmly rooted the right-to-work cause within the context of the broader African American struggle for civil rights: "No logical mind *can find an acceptable difference between the Faubuses in Arkansas and the union leaders in California, or Ohio, or New York, or Pennsylvania, who [bar] Negroes from membership.* . . . Against whom should federal troops be sent? Men who bar children from school, or men who bar other men from making a living?"[48]

Baker's pamphlet was a remarkable piece of public relations. It focused on discrimination that would have been particularly salient to African Americans in California: the ongoing dispute between civil rights groups and Teamsters locals in Los Angeles and the history of segregated craft unions in San Francisco.[49] It pricked African Americans' pride in their own industriousness and patriotism (the pamphlet repeatedly refers to African American veterans) while representing white union members as ignorant, foreign, unreconstructed racists ("the worst kind . . . who could not spell their names, or pronounce clearly the streets on which they lived").[50] Union leaders were autocratic royalty (Walter Reuther is "labor's crown prince") exacting "tribute." They were also hypocrites, who demanded that employers hire African Americans in executive positions while they themselves refused to do so.[51]

Baker invoked the heroic work of the NAACP and A. Philip Randolph, cleverly eliding the fact that both were unalterably opposed to Proposition 18. Indeed, it is not possible to read "The Negro and His Right to Work" without getting the impression that the civil rights establishment endorsed the proposition. Similarly, as Les Bailey noted in his panicked memo to the Citizens Committee Against Proposition 18, the pamphlet strongly implied that the proposition actually prohibited discriminatory practices by unions, when, in fact, it did nothing more than allow an employer to hire African American workers even if the union representing his employees discriminated.

Baker's pamphlet was not the only pro-18 argument made by an African American to the African American community. The right-to-work forces were active in California's many black communities. In Southern California, the main spokesman was Claude V. Worrell, head of the Los Angeles NAACP's legal redress committee.[52] In the Bay Area, the proponents were represented by Fred Marcus, the first African American deputy sheriff in Marin County. In May 1958 the *Sun-Reporter*, San Francisco's African American newspaper, ran a four-part debate between Marcus and William Chester, the African American regional director of the International Longshore Workers' Union, on the merits of the proposition.[53]

Marcus's contribution to the debate was nowhere near as polished as Baker's, but it had more substance. A large part of his argument rehashed the non-race-specific points that were part of the pro-18 materials aimed at the general public: right to work promoted freedom of association; it limited the power of corrupt or subversive union bosses who had become too powerful since the passage of the NLRA; it would create jobs and promote economic growth in California. However, Marcus also addressed concerns specific to the African American community: "Last month an expert waiter, Negro, was offered a job at the Mark Hopkins Hotel. He was to begin as soon as the Union gave its blessing. . . . Upon applying for membership in the waiters union, he was told by the business agent that they (the union) had not begun to accept Negro members yet, but that his name would be kept on file. The Local then proceeded to send a white waiter to the Mark Hopkins to fill the position."[54] Such incidents were inevitable in a racist society when too much power was put in the hands of white union bosses, Marcus argued: "Compulsory Unionism gives one man, or a small group of men, the power to reject without explanation other men, thus denying them the right to work and survive merely because he, or they, as individuals, do not like the color of his skin."[55] If unions were to be made genuinely democratic and racially egalitarian, then two things had to happen: unions had to be forced to allow African Americans into the bargaining units they represented, and their leadership had to be made responsive to the members of that bargaining unit. Only a system of labor relations that allowed individuals to decide for themselves whether they would join a union or not would accomplish these ends.[56]

While the arguments made by the African American proponents of Proposition 18 may have been slick and more than a little misleading, they surely stung, for their most basic assertion—that there was widespread racism in the labor movement—was unquestionably true.[57] Despite repeated calls to end racist practices from the AFL-CIO leadership, and despite much progress toward a more racially egalitarian labor movement, many AFL-CIO-affiliated unions still discriminated. As late as 1963, several railroad unions formally prohibited African Americans from joining. Many other unions, particularly in the South, maintained segregated locals or, less frequently, black auxiliary locals. Even more potent a barrier to African Americans in the labor movement than formal discrimination, which was clearly on the decline by the late 1950s, was a variety of informal mechanisms that kept blacks out of a vast number of unionized jobs, particularly in the building trades. Indeed, even as he decried right-to-work laws, the NAACP's labor secretary, Herbert Hill, was unable to restrain himself from scolding the AFL-CIO's leadership for "a tendency to substitute hollow ritual for vigorous action when conflicts develop within local unions involving the rights of Negro workers."[58] If the House of Labor did not clean up its act, Hill wrote, it should not be surprised if African Americans supported anti-union legislation.[59]

Proposition 18's opponents recognized this vulnerability and sought to prevent the right-to-work forces from exploiting it. To do so, they turned, first and foremost, to the NAACP. By the late 1950s the AFL-CIO had developed an intimate working relationship with the NAACP.[60] Indeed, as early as 1947 the NAACP had indicated its strong opposition to right-to-work laws.[61] In the face of the spate of right-to-work campaigns during the 1958 election season, the association threw its weight against these referenda, publishing anti-right-to-work editorials in the *Crisis*, forbidding Proposition 18 endorsements by any of its California branches, and urging all of its members to "join hands with local AFL and CIO unions in fighting against the Right-to-Work movement."[62] That movement, the NAACP asserted, was no friend of African American workers. To the contrary, the main effect of the passage of such laws was to drive down wages, which would have a disproportionate impact on black workers. By keeping labor unions strong and joining them, the NAACP argued, African Americans could address such wage disparities.[63]

The NAACP also helped the anti-18 forces within the labor movement to reach out to the African American community. Both groups sent speakers into black neighborhoods, advertised in black newspapers and on radio stations that catered to a black audience, and addressed (usually somewhat obliquely in the case of union leaders) issues of racial discrimination when presenting arguments against the proposition.[64] The specifics of the strategy that they used are nicely illustrated by the materials both groups distributed.

When addressing the African American community, Proposition 18's opponents took a page from the playbook of the proposition's supporters. They attempted to place the campaign against the proposition in the context of the civil rights movement, though, obviously, their perspective was reversed: the proponents of right-to-work were the allies of the southern segregationists, not their enemies. In making this argument, opponents were aided by the fact that right-to-work laws were prevalent in the South. Indeed, in August 1958, Franklin Williams, the director of the NAACP's West Coast Regional Office, wrote to the branch presidents throughout the South, asking them for information about the effect of right-to-work laws on African Americans in their state.[65] Similarly, the counsel of the NAACP's Washington Bureau wrote to Hill, inquiring if he knew of links between the supporters of right-to-work legislation and "white supremacist groups."[66]

These inquiries resulted in information that quickly made its way into two pamphlets published by the NAACP and distributed in California. "Keep Mississippi out of California!" one pamphlet announced above an illustration of a kneeling man ("California Worker"), lash marks on his back, prostrate before his tormentor, a sinister fellow wielding a swastika-tipped whip, the cord of which spelled out the words "Right to Work."[67] Sprinkled through the illustration were the names of southern right-to-work states—"Tennessee, Georgia, Alabama, Texas, Virginia, Florida, Carolina, Arkansas." In addition to linking the right-to-work movement with the forces of southern racism, the pamphlet attempted to rebut the idea that Proposition 18 would prevent employment discrimination. It included a "Scorecard" and a "Tally Sheet" demonstrating that the supporters of the right-to-work law were the same organizations that opposed fair employment practices legislation. Finally, while the pamphlet followed the more general strategy of equating right-to-work laws with low wages, the NAACP added language that was designed to motivate African Americans in particular. Only by opposing Proposition 18 could Californians "Fight Sharecropper Wages" that southern business interests and other "Dixie-minded businessmen" were trying to foist on the state.

The NAACP's other pamphlet was even more explicit about the connection between right-to-work advocates and southern, racist extremism.[68] "THIS Happened in a RIGHT-TO-WORK State," the pamphlet read over a photograph of two police officers manhandling Martin Luther King, Jr. in Montgomery. "It Could Happen Here! But YOUR Vote AGAINST Proposition 18 Can Keep Bigotry and Tyranny from California." The pamphlet contained quotes from African American leaders (including King, Randolph, NAACP executive director Roy Wilkins, Lester Granger of the Urban League, and J. H. Jackson of the National Baptist Convention) decrying the right-to-work movement. Indeed, these seem to have been the quotes that the California Labor Federation solicited in response to Les Bailey's September memo.[69]

On the inside of the pamphlet was a photograph of federal troops escorting African American students into Little Rock High School. The caption reinforced the link between massive resistance and the right to work: "Don't Bring Little Rock's Bigotry and Shame to California. 'Right-to-Work' Promoters Are the Same People Opposing School Desegregation in Southern States." The pamphlet then listed, in some detail, "Seven Reasons Why Every Negro Citizen Should Vote Against Proposition 18." These echoed the arguments in the NAACP's resolution: right-to-work laws depressed wages in the states where they had been enacted, and African Americans bore the brunt of this depression. Right-to-work laws did not prohibit racial discrimination. In fact, they "worsen the lot" of black employees, by putting them at the mercy of their employer. Strong unions and collective bargaining, on the other hand, brought higher wages, fair hours, and job security.

The NAACP was not the only organization that designed literature especially for the African American community. The California Labor Federation distributed a two-sided broadsheet.[70] One side printed the text of the NAACP's anti-right-to-work resolution and a quote opposing Proposition 18 from the Urban League. The other side began with a banner headline: "Read What Southern Racists Think About 'Right to Work Laws!'" What followed was an edited reproduction of a letter on the stationery of an organization known as the Arkansas Free Enterprise Association addressed to a certain Walter McLogan of Los Angeles from the association's executive director, J. B. Withee: "The Executive Secretary of the Citizens Council here in Little Rock, gave me your letter regarding Negroes securing jobs in Arkansas, etc. . . . [Right-to-work] laws have been adopted for many years and have been successful in creating a good labor climate, as well as bringing into the State a host of new industries and businesses." After omitting two paragraphs, the Labor Federation reproduced the rest of the letter, which veered from the merely mercenary to the barely coherent and profoundly disturbed:

> This race-mixing, as you know, is one of the Nation's big problems, because of the decision of the Supreme Court in integrating public schools and we might say that your fellow citizen, Earl Warren, was the main instigator and now he is attending the Jewish College in New York City, learning the Talmad [sic] and what it has to say about it.
>
> I hope you will be able to get back of Senator Knowland in connection with your Right-to-Work program. It is our only hope at the moment. Also you might check your own laws in California and see if you have an active FEPC law. If you have one, this makes trouble and every employer [sic]. Let me say also, that the new Civil Rights Law recently passed in Congress by a big majority with a big budget and a well organized Gestapo, will see to it that the races will be mixed, not only in the South, but also in the North.

It is unclear how the letter came into the possession of the federation. Indeed, it was so perfect for their campaign that one might be inclined to believe that the anti-18 forces made it up. It touches every possible nerve of a progressive Californian, whether black or white, by linking the right-to-work movement to the worst excesses of southern extremism: absurd, Bilboesque miscegenation fears; paranoid opposition to FEPC (Fair Employment Practice Commission) legislation; Citizens Councils; barely literate anti-Semitism; a bizarre attack on Earl Warren. However, the paragraphs that the federation edited out before distributing it in the African American community suggest that the letter was indeed authentic, for they contain information that Proposition 18's opponents most certainly wished to keep out of the consciousness of California's African American voters. Withee wanted McLogan to know that "no unions in Arkansas have Negroes," and that "the members of organized labor who are affiliated with the AFL-CIO are not anxious for Negroes to be in the union at all," and that "Negroes . . . receive common labor pay, while members of organized labor unions receive all the way from $2 to $3 per hour."[71]

The facts that the California Labor Federation had to edit out of Withee's letter illustrate the problem that the anti-18 forces encountered whenever they sought African American votes for a pro-union position. It was difficult to emphasize the various ways in which African Americans benefitted from the labor movement without raising in the minds of black voters how they were being held back by the self-same movement. Consequently, it was not surprising that when the African American press editorialized against Proposition 18, it did so either in a lukewarm fashion or with some reservations. The African American newspaper in Los Angeles, the *Sentinel*, recommended voting against 18, but only as part of an editorial endorsing Pat Brown for governor.[72] San Francisco's black-owned newspaper, the *Sun-Reporter*, was much more vociferous in its condemnation of Proposition 18. A week before the election it published a "special supplement" in conjunction with the racially progressive longshore workers union, with a front page editorial attacking the proposition.[73] The issue was filled with news stories about African American leaders who opposed the right-to-work movement and progressive unions that supported equal employment opportunity. Nonetheless, Carlton Goodlett, the *Sun-Reporter*'s owner and editor, had to temper his endorsement: "We do not want to give the impression that there are not unsolved problems for Negro workers within unions in California. Although there are tens and tens of thousands of Negro Workers in trade unions—there are still a number of lily-white unions or unions where the number of our people are still too few for this year of 1958."[74]

Earlier in the year, Goodlett had been less circumspect. Unions, he wrote, must stop taking the votes of African Americans for granted: "It is going to be very difficult to convince a Negro that he should vote against 'right-to-work' legislation if he has . . . [been] turned down by a union because of his race."[75] The fact that Proposition 18 was causing much discussion in the black community indicated that "the day when minority groups will accept the blank checks of a labor movement permeated with racial bigotry, it seems, has come to an end." Like Herbert Hill, Goodlett concluded with a threat: "Time is running out for leaders in the labor movement to bestir themselves and clean house before the voting begins."[76]

Goodlett's ambivalence was reflected elsewhere in the African American community in the weeks leading up to election day. The Citizens Committee Against Proposition 18 reported receiving an unenthusiastic reception at an NAACP meeting in Berkeley at the end of August.[77] It also noted that the Richmond NAACP president was "strongly Republican" and "might need some working on . . . re: policy position on Right-to Work."[78] Fred Marcus's position within the San Francisco NAACP branch created dissension there, and Claude Worrell's pro-18 stance resulted in his removal as the head of the Los Angeles branch's legal redress committee.[79] Similarly, the National Office had to scold its San Diego branch when its officers suggested having a debate on the right-to-work issue. "NAACP branches," Wilkins wrote, rather patronizingly, "do not customarily sponsor debates on a question on which the NAACP has adopted a policy. For example, we are opposed to racial segregation. We would not stage a debate to hear both sides of the segregation question."[80]

George Beavers, an African American insurance executive and fundraiser for the NAACP in California, stated his objections privately to his friend Wilkins.[81] The association's campaign against Proposition 18 had veered dangerously close to partisan politics. Beavers enclosed with his letter a copy of the anti-18 pamphlet featuring the photograph of Martin Luther King, Jr. being arrested in Montgomery, which he characterized as "an example of gross misuse of N.A.A.C.P. causes and racial incidents to influence action in connection with the so-called 'Right-to-Work' measure." The use of such tactics, Beavers believed, demeaned the fight for integration by focusing the association's attention on other issues. It also risked alienating business interests, whose support the NAACP needed. Taking sides in such a fight was not "sound" when "it is no secret that both groups are guilty of racial discrimination." As proof of this fact, Beavers noted that "this one leaflet caused me to lose, at least for the present, two life memberships."

Indeed, Wilkins was aware that the association paid a price for its attack on right-to-work measures. In the aftermath of the 1958 election, Wilkins wrote to James McDevitt, the director of the AFL-CIO's Committee on Political Education, requesting its financial help for voter registration drives in African American communities. The request was stated as a subtle quid pro quo. Wilkins pointed out that the NAACP's support of labor had not been without costs: "In both California and Ohio certain elements of the Negro population were vigorous in their denunciation of the NAACP for taking such a stand, holding that the issue was outside the area of civil rights."[82]

Ultimately, the dissatisfaction with the NAACP's stand on Proposition 18 by African American elites like Beavers, Worrell, and Marcus made little difference to the outcome of the election. African Americans voted against the proposition in overwhelming numbers. A Harris poll conducted prior to the election revealed that only one in ten African Americans supported the proposition.[83] Similarly, voting results from predominantly African American precincts (e.g., the Western Addition in San Francisco and South Central Los Angeles) showed that black voters opposed the proposition by significantly larger margins than the population at large.[84] They were willing, for the time being, to put aside their reservations about racially discriminatory labor unions and join with workers of all races to support the union shop.

The Saturday after Election Day, the *Sun-Reporter* editorialized about the role African Americans played in Proposition 18's defeat. The editorial was a threat, not a celebration. Black support for the campaign against the proposition was not a "tribute to labor by Negro voters for . . . services rendered." Instead, this support placed "squarely upon the shoulders of labor, the responsibility of cleaning up its own house." The overwhelming vote against Proposition 18 by African Americans "should warn organized labor that cooperation is a two-way street, and that Negroes expect labor to really give every American 'The Right To Work' by outlawing Jim Crowism in the trade union movement in the State of California."[85] Even in victory, tensions within the African American–labor alliance were obvious.

Indeed, the tension was vital to the California Right's post-1964 reinvigoration. Although the outcome of the 1958 referendum appeared to suggest that accommodating labor, rather than attacking it, was the path to electoral success, this was not the one that the Republican Party, either in California or nationally, would take in the decades that followed. Despite the electoral victories in 1958, both in Ohio and California as well as in other states, the cleavages in the alliance between the labor movement and the African American community proved helpful to the Republican Party as it reconstituted itself in a new, hard right guise. Over the next decade, the promise of the *Sun-Reporter's* version of "the right to work"—fair employment opportunity—was not fulfilled by the labor movement (or by liberalism in general), and many African Americans would run out of patience.[86] "Mr. Divide" and "Mr. Conquer" would be there to exploit these divisions. The Right would use racial antagonism once again, this time to get white votes rather than black ones, and the events of 1958 would come to look different in retrospect than they did at the time. They did not, in fact, signal the weakness of the conservative wing of the Republican Party. Instead, these events generated fissures in the fragile alliance between African Americans and the labor movement—fissures that the Right would learn to exploit.

Chapter 8

Whose Rights? Litigating the Right to Work, 1940–1980

Sophia Z. Lee

"We're Working to Protect Human and Civil Rights for America's Wage Earners," the 1972 pamphlet read. Inside, it presented the "Landmark Cases" a legal organization with the initials LDF was pursuing in the courts. Under the heading titled "Employment Discrimination," the pamphlet listed cases on behalf of "Mexican-American grapeworkers" and "a Black Philadelphia movie projectionist." Given the organization's name, plaintiffs, mission, and presentation of its cases, one might expect that this pamphlet was put out by the leading civil rights litigators, the NAACP Legal Defense Fund, Inc., commonly known as LDF. It was not. Instead, the pamphlet was the work of the National Right to Work Committee's Legal Defense Foundation, Inc. (NRWLDF), an organization committed to ending "compulsory" unionization. The confusion, however, was intentional.[1]

Most historians associate American postwar conservatism with more or less blatant racism. Scholars have described how conservatives used everything from racially coded "law and order" campaigns to racially explicit rousting to build the New Right coalition. Race, many argue, played a particularly potent role in conservatives' efforts to court white working-class voters. Recently, however, historians have questioned this consensus, arguing that race, although not irrelevant to conservatives' postwar mobilization, was less central than previously thought. These historians emphasize the laissez-faire, anti–New Deal politics that fed the rising Right, particularly outside the South. The history of right-to-work litigation adds a further twist to the evolving understanding of postwar conservatism, by reinserting race into the history of pro-business conservatism, albeit in a quite different role than it plays in the traditional narrative of race and postwar conservative politics. The national right-to-work movement sought to align itself with, rather than mobilize against, the civil rights movement.[2]

As early as the 1940s, right-to-work supporters used constitutional litigation to advance their cause. Beginning in the 1960s, the National Right to Work Committee (NRWC) and later the NRWLDF used this litigation to strategically link their right-to-work agenda to the black freedom struggle. Awkward at first, during the 1970s, these anti–New Deal conservatives made increasingly savvy use of black workers' support as they styled themselves champions of civil rights. In doing so, NRWC and NRWLDF altered the racial politics of New Right conservatism.

Litigation and the Formation of a Right-to-Work Movement

Alarmed by the rapid midcentury growth in union power, an increasingly well-coordinated coalition mobilized to fight the "union bosses" and "big labor." Their campaigns for state "right-to-work" laws are well known. Less known is that these legislative efforts were accompanied by increasingly coordinated litigation that sought a constitutional bar against having to join or support a union as a condition of employment.

During the 1930s and 1940s, union density, reach, and power grew dramatically. In the 1930s the nation's labor laws for the first time guaranteed workers a right to organize, granted unions that demonstrated sufficient employee support the power to bargain on behalf of all workers in a designated unit, and required employers to recognize and bargain in good faith with these exclusive bargaining representatives. The American Federation of Labor (AFL) traditionally organized only craft workers. A breakaway group, the Congress of Industrial Organizations (CIO), used the new labor laws, along with vigorous organizing campaigns, to unionize a much wider swath of industrial workers. In addition, through a growing array of employer-union agreements, unions vastly expanded their membership and their base of financial support. Closed-shop agreements, long favored by AFL unions, required employers to hire only union members. In a union shop, championed by the CIO unions, every new employee had to join the union soon after starting work. Finally, under an agency-shop agreement, workers did not have to join the union, but had to pay the union fees. As a result of these labor law protections, aggressive organizing drives, and membership- and fee-building agreements, about a third of American workers belonged to a union by the 1950s.[3]

No sooner had workers won the right to organize, however, than an assortment of businessmen, academics, management-side lawyers, free-market idealists, anti-union workers, and grassroots supporters, some of them longtime opponents of the closed shop, challenged unions' newfound power. They adopted the slogan "right to work" and focused their energies on banning "compulsory unionism": any employer-union agreement that required workers to join or support a union. Some opposed unions for ideological reasons, viewing them as a monopoly power and socialistic threat, more un-American than the business cartels fought by earlier generations of Progressives. Others were businessmen concerned with their bottom line and protecting their right to manage. Still others were former trade unionists who opposed union shops and their former unions.[4]

Many right-to-work supporters would say that they were not anti-union, just opposed to "compulsory" unions. Friedrich A. Hayek, one of the intellectual godfathers of the right-to-work movement, insisted that he challenged "neither the right of voluntary agreement between workers nor even their right to withhold their services in concert." Instead, he opposed "the coercion which unions have been permitted to exercise . . . [against] fellow workers." Labor supporters countered that that this was an untenable line to draw. Unions needed union- and agency-shop agreements to address free riders: those workers who benefited from the terms unions won on their behalf but saw no need to support the unions' efforts. Open shops would bankrupt unions and render them powerless. Right-to-work supporters spent quite a bit of ink challenging this free rider argument, pointing out, for instance, that the unions at General Motors and on the railroads were powerful long before they won union-shop agreements.[5]

Right-to-work advocates' campaigns to pass laws and amend constitutions to require that no one be denied a job based on union membership (or lack thereof) accelerated during the 1940s. In 1941, they proposed amending the United States Constitution to include a "right-to-work" provision. They followed up by seeking similar state-level statutes and constitutional amendments. By 1947 right-to-work advocates had secured laws in fourteen states. They were most successful in the South and West, where unions were weak. That year they also achieved a major victory in Congress. Republicans had swept the 1946 midterm elections. The increase in Republicans' numbers helped produce a bipartisan coalition that, in 1947, garnered enough votes to amend the Wagner Act, the labor law that governed most workplaces.

In a resounding defeat for labor, Congress passed the amendments despite unions' cries that Congress was enacting a "slave labor law," and over President Harry Truman's dramatic veto. Right-to-work advocates, on the other hand, had much to celebrate: even if they did not secure open shops, the amendments to the Wagner Act went a long way toward this goal, barring closed shops, limiting enforcement of union-shop agreements, and allowing states to prohibit union shops. The legislative battle lines between labor and right-to-work activists had been drawn; thereafter their state and federal campaigns would center on the viability and legitimacy of union security provisions, primarily union and agency shops.[6]

While some right-to-work advocates were seeking legislative victories, others went to court, challenging mandatory union activity under existing laws. There was nothing new about litigating against unions. National employer-funded groups had been using tort law to challenge closed shops since the early twentieth century. But the post–New Deal generation added something new: reflecting a growing rights consciousness, they brought their claims under the United States Constitution.[7]

In 1944, Cecil B. DeMille, a famous movie producer and radio personality, sued his union, the Los Angeles local of the American Federation of Radio Artists. The union had levied a fee upon its members to fund its opposition to California's right-to-work ballot initiative. DeMille refused to pay and his union suspended him. DeMille argued that the union violated his First and Fifth Amendment rights. DeMille *supported* the right-to-work initiative. He argued that he should not have to give his union money to *oppose* it. DeMille also argued that his union, by suspending him, was violating his constitutional right to work. The California courts dismissed DeMille's claim, easily finding that DeMille, like a member of any other association or club, was free to withdraw from membership, but was obligated to respect the majority will of his union so long as he remained a member.[8]

Right-to-work advocates were soon organizing to secure the constitutional win that had eluded DeMille. In 1951, Congress amended the Railway Labor Act (RLA), the federal labor law that covered the railroad and airline industries, to allow unions to negotiate union-shop agreements with the railroads.[9] Traditionally, the railroad unions were among the most exclusive. Some railroad workers opposed the union-shop agreements that soon prevailed, either because they opposed unionization or worried that the new regime would threaten railroad unions' old, exclusive membership policies. These outraged workers helped to form the National Committee for Union Shop Abolition. The group adopted the credo, "the right to earn a living, with or without benefit of union membership is an inherent Constitutional right of every citizen of the United States." The group's primary goal was to finance litigation that could get the Supreme Court to "once and for all declare the Union Shop to be in conflict with the Bill of Rights and therefore un-Constitutional."[10]

In the mid-1950s, anti-union-shop railroad workers achieved victory in the courts. The Union Pacific Railroad Company had signed union-shop agreements with a number of the unions that bargained on its employees' behalf. Railroad workers who objected to being required to join a union sued their employer and its unions, claiming that the RLA amendments were unconstitutional. In 1955, the Nebraska Supreme Court held in favor of the railroad workers, finding that the RLA amendments violated workers' First Amendment freedom of association and Fifth Amendment right to work.[11] Right-to-work litigators had won the constitutional victory that had eluded DeMille.

As the Nebraska case wound its way toward the United States Supreme Court, a new, more powerful, right-to-work organization promised to extend this state-level victory into a national open-shop mandate. In 1955, both sides of the right-to-work struggle consolidated. The two major labor organizations joined forces to form the AFL-CIO, while right-to-work advocates came together to form the National Right to Work Committee. Among NRWC's goals was to "help make the public aware of the fundamental rights which are violated by compulsory unionism."[12]

NRWC got off to a shaky start. Right-to-work advocates continued to win state right-to-work laws in the early 1950s. After the AFL-CIO formed in 1955, however, labor developed a national strategy and more effective state-level organizations to vigorously oppose state right-to-work campaigns. The newly united labor and right-to-work forces faced off in the 1958 elections. NRWC joined business groups like the National Association of Manufacturers and Chamber of Commerce to inject the right to work into state and national elections.[13]

Labor launched a counteroffensive. The AFL-CIO's Executive Council convened a Subcommittee on Right-to-Work Laws. Over the summer and into the fall, the AFL-CIO distributed eight million pamphlets. It also produced two movies that were shown at over two thousand civic meetings and were aired by state and local television stations. Twelve television spots created by the AFL-CIO aired twenty-six hundred times in California alone. The AFL-CIO also called on its ally, the NAACP. The NAACP was a long-time supporter of union security agreements and opponent of right-to-work efforts. In 1947, when Congress was considering amending the Wagner Act, the NAACP defended closed and union shops, arguing that they not only strengthened labor generally but also benefited African American workers in particular. "It is a delusive misstatement of fact," the NAACP warned Congress, "to say that the elimination of the closed shop will cut down discrimination against any minority." In 1958, the NAACP again came to the AFL-CIO's aid, mobilizing black voters who provided decisive votes in a number of state right-to-work campaigns. In a blow to right-to-work advocates, labor and its civil rights allies defeated all but one state right-to-work law and Democrats gained many congressional seats.[14]

The widespread losses energized, rather than crushed, the fledgling NRWC. In its first years of existence, NRWC developed an effective media campaign that countered the right-to-work movement's elite image by featuring the support of disgruntled union members such as the railway workers that founded the Committee for Union Shop Abolition. This publicity campaign was not enough to win elections in 1958, but it had the labor movement worried. The 1958 fight also gave NRWC a tireless and battle-tested leader. Reed Larson's zeal and pugnaciousness matched his wiry frame, if not his Kansan origins and training in electrical engineering. Larson found politics and the right-to-work cause as a state and national leader of the Junior Chamber of Commerce. He was soon directing Kansans for

Right to Work. Under Larson, the Kansas group pioneered an exceptional, and exceptionally successful, strategy involving intensive grassroots mobilization, prolific advertising, and outreach to Democrats as well as Republicans. In 1958, as right-to-work laws met defeat elsewhere, Larson secured a singular victory in Kansas. Larson took the lead at NRWC in 1959, bringing with him the determination and strategic savvy that led to his Kansas success.[15]

If Larson brought organizational skills and political vision to NRWC, the organization also benefited from a different sort of tactician. Edward A. Keller was a Catholic priest and professor of economics at the University of Notre Dame who joined the right-to-work fight out of religious as much as worldly conviction. During the 1950s, Keller participated in vigorous debates among Catholics regarding the theological merits of unions and published works defending the right to work according to ecclesiastic and natural law. Keller was also an apostle of the right-to-work cause to non-Catholics, hewing his arguments from the United States Constitution, not only canon law. Indeed, Barry Goldwater, one of the most visible right-to-work proponents in the Senate, credited Keller with helping him formulate his right-to-work position. Keller became a legal hub in the right-to-work network, passing briefs and court opinions among businesses such as the Santa Fe Railway and Ford Motor Company. He was also a board member of NRWC. With a broader right-to-work base than the Committee for Union Shop Abolition, a vigorous advocate at its helm, and one of the foremost right-to-work legal theorists on its board, NRWC provided a new means to both coordinate and support right-to-work litigation.[16]

In the wake of their 1958 losses, right-to-work advocates' state legislative campaigns stalled, but their legal advocacy gained traction. NRWC took notice, assigning litigation an increasingly prominent place on its agenda. By 1960, NRWC lawyers had participated in two cases before the United States Supreme Court, including defending the railroad workers' Nebraska win. The Supreme Court did not declare the RLA union-shop amendments unconstitutional, as the right-to-work litigants argued and the Nebraska court had found. Instead, the Court interpreted the RLA to require unions to refund to dissenting workers any dues that the unions used for political speech.[17] Right-to-work advocates had not won the constitutional victory they had hoped for. Nonetheless, this statutory means to challenge payments workers made to unions was hardly a loss. Equally heartening to right-to-work advocates, for the first time the Supreme

Court adopted their pejorative term for the union shop, "compulsory unionism."[18]

Encouraged by the Supreme Court's decision, NRWC deepened its commitment to litigation. In 1962, litigation was already a significant part of NRWC's work. The organization spent $35,000 (a little less than 10 percent of its budget) on reviewing possible test cases, arranging for counsel, assisting local attorneys, and paying legal fees.[19] During the 1960s, litigation's appeal grew. These were fallow years for right-to-work legislative campaigns. Only Wyoming passed a right-to-work statute during the 1960s while an Oklahoma ballot initiative failed and Indiana repealed its right-to-work law. At the national level, right-to-work advocates helped thwart labor's efforts to end the federal ban on closed shops. But NRWC strategists did not think it likely that the organization would achieve its own legislative agenda: a national right-to-work law. They viewed both Republicans and Democrats in Congress as beholden to labor. As a result, they reasoned that the "best hope for outlawing compulsory unionism in America must lie with [the] courts."[20] The group's Washington counsel, John Kilcullen, thought right-to-work plaintiffs' chances of success had improved since the Court decided the first RLA cases. The Supreme Court, he noted, had since recognized an increasing array of individual rights. Kilcullen found it "highly probable that if the compulsory unionism question were again presented to the Supreme Court the Court would be virtually compelled to squarely face the constitutional issues presented."[21] The time seemed ripe for NRWC to litigate.

These political realities and doctrinal opportunities prompted NRWC to create a new institutional home from which to develop its litigation campaign. In the late 1960s, NRWC formed a separate nonprofit corporation to handle right-to-work litigation—what it eventually named the National Right to Work Legal Defense Foundation. According to its charter, NRWLDF would help "workers who are suffering legal injustice as a result of employment discrimination under compulsory union membership arrangements" and protect their "rights guaranteed to them under the Constitution and laws of the United States."[22]

NRWLDF began with a bare-bones leadership that mirrored NRWC's mix of business, activist, and conservative academic support. Louis E. Weiss, president of Midland Industries in Wichita, Kansas, chaired the new foundation. Dr. Ernest Wilkinson, president of Brigham Young University, was its president. Reed Larson, who also headed NRWC, became NRWLDF's executive vice president. Legal theorist Edward Keller joined its board and Edith Hakola, who had been a professor at Delaware Law School, was its first legal director.[23]

During the next ten years, NRWLDF grew rapidly. After receiving tax-exempt status in 1969, it began fund-raising in earnest, bringing in over $100,000 in its first campaign. By 1971, nearly three hundred corporations had pledged their support and NRWLDF had an "Advisory Council of Business Leaders." NRWLDF started off the 1970s with a score of cases and five staff members. By 1975, it was handling sixty-five cases, its staff had nearly doubled, and it had a network of one hundred cooperating attorneys dedicated to the right-to-work cause. In 1979, NRWLDF's ten-year anniversary, it dedicated a new building, wrote an institutional history, and presided over a growing docket of cases—one that would include over three hundred pending actions by the mid-1980s. Litigation had become a key component of the right-to-work movement.[24]

Creating a Constitutional Right to Work

From the 1940s through the 1980s, right-to-work litigators maintained a focused campaign to have union security agreements declared unconstitutional. This goal was set as early as DeMille's lawsuit in the 1940s, and continued into the 1950s with the National Committee for Union Shop Abolition. NRWC carried on this constitutional campaign in the 1960s, seeking and funding cases to this end; later, it created NRWLDF in order to more effectively make its constitutional attack on the "outmoded concept of compulsory unionism."[25]

In pursuing its claims, NRWLDF treated each win as a step toward reaching its ultimate goal, "affirmation by the courts that compulsory unionism violates the freedom to pursue the occupation of his choice of every American working person." Reed Larson argued that NRWLDF's success in a case on behalf of public school teachers augured well for the open-shop rights of *all* workers. Larson was certain that "a succession of favorable rulings could place the whole compulsion-oriented federal labor policy on very shaky Constitutional ground."[26]

Larson's enthusiasm glossed over two significant problems NRWLDF faced in getting courts to recognize its constitutional claims. Right-to-work advocates who wanted to challenge the actions of unions and employers faced a high constitutional hurdle: the "state action doctrine." Right-to-work advocates' constitutional claims primarily relied on the First, Fifth, and Fourteenth Amendments. When they began bringing their claims in the mid-twentieth century, courts limited the reach of all three amendments to actions taken by the state and its agents. This state action doctrine drew a strict line between public and private acts, restricting the former and protecting the latter from constitutional attack. Traditionally, the Supreme Court deemed economic transactions, including decisions about whom to sell to and whom to hire, quintessentially private. Likewise, clubs and other associations were considered private and outside the Constitution's reach. Right-to-work litigators needed to find a way to bring seemingly private union- or agency-shop agreements within the ambit of state action. If they could not link these agreements to the state, their clients would have no constitutional rights to assert.[27]

By the 1950s, waves of Progressive Era and New Deal regulation threatened to change how the state action doctrine differentiated between public and private action, bolstering right-to-work advocates' claims. In particular, the Wagner Act and the RLA guaranteed workers' right to organize. These laws empowered federal labor boards to oversee many aspects of unionization from organizing campaigns to the negotiation of workplace contracts. Much to right-to-work advocates' chagrin, these laws permitted union- and agency-shop agreements. Much to their benefit, however, these laws also provided them a means to argue that these agreements now involved state action. Congress had made these agreements attributable to it, right-to-work advocates argued, by empowering unions, preempting state right-to-work laws, or permitting these agreements. Thereby, right-to-work litigators contended, the government triggered workers' First, Fifth, and Fourteenth Amendment rights.[28]

Right-to-work advocates also had to fight to shore up their claim that their clients had a constitutionally protected right to work free from government interference. This kind of substantive due process claim had its heyday in the decades preceding the New Deal. Most famously, courts struck down Progressive Era labor laws because these workplace regulations violated workers' rights under the Fifth and Fourteenth Amendments' due process clauses. The Supreme Court's embrace of New Deal legislation in the late 1930s threw this line of cases into doubt, making it difficult for right-to-work litigators to defend their substantive due process claims.[29]

Right-to-work advocates' constitutional claims stood in uneasy and conflicting relationship to the New Deal. On the one hand, their claims attacked the legitimacy of New Deal labor laws and were weakened by the New Deal Court's repudiation of substantive due process. On the other hand, the New Deal bolstered their claims by helping them stretch the state action doctrine to reach employers and unions. This broadened notion of state action, in turn, expanded the sphere of right to work, allowing them to assert their substantive due process claims, ones the New Deal had eroded but not extinguished, against traditionally private union and employer defendants.

Midcentury shifts in the trade union movement and workers' politics also shaped the course of right-to-work litigation. Unions were still powerful in the Northeast and Midwest where their membership continued to grow, as it did in parts of the South and Southwest. Still, organized labor was embattled. A coalition of Republicans and southern Democrats sought to chip away, even repeal, the New Deal labor laws. Some workers opposed all unions, while others found many of the new unions distastefully bureaucratic and undemocratic. Right-to-work litigators targeted industries where they could find workers who were opposed to unionization or where labor was particularly strong. Along the way, they gained support from gathering grassroots conservatism.

In the 1950s, right-to-work cases were brought primarily on behalf of the railroad workers whose opposition to the RLA's union-shop amendments had inspired them to form first the National Committee for Union Shop Abolition and later NRWC. By the 1960s, the decades-long growth of conservatism in the Sunbelt had created a new source of litigants: upwardly mobile defense-industry workers. NRWC lawyers took industry giant McDonnell Douglas and the nationally prominent UAW to court on their behalf, challenging agency-shop agreements at plants in Southern California and Oklahoma. The lead plaintiff in the California case, George Seay, typified conservative defense-industry workers' support for the right-to-work movement. Seay was an aerospace worker and a former member of the Hod Carriers Union who was immersed in conservative politics and the right-to-work cause. He was a leader of the California Southern Baptist Convention, whose churches were crucial nodes in Southern California's growing grassroots conservative network. Seay also led his plant's Employees Right-to-Work Committee in its fight against the agency shop and went on to help lead NRWC and the California Right to Work Committee.[30]

Right-to-work litigators also focused on the most dynamic sectors of the labor movement. Public employee unions flourished in the 1960s and 1970s. In 1969, NRWLDF sued on behalf of school teachers in Detroit. Seven years later, the Supreme Court found meritorious its argument that the Constitution prohibited unions from using public employees' fees for political expenses that were unrelated to unions' duties as exclusive bargaining representatives. During the 1970s, NRWLDF and its network of attorneys represented a range of public sector workers, including teachers, professors, postal employees, and civil servants, who claimed that mandatory union dues violated their constitutional rights. NRWLDF lawyers also turned their attention to California's farmworkers. In the 1960s and 1970s, Chicano and Filipino labor leaders, most famously Cesar Chavez, led an astonishingly successful organizing campaign, which included nationwide boycotts of farm produce. NRWLDF responded by targeting Cesar Chavez and the farmworkers' union he organized. Farmworkers were excluded from the federal labor laws, but in 1975, California created a state labor board to regulate this union drive. In lawsuits brought both before and after the state board was created, NRWLDF lawyers challenged the constitutionality of agency-shop agreements between the United Farm Workers' and growers.[31]

In the early 1970s, NRWLDF could proudly announce that it was "working in three separate areas of attack on the constitutionality of compulsory unionism": First, it was targeting private industry through cases like George Seay's. Second, it was challenging mandatory union membership and dues for public workers through cases like the Detroit teachers'. Third, it was opposing the agency shop for agricultural workers through its suit against Chavez and the farmworkers' union. NRWLDF hoped that these cases would establish "the right of citizens to earn a living without paying money to a union."[32]

Adopting a Civil Rights Mantle

In the 1950s and 1960s, as litigation became an increasingly prominent part of the right-to-work movement, these activists looked to the civil rights movement for litigation strategy and constitutional theories. By the late 1960s, however, they also began to link right to work's substantive goals with African Americans' freedom struggle.

In the 1950s, right-to-work litigators relied on civil rights precedents. Beginning in the 1930s, civil rights litigators used the nation's labor laws to establish black workers' constitutional right to join unions and access decent jobs. These attorneys argued that government regulation of workplace organizing made unions' and employers' racially exclusive practices a matter of state, not merely private, action. This campaign met with mixed results. In 1944, the Supreme Court ruled that unions must represent the interests of black workers in their bargaining units, known as a union's "duty of fair representation." But the Court was unclear whether the labor laws had created sufficient state involvement to make the Constitution the source for this duty. The Court expanded unions' duty of fair representation over subsequent years, but it continued to equivocate as to whether state action, and thus the Constitution, was its source.[33]

Right-to-work litigators took up this duty in their first cases, arguing that it had constitutional roots and should reach their right-to-work claims. In 1956, J. C. Gibson, the president and general counsel for the Santa Fe Railway Company and a member of Edward Keller's network of right-to-work lawyers, gave a speech at an American Bar Association meeting. Gibson had recently supported his workers' successful effort to enjoin several unions from striking to win a union-shop agreement. He now told his audience of labor lawyers that union-shop agreements involved state, not private, action. Gibson relied on the same post–New Deal constitutional logic, and race-based precedents, as civil rights attorneys. Unions wielded a "great complex of powers placed in their hands by modern labor law"; to call these agreements "purely private action [would be] to substitute fiction for reality," Gibson argued.[34]

These early right-to-work litigators did not suggest that they were bringing civil rights claims. Instead, they urged that their plaintiffs' rights were as important as African Americans' equality rights. In 1956, the dean of Duke Law School, J. A. McClain Jr., proclaimed that the right to work had traditionally been "an individual liberty of the highest order."[35] He noted that the Court's recent *Brown v. Board of Education* decision struck down public school segregation statutes despite states' arguments that these laws promoted the general welfare. Yet two years later, the dean observed, the Supreme Court upheld the RLA's union-shop provisions because Congress determined that these provisions advanced the public interest. In other words, the Constitution trumped public interest arguments in *Brown* but not in the RLA cases. In McClain's estimation, if African Americans' claim to equal treatment had defeated arguments about the general welfare in *Brown*, then right-to-work claims should defeat Congress's public interest defense of the RLA amendments.[36] Thus, right-to-work litigators relied on civil rights precedents to argue that right-to-work claims were superior to the general welfare, just like the equality claims of black Americans.

In the 1950s and early 1960s the analogy that right-to-work advocates drew between their cause and civil rights stopped at legal arguments, however. In nonlegal venues, right-to-work advocates described themselves not as civil rights warriors, but as adherents of a Cold War conservatism dedicated to god, country, and anti-Communism. In 1956, Edward Keller published his right-to-work treatise, *The Case for Right-to-Work Laws: A Defense of Voluntary Unionism*. Although Keller's book surveyed the extant right-to-work constitutional arguments, in this and other writing, he also based his case against mandatory unionization on Catholic teachings and natural law. In particular, Keller argued that union shops impermissibly required Catholic workers to belong to "immoral unions, such as communist, socialist, racketeer or mobster-controlled unions." Keller also defended right-to-work laws using the words of Popes Leo XIII and Pius XII. Other NRWC leaders similarly invoked God and country in defense of the right to work. Reed Larson often asserted that it was the "individual's God-given privilege" to decide for himself or herself whether to join a union. Elsewhere, early NRWC literature predicted that "unless . . . union compulsion is checked and outlawed" it would lead to "a socialistic labor dictatorship."[37]

In the mid-1960s, as the civil rights movement gained national prominence and political support, right-to-work advocates changed their tactics. Instead of using the religious and patriotic rhetoric of Cold War conservatism, NRWC began to secure popular support by linking the right-to-work and civil rights movements. According to NRWC and NRWLDF publicity, the fight for a right to work and the black freedom struggle were both part of a broader struggle for human and civil rights. In addition, NRWC and NRWLDF argued that the struggle for the right-to-work was not merely *like* the black freedom struggle, it was *part* of it.

NRWC's new view of itself as a civil rights warrior had its most concrete expression in NRWLDF itself. From its name to its institutional structure to its mission, NRWLDF was self-consciously styled after the predominant civil rights legal organization, the NAACP Legal Defense Fund, Inc. Reed

Larson studied the Legal Defense Fund before establishing the like-named National Right to Work Legal Defense Foundation. Larson even modeled NRWLDF's charter after the Legal Defense Fund's. Nor was the similarity between these two organizations a secret. Instead, NRWLDF publicized the Legal Defense Fund's role in its origin story.[38]

In addition to institutionally linking NRWC and NRWLDF to the civil rights movement, right-to-work advocates continued to build on civil rights precedents, but they now positioned their claims as part of this civil rights tradition. NRWC and NRWLDF relied on their similarity to the NAACP to defend themselves against a multi-union lawsuit that sought their membership lists. The unions wanted to prove that NRWC and NRWLDF were supported by the employers of their worker clients, in violation of the Wagner Act. Before the public, right-to-work advocates likened this lawsuit to the legal harassment the NAACP had faced throughout the South in the 1950s and 1960s, and they compared right-to-work litigators to the NAACP's beleaguered attorneys. In the courts, NRWLDF lawyers relied on the protective precedents the NAACP had won to fight off the unions' request.[39] NRWLDF replicated the NAACP's affirmative, as well as its defensive, strategies. Soon after the NAACP challenged the tax-exempt status of racially exclusive private schools, NRWLDF attorneys adopted the logic, claims, and cachet of these cases to bring their own challenge to unions' tax-exempt status. In its publicity about the cases and in court, NRWLDF emphasized that the right-to-work cases built on the NAACP's "landmark" private school suit.[40]

NRWLDF also increasingly used civil and human rights rhetoric to describe its work. From its charter, which promised to represent "workers who are suffering legal injustice as a result of employment discrimination under compulsory union membership arrangements," to promotional materials that touted its mission to "Protect Human and Civil Rights for America's Wage Earners," NRWLDF positioned itself as a civil rights champion. This view was endorsed by its most prominent client, William F. Buckley Jr., the nationally famous broadcaster, founder and editor of the conservative magazine *National Review*, and a general champion of postwar conservatism. In the early 1970s, he sued the American Federation of Television and Radio Artists, charging, as Cecil B. DeMille had thirty years earlier, that it was unconstitutional to require Buckley to pay dues to the union in order to broadcast his commentary. Buckley pronounced that he was fighting for "a fundamental civil and human right." NRWLDF also emphasized that a 1975 attack on the agency shop was "not a labor law suit, and was not filed as such. It was filed as a civil rights suit."[41]

At times, Larson even suggested that NRWLDF was a more pure civil rights advocate than the NAACP. Before World War II, many unions had excluded African Americans from membership and used their power to bar them from well-paying and skilled work. By midcentury, most unions had dropped their color bars and national labor leaders advocated for laws prohibiting discrimination by employers and unions. In the 1940s and 1950s, African Americans joined unions in droves. Nonetheless, many black workers still found themselves relegated to low-skilled, low-paying jobs, in part because of union practices. Despite vigorously challenging this trend and the union practices that helped cause it, the NAACP remained an ally of labor and an opponent of right-to-work. This meant that the NAACP, Larson argued, did not always put African Americans' interests first. Instead, he argued, the NAACP's alliance with labor compromised its freedom mission.[42]

NRWC and NRWLDF described themselves not only as part of a broad movement for civil rights but also as participants in the black freedom struggle. In 1967 Larson gave a speech, which NRWC publicized heavily, to the California Negro Leadership Conference. Larson's speech had its awkward moments (note his references below to "your people"). Clumsy as he may have been, Larson was trying to connect the right-to-work movement to African Americans' political goals. He peppered his speech with quotes from the NAACP's labor secretary, who was a vociferous critic of unions' racially discriminatory practices. Larson urged his audience to recognize their common mission. "Your dedication to freedom of the individual coupled with the unchallengeable fact of union discriminatory practices," Larson observed, "meant that eventually people like you would . . . tak[e] a long, hard look at your position on compulsory unionism." While the civil rights movement had long allied itself with labor, Larson advised, "it is in the interest of your people and all minorities to disperse, not enhance, a power structure through which the prejudices of fallible human beings can be brought to bear against the employment opportunities of your people."[43]

It is unclear how effective Larson's early outreach was, but soon NRWC and NRWLDF grew more sophisticated in their efforts to link their struggle to the black freedom movement. NRWC publications quickly substituted black speakers' and writers' own words for Larson's missives to African Americans. Publications featured reprints of articles with titles like "Black

Power and Right to Work" and "Unions Like 'Massah,'" which argued that right-to-work advocates, not unions, were black workers' real allies. "The only true friends we have in America," one writer opined, "are those who sincerely believe that blacks have a right to an opportunity to endeavor within the free enterprise system. All that we have slaved, struggled, sacrificed and died for is the privilege of being a citizen with a freedom of choice."[44]

African American workers also appeared in NRWC's publications, linking their support for a right-to-work with the civil rights movement. One early article quoted Ben Howard, a former United Auto Workers steward and member of the Black Workers Alliance, an organization that "'combats compulsory unionism for black people.'" In a coauthored statement, Howard argued that the combination of mandatory unionization and union discrimination meant that, "in effect, the black worker . . . has to pay the cost of actions which discriminate against him." In 1969, NRWC featured its first black leader: Ruth Johnson, a poultry worker from Missouri. Johnson became a prominent local and national spokesperson for NRWC. She consistently linked her support for the right-to-work cause with African Americans' civil rights struggle. According to Johnson, mandatory unionism was "almost like a new kind of slavery." In a letter to *Ebony* magazine, she even argued that Martin Luther King Jr., who was killed while supporting black sanitation workers' fight for a union in Memphis, Tennessee, would have fought for right-to-work laws had he lived.[45]

NRWC's efforts to link its struggle with black Americans' became more elaborate, institutionalized, and sophisticated during the 1970s. NRWC developed educational materials targeted to a "minority" audience and cultivated relationships with black columnists to help NRWC's view reach an African American public. Larson also grew savvier. In a 1980 article titled "Blacks and Compulsory Unionism: 'The Classic Double Bind,'" Larson constructed his argument from African American speakers' words. Then, switching into his own voice and adopting the nomenclature preferred by many African Americans, Larson exhorted, "In standing up for such principle, Blacks throughout America are proving themselves unwilling to shuffle their feet and 'bear their fortune.'"[46]

NRWLDF, like NRWC, fostered a right-to-work civil rights image. NRWLDF featured black litigants in its cases, publications, and leadership. Two of its early public worker cases featured African American plaintiffs who tied their right-to-work claims to a broader fight against racial discrimination. The organization publicized an African American plaintiff's opinion that "any fair-minded educator who pays dues money to a unit of the AFL-CIO . . . is paying those unions to further discrimination." The title of an article featuring a different black plaintiff explicitly associated right to work with the civil rights movement: "Free Choice: Another Area of Civil Rights That Jim Nixon Deeply Believes In," it read. "Are we to die to erase one barrier and close our eyes to the erection of another— Compulsory Unionism?" queried another featured civil rights veteran turned right-to-work litigant.[47] NRWLDF's African American plaintiffs joined state and national right-to-work leadership. Jim Nixon became a NRWC board member as well as a leader of his state's right-to-work organization. Henry Austin was another black litigant turned NRWC board member.[48]

NRWC and NRWLDF, by depicting their fight as a fight for civil rights, one that both carried on and was fed by African Americans' freedom struggle, pioneered a tactic later generations of conservative legal countermobilizers. At a time when the white working class was associated with backlash, right-to-work advocates calculated that connecting their cause with the civil rights movement in general and black workers in particular would help, not hurt, their fight.

This proved a shrewd calculation. During the 1970s, NRWC and NRWLDF grew in size, legitimacy, and effect. Linking right to work with civil rights facilitated their growth by helping advocates spin themselves as pro-worker and by framing their fight in a popular rhetoric that was already familiar to both the press and the courts. At the same time, fostering and featuring African Americans' support helped to weaken the right-to-work leadership's ultimate enemy, the Democratic Party, by aggravating growing tensions in the labor–civil rights alliance.

NRWC grew dramatically during the 1970s, mushrooming from under fifty thousand to three hundred thousand members in 1975 alone. Thanks to their exhaustive direct mail campaigns, the organization brought in a broad base of small contributors, with their average donation falling from forty dollars to twelve dollars. The organization also gained cultural legitimacy. By the mid-1970s, right to work had entered the mainstream. Reed Larson was featured in glossy biographical articles, popular magazines wrote features on NRWLDF's work, and the major national newspapers reported on its wins and losses.[49]

Associating right to work with civil rights helped NRWC and NRWLDF project a pro-worker, rather than pro-business, image and depict themselves as serving a public, rather than special, interest. NRWC and NRWLDF stressed their independence from big business. In interviews and speeches, Reed Larson derided big business as a fickle ally to the free market conservatism he preached. Big corporations were bureaucratic and non-ideological, he argued, just as happy to cozy up to unions as to oppose them, if doing so would benefit the corporations' bottom line. These businesses, according to Larson, were "not trying to solve problems basically for society." Instead, "they adjust to the set of monopolies that exist." Because "union monopoly is one of them," Larson contended, "they may find it in their interest to accommodate with union officials." Small and medium-sized businesses were another matter, and Larson often described them as right-to-work allies. Overall, however, NRWC and NRWLDF promoted themselves as "representing the interests of a vast majority of the American people as distinguished from special interests of some employers."[50]

To cultivate a populist image, NRWC and NRWLDF promoted their cause to workers and championed workers' support for right to work to the public. Beginning in the mid-1960s, NRWC began distributing a newsletter titled *Free Choice*. Advertised as a "Monthly Round-up of Labor News for Employees Who Think for Themselves," *Free Choice* featured stories about the misdeeds of "big labor bosses" and profiled workers who supported the right-to-work cause. NRWC and NRWLDF also gave awards to workers who fought for open shops. The winners were fêted at national ceremonies and celebrated on the pages of the organizations' multiple newsletters. The honorees were also often elevated to the organizations' boards of directors, leading to another round of stories commending their achievements. NRWLDF's cases played a key role in cultivating this pro-worker image. Many of the featured workers turned board members were also NRWLDF plaintiffs. In addition, *Free Choice* regularly used NRWLDF's cases to solicit subscriptions. Stories about William Buckley Jr.'s case and lawsuits brought by Wisconsin teachers and secretaries were among the many paired with an invitation to subscribe to *Free Choice*.[51]

NRWC and NRWLDF used their civil rights–themed material to advance right to work's pro-worker, pro–public interest image. African Americans were among the worker leaders, litigants, advocates, and awardees the two organizations featured. Jim Nixon, a disaffected Detroit civil servant; Philip Wallace, a Connecticut aerospace worker; and Henry Austin, a Virginia postal worker, all graced the pages of *Free Choice*, won NRWC awards, and joined the organizations' boards. These were also workers who described their right-to-work politics as an extension of their civil rights activism. By linking their fight to the black freedom struggle, NRWC and NRWLDF affiliated themselves with the disempowered and distanced themselves from the elites with whom they were traditionally associated.[52]

Framing right to work as part of the civil rights movement helped right-to-work advocates shed their "ultra-right," as well as elite, reputation. According to one mid-1970s profile of Reed Larson, even opponents credited NRWC and NRWLDF "with dissociating the movement from the right wing generally and with appealing to liberals," in part by creating "right-to-work ads [that] featured women and blacks who had had union trouble." The *New York Times* replicated this careful packaging when it printed an impassioned letter to the editor favoring national right-to-work legislation under the heading "(Civil) Right to Work." NRWLDF's rights claims also won the support of judges whom liberal litigators had long seen as their allies. Joseph Rauh was a veteran labor lawyer who defended unions against NRWLDF's lawsuits. Remarking on an argument in a dues case, Rauh observed that he had "argued cases on civil rights before Southern judges, cases on civil liberties before ex-prosecutor judges and cases for labor unions before ex-management judges." Nonetheless, he lamented, he had "never seen the level of hostility . . . exhibited" by what he had expected would be a friendly Ninth Circuit Court of Appeals panel.[53]

NRWC and NRWLDF usually presented themselves as fighting for workers, liberty, and a free market, but not for any particular political party. Indeed, Reed Larson said his cause transcended labels of "liberal" and "conservative." Nevertheless, every so often right-to-work advocates expressed a more crassly partisan goal. In 1974, while the Supreme Court was deciding whether to review one of NRWLDF's cases, an article in an NRWC newsletter took stock. With four new Republican appointees on the Court, their odds seemed good. And if they should win, the article thrilled, "the Democrats conceivably could lose the largest block of cash that fuels their election campaign machinery."[54]

To the extent that wresting power from the Democrats was their goal, NRWC and NRWLDF had much to gain from courting and promoting African American support for their cause. Since the 1930s, labor and civil rights organizations had formed the backbone of the post–New Deal Democratic Party. By the 1960s, however, relationships between labor and civil rights groups were growing increasingly frayed over the contentious issue of discrimination on the job and in the union. Right-to-work advocates took advantage of the opportunity. They began cultivating African American support and associating right to work with the civil rights movement just as tensions between the labor and civil rights movements grew more public and rancorous. In the 1970s, NRWC and NRWLDF continued these efforts, no longer simply using civil rights to moderate their own ultraright image, but also using union discrimination to siphon off black support for the Democratic Party. During the 1970s, NRWC and NRWLDF cultivated relationships with black conservatives. By the late 1970s, they had teamed up with one of the first African American conservative policy organizations, the Lincoln Institute for Research and Education, to promote the right-to-work cause to a black audience. NRWC and NRWLDF linked their goals to African Americans' civil rights struggle not only to moderate right to work's image but also to fester divisions in the Democrats' New Deal coalition.[55]

Conclusion

Litigation was a major part of the right-to-work movement, providing it with doctrinal victories, a potent means of publicity, a tactical weapon against its sworn enemy, "big labor," and a more subtle means of weakening its implicit foe, the Democratic Party. Along the way, right-to-work advocates redeployed the civil rights movement's constitutional claims and adopted its political mantle. By using the tropes of liberal legalism, right-to-work litigators pioneered what would become a key method of the conservative legal movement. In his recent pathbreaking book on conservatives' legal mobilization, Steve Teles writes that, in the 1990s, the newly founded libertarian Institute for Justice "judged that placing poor, black clients against large government institutions would improve their odds of success in the courts, magnify their public profile, and help change the reputation of conservatives and libertarians." As it turns out, this was a well-worn tactic, one that helped the right-to-work advocates of the 1950s through the 1980s gain legitimacy, thwart liberal attacks, and exacerbate divisions within the Democratic Party.[56]

"Such Power Spells Tyranny": Business Opposition to Administrative Governance and the Transformation of Fair Employment Policy in Illinois, 1945–1964

Alexander Gourse

In the spring of 1978, future U.S. appellate judge Laurence H. Silberman asked readers of the American Enterprise Institute's new journal *Regulation* a sobering question: "Will lawyering strangle democratic capitalism?" Silberman, a practicing lawyer himself, counseled that the legal process was "antithetical" to both capitalism and democracy. Almost all forms of governmental regulation warranted contempt, but courts and quasi-judicial bodies merited particular concern for the threat they posed to individual liberty. Legal disputes often posed competing claims of rights, explained Silberman. But rather than letting the market determine whose rights would prevail, the legal process allowed a government official to determine the "superior claim . . . in terms of priority of rights." "The adversary procedure," he argued, "deceptively suggests a neutral umpire-like role on the part of adjudicators and merely an advocate's role for lawyers." In reality, "the winner is the one deemed to have the 'better' position in accordance with a legal-moral standard." Silberman deemed this outcome incompatible with free enterprise.[1]

Silberman's argument against a litigation-dominated system of regulation reveals an ironic twist of American political history: business lobbyists and conservative intellectuals played a central role in creating the same institutional arrangements they now decry. For decades, conservatives have warned that employee and consumer litigation threaten economic growth. Political commentators who lament judicial involvement in the legislative and administrative processes or an increase in discrimination, personal injury, or medical malpractice litigation point to liberal judges, idealistic law students and professors, and opportunistic plaintiffs and trial lawyers as the forces increasing the "litigiousness" of American culture.[2] Yet during the first two-thirds of the twentieth century, business associations were powerful advocates of an adversarial, litigation-centered system of dispute resolution. This system has become, in the words of legal historian John Fabian Witt, "a kind of Frankenstein's monster haunting the managers who invented it."[3]

In this essay, I argue that business groups played a decisive role in pushing disputes over employment discrimination into the courts. For two decades following World War II, business associations such as the National Association of Manufacturers and the United States Chamber of Commerce fought against legislation to create state and federal administrative agencies, dubbed fair employment practice commissions (FEPCs), that would centralize the enforcement of civil rights law in the executive branch of government. They insisted that the "free enterprise system" depended on preserving the judicial process and expanding judicial checks on administrative power. The senators and congressmen who amended Title VII of the 1964 Civil Rights Act to ensure judicial involvement in the regulation of hiring practices did so primarily at the behest of organized business.

Nowhere was the campaign against FEPC more significant than in Illinois, where Everett Dirksen, future Senate minority leader and Republican intermediary in congressional disputes over the Civil Rights Act, developed his views on fair employment policy. Illinois was the site of a protracted legislative battle over a state-level FEPC during the postwar decades. Introduced in every legislative session between 1945 and 1961, FEPC became both a centerpiece of the state Democratic Party platform and a rallying point for conservative opponents of the liberal agenda.[4] Sensationalist rhetoric about the threats of racial integration and Communist subversion were not uncommon among FEPC foes, but the most consistent and active opponents of FEPC were organized business associations like the Illinois Manufacturers Association (IMA) and the Illinois State Chamber of Commerce, which argued that the creation of an agency would lead to the persecution of business owners by "biased" commissioners.

My study of the legislative politics of FEPC in Illinois builds on the work of the sociologist Anthony S. Chen, whose recent study of fair employment politics from World War II through the 1970s argues persuasively that conservatives' opposition to fair employment legislation had unintended consequences, ultimately "laying the foundations for affirmative action."[5] Chen's study should redirect scholars' attention toward conservatives' influence on policy outcomes, which was significant even at the height of the "liberal consensus" of mid-twentieth-century American politics. Yet his investigation of how the Republican Party and allied business associations stymied fair employment legislation largely misses the origins of this conservatism in the politics of labor and administrative law. I argue that Illinois business leaders' opposition to fair employment legislation developed from wartime struggles to dissolve what they saw as an alliance between the Congress of Industrial Organizations (CIO) and federal administrative agencies such as the National Labor Relations Board (NLRB). As law professor Sylvester Petro wrote in 1961, business leaders' "bitter experience" with the NLRB proved to them once and for all that "the personnel of administrative agencies are more often than not rigid, doctrinaire bureaucrats who place ideological and political objectives above law and justice."[6] In drawing this connection between anti-labor and anti–civil rights politics during the postwar era, I show how the "racial conservatism" that Chen and others have documented as a major political force in the 1940s and 1950s aided and was aided by business leaders' larger post–New Deal campaign to preserve their "right to manage."[7]

Organized business groups in Illinois played an outsized role in shaping fair employment legislation at both the state and federal levels. By examining the 1945, 1949, and 1961 campaigns for FEPC legislation in Illinois, I trace the influence of business lobbyists on fair employment politics between World War II and the Civil Rights Act of 1964. Adopting the views of groups such as the IMA, the Illinois Republican Party and congressional conservatives such as Dirksen became committed to court enforcement as preferable to what business leaders deemed "administrative tyranny."

Spring 1945: The Fight over Administrative Procedure

"The time to fight for jobs after the war is now—while the war is still on," asserted the editors of Chicago's widely respected black newspaper, the *Defender*, in May 1945. "It is up to the voters of Illinois to insure the passage of FEPC in this state by flooding the state capitol with letters and demanding S.B. 254 be passed without crippling amendments—now."[8] Confident that white supremacy had lost political legitimacy on the battlefields of World War II, civil rights activists committed themselves to fighting legislative battles to open good jobs to racial minorities. Those who supported the creation of FEPCs did not abandon other tactics that activists and lawyers had pioneered during the Great Depression and World War II, such as organizing consumer boycotts, joining radical industrial unions, or challenging economic and racial inequality through the courts. Yet the expansion of state and federal regulatory authority during the Great Depression and World War II provided new tools for activists to demand equal treatment for racial minorities in the labor market. The problem of racial inequality could now be approached in much the same way that Progressive reformers and New Deal liberals had previously sought to rein in the excesses of industrial capitalism: through administrative regulation.

Proponents of fair employment practices legislation believed racial inequality demanded the attention of experts trained in the fields of labor economics, race relations, and public administration.[9] Judges—"jacks-of-all-trades and masters of none," as the influential Harvard Law School dean James Landis wrote in 1938—were ill equipped to adjudicate such matters, having been trained in formalist legal doctrines that failed to recognize how individual autonomy could be subsumed by dominant economic and social forces in an industrial economy.[10] Only an administrative agency, whose appointed commissioners could consider the myriad factors that contributed to racial and economic inequality, would be able to resolve complaints in an effective manner. The notion that social problems required expert management of the kind that courts could not provide was a core ideological underpinning of the New Deal, and between the 1930s and the 1960s leading black lawyers and intellectuals viewed the administrative state as a site where key victories could be won on behalf of black workers.[11] By working through these agencies, civil rights activists hoped to incorporate protections against racial discrimination by private actors into the corpus of positive rights to economic security that would be administered by the New Deal state.[12]

FEPC supporters in Illinois argued that employment discrimination was a matter of *public* concern. "Such discrimination," according to the leaders of the Illinois Fair Employment Practices Committee, "fails to utilize the productive capacities of individuals to their fullest extent, deprives large segments of the population of earnings necessary to maintain decent standards of living, necessitates their resort to public relief, and intensifies group conflicts, resulting in grave injury to the public safety, health and welfare." Social problems such as urban decay, overcrowded schools, disease, and crime "are all byproducts of discrimination," they argued. "It would be futile to clear slums, if by permitting and abetting discrimination in employment we doom untold thousands to joblessness and privation." Most gravely, fair employment was crucial to the national interest in the Cold War world. "Communist propaganda cleverly exploits all our shortcomings and weaknesses. . . . Fair employment practices can be a weapon either for or against us. We must not allow our enemies to use it."[13]

Because fair employment served vital public interests, FEPC supporters believed that discrimination claims should be handled by a centralized administrative body that would provide "the impartial machinery for the orderly address of grievances."[14] "Why shouldn't federal courts handle the problem instead of a new administrative agency?" asked an NAACP press release, rhetorically. An "administrative agency is necessary," the organization concluded, "to prevent the flooding of courts; to screen out worthless complaints; to protect the rights of employees without compelling them to hire their own lawyers; to ensure speedy action; to ensure uniformity by having one agency interpret the bill instead of 94 federal district courts; to avoid the necessity of criminal penalties."[15]

Civil rights activists in Illinois developed their views on administrative enforcement through their experiences with nondiscrimination policies in public contracts during the 1930s and 1940s. The black struggle for jobs in Illinois developed from the protest politics of organizations like A. Philip Randolph's Brotherhood of Sleeping Car Porters (BSCP). During the Depression, the BSCP and the militant National Negro Congress waged a campaign to integrate Chicago's public transit system that turned activists' attention toward state and municipal governments as potential allies in the fight against discrimination.[16] Illinois officially banned discrimination in public works contracts in 1933, but fair employment advocates such as

Chicago labor lawyer (and future NLRB chairman) Frank McCulloch found that private enforcement of nondiscrimination clauses did little to effect change on a mass scale. In late 1941, after President Franklin Roosevelt issued an executive order banning discrimination in defense contracts in response to Randolph's threatened March on Washington, the black alderman Earl Dickerson demanded municipal action to implement the order. In November, McCulloch formed the Fair Employment Council of Metropolitan Chicago to assist the federal Committee on Fair Employment Practices in its investigations.[17]

The wartime Fair Employment Practice Committee demonstrated to Illinois activists the strengths and weaknesses of administrative enforcement. Created under Roosevelt's wartime legal powers, the commission lacked the same authority to subpoena witnesses and issue cease-and-desist orders that Congress granted to agencies like the NLRB. Instead, the staff of the wartime FEPC investigated complaints and conferred with individual employers, pressured other federal agencies to withhold contracts from recalcitrant businesses, and worked with activists to publicize discriminatory practices. While such tactics were no substitute for coercive enforcement mechanisms, the wartime FEPC was, in the words of historian Nelson Lichtenstein, "one of the New Deal's great mobilizing bureaucracies."[18] With support from the Chicago chapter of the NAACP and CIO unions like the United Packinghouse Workers of America (UPWA), the FEPC worked with racially liberal business leaders like Fowler McCormick of International Harvester to open thousands of jobs to blacks in northeastern Illinois between 1941 and 1945.[19] Yet the FEPC was more successful in Chicago than in southern Illinois, where African Americans saw little improvement in their job prospects. When the FEPC held hearings in East Alton to publicize the discriminatory practices of Western Cartridge, members of the lily-white American Federation of Labor (AFL) local shut down the meeting by force and the company simply ignored the committee's findings. Unable to compel employers or unions to alter their practices, the wartime FEPC was most successful where it had strong grassroots backing to make compliance a public relations necessity.[20]

Legislation to create a permanent federal FEPC met resistance from southern Democrats and northern Republicans at the end of the war, but civil rights activists remained adamant that racial justice would best be achieved through the administrative state. As a result, fair employment

advocates looked to municipal and state governments to create fair employment practices agencies. Hoping to avoid the fate of cities like Detroit,
where a 1943 race riot left thirty-four dead and nearly seven hundred
injured, Chicago mayor Edward Kelly established the Mayor's Commission
on Race Relations (MCRR) in 1943 to study race relations and promote
policies that would prevent racial violence. The MCRR quickly became "a
reforming agency of some zeal," and by 1945 it had identified employment
discrimination as a problem that local government might tackle.[21] The Kelly
administration proposed a municipal ordinance to ban discrimination by
private employers, which passed the City Council with little public controversy in August 1945. The only enforcement provisions, however, were
meager financial penalties, and the law created no agency to prosecute
violators.[22]

Discrimination was not suffered by African Americans alone, and during the mid-1940s a wide coalition came together to lobby for a state FEPC.
Investigators from the Illinois Interracial Commission found that both
Catholic and Jewish job applicants "faced serious discriminatory barriers."
Of eleven thousand Chicago businesses visited by the commission, forty-
five hundred required Jewish applicants to state their religion; 95 percent
of private employment agencies reported that they had trouble finding
positions for Jewish applicants. Blacks undoubtedly faced the most thor-
ough exclusion. Only 51 percent of Illinois industrial firms employed a
single non-white employee, and 97 percent refused to hire blacks for managerial or other professional positions. Most black workers clustered in those
firms that hired nonwhites in large numbers, and the commission found
that 90 percent of nonwhite employees worked in only 25 percent of the
state's businesses. Yet widespread discrimination against religious minorities meant that African Americans in Illinois had diverse allies in their fight
for fair employment legislation. In addition to the NAACP and radical
industrial unions like the UPWA, FEPC advocates ranged from religious
groups like the American Jewish Congress and the Catholic Interracial
Council to the leaders of neighborhood organizations in Chicago.[23]

The Chicago labor lawyers who drafted the initial Illinois FEPC bills
sought to put "teeth" into a state fair employment law and overcome the
shortcomings of the well-meaning but largely powerless ordinance passed
in Chicago. Drawing on the model of the National Labor Relations Board,
they closed many of the loopholes that made other fair employment statutes
relatively weak. The Illinois commission would have jurisdiction over all

private businesses that employed more than six persons, whereas the war-time federal FEPC had been limited to defense contractors. The Illinois FEPC would also have the authority to subpoena witnesses and issue cease-and-desist orders that would be backed up with criminal penalties for persons who "willfully resisted" its orders. Civil rights organizations like the NAACP would be given standing to pursue complaints on behalf of individual workers, a provision that FEPC advocates considered vital since the process of adjudicating complaints frequently took more time than individual workers could spare. Finally, the commission was to have the same powers as the NLRB to "take such further affirmative action or other action as will effectuate" the ends of racial integration in the labor market.[24]

In contrast to the ease with which the Chicago FEP law passed, state FEPC legislation met vehement resistance in 1945. "None of the 1,000 other bills introduced this session brought such an avalanche of telegrams, letters, and telephone calls to the legislators," reported the *Chicago Tribune*.[25] The bill provoked opponents of the measure "to begin the familiar tactics of race-baiting and dragging in red herrings," according to the *Chicago Defender*.[26] Yet while "race-baiting" mobilized some white workers to express their opposition to FEPC, the greatest obstacle was organized business. The IMA and other employer associations were highly effective lobbying organizations at the state level. Historian Lizabeth Cohen notes that the state government enacted only one piece of legislation between 1911 and 1929 that was "seriously opposed" by the IMA.[27] In 1945, dozens of business associations, representing nearly all sectors and regions of the Illinois economy, sent representatives to speak before the House and Senate Judiciary Committees, where they expressed a shared fear that the FEPC bill "would be impractical in operation, would seriously interfere with employment practices, and would promote unnecessary strife and dissension."[28]

Individual businessmen in Illinois reacted to fair employment bills in a variety of ways. Business leaders remained divided on both the desirability of racial integration in the workplace and the relationship of private enterprise to the state. Most claimed to support the position of the IMA, which argued that fair employment legislation "stated a worthy purpose, namely to relieve oppression and eliminate discrimination," but maintained that "such [an] objective could be better accomplished through education than through legislation."[29] Members of the City Club of Chicago worried that "democracy is menaced by its apparent inability to overcome racial inequalities in opportunity," and implied that some form of state action to eliminate discrimination was necessary.[30] Fowler McCormick of International Harvester instituted official nondiscrimination policies to improve his firm's public image at a time when his anti-union campaign was attracting negative attention.[31] Chicago civic leader Marshall Field III supported fair employment legislation because he believed it would allow employers *greater* latitude in hiring decisions by shifting the ire of white workers away from management and toward the state. FEPC legislation, Field explained to NAACP executive secretary Walter White, "would be of infinite value to those employers who would like to go forward in this matter and are fearful of public opinion."[32]

While the executives of large corporations in Chicago and northern Illinois were generally more supportive of racial integration than smaller manufacturers downstate, both groups firmly opposed legislation to create an administrative agency with powers to limit their prerogatives as managers.[33] Business leaders developed their staunch opposition to administrative governance through their experiences with the NLRB and the War Labor Board (WLB) over the preceding decade. The Chicago retailer Montgomery Ward's was charged with unfair labor practices in half of its forty disputes before the NLRB between 1937 and 1947. In 1944, after Roosevelt directed the army to seize Ward's for violation of three WLB orders, company president Sewell Avery locked himself in his office overlooking the north branch of the Chicago River and had to be removed by force.[34] "Our plant has been shut down by the Commander in Chief of the CIO," Avery told reporters from the *Tribune*.[35] The following week the company published a full-page ad in newspapers nationwide, asserting that "Wards' experience with the War Labor Board over a period of two years has convinced Wards that the Board is a means by which special privileges are granted to labor unions."[36]

The seizure of Ward's provided a powerful symbol for business opponents of the New Deal and the wartime state. Anti-union firms became convinced that an inherently liberal bureaucracy had emerged during the Great Depression and World War II. Employers appropriated AFL accusations that NLRB commissioners were "biased" toward the CIO, and echoed the AFL's demands that the board's determinations be subject to judicial review.[37] The IMA began lobbying Congress for mandatory court review of NLRB rulings in the early 1940s. The "prejudiced views of individuals who are unfriendly to industry" made the board "a Supreme Court unto itself," the IMA charged in 1943. Allowing unelected "bureaucrats" to manage labor relations without "an independent consideration of the facts" was an affront to traditions of American entrepreneurship, and was "encourag[ing] that body in its determination to unionize American business through government compulsion."[38]

Concluding that regulation by administrative agencies was a greater threat to managerial prerogatives than regulation by courts, Illinois business advocates joined a growing nationwide movement of lawyers, business leaders, and intellectuals who advocated expanded powers of judicial review to prevent "administrative absolutism."[39] "Administrative law has received its worst black eye from the openly prejudiced and unfair New Deal agencies," opined the editors of the *Tribune*. With state fair employment legislation looming on the legislative horizon, businesses demanded protection from state-level administrative bodies as well. "Altho the misdeeds of the New Dealers have focused public attention on federal administrative procedure," asserted the *Tribune*, "the same system of law extends down thru our state and municipal governments and is subject to the same, tho usually less flagrant, abuses of official power."[40] On May 8, 1945, Republican governor Dwight Green signed into law the Illinois Administrative Review Act, making the final determinations of any state administrative body reviewable (and reversible) by state circuit or superior courts.[41] Although supporters framed the Review Act as a politically neutral means of standardizing legal procedure throughout state government, most commentators viewed it within the larger struggle over power in the administrative state.[42] The *Tribune* hailed the Review Act as a victory for the "citizen who was the victim of arbitrary action" by government.[43] The editors of the *Defender*, by contrast, worried that the act would hinder the enforcement of fair employment legislation. "The cost of bringing violators into court would be prohibitive," they wrote. "The delay of court trials would render the [FEPC] law ineffective."[44]

The 1945 FEPC hearings before the Illinois General Assembly mirrored the debates over administrative procedure that had divided the business, labor, and legal professions since the late 1930s. On May 8, the same day that Green signed the Administrative Review Act into law, Chicago attorney Charles F. Hough testified before the Senate Judiciary Committee on behalf of thirty-eight employer organizations, arguing that "at no time in the history of Illinois has the legislature been faced with a more momentous decision than it has to make on this bill. It is the first time . . . when it has been proposed to make it possible to throw the citizens of Illinois in jail or make them pay fines without the time honored and tried protection, guaranteed by the state constitutions, of trial by jury, rules of evidence, right to change of venue, and other protective measures." The proposal would lead to persecution of Illinois business owners, argued Hough: "The Act violates all of our known principles and sense of fair play in that it makes members of the proposed Board investigators, prosecutors, judge and jury." Responding to claims that administrative law would "streamline justice," Hough said bluntly: "*Well, Hitler* streamlined justice—and we did not like it." Hough concluded with a plea for the courts to reestablish their jurisdiction over labor-management affairs: "If such a bill is absolutely necessary or is desirable let the judicial process of our government, including the right to trial by jury, be preserved."[45]

The fight over administrative procedure in Illinois shifted debate over fair employment legislation toward a concern for the rights of employers. Faced with strong opposition from the business community, Illinois lawmakers rejected FEPC in 1945. The Senate bill died in committee in late May, and the House bill was voted down in early July. And while many civil rights activists vowed to continue the struggle for fair employment legislation, the battle over administrative procedure that dominated the 1945 FEPC campaign narrowed the political and legal horizons for FEPC laws in Illinois. With the passage of the Review Act all subsequent FEPC bills in the state would include easy access to judicial review as a fundamental protection of employers' rights.

Winter 1949: Free Enterprise and an Alternate Rights Discourse

The elections of 1948 proved a turning point in American political development, as Democratic victories encouraged liberals who feared that the reform agenda would wither once the Great Depression and war emergencies had passed. Conservative opposition to trade union power and administrative governance had already produced legislation such as the 1946 Administrative Procedure Act and the 1947 Taft-Hartley Act, and the battle over a state FEPC in Illinois reflected the continuing struggle over the role of government in the American economy.[46] FEPC advocates were optimistic that state-level Democratic victories in northern industrial states such as Illinois, Ohio, Wisconsin, and Michigan had opened the door for a series of "little New Deals" that would expand the New Deal economic and civil rights program without the encumbrances of conservative southern Democrats. Activists in Illinois believed that Democratic gubernatorial candidate Adlai Stevenson's victory over Dwight Green represented a "new birth of freedom" for minorities. Civil rights at the state level was a distinctly partisan issue for liberals like Gilbert Gordon of the American Jewish Congress. "Unlike the situation in the presidential election where both candidates were pledged to civil rights measures," he argued, "the differences between Democrat Stevenson and Republican Green on civil rights were apparent." While Stevenson had made an Illinois FEPC a central element of his candidacy, "Green, through his eight-year tenure, had not taken a single significant step" toward guaranteeing fair employment. But with Democrats in power, "the forecast is definitely one of success" for "a New Deal for minorities in Illinois."[47]

Stevenson's victory also represented a chance for liberal Democrats to stanch the erosion of administrative authority that organized business groups championed. Stevenson owed his impressive margin of victory to the CIO and the more progressive Chicago Federation of Labor and AFL internationals, as well as the increasingly pivotal black vote. The Illinois Federation of Labor, early critics of a supposed alliance between the NLRB and the CIO, had thrown its support behind Green and the state Republican Party. [48] Liberals hoped that this would allow the Stevenson administration to utilize its authority over the administrative state to pursue the intertwined goals of racial integration and economic citizenship. "The real test of Stevenson's pledges," argued Gordon, "will come in the purely administrative aspects of his governorship." Appointing officials who would "militantly" administer antidiscrimination laws while upholding the rights granted to unions by New Deal labor legislation would allow Stevenson to hold together the labor–civil rights coalition that had elected him.[49]

Yet the new governor's political debt to the CIO and Illinois's black population did not immunize him from competing interests, particularly because the state Senate remained under Republican control. Hoping to avoid the factional disputes that complicated the 1947 FEPC campaign, the administration drafted its own fair employment bill for the 1949 legislative session.[50] After meeting with legislators in early February, the administration sent a bill to the House that bore the marks of political compromise.[51] The bill exempted from the FEPC's jurisdiction employers of fewer than six workers, as well as all agricultural and domestic laborers.[52] Legislative aides warned Stevenson that the "exclusion of agricultural labor may well invalidate the entire act, since discriminatory labor practice in this phase of our economy seems to come within the very heart of evils condemned."[53] Leftist supporters condemned such exemptions as well. Amalgamated Local 453 of the United Auto Workers in Cicero charged that "those sections of the proposed bill . . . are a flagrant violation of the World Bill of Human Rights that was introduced in the Social Council of the UN."[54] The administration also considered changes in the enforcement powers the bill would grant to a commission. Taking note of the concerns expressed by business and lawyers' organizations, Stevenson removed the portions of the 1945 bill that provided criminal penalties for offenders. The commission would retain the power to issue cease-and-desist orders, but would have to seek a court ruling to compel employers or unions who ignored such orders.[55]

Despite such compromises, Stevenson's proposed bill preserved many of the powers granted to New Deal agencies like the NLRB. The commission would have the authority to hold public hearings upon receiving a complaint, subpoena witnesses, issue cease-and-desist orders, and initiate contempt proceedings through the courts against recalcitrant employers or unions. It would be authorized to work with other state agencies to craft policies that would "take such further affirmative action or other action as will effectuate" racial and religious integration in the workplace. The bill defined discrimination broadly and covered private employers, labor organizations, and state and private employment agencies.[56] The administration rejected business requests for an "FEPC guide" that would create statutory benchmarks that employers could use to "guard against crackdowns" by the agency. An administrative commission comprising social science, human relations, and public administration "experts" would be created that could issue legally binding orders and work with organizations like the NAACP or the CIO to investigate and eliminate discrimination.[57]

Business leaders campaigned against FEPC in 1949 by charging that administrative regulation of hiring practices violated the "civil rights" of employers and employees alike. Free enterprise depended upon the manager's "inherent right to hire whomever he may wish to hire," asserted the Illinois State Chamber of Commerce, which spearheaded the employer effort. The chamber argued that "the phrase 'civil rights' has ordinarily been used in connection with fundamental principles of liberty. . . . *It may be that the employer is entitled as a matter of 'civil right' to employ whomever he pleases and that a denial of that right may violate the constitutional guarantees he now enjoys.*"[58] Businessmen throughout the state echoed the chamber's invocation of the right to manage as a natural right. "The fair employment practice [act], if it becomes law, would be unconstitutional," wrote R. M. Westcott of Peoria to Adlai Stevenson. "An employer has a moral right to hire whom he pleases."[59] Frank Koch of the LaSalle Motor Company pleaded with the governor to consider the rights of business owners: "On the one hand the bill says discrimination threatens this state. What about threatening the rights and privileges of the employers of this state— aren't they inhabitants too? Shouldn't the employer have the same right to hire and upgrade whom he wants without being told what to do by some state appointee?"[60] Former Illinois Supreme Court justice Floyd Thompson testified before the House Executive Committee that the bill entailed "a restriction of civil rights and a slander against the American employer." FEPC threatened the "freedom of the individual to conduct business under the American competitive system," Thompson warned. "Free enterprise is not dead, but it is badly mauled and all that is needed to finish it are a few quack doctors."[61]

Most Illinois opponents of FEPC claimed to support the principles of tolerance. The State Chamber of Commerce asserted that "no one can have any objection to the principle of non-discrimination," while some businessmen argued that the interests of minorities would best be served by keeping an open shop. "Rights of minority employees should be protected," according to C. S. Craigmile, president of the Belden Manufacturing Company, by preserving "the present right to settle grievances without union intervention."[62] But these business leaders viewed the civil rights of minorities, the public interest, and the property rights of business owners as existing in delicate balance. And because they considered the "right to manage" as coequal with (if not superior to) both the public interest and minorities' rights to racial justice, they demanded procedural safeguards against the abuses of power they believed were inherent to administrative governance.[63] They insisted that judicial disposition of hiring disputes was necessary to prevent "petty tyranny" by bureaucrats.

The procedural reforms included in the 1945 Administrative Review Act did not go far enough to allay the fears of business leaders that the FEPC would wield "dictatorial powers." "There is no adequate court review of the commission's administrative functions," complained the Fox River Valley Manufacturers Association, "since the commission is not bound by the technical rules of evidence and courts must accept the commission's findings of fact as final."[64] This represented a "complete abandonment of legal procedure," protested Clarence Mark Jr. of Clayton Mark and Company in Evanston.[65] Earl Kribben, vice president of Marshall Field & Company, disapproved of the committee's authority to determine the facts of discrimination in a case. The commission would operate as "investigator, prosecutor, and judge" through a "kangaroo court," warned Kribben. "As findings of fact are not subject to adequate court review under the current Administrative Review Act, the seriousness of the situation is apparent."[66]

While the IMA and the Illinois Chamber of Commerce remained unwilling to negotiate on any FEPC law, some employers suggested amendments that would make the bill palatable to the state's businesses. Existing powers of judicial review of the commission's findings of law would not be sufficient to prevent the commission from harassing employers. The Associated Employers of Illinois sought to expand an employer's right to obtain court review of findings of fact, and submitted an amendment to the administration that would limit the power of the committee to initiate contempt proceedings through courts (a penalty that was "the most severe that could be imposed").[67] Earl Kribben demanded a narrower definition of discrimination under the law and a statute of limitations that shortened the period during which workers could file claims from one year to sixty days. "Too long a time period will encourage abuse, inefficiency, or both," he predicted. Kribben also insisted that third parties be banned from working with the commission to investigate and eliminate discriminatory practices. "As written," said Kribben, the bill "would permit the Communist Front, or any other kind of organization, legitimate or otherwise, sincere or not, to use the Commission as a tribunal for its propaganda." As a final safeguard against harassment, Kribben demanded that the "ambiguity of language" that gave the commission authority to pursue systematic solutions to discrimination be removed so as to avoid "an opportunity for unlimited despotism through conferring unlimited discretion."[68]

In the spring of 1949, Illinois civil rights activists were optimistic that the ominous predictions of business leaders would fall on deaf ears in state government. Gilbert Gordon expected that New Deal liberalism "free from Dixiecrat influence" would flourish at the state level.[69] Albert J. Weiss, executive secretary of a lobbying group that called itself the Illinois Fair Employment Practice Committee, predicted in early April that the Stevenson administration's FEPC bill would receive the unanimous support from

Democrats in the House, and all but one Democratic vote in the Senate. Opposition was strongest among downstate senators, but Weiss believed the administration could rely on the support of at least nine Republicans and five Democratic senators from downstate districts.[70] As these activists expected, the House rejected virtually all the amendments demanded by business and passed the FEPC bill in late May.

A last-minute media campaign coordinated by the IMA raised the political stakes of FEPC for senators, however. The *Tribune* provided a platform for IMA counsel David Clarke, who warned that "enactment of the FEPC bill would place a cloud of fear over all employers." The bill "would create a fearful bureaucracy, conducting inquisitions with the commission acting as prosecutor, judge, and jury all in one. Such power spells tyranny."[71] In preparation for the bill's expected passage, conservative Republicans in the Senate passed an amendment that would require two of the five commissioners of the FEPC to be appointed by the minority political party.[72]

The 1949 campaign for FEPC in Illinois ended in the state Senate in late June after what one observer described as "one of the most dramatic sessions ever held in that chamber." In an "explosion of emotions on the floor of the Senate," the only Democrat who voted against the measure complained that "I am under tremendous pressure. If I am voting wrong, I pray to God to forgive me." One pro-FEPC senator reported having been offered $4,000 to change his vote. The bill fell three votes short of passage as a result of the "sudden absence" of one Democrat and the unexpected opposition of three Republicans who previously "had been counted on for FEPC."[73]

1961–1964: Moral Imperatives and Political Compromises

The defeat of FEPC legislation in 1949 represented a major disappointment for liberals who had placed their hopes for reform in the labor–civil rights coalition united behind Governor Adlai Stevenson and the Illinois Democratic Party. Although Stevenson's Republican successor, William Stratton, expressed support for FEPC during the 1953, 1955, 1957, and 1959 legislative sessions, fair employment advocates questioned the sincerity of his civil rights platform. Stratton did little to challenge "the almost 100% negative vote of Republican Senators" that defeated FEPC in every legislative session during the 1950s.[74] Business leaders exerted a powerful influence over the public discourse of FEPC debates during the 1950s, and the memory of the New Deal and World War II continued to shape opponents' views of administrative governance. Republican senator Hayes Robertson of Flossmoor explained in 1957 that his own business's dealings with "federal officials" during World War II turned him against fair employment laws. If such a law passed in Illinois, he argued, "Employers would be faced by a Gestapo type of official in every town." Compulsory fair employment legislation was "inimical to freedom," echoed Republican senator Robert McClory of Lake Bluff. [75] The *Tribune* nearly always discussed FEPC in the context of New Deal labor legislation. "In many respects," argued the paper's editors in April 1961, "what's wrong with FEPC laws is the same thing that's wrong with closed shop laws: they restrict what should be a freely chosen relationship."[76] Summing up their reasons for opposing fair employment laws, the editors explained, "We do not believe that it is the right of the state to dictate to an employer whom he must hire. An employer who chooses to believe that all Negroes, Catholics, Jews, Italians, or Christian Scientists are undesirable employes has proved that he is a jackass, but it is not the business of the government of Illinois to keep men from being jackasses."[77]

By the early 1960s, however, the near-unified opposition of Republican state senators began to dissipate. Democrat Otto Kerner backed strong FEPC legislation during his successful 1960 gubernatorial campaign, and "Republican liberals," according to Joseph Minsky of the American Jewish Congress, were "anxious to attempt to obtain some Negro votes" in the wake of the year's Democratic victories.[78] As civil rights protests in the South gained national attention and federal action on job discrimination began to appear imminent, a group of moderates that included senators Arthur Sprague of La Grange, W. Russell Arrington of Evanston, and John P. Meyer of Danville concluded that the passage of a fair employment bill in Illinois was inevitable. Arrington presented a revised bill to the Senate Industrial Affairs Committee that he hoped would be merged with one favored by state Democrats. "Months ago I advised my friends that we were going to have FEPC," he explained. "I told them to help us make it an orderly thing. Thus I have tried to make the provisions in my bill . . . to prevent harassment [of employers]."[79]

The provisions proposed by Arrington and Sprague in exchange for their support reflected twenty years of business resistance to New Deal liberalism. Only employers of more than twenty-five persons would be covered by the law, and instead of creating an administrative agency with powers to issue cease-and-desist orders and initiate complaints, the Republican amendments eliminated a commission entirely and placed enforcement in the hands of state's attorneys. "Creation of the commission is perhaps the greatest obstacle to passage of the bill," Sprague commented to the *Tribune*.[80] Directing complainants to state's attorneys in each county would reduce the dangers of an "inquisitorial" commission and restore the rights of due process to the regulatory system. Democrats on the Committee rejected GOP amendments that eliminated an agency, however. Chicago NAACP activist L. H. Holman protested that the bill would effectively exempt employers from rural downstate districts: "every individual who files a complaint must have a lawyer," Homan observed, so "outside the big metropolitan areas this bill will have little meaning."[81]

In early May, Senate Democrats agreed to a second round of amendments that earned the support of prominent Chicago-area executives. The commission's jurisdiction would be limited to employers of more than one hundred for the first two years of its operation, and commissioners would be required to adhere to "strict rules of evidence." These businessmen also stipulated an "implicit three-point compromise," according to one participant in the negotiations, that would "regulate the Commission's activities in its beginning years." The FEPC would not initiate its own complaints; aggrieved workers and employers would be treated as adversaries, with the commissioners being "limited to an adjudicatory role"; and the state business associations would administer the educational programs in which the commission could order employers to participate. Seeing a chance for business to establish a system of self-regulation, future U.S. senator Charles Percy, then president of Bell and Howell Company, told the Senate Industrial Affairs Committee that "the philosophy of FEP Commissions in other states . . . has been to use the law for friendly persuasion for employers, labor unions, and employment agencies to change any discriminatory hiring practices."[82] The revised FEPC bill passed the Senate in late May with four Republican votes, and the governor signed it into law in July 1961.

The sixteen-year legislative battle over a state FEPC affected more than state-level fair employment policy. The Illinois FEPC proved more aggressive than moderates like Percy had hoped. In the fall of 1963, the agency decided a case against the Motorola Corporation that rallied conservative critics nationwide against the administrative approach to fair employment. Attorneys for Motorola, contending that the company could not receive fair consideration before the commission because the hearing officer was black, pledged to appeal the agency's ruling to the U.S. Supreme Court. Arthur Krock of the *New York Times* warned that civil rights legislation pending in Congress would "project the rationale of the Illinois FEPC throughout the free enterprise system of the United States."[83]

As Congress debated the enforcement provisions that would be included in the employment section of the 1964 Civil Rights Act, business lobbyists turned to Illinois's Republican senator Everett Dirksen to prevent a federal version of the Illinois FEPC from being created. The Illinois Manufacturers Association contacted Dirksen in the spring of 1964 to demand that all employment sections be removed from the act, and directed its fifteen hundred member firms to flood the senator with mail expressing their belief that the act's employment provisions were "particularly drastic and unwarranted." Dirksen replied that "civil rights legislation was due to pass in some form" and that "a Title VII would be incorporated in such measure." The most prudent course for Illinois businesses, Dirksen advised, would be "to cooperate in an effort to moderate the provisions of Title VII."[84]

The amendments that Dirksen secured for the Civil Rights Act were drawn directly from the two decades of legislative disputes over FEPC in Illinois. The senator had developed a close relationship with Illinois manufacturers during his thirty-year political career,[85] and as Senate minority leader he advocated crucial policy compromises to civil rights legislation that would, in the words of historian Hugh Davis Graham, "yield to the moral imperative of [equal opportunity] while still constraining federal intrusion in commerce."[86] Building on a House bill that conservatives had already amended to require federal courts—not officials from the Equal Employment Opportunity Commission (EEOC) itself—to weigh the merit of complaints and determine appropriate punishments for offenders, Dirksen added limitations on the role of third parties in the complaint process and eliminated all prosecutorial powers for the agency, replacing the EEOC's ability to sue offenders with a right of action for private litigants to enforce the law.[87] After President Lyndon Johnson signed the Civil Rights Act into law on July 2, 1964, IMA vice president James L. Donnelly reassured member firms that "most of the major amendments suggested by the

IMA were eventually incorporated into law."[88] Although business associations such as the IMA preferred for the state to abstain entirely from involvement in hiring decisions, they succeeded in implementing a regulatory model that they believed would result in fewer encroachments on management autonomy.

Conclusion: Organized Business and Adversarial Legalism

The arguments of civil rights activists and business leaders during the sixteen-year struggle for fair employment legislation in Illinois appear strange in hindsight. In the years following the Civil Rights Act, the courts provided powerful tools for civil rights activists and lawyers who fought to break down racial and gender barriers to employment and union membership. By the turn of the twenty-first century, job discrimination lawsuits constituted the second largest source of litigation in the federal courts.[89] Class-action lawsuits forced many of the most obstinate employers and craft unions to alter their practices, judges broadened the meaning of Title VII to sanction affirmative action as a solution to entrenched patterns of discrimination, and for a time the language of due process was more often associated with the "positive liberty" of welfare rights than with the property rights of business owners.[90] Conservative critics of the liberal legal order, for their part, founded new right-wing public interest law firms during the early 1970s to provide a counterweight to what they saw as a rights revolution run amok. "Strict constructionism" and "judicial restraint" became the founding principles of a new conservative legal movement that served many of the same corporations that had once demanded active court supervision of the New Deal administrative state.[91]

Most historians have interpreted the striking reversal in thinking about legal procedure and fair employment that occurred during the 1950s and 1960s as part of a broader ideological or tactical shift on the left.[92] State FEPCs made little more than a minor dent in the broader edifice of racial inequality.[93] Hindered with statutory limitations on their jurisdiction and enforcement powers, and staffed by commissioners who were subject to the political considerations of the elected officials who appointed them, FEPCs provided evidence for civil rights activists like NAACP labor secretary Herbert Hill who believed that a pragmatic alliance with organized labor and the New Deal state would reap few rewards for black workers.[94] New Left activists and liberal intellectuals noticed a broader tendency toward "industry orientation" in the administrative state that reached beyond fair employment policy. "Agency capture," in the words of the legal scholar Louis Jaffe, was "a condition endemic to any agency."[95] Only the judicial process could prevent powerful business interests from controlling their own regulators.

Yet the expansion of judicial authority was, in part, the result of an earlier conservative campaign to save "free enterprise." While many business leaders rejected any enforcement of antidiscrimination law, those not categorically opposed to fair employment legislation advocated court enforcement because they believed a Democratic administration would stack an agency with appointees hostile toward managerial autonomy. In instances where legislation creating an agency appeared likely to pass, business groups demanded extensive judicial review of agency actions. These businessmen channeled the demands of civil rights activists into particular legislative forms, demanding judicial protection of their rights and arguing that their "right to manage" constituted a civil right worthy of heightened standards of procedural due process. Ironically, their challenge to the labor and civil rights movements aided the expansion of judicial power that dogged them for the remainder of the century.

My purpose in making this argument is not to uncover hypocrisy in the thinking of libertarian intellectuals or businessmen. I intend no moral judgment when I point to the inconsistency of their views (at least insofar as the inconsistency itself would be the subject of judgment). My only normative claim is simple: that we should not view as adequate political or philosophical arguments that focus on procedural matters alone, without reference to the substantive social and economic consequences of the procedures in question. This view is hardly new to American political or legal thought. As the eminent legal historian Morton Horwitz notes, legal scholars of widely varying ideological and partisan persuasions have understood "that there has always been a trade-off between substance and procedure." In any dispute over economic, social, or political power, "one man's due process is another man's delay."[96]

Rather, my purpose is historical. We cannot understand the changes in postwar social movements and politics, on both the left and the right, without understanding the ways in which powerful actors shaped political institutions. Political scientists such as Paul Frymer emphasize the role of trial lawyers, beginning during the 1930s, in facilitating the development of a "legal state" by advocating changes in the federal rules of civil procedure that expanded lower income groups' access to the courts.[97] While lawyers certainly supported procedural changes that would lead to higher volumes of litigation, Frymer's assertion that "non-ideological and purely institutional factors explain why lawyers and courts became the chief enforcers of labor civil rights" overlooks the ideological aversion to administrative governance that influential business groups developed during World War II and the postwar decades.[98] The modern enforcement regime of fair employment law resulted from two decades of business campaigns against the New Deal legal and political order. Long before Great Society liberals expanded the New Deal's positive liberties to include protections against racial and gender discrimination, business groups devised strategies at the state level that they thought would limit the burdens such legislation placed on managerial autonomy. By demanding extensive judicial involvement in the administrative process and advocating court enforcement as preferable to administrative governance, business groups like the Illinois Manufacturers Association played a crucial role in developing the adversarial, litigation-dominated style of modern American government.

PART IV

The Specter of Union Power and Corruption

In the fourth part of this book we examine case studies in which employers and conservatives chose to battle unionism, either in the public sphere, within their own enterprise, or in terms of a transformation of national law and politics. Their charges did not center on either the presumptive radicalism of organized labor or the union threat to the racial order but instead targeted what many conservatives defined as the corruption of the union leadership and the illegitimate power wielded by virtually all trade unions, especially those in the public sphere.

In his study of the labor beat in the 1950s and 1960s, David Witwer explains how Victor Riesel, Clark Mollenhoff, and other high-profile reporters worked in partnership with editors, legislators, and some employers to move debate over the labor question from one that emphasized the economic and political influence of the trade unions to a discourse that highlighted violence, corruption, and autocratic leadership. Corruption, institutional and personal, was certainly present within organized labor, but Witwer argues that these midcentury investigators failed to offer a proportionate analysis. This was especially true when the Senate convened a special, televised inquiry chaired by John McClellan of Arkansas, designed to investigate abuses and racketeering within both labor and management. Both journalists and legislators proved remarkably uncurious about management activities, but focused instead on a rogues' gallery of unseemly labor leaders, most notably Jimmy Hoffa, whose persona became a symbol for union corruption, autocracy, and thuggish power.

Sylvestor Petro identified another kind of union corruption, more legal and political, in these years. Joseph McCartin and Jean-Christian Vinel examine this conservative libertarian's career, a calling that linked the ideas of the Austrian school of economics to the venerable American antimonopoly tradition. Drawing upon the midcentury debate over union violence and corruption, Petro forged an updated rights talk that condemned "compulsory unionism" and challenged the collective logic inherent in the Wagner Act. Unionism was coercive and undemocratic, argued Petro, not because of any rotten apple leaders, but because it deployed New Deal–born state power on its behalf. Hence his most notable contribution to conservative anti-union argumentation came after 1960 when Petro denounced collective bargaining in the public sector, which he thought a subversion of government sovereignty. Elements of this Petro assault would soon be found in the rhetoric of President Ronald Reagan when he broke the Professional Air Traffic Controllers' Organization in 1981.

Anti-union language also infused Wal-Mart's corporate culture. A product of the rural South, the company nevertheless required an ideologically and organizationally sophisticated strategy to stymie organizing when it began to put its stores in metropolitan America. John Tate, Nelson Lichtenstein shows, proved his worth in this regard. The anti-union strategist's ideas had been shaped, directly or indirectly, by Elton Mayo, Petro, and the most intransigent anti-union employers of the textile South and the small town Midwest. In the early 1970s Tate codified for Wal-Mart and other service sector firms the key elements of a successful union avoidance strategy: construct a business ethos that mimics the sense of community found in monoracial, small-town America; deploy a pension scheme that rewards loyalty for a core of longtime employees; and use the "free speech" rights of employers to paint unions as corrupt and self-serving institutions incapable of improving the wages or work life of employees.

When the Democratic Party achieves electoral success, labor and its liberal allies have invariably tried to change the law so as to facilitate union organizing. But in two of the most high-profile recent instances, employers and conservative politicians have easily maintained the status quo. John Logan's review of the Clinton-era Commission on the Future of Worker-Management Relations (Dunlop Commission) demonstrates that labor's willingness to permit a form of company unionism—so as to create the high-performance workplace needed to compete in a newly global market-place—generated no corresponding employer concession, which might have eased the barriers to trade union organizing. The "deal" was off because corporate leaders in the United States, in contrast to those in many other industrialized countries, were convinced that trade unionism per se was detrimental to the interests of their firms. Labor's independent voice inside their enterprise represented, in fact, a failure of management and was thus harmful to their careers. Thus the final recommendations of the Dunlop Commission did little to expedite union recognition, improve collective bargaining, enhance employee productivity, or penalize the use of temporary, part-time labor.

The Chamber of Commerce and others in management have vociferously opposed efforts to enact an Employee Free Choice Act (EFCA), often on the grounds that alternatives to the National Labor Relations Board election—such as majority sign-up or card check—are undemocratic on their face. But in the concluding essay Susan Orr explains how this framework actually distorts the key issues: those of representation, democracy, and privacy that lie at the heart of the controversy. NLRB elections, designed to determine if workers want to form a union, are not analogous to contests for elective office. Rather, they are similar to the process by which a constitution is written or a new nation's independence is declared. Union representation elections are therefore "constitutional moments." Shifting the analogy in this way draws attention to the fact that the major threats in union certification campaigns are directed toward workers as a group, as a consequence of forming a union. The secret ballot, which opponents of EFCA mistakenly champion as fundamental to democracy, affords no protection from such threats. Orr concludes that the majority sign-up process thereby enhances the democratic nature of union formation as it allows workers to deliberate among themselves and minimizes the opportunity for employers to engage in the sort of coercive speech deployed by John Tate and latter-day anti-union operatives. Orr's work reminds us that the fundamental issues at stake in the century-long debate between the American Right and organized labor are as much about the meaning of democracy, civil rights, and free speech as they are a contest over wages, working conditions, and the American standard of living.

Pattern for Partnership: Putting Labor Racketeering on the Nation's Agenda in the Late 1950s

David Witwer

In the spring of 1954, a nonunion contractor named Edward Pozusek, from Wilkes-Barre, Pennsylvania, was building a house in nearby Scranton. Three local union officials came by the construction site in late April and talked to Pozusek, warning him that he could expect to encounter problems if he continued working this job as a nonunion contractor. An obdurate Pozusek told them that he had no intention of either signing with the union or giving up the job and two days later a dynamite blast damaged part of the house's foundation.[1] No one thought the two events were unconnected. But it seems safe to assume that few people at the time would have expected the episode to be featured in front-page news stories across the country, or in the leading weekly news magazines, *Time*, *Newsweek*, and *U.S. News & World Report*. *Life* magazine even carried a photograph of the damaged basement foundation of Pozusek's Scranton job site.[2]

The front-page treatment accompanied congressional hearings held in April 1957 that focused on Scranton and made Pozusek's story the center-piece of a "case history of 'Teamster terrorism' in a typical city."[3] Three years after it happened, this otherwise obscure event in Scranton had come to symbolize a dangerous pattern of aggressive union tactics. *U.S. News &*

World Report's headline for the magazine's seven-page spread on the Scranton hearings read, "Strong-Arm Tactics in Unions: Case History of a City."[4] A newspaper editorial asserted that the Scranton hearings had "served the useful purpose of bringing the 'goon' into the spotlight," demonstrating how organized labor's "resort to violence" now constituted "a sort of Nation-wide plague."[5]

Framed in this way, the story had significant political impact. In the wake of the Scranton hearings, *Newsweek* magazine noted how "demands for legislation to curb the power of union bosses [were] rising to a roar," fed by the "revelations concerning racketeering and terrorism in the Teamsters Union."[6] President Dwight Eisenhower responded to this public outcry by declaring that "labor racketeering" was "an abomination, which must be eliminated if and whenever it occurs." He promised that his administration would begin the work of drafting an effective legislative response.[7] The Scranton story, and the way it was framed, had helped put the issue of labor racketeering squarely on the national agenda.

The episode highlights the larger forces that shaped media coverage of organized labor and which in turn influenced the content of political discourse about unions. *Time* magazine raised this issue in an article in May 1957 entitled "Pattern for Partnership." The article appeared in the immediate aftermath of the Scranton hearings and it focused on the recent history of the committee that had held those hearings, the Senate's Select Committee on Improper Activities in the Labor or Management Field, a group better known as the McClellan Committee (1957–1959). *Time* credited the committee's recent hearings with drawing national attention to the problem of labor racketeering, but it noted that "in a society as complex as the U.S., it takes more than one man, or one newspaper, or one committee to focus the national attention on a serious problem." This had been a cooperative effort: "While the U.S. Senate's McClellan committee has produced the national headlines on labor racketeering, it was vigilant newsmen, from Des Moines to Portland, Ore. and back to Scranton, Pa., who sparked the Senate investigation and provided the scattered local fragments that fell into a nationwide kaleidoscope of corruption and violence."[8]

This essay explores the cooperative effort that produced that "nationwide kaleidoscope of corruption and violence," and the political implications that lay behind such media coverage. It uncovers the story behind the story of the Scranton hearings and in the process traces the way in which labor racketeering became an important issue in the late 1950s, one with serious political ramifications for the union movement. This history will highlight the influence of the news media, but also the strategic alliances between journalists, political leaders, and congressional investigators that shaped the news and shifted the nation's political agenda.

In this case it was a shift very much to the benefit of anti-union forces, as coverage of the McClellan Committee hearings produced what one news article in May 1957 described as a "cloud of suspicion of corruption and racketeering [that] hovered over some elements in labor." Or, as a top official in the AFL-CIO explained the matter to the *Los Angeles Times*, two weeks later, "Exposures before the McClellan committee on racketeering in the Teamsters Union forced the rest of organized labor into the enormous task of overcoming the public's anti-union reactions." In late April 1957, *Newsweek* surveyed correspondents across the country and concluded "the Senate probe has given the impetus to right-to-work and other labor laws restricting unions."[9]

For the conservative National Association of Manufacturers (NAM), that outcome amounted to an almost perfect fit with the group's public relations agenda. In internal documents from 1956, NAM leaders had laid out the need to undercut the growing power of organized labor. A policy memorandum from February that year set out plans for a "broad public relations program to educate the public to the abuses and evils of organized labor." In describing the issues it wanted to emphasize in this educational program, NAM's document put labor violence second on the list, after compulsory unionism. The central theme was the power of the labor movement. Or as the group's public relations expert put it, "The program will emphasize . . . [the] vast uncontrolled power of labor unions."[10]

NAM's public relations program document laid out an ambitious agenda for raising public concerns about union power through cooperative efforts with sympathetic elements in the news media. These efforts included supplying potential subject matter to editorial writers and opinion columnists as well as encouraging "editors and publishers of leading newspapers and/or newspaper chains to assign writers and photographers to research and write series of articles on the various areas of labor abuses." The document put forward a similar program for national magazines: "A selected list of national magazine editors and publishers will be contacted to interest them in publishing articles that will dramatize and document the labor monopoly abuses story, especially in relation to the 1956 political actions." The document referred specifically to contacts with editorial writers at the

Saturday Evening Post and *Collier's.* It also suggested efforts to "stimulate roundup stories on labor-politics in *Newsweek, Time, Town Journal, Grit,* etc."[11]

A year later the McClellan Committee hearings had provided potent material for editorials and articles that conveniently meshed with NAM's public relations program. Although there is no evidence the business group played a direct role in launching the probe, its public relations campaign benefited immensely. For instance, in April 1957, the same month as the Scranton hearings, the *Saturday Evening Post* ran an editorial arguing that the revelations of the McClellan Committee demonstrated the evils of compulsory unionism and the prevalence of labor violence, justifying efforts to pass right-to-work laws. "In the future," the *Post* asserted, "it will be just a little more difficult to persuade legislators, governors or the people generally that no right to work exists until the worker has made his peace and shared his wages with any set of goons who have managed to muscle into his union."[12] Later that month, *Newsweek* featured a roundup article headlined "Labor Rackets: 48-State Survey."[13]

For the conservative businessmen who ran the NAM, the McClellan Committee represented a godsend. However, other parties played a much more prominent role in initiating this congressional investigation. In particular, the McClellan Committee grew out of the efforts of two newsmen operating in an environment that was already ripe for promoting such an investigation.

Victor Riesel was one of those newsmen. In the 1950s he produced a syndicated daily column entitled "Inside Labor" that appeared in the *New York Mirror* and a couple hundred other newspapers across the country. His column portrayed a labor movement under siege from intertwined threats of Communism and organized crime. Riesel warned that this ominous alliance endangered the nation's security.[14] His claims gained credibility in April 1956, when a hired thug threw acid in his face and permanently blinded him, apparently in retaliation for his "Inside Labor" newspaper columns. Law enforcement attention soon focused on organized crime's role in the attack and Riesel became a symbol of the menacing power of labor racketeers. As the *Des Moines Register* put it, "The circumstances make it impossible to separate the attack from Riesel's crusade against the labor mobsters."[15]

The episode had important political results. Riesel's plight dramatized the problem of union corruption while apparently vindicating his claims about the existence of a powerful criminal conspiracy. Brought into the national spotlight, Riesel insistently called for a congressional investigation of labor corruption. In June 1956, he spoke out forcefully on the issue during an appearance on *Meet the Press*.[16] Many found his argument convincing. This group included President Dwight Eisenhower, who voiced support for a powerful congressional investigation of labor racketeering. By the summer of 1956, prominent congressional figures were echoing his call, including moderate Republicans like Senator Irving Ives of New York, who sat on the Senate's Labor Committee. He submitted a formal resolution calling for a congressional investigation of labor racketeering in early July, citing the attack on Riesel and warning that "no one knows the extent to which racketeers have moved in on the labor movement."[17]

Accompanying these calls for a new congressional probe, the Senate's Permanent Subcommittee on Investigation (PSI) launched a series of preliminary investigations into labor racketeering in the latter part of 1956. These were apparently speculative ventures, meant to determine the viability of a full-scale investigation and also to stake a claim to what could be a politically valuable investigation. The PSI was a subcommittee of the Senate's Government Affairs Committee and it had gained prominence in the early 1950s under the leadership of Senator Joseph McCarthy by focusing on the menace of internal Communism. By1956, a conservative Democrat from Arkansas, Senator John L. McClellan, chaired the committee, while Robert F. Kennedy, then in the conservative, youthful phase of his career, served as the PSI's chief counsel. The group had moved toward labor racketeering in the previous year as it followed the leads in an investigation into a cartel of garment manufacturers who dominated the production of military uniforms. The Mafia figures involved in that cartel included John Dioguardia, the man federal authorities charged with ordering the acid attack on Riesel. In this way, the PSI's investigation of military procurement practices had wandered onto a high-profile target; by the summer of 1956 Dioguardia had become the villainous symbol for the menace of labor racketeering. The PSI soon moved to focus its attention on him and began tracing his connections to a prominent figure in the nation's largest labor union, James R. Hoffa, a vice president in the International Brotherhood of Teamsters.[18]

In following that particular investigative path, Senator McClellan and his chief counsel Kennedy presumably were guided by sound political instincts that drew them toward what one newspaper predicted was "potentially the most sensational congressional probe in 1957"; but they also received encouragement and assistance from a well-connected investigative journalist, Clark Mollenhoff.[19] Indeed, Mollenhoff would later claim credit for initiating the McClellan Committee's investigation of Hoffa and the Teamsters.

Mollenhoff had gone to work as a reporter for the *Des Moines Register* in 1944, soon after receiving his law degree from Drake University. The newspaper's parent company, Cowles Publishing, moved him to its Washington, D.C., bureau in 1950 and he promptly began covering the Kefauver Committee's hearings, the Senate's investigation of organized crime. It was, Mollenhoff later recalled, the beginning of his experiences "learning how to work with congressional committees." Mollenhoff's personal papers contain a draft chronology for his career in the 1950s and it documents a consistent pattern of cooperating with congressional committee members and investigators to promote their investigations, while acquiring the inside information that would make splashy exposés. He was by the mid-1950s the consummate Washington insider, who had valuable contacts with congressmen on both sides of the aisle as well as officials in a range of government agencies.[20]

When the occasion arose, he cooperated with groups outside the capital to build support for a congressional investigation he viewed as potentially useful. His papers contain a couple of intriguing letters from 1953 and 1954, correspondence that was copied to him by a wealthy trucking company executive from Sioux Falls, South Dakota, named William Wilson. The letters reveal a behind-the-scenes effort by businessmen to restore investigating authority to the notoriously anti-union congressman Clare Hoffman, who chaired a series of labor racketeering investigations in the mid-1950s. A bipartisan group within the House of Representatives Government Affairs Committee had rebelled against Hoffman's power as chair of that committee and in so doing blocked his racketeering investigations.[21] Mollenhoff's records reveal a determined effort to get the congressional probes restarted. "I think it is very important," reads one of the Wilson letters, addressed to an official at Standard Oil Company, "and I have talked to a large number of industry men throughout the country and they feel the same way that we must have a Committee in Washington that can investigate and prosecute when necessary racketeering in labor unions." Wilson later asserts, "I think we can do much to convince the members of this Committee [on Government Operations] that they should vote on

January 20 to restore the authority that they took away."[22] Wilson listed particular congressmen and Republican Party officials to contact.

He closes the letter, however, by referring the Standard Oil executive to Mollenhoff for further information: "I do not have the exact details on the controversy [involving Congressman Hoffman] and it would be my suggestion that your representatives call on Clark Mollenhoff. . . . You can depend on him being reliable, trustworthy, and a man who knows all the details on this matter." Mollenhoff's own chronology refers to his role in this episode, by noting, "January 1954: Wrote stories and brought pressure for full Teamster hearing in Minneapolis, in addition to a nation-wide probe."[23]

Labor was not Mollenhoff's usual beat, but in January 1953, an executive editor at Cowles's newspaper in Minneapolis brought him into that city to investigate racketeering allegations involving a local Teamster leader. Mollenoff later noted that "this was the first step in the five-year probe of the Teamsters."[24] It is not clear what led Cowles's executives to set one of their ace reporters onto this story of local union corruption, thus shifting him at least temporarily away from his national political beat. Mollenhoff had not angled for the story and he later wrote that he was "unenthusiastic about the assignment" as he travelled to Minneapolis that January.[25] The publishers he worked for were prominent Republicans, but they bore little resemblance to such flamboyant conservative media figures as Colonel Robert R. McCormick of the *Chicago Tribune* or Frank Gannett of the Gannett Newspaper chain. The brothers who ran Cowles Publishing, John Cowles and Gardner Cowles Jr., were liberal Republicans, known for their influential support of Wendell Willkie in 1940 and later for Dwight Eisenhower in 1952.[26] The push for a journalistic campaign against labor does not fit their style.

Instead it seems more likely that local employers helped engineer Mollenhoff's assignment. There is one intriguing reference in Mollenhoff's correspondence from February 1953 (a few weeks into his research on the story) to the case of Wilson Trucking, which was apparently being squeezed out of some of its shipping routes by a rival company with links to a Teamster official in Minneapolis. This was the same Teamster official whom Mollenhoff had been sent in to investigate. And Wilson was the same trucking executive whose letters described his role in coordinating business efforts to lobby Congress for an investigation into labor racketeering.[27] It seems possible that Wilson and his business allies had waged a similar lobbying effort with local newspaper executives. Indeed, Mollenhoff later described how during his initial visit to Minneapolis he worked closely with Gid Seymour, the executive editor for Cowles's local paper, the *Minneapolis Star and Tribune*. According to Mollenhoff, Seymour was "personally interested" in the story and the editor described the resentment felt by "many of his friends in the business community" in the face of local "Teamster power."[28]

However his assignment happened, Mollenhoff soon came to embrace his particular portion of the labor beat. It became a journalistic crusade against labor racketeering. He focused on the Teamsters, warning of the dangerous power wielded by Dave Beck and especially James R. "Jimmy" Hoffa. In a note accompanying a series he wrote in 1955, Mollenhoff suggested that Cowles's editors should include "a map of the United States to run with the series on Jimmy Hoffa. This map would have the Central States, Southeastern States and Southwestern States [Teamster conference jurisdictions] shaded and the word 'Hoffa Land' printed across it."[29] But Mollenhoff's pieces in this era also pictured a nationwide pattern of corrupt labor leaders operating with impunity. The solution, he argued as early as 1954, should be congressional hearings that would lead to legislation that would strengthen the legal restrictions on organized labor. "The Taft-Hartley Act and the rules of the unions themselves were designed to stop some of the sidelines of plunder," Mollenhoff argued in a magazine article that year, "but the Act is often inadequate or it is improperly enforced by the politicians who fear the labor bosses." He then added, "It is up to Congress to expose fully what has happened under the present laws," and then "to draft new laws" that would curb these abuses.[30]

Mollenhoff's efforts occurred in a particular context that lent credence to his charges and gave them more potency. Ever since the early 1900s, critics of organized labor had underlined the menace of union power by charging labor leaders with widespread corruption. These charges purposely blurred the lines between criminal acts that betrayed the union membership, such as bribe taking, and aggressive organizing tactics like the secondary boycott. In the early 1940s, the newspaper columnist Westbrook Pegler had helped popularize the term *racketeering* as an all-purpose denunciation for a union movement whose rebirth during the New Deal had become a central concern for conservatives. This broad usage of the term soon developed into an accepted convention. It became common practice to tag aggressive labor leaders with the label racketeer, even when no allegations of corruption were involved. Writing in a private letter home to his family during the World War II, then senator Harry Truman referred to John L. Lewis as a "racketeer," complaining that the Mine Workers' decision to violate labor's "no strike pledge" had hurt the country's war effort.[31]

In the post–World War II era, warnings about the need to limit union power often utilized this broad construction of the word *racketeering*. Antiunionists justified the restrictions imposed on the labor movement by the Taft-Hartley Act (1947) with the claim that the law "meant the end of the day of the labor racketeer." In the years that followed, conservatives continued to invoke the potent image of a labor movement subverted by racketeers.[32]

In this way, Mollenhoff's intertwined warnings about union corruption and union power tapped into a rhetorical trope that others had helped to popularize long before he began his crusade. The longevity of this trope—and its continued potency—reflects the coexistence of two different phenomena. Actual corruption, including organized criminal activity, had a long history within some segments of the labor movement. Although the scope of corruption was far smaller than what critics such as Pegler alleged, real abuses did exist that belied the movement's idealistic goals and provided fodder for its opponents. At the same time, many Americans felt uneasy about the distinctive power union officials held, an authority that existed outside the more accepted venues of political office or the corporate boardroom.[33] That such power often was wielded by individuals from a lower socioeconomic background heightened that unease. In his study of cartoon caricatures of union leaders, William J. Puette observes that the figure "cartoonists have come to favor is male, muscle-bound but overweight, unkempt, and violent by nature." Puette explains that cartoonists employ that figure "because the public has come to accept the image as a depiction of working-class people. . . . This image is a class-based projection of ignorance and vulgarity."[34] This enduring, negative image of the working class undercuts acceptance of the power held by labor leaders who epitomize that class. As Pegler put it in 1943, "There is no national union leader big enough or good enough as a man for the job he holds."[35]

At the same time, by the mid-1950s, business efforts to turn back the tide of organized labor were beginning to grow into a full-fledged counteroffensive. NAM started conducting management training sessions on effective strategies for defeating union organization drives. Reflecting this new spirit of aggressiveness, the number of unfair labor practice charges filed against employers by the National Labor Relations Board nearly doubled in the second half of the decade. In some areas, this push-back by employers began to have an impact. Union declines in residential construction and in rural agricultural trucking presaged the defeats in other sectors that would come in later decades.[36]

Operating in this particular political context, Mollenhoff worked steadily for the next several years to promote a large-scale congressional probe into labor racketeering. His motives in doing so were mixed. Like others who encountered the reality of labor union abuses, Mollenhoff expressed sympathy for the victims, including rank-and-file union members denied basic democratic rights in their organizations and bilked of their hard-earned dues money. In addition, he was uneasy about the power that union leaders such as Hoffa wielded. But Mollenhoff also cited the professional advantages that a congressional investigation of labor corruption would bring. It would allow him to write a hard-hitting story about Teamster leaders without fear of a libel suit. Recalling his early days on this story in January 1953, Mollenhoff remembered his concern that even as he gathered evidence of wrongdoing by Teamster leaders, "we could still be subject to losing a few million dollars in libel suits." Under pressure, his sources might change their stories: "In fact, I wouldn't even be sure that all our employer-witnesses would remain firm on their stories unless we had them under oath." It would be safer and surer, he argued, to "pull the story out through a Congressional committee." Witnesses would then be locked into their story and any allegations produced by a congressional hearing would be protected from libel.[37]

Even as he worked to promote a congressional probe, Mollenhoff cultivated a network of investigative journalists pursuing similar stories on corruption in the Teamsters Union. For instance, in 1954, he began cooperating with Ed Guthman and Paul Staples, two reporters with the *Seattle Times* who were pursuing an investigation of Dave Beck. Guthman remembered how his relationship with Mollenhoff began: "We decided we might be able to help each other and began exchanging information about the two Teamster kingpins [Beck and Hoffa]." In Portland, two other reporters, Wallace Turner and William Lambert, writing for the *Oregonian*, were working on stories involving local Teamsters leaders in that city.[38] Mollenhoff's papers reveal similar arrangements with reporters in other cities, including Detroit, which was Hoffa's home base.[39]

This network meant that in 1956 Mollenhoff brought something valuable to the table as he urged the Senate's Permanent Subcommittee on Investigation to pursue a probe into labor racketeering that would focus on the Teamsters' leadership. For the PSI's chairman, Senator McClellan, and his chief counsel, Robert Kennedy, Mollenhoff's advice offered them the chance to draw on a series of ongoing investigations. It was a shortcut to producing impressive results quickly, to demonstrate the viability of the committee's investigation. It also allowed Kennedy and McClellan to claim the key leadership roles in January 1957, when Congress resolved a jurisdictional dispute over who would conduct the new labor racketeering probe by drawing on members from both the PSI and the Labor Committee and forming a temporary select committee. In return, all that was required was that McClellan and Kennedy follow Mollenhoff's lead.

In late 1956, Kennedy dispatched teams of investigators to begin work on congressional hearings that would draw on these local journalistic efforts. Mollenhoff acted as the go-between. He called Guthman in November that year to tell the *Seattle Times* reporter about the new congressional probe that was beginning to take shape. In Guthman's later rendition of this call in his memoir of this period,[40] Mollenhoff told him, " 'I've suggested they [the PSI] start with Dave Beck and the Teamsters in the Pacific Northwest,' he said. 'A young lawyer from the committee [Kennedy] would like to come out and see you and I hope you will help him.' " Mollenhoff "vouched strongly for Bob Kennedy as a person who could be trusted completely."

He also reminded Guthman of the advantages that would come from working with a congressional committee. Guthman added that Mollenhoff "went on to point out that the committee, with its subpoena power could get Beck's financial records, which we had practically no hope of ever obtaining. That was the real clinching argument," Guthman remembered, "and I agreed to see Bob [Kennedy]." They ended up working quite closely together to gather material for hearings on Beck that took place early in 1957.[41] In Portland, Kennedy's investigators teamed up with the *Oregonian* reporters Lambert and Turner, digging through the materials that the journalists had accumulated and following up their leads.[42]

The hearings in Scranton followed this same scenario in most respects, except for the fact that Mollenhoff had not steered Kennedy to this particular locale. Instead, it was the conservative anti-union columnist Westbrook Pegler who brought the story of the Pozusek bombing to the attention of

Kennedy's investigators. For years Pegler had mined local news reports of union misdeeds to provide fodder for his ongoing campaign that denounced the labor movement as violently predacious and ridden with corruption. The few labor leaders not mired in corruption, Pegler claimed, were too complaisant to conduct any kind of meaningful reform.

In September 1956, just as Kennedy and McClellan were beginning to turn their committee toward a probe of labor racketeering, Pegler ran a syndicated column that drew on a local news report from the *Scranton Tribune*. Headlined "Big Union Dinner Honors 4 Felons," Pegler's piece retold the story of a benefit dinner held by Scranton labor leaders to raise money for the legal defense fund of four union officials charged with conspiracy in the case involving Pozusek's construction site. Pegler emphasized the issue of complaisance by detailing the number of prominent labor leaders who attended this gathering. He mocked the hypocrisy of their claims to champion "the sacred cause of labor," and he asserted that the case reflected a widespread pattern of outrageous union violence. In particular Pegler cited "an identical crime" that occurred one month after this benefit dinner when a man in East St. Louis who was building his own family home was threatened by local union officials. When the man persisted, an explosion severely damaged the structure.[43]

Although Pegler was not close to either Kennedy or McClellan, a clipping of this one particular column appears in Kennedy's working files, in a period when very few news clippings were kept.[44] Six months later, when the McClellan Committee held hearings on labor violence in Scranton, it followed Pegler's line of emphasis, using Pozusek's case to demonstrate both the widespread nature of union violence and the complacency of the union hierarchy.

Both Pegler and the McClellan Committee were drawing on the investigative work of J. Harold Brislin, a reporter at the *Scranton Tribune*. Brislin had cracked open a case that had seemed destined to end with the conviction of one lone perpetrator, Paul Bradshaw, who had been spotted along with three other unidentified men in the vicinity of Pozusek's construction site around the time of the explosion. A former boxer who had become a Teamster steward, Bradshaw was part of a crew of men that local Teamster officials used to intimidate opponents in the union and to commit acts of sabotage against nonunion operations in the area. He was the only one arrested for the explosion and the local authorities had essentially closed the case after his conviction. Brislin convinced an embittered Bradshaw to reveal who else had set the explosives and to name the union officials who had ordered the sabotage. Still better, Bradshaw managed to secretly record conversations with his coconspirators that confirmed his version of this episode. Despite threats against him, Brislin used the tapes—and Bradshaw's information—to write an exposé that led to more arrests and eventually the conviction of several local union officials on conspiracy charges growing out of the explosion at Pozusek's construction site.[45]

It was good investigative reporting, but it was still very much a local story, and as Brislin wrote it up, the exposé focused on the apparent lack of diligence on the part of the district attorney. A former official in the Newspaper Guild, Brislin had no animus toward the labor movement. Nor did a case involving damage to one homesite in Scranton get any coverage outside that city. It was Pegler who gave Brislin's story a national profile and who cast it in terms of an indictment of unions in general. The McClellan Committee drew on Brislin's research, but framed the resulting hearings in terms first set out by Pegler.

As had been the case in Seattle and Portland, Kennedy mined the work already done in Scranton by the fourth estate, and a member of his staff reached out to Brislin in January 1957. In response, Brislin wrote to Kennedy, "I am certain that your staff as well the subcommittee will find much information here which will fite [sic] into the pattern of your investigation." The Scranton reporter made his research materials available to the committee and promised "to line up" individuals "who can provide the type of information needed." The committee sent its investigator into Scranton later that month armed with Brislin's research and assisted by the reporter's introductions to the key witnesses needed for the hearings.[46]

Even before the Scranton hearings began, the committee's chairman, McClellan, framed the case in terms of a larger indictment of organized labor. Like Pegler, McClellan depicted the case as emblematic of a pattern of complicity on the part of a labor movement that had done nothing to strip the convicted union officials of their offices. Two days before the hearings began, McClellan told reporters that the "case will present a very grave question of ethics in that there have been court convictions of union officials for offenses that should disqualify them from [any] longer holding office in the unions. However, they are still in office, probably just as much, or in greater control of their unions than before the convictions."[47]

McClellan and another committee member, Senator Barry Goldwater, hammered away at the same point during the actual hearings. As one newspaper report described it, "Both McClellan and Senator Barry Goldwater (Rep. Arizona) bore down indignantly on the presence of convicted union officials in Scranton in high positions of trust in their organizations." McClellan and Goldwater both argued that this situation belied the claims by national AFL-CIO leaders that they were moving against corruption.[48] The headline for the United Press story on the hearings put it simply, "Probe Challenges Labor's Pledge."[49] The inability or unwillingness of union leaders to achieve real reform was a theme frequently used by union critics, including Pegler, to justify new restrictions on union power.

Similarly, Chief Counsel Kennedy previewed the Scranton hearings as an example of a nationwide pattern of union violence. The *Wall Street Journal*'s article describing the forthcoming Scranton hearings quoted "a committee official [who] says this reported case of violence is 'not an isolated incident.'"[50] And McClellan opened the hearings by making a similar claim. The hearings were going to present a "classic example of the use of force and violence" by unions, he asserted. The Scranton case would be representative of the "many reports from areas throughout the country" the committee had received. "For the most part," McClellan said, the complaints received by the committee "are directed against officials or hired thugs and goons of labor unions."[51] The news coverage of the hearings in turn faithfully promoted this version of the significance of the Scranton hearings: convicted union leaders remained in office despite the reform claims of the newly merged AFL-CIO and union violence was rampant.

There were other stories that might have been told about improper practices in the fields of labor or management in the Scranton area. The Teamster steward Bradshaw had information about employers who approached him offering bribes to evade the union's contract restrictions. When interviewed by the committee's investigator in early February 1957, Bradshaw named one prominent employer who "asked me if I'd take $200 a week to leave his trucks go in [to a unionized depot]" in contravention of the union's contract. He described how that employer later bragged about paying off the local Teamster officials.[52] But in the detailed prehearing memo in which the committee's staff laid out the issues and questions that would be raised during the Scranton hearings, no mention was made of employer involvement in union corruption.[53] Instead the staff memo detailed the examples of union violence that Bradshaw's testimony would highlight and his knowledge of rigged union elections. The memo made it clear the committee had an intended story line for the hearings. It declared, "Bradshaw will be playing the role of a man who desires to tell all he knows about labor racketeering in Scranton, Pennsylvania." But labor racketeering, in this case, would be the story of union misdeeds and nothing else.[54]

For that reason, the committee failed to look at a dramatic example of large-scale corruption that had recently occurred in the local Scranton scene. A number of employers, a member of Congress, and a former congressman were all indicted in December 1956 on corruption charges stemming from the construction of a $33 million military depot outside Scranton.[55] No mention of this appeared in the Scranton hearings. The committee also never used its hearing to present the emergence of an internal reform movement within the Scranton Teamsters, one that swept out of office the union officials convicted for conspiracy in the explosion at Pozusek's construction site.[56] Had the McClellan Committee or the news media highlighted these developments it would not have absolved the local labor movement, but it would have provided a more balanced perspective. Union misdeeds would look less like a dangerous aberration, if they were placed alongside abuses in other social sectors, including Congress and the business community. Nor was the union movement incapable of reform.

In conclusion, it should be noted that neither the McClellan Committee nor the news media operated in a historical vacuum. As Lawrence Richards has recently pointed out and other scholars have noted as well, antipathy to unions has a long history in the United States and popular concerns about union practices, from labor strikes to closed shop contracts, predated the hearings in Scranton.[57] Elsewhere I have noted how in the immediate post–World War II era congressional Republicans drew on a broad construction of the term *racketeering* to campaign against the New Deal and for the Taft-Hartley Act. As they regained a majority in Congress, the Republicans launched the first congressional probe into labor racketeering in 1947, with hearings that occurred at the same time as debates over the Taft-Hartley Act. In the years that followed congressional investigations into racketeering proliferated along with news coverage of the problem.[58]

But the McClellan Committee hearings were different in ways that heightened the significance of this episode. First and foremost, this was a much bigger investigation than anything previously seen, dwarfing other comparable efforts. The committee had a staff of over one hundred people,

including eighty investigators, with about half of them specializing in foren-
sic accounting. By way of contrast, the Senate's Permanent Subcommittee
of Investigation, Joseph McCarthy's committee, had about fifteen investigators and the House Un-American Activities Committee had about twenty.[59]
The size of this staff reflected the committee's early successes, its ability to
produce headline-grabbing revelations during the first few months of the
hearings. In late March 1957, Kennedy announced that he was tripling the
number of people working for the committee.[60] Thus, the committee's early
partnership with Mollenhoff's colleagues in Seattle and Portland had
brought tangible political benefits.

The hearings came at a pivotal political moment. Conservative business
forces had reacted to the merger of the AFL and the CIO in 1955 with
alarm and then with a renewed commitment to stage a counteroffensive
against organized labor. As Elizabeth Fones-Wolf observed, many in the
business community "saw in the merger the specter of a labor jugger-
naut."[61] The National Association of Manufacturers had decided by 1956
that the news media represented a critical venue for waging this counteroffensive and the McClellan Committee hearings provided NAM with a
wonderful opportunity for broadcasting its message. Meanwhile, in the
Republican Party, President Eisenhower's administration was abandoning
its earlier efforts to build a political bridge to moderates in the labor movement. The president's political advisors had concluded that the Republican
Party's best hope for regaining a majority status lay in an "attempt to separate the leaders of labor politically from the rank and file."[62] The McClellan
Committee's revelations offered a choice opportunity to do just that and
Eisenhower soon embraced a focus on the problem of labor racketeering.
The *New York Times* columnist James Reston reported that the Republican
National Committee believed "the President's tactics will split many workers from their labor union bosses."[63] Further to the right, Barry Goldwater
staked his 1958 Senate reelection campaign on an attack against the racketeering bosses of big labor, demonstrating the populist appeal this issue
could have.[64]

Finally, the close partnership between the committee and the press
heightened the impact of the hearings while allowing the conservatives who
dominated this probe to promote a menacing depiction of the labor movement. Newsmen who teamed up with the McClellan Committee became

equivalent to a later generation of embedded reporters; they gained unparalleled access but in the process they were co-opted. The rules of this partnership were usually implicit but occasionally Kennedy would spell them out in correspondence that marked the end of a successful set of hearings and would thank the journalists for their assistance. Journalists like Mollenhoff, Guthman, and others who agreed to this arrangement gained exclusive access to the privileged information that committee staff members were able to gather with the power of subpoena and access to government records. These reporters also could use the committee to help track down promising leads. In return they agreed to a kind of prior restraint on what they would publish and when they would publish it. For example, in a letter to John Siegenthaler in 1958 that followed a set of hearings on Teamsters violence in Tennessee, Kennedy noted that the Nashville journalist was "responsible for much of the information which was the basis for our hearings." Summarizing Siegenthaler's embedded role in the committee's investigation, Kennedy recalled, "During the course of the investigation, when you were aware of many things that we had uncovered, you worked closely with the investigators without revealing information that would have been harmful if it had been made public prematurely."[65]

For these journalists, the working arrangement with the committee's staff often yielded dramatic professional benefits. William Lambert and Wallace Turner (the reporters at the *Portland Oregonian*), Mollenhoff, and Scranton's Brislin all won Pulitzer Prizes for their reporting on the Teamsters scandals. Beyond that close immediate circle, Kennedy cultivated a larger group of reporters who received advanced briefings on the content of the hearings, access to committee information, and a range of useful tips and leads.[66]

In return these reporters carefully stayed on message. Kennedy's working files are replete with correspondence from this circle of journalists offering their assistance and running their stories by the committee's chief counsel. In June 1957, for instance, Ed Guthman wrote Kennedy and enclosed clippings of the *Seattle Times*'s most recent articles on the McClellan Committee hearings. Referring to a piece that had touted the committee's allegations regarding a Hoffa ally in Los Angeles, H. L. Woxberg, Guthman noted, "We did fine with the Woxberg story as the attached clips will show. The wire services however did not attach much significance and didn't pick it up. I talked to the AP this morning and perhaps they'll do it today. We can't tell them how to run their railroad, but we can try." Guthman closed his note with an offer that in various forms other reporters also made: "If you can see any other move we can make in the Woxberg-Hoffa situation, please drop me a line or call collect."[67]

For his part, Kennedy worked assiduously to maintain this close relationship and noted its importance to the committee's efforts. In early May 1959, he wrote to thank the national affairs editor at *Life* magazine, Hugh Moffett, for their meeting the previous day for a "talk about the Teamsters." Kennedy noted, "*Life* has been very good to this Committee over its two years of existence—of this of course I am very much aware." With a circulation of six million subscribers in the late 1950s, *Life* magazine blanketed the nation.[68] Kennedy wrote of his satisfaction that "an article such as this is in good hands and in my estimation can and will have a most worthwhile effect—far better than weeks and weeks of our hearings on the subject." For his part, Moffett wrote back to make sure Kennedy approved of the article the magazine was preparing to run on the Teamsters: "Although we think you will like the story as it finally appears, we cannot be sure at this point. Therefore, I hope we can hear from you through our Washington associates or directly if you care." The article in question was featured on *Life*'s cover, May 18, 1959, headlined "A National Threat: Hoffa's Teamsters."[69]

In effect, and not for the last time, the press had ceased to function as an independent voice, capable of offering the general public a balanced perspective. It was not that corruption did not exist in the Teamsters Union, or that sabotage had not occurred in Scranton; the committee profiled a series of incidents that included the damage done to Pozusek's house construction site, the stink bombing of a local bakery, and efforts to sabotage some road construction equipment.[70] But in its coverage of labor racketeering, the press had essentially abdicated the role of deciding the scale and the significance of these phenomena, acceding to the claims of a congressional committee dominated by anti-union conservatives.[71]

John Siegenthaler, one of the reporters who had teamed up with the McClellan Committee in 1957 and 1958, later warned about the dangers presented by the "mutual cooperation between the press and congressional investigators." In 1963, he told a gathering of newspaper editors that "this relationship should never become too intimate or cozy." He asserted that, when it did, the relationship undermined the ability of the press to perform its "relevant responsibilities," which included offering the public a critical perspective on the investigative efforts of Congress.[72] Though he did not intend it as such, Siegenthaler's warning has the feel of a rueful admission, and perhaps an epitaph for what *Time* magazine had labeled "The Pattern for Partnership."

"Compulsory Unionism": Sylvester Petro and the Career of an Anti-Union Idea, 1957–1987

Joseph A. McCartin and Jean-Christian Vinel

In 1959, a forty-two-year-old labor law professor from New York University traveled to Washington, D.C., to testify in the McClellan Committee hearings. Sylvester Petro had caught the attention of conservative policymakers two years earlier by publishing *The Labor Policy of a Free Society*, a scathing critique of the New Deal labor relations regime, which he had concluded with a detailed analysis of the Taft-Hartley Act as interpreted by the National Labor Relations Board (NLRB). Petro had made a name for himself as an expert on labor unions under Taft-Hartley, particularly on their financial contributions to the electoral process, but for the committee's purposes, it was no doubt an added bonus that he had been a steelworker and a union activist in the 1930s before attending law school at the University of Chicago and adopting libertarian, anti-union views.[1]

That conservative policymakers such as Senator Barry Goldwater were able to draw on the expertise of a former union activist sheds considerable light on the post-New Deal relationship between the Right and labor. For Petro's rise as a union critic in the late 1950s occurred at a decisive moment in the history of American labor relations, when the pluralist, pro-union framework championed by a generation of liberal politicians, jurists, and academics had just begun to falter.[2] Then or now, Petro achieved none of the recognition that came to the Ivy League theorists of the American system of postwar industrial pluralism, but his appearance in a Capitol hearing room in 1959 nonetheless symbolized the growing vitality of ideological anti-unionism in the United States. Indeed, Petro's school of economic and constitutional analysis played a crucial role in legitimizing a libertarian outlook in the 1970s and 1980s that would effectively challenge much that had once been considered hegemonic and progressive within the world of industrial relations law and scholarship.

Yet the contribution of this former steelworker to the growth of the anti-union idea is still largely unknown. Scholars rarely mention his books, and he is mostly remembered for his denunciation of labor racketeering. While labor historiography is rich with accounts demonstrating the sobering effects of industrial pluralism on the American union movement, so far there are almost no studies of the intellectual movement that gave the New Right its anti-union agenda. In this field, conservatism is still somewhat of an "orphan," its existence usually acknowledged only in studies of businessmen and business associations.[3]

Tracing Petro's long career, one catches a glimpse of the complex intellectual and political dynamics that nourished a libertarian conservative critique of the New Deal labor relations regime in the postwar era. This critique, we argue, was not merely a refurbished expression of American individualism. It linked the ideas of the Austrian school of economics to the venerable American antimonopoly tradition, drew on the midcentury debate over union violence and corruption, and ultimately forged a form of rights talk that challenged the class-based, collective logic of the Wagner Act and asserted the worker's right to be free of union "coercion" based on the First Amendment. This critique, which developed in conjunction with the right-to-work struggle in the 1950s and 1960s, generated a series of crucial legal battles in the next decade that weakened union protections and continues to provide a powerful intellectual resource in anti-union struggles down to the present day.

Theory: "Every Union Man Is a Serf"

"Questioning the virtues of the organized labor movement is like attacking religion, motherhood, monogamy, or the home. Among the intelligentsia, any doubts about collective bargaining admit of explanations only in terms of insanity, knavery, or 'subservience to the interests.' Discussion of skeptical views runs almost entirely in terms of how one came into such persuasions, as though they were symptoms of a disease."[4] With these words, the University of Chicago economist and free marketeer Henry C. Simons pithily summarized the isolation and political impotence of anti-union ideas in the United States in 1944. Like other conservatives, Simons watched with anxiety as World War II drew to a close, leaving in its wake an expanding labor movement and a set of near hegemonic liberal ideals best exemplified by President Franklin Roosevelt's determination to use government power to ensure "freedom from want" and "economic citizenship." To conservatives, these were no more than shibboleths, "fools' gold words," as John Chamberlain dubbed them.[5] But there was no denying the reality of the unions' newfound legitimacy. Indeed, Simons thought of himself as a lonely voice, a producer of heterodox ideas whose role was to challenge common wisdom.

A former machine shop worker who was once steeped in the liberal culture bewailed by Simons, Sylvester Petro was in his origins a most unlikely libertarian. Born in 1917 to an immigrant working-class family of steelworkers on Chicago's South Side, Petro took part in the political awakening that led many white ethnic workers during the 1930s to join the ranks of unions and support the New Deal. At Republic Steel, Petro contributed to the union impulse at the very moment when the assistance of the federal government helped the Steel Workers Organizing Committee (SWOC) overcome the deeply entrenched anti-unionism in this bastion of the open shop.[6]

Given the violent anti-unionism of so many "Little Steel" executives, Petro's organizing work was the kind of social experience that might well have built faith in industrial democracy and the power of collective action in the service of social justice. But unlike the hundreds of thousands who lent their allegiance to SWOC and the new Congress of Industrial Organizations, Petro gradually grew disenchanted with unionism as it operated under the Wagner Act. A government-enforced model of exclusive representation that countenanced the closed shop was dangerous in his view: "further experience, education and reflection led me to believe that unions, whatever their capacity for good, had to be watched and subjected to the same laws and rules of conduct that apply to others," he explained.[7]

To be sure, at midcentury there was no dearth of defectors from the proletarian Left: men like John Burnham, Max Eastman, or Whitaker

Chambers exemplified the importance of converts to the resurgence of the Right. Petro, however, was no born-again intellectual fleeing a youthful radicalism. His was an estrangement from the culture of unionism as it was lived and practiced on the shop-floor—one that arose from the conflict he perceived between the collective logic of unionism and the constitutional rights of the individual. So far there is no accessible archival material to trace precisely the events that led to Petro's move away from unionism. But one thing is clear: he drew on his "personal experience in unions and in industry" to frame his repeated denunciation of "compulsory unionism" and "union violence," and his defense of workers' individual rights.[8]

Petro's uneasiness with union strategies need not surprise us. Lizabeth Cohen reminds us that some workers resented the rise of industrial unionism and the forceful persuasion of their activists: "They approached you, kept after you, hounded you. To get them off my neck I joined," recalled an irritated worker at Chicago Inland Steel. And as David Witwer has shown, a similar resentment informed the rise of the anti-union columnist Westbrook Pegler, who had once belonged to the Newspaper Guild.[9] More intriguing, however, is the social process whereby Petro slowly morphed into a recognized libertarian expert on labor relations.

Petro's Libertarian Conversion

Discontented with the jobs he held in the steel industry, Petro worked his way through the University of Chicago Law School, from which he graduated in 1942. He earned an LLM degree from the University of Michigan three years later. These were remarkable achievements, but such educational triumphs did not necessarily put a young working-class student on a path toward the legal and political Right. The law school itself was not yet a libertarian stronghold. It had briefly been home to Roscoe Pound, one of the fathers of legal realism, and Chicago had trained its share of New Dealers, like Harold Ickes and Jerome Frank. While the school would later become a bastion for the followers of Friedrich A. Hayek and Ludwig von Mises, in the early 1940s Chicago taught law very much within the legal realist tradition, a commitment signified by the school's recruitment of Karl Llewellyn in 1951.[10]

At Chicago, however, Petro attended the classes of William Winslow Crosskey, an iconoclast whose work roiled the waters of constitutional scholarship in the 1950s. Crosskey contended that it was possible to demonstrate how Americans understood the Constitution in 1787. In his rendition of their designs, the framers had meant to create a strong, central government—one capable of regulating commerce—and had left the states with no real autonomy. However, he maintained that the fathers of the Constitution expected the Congress, not the presidency, to be the preeminent institution in this strong central government, and that this legislative domination was to be strictly protected by the separation of powers. Crosskey's teaching made a strong impression on Petro, who embraced the idea that separation of powers and a strong legislative branch were the only safeguards against tyranny. Unlike many conservatives who fretted over the rising imperial presidency, however, Petro identified federal agencies as the sources of tyranny—reading Crosskey, he later argued, one could only come to the conclusion that the "quasi-judicial" agencies created during the Progressive Era and the New Deal were both unconstitutional and dangerous.[11] Indeed, Petro would come to contend in the *Labor Policy of a Free Society* that the role of Congress was to intervene in the economic sphere by prescribing a rule of law that would uniformly protect the free exchange of goods, while the task of arbitrating labor relations should devolve to the courts—federal or otherwise.[12]

Petro's libertarian conservatism deepened after his graduation from law school, especially with regard to labor issues. Admitted to the Illinois bar, he practiced law but also took a job with the Commerce Clearing House (CCH), a Chicago-based company that published guides to commercial and tax regulations. Founded by William KixMiller, a famous exponent of American business civilization who opposed the statist approach of the New Deal, the CCH was firmly rooted in Chicago's conservative corporate circles, an environment that fed Petro's anti-union views. While at CCH, Petro also served as editor of the Labor Law Reports, authoring a guide on the Taft-Hartley Act that served as the basis for a study published in 1958 under the aegis of the Labor Policy Association. In *How the NLRB Repealed Taft-Hartley*, he explained that the board had constantly violated congressional intent, which, since the passage of the 1947 law, was no longer intended to promote unionism. Petro's critique of the board gained little traction at first, but in time it found a wider audience and by 1970 Petro was back in front of Congress, testifying in favor of the Tower Bill, a failed effort to strip the NLRB of the power to adjudicate unfair labor practices.[13]

In 1950, the year that John Chamberlain and Henry Hazlitt revived the publication of *The Freeman*, which would soon become the leading vehicle for the articulation of libertarian conservatism, Petro took a post at the New York University (NYU) School of Law. At the time of Petro's arrival,

NYU had already attracted a nucleus of committed libertarians, including one of the leading figures from the Austrian school of economics, Ludwig von Mises, who had emigrated to the United States in 1940.[14] The tenets of the Austrian school contradicted the Keynesian approach that had swept through the polities of most Western countries in the course of the 1930s. Indeed, the followers of the Austrian school were heirs to the older neoclassical strand of economic theory, which viewed economic relations apart from social relations. Preaching a methodological individualism (an agent-based approach to economics), they argued that the market was a harmonious space in which economic phenomena necessarily reflect the decisions made by rational individuals exemplifying universal and predetermined rules of behavior exempted from time and history. According to this vision of the market, producers or consumers simply tried to maximize their satisfaction given their constraints in a self-contained system that the intervention of the state could only disrupt. Mises and Hayek had devoted much time in the 1920s and 1930s to demonstrate that socialism was inefficient, using the theory of marginal utility to argue that to rationally allocate resources in an economy, it was necessary to rely on market-based prices because they reflect both the amount of resources and their desirability. Hence the two most important tenets of the Austrian school: the sovereignty of the consumer and the necessity of economic freedom to buttress political freedom.[15]

After Crosskey, Mises would be the most important intellectual influence on Petro, and an important connection as well. In 1958, Petro was invited to join the Mont Pelerin Society (MPS), the international group founded by Hayek to promote free-market ideas. Petro earned this invitation with his 1957 *The Labor Policy of a Free Society*, but his new membership reflected the broader impact of the Austrians' ideas on the growing infrastructure of the New Right. Thanks to funding from the former DuPont executive Jasper Crane, the MPS annual conference that year was held in the United States for the first time, and a number of American businessmen traveled to Princeton to join the elitist intellectual group. As Kim Phillips-Fein has recently argued, libertarian intellectuals, particularly Hayek and Mises, provided corporate America with an intellectual and conceptual framework to fight the emerging welfare state.[16] Petro's own contribution was to apply Mises's theories to labor relations, arguing that unions were inimical to the spontaneous and unpredictable order that consumers generated and that unions corrupted the political system that made the free market possible.[17] In using the concept of "compulsory unionism" in his critique of the New Deal labor relations regime, he provided a useful link between the intellectuals agitating for the free market and the emerging "right-to-work" movement.

Anatomy of a "Free Collective Bargaining Rule"

Like many Americans at midcentury, Petro defined liberty and civilization through the prism of consumption, celebrating the American standard of living and contrasting it to that of the Soviets.[18] Because they were a relatively new phenomenon, he argued, unions could not be credited for helping to produce the highest standard of living in the world. Rather, what made America exceptional was first and foremost the amount of capital invested per worker, and the economic system that had made such investment possible. "Our nation-wide free market, based on private property and freedom of contract, is the institution which most clearly distinguishes the United States from other societies," he asserted.[19]

Unlike many conservatives, however, Petro had no use for religion and had no qualms about defending the materialism that many lamented in America, claiming that it was the very evidence of American superiority over European nations. Like Ayn Rand, Petro departed from the fusionism expounded by William Buckley and Frank Meyer in the pages of the *National Review*. He placed himself on the libertarian side of the conservative debate—he never mentioned religious concerns in his writing, arguing instead that the two pillars of American civilization were the free market and the rule of law, both of which were jeopardized by Keynesian economics and the government's empowerment of unions.[20]

Reaffirming the virtues of the free market in the 1950s, however, was no easy task once one left the confines of specific academic campuses and seminar rooms. The world of rugged individualism that prevailed before the Great Depression had been supplanted. Petro himself acknowledged as much in *The Labor Policy of Free Society*, which opened with an endorsement of the notions that had animated much of New Deal reform— security, stability, freedom, and well-being—which he saw as the motives animating people's lives: "The worker turns out to be a human being, even as you and I, with the same instincts, desires and habits. The worker wants more money, meaning more things, usually; but he would also like to work fewer hours and have better and longer vacations. He would like to have a secured income. . . . Workers tend to prefer stability and security to instability and insecurity. . . . Here we are, all of us, wishing material goods plus freedom, plus opportunity; and at the same time strongly desiring personal security and stability."[21]

To Petro, the "great society" (a phrase he borrowed from Mises) would be a society in which these aspirations were fulfilled, but this could be done only in an unregulated market, because whatever form they might take (food, leisure, or even medical services), the quests for well-being and security were necessarily expressed through the act of consumption. True to the reductionist logic of the Austrian school, Petro argued that the market was a democratic space where individuals harmoniously realized their private choices through consumption—as consumers voted for or against the products offered by companies, they generated a "spontaneous order" based on subjective motives for which there could be no planning. Only an economic system in which entrepreneurs were free to respond to the fluctuating desires of consumers could ensure the liberty of people to improve their well-being. The mainstay of this democratic system was the sanctity of property rights, which alone ensured a citizen's ability to compete in the marketplace and to enjoy its fruits. According to Petro, property rights were indispensable to American civilization because they acted as a Durkheimian *social bond* mediating relationships between people and coordinating private goals and collective aspirations.[22]

The idea that the market produced a harmony of social interests naturally led Petro to ignore the idea of the "working class" and to dispute the contention that industrial society was inherently violent. In a line of thinking going back to David Ricardo's law of association, Petro argued that society was by essence "cooperative," by which he meant that the division of labor was the very source of the material progress of the United States, and was necessary to provide the most adequate answer to men's and women's desires.[23] More, this perspective on the economy allowed Petro to deny as illogical the very premise of the Wagner Act—that it was necessary for the state to redress the imbalance in the bargaining power of employers and workers: "Workers and their employers *share* the same bargaining position *vis à vis* the consumers and other producers," he argued. Drawing on the recent research of conservative economists such as Milton Friedman and Edward Chamberlin, who denied that unions could help workers increase their share of the national income, he concluded that to improve their lot, workers should try to improve the position of their employer in the market.[24]

Here lay the very foundation of Petro's fight against "compulsory unionism" and his struggle for "free employee choice": unions took advantage of majority rule and the union shop to "impose" a collective bargaining contract on all workers, thereby depriving them of the freedom to pursue their own ends in the marketplace. Having placed workers under their control, labor organizations then pursued interests of their own. He made this point at length in *The Kingsport Strike,* in which he took the union of the printers working for the Kingsport Press to task for agreeing to a "sweetheart deal" that brought no real benefits to the printers. As for the long and bitter strike called by the union in 1963, Petro argued that it was undertaken only to reduce the company's competitive advantage, not to promote the workers' immediate interests. Hence to Petro making unions more democratic was pointless—what was needed was to reduce them to their marketplace voluntaristic and individualistic dimension, that is, allow workers to join them and leave them at will.[25]

Reading Petro's analysis of the free market, one is struck by the abstract character of his thought. But we must remember that he was heir to an intellectual tradition—the Austrian school—that rejected empirical analysis and instead held that for a theory to be valid, it had to be intellectually coherent.[26] This theoretical perspective, which was at odds with the mathematical models developed by neo-classical scholars such as William Stanley Jevons, harkened back to the influence of Karl Popper (another member of the Mont Pelerin Society), and largely fit in the midcentury American context, for in the 1950s empirical research was often associated—particularly within the social sciences—with "totalitarian" science.[27]

This theoretical background matters enormously to understanding Petro's work, for he developed his critique of labor relations during an intense period of anti-Communism. In the 1950s, the conservatives whose voices mattered most dealt with the threat of Communism. This feature of American political life was illustrated by the success of Robert Welch's "May God Forgive Us," a speech that sold over two hundred thousand copies in the aftermath of the debate over President Harry Truman's dismissal of General Douglas MacArthur during the Korean War. Reading Petro, however, we see that he was unimpressed with the achievements of the anti-Communist crusade at home. He understood that many on the left as well as the right embraced anti-Communism. This was particularly true of unions, for the Taft-Hartley clause mandating their signing affidavits that they were not Communists had received strong backing from many liberal union leaders.[28] As Petro noted, many union leaders, such as George Meany or John L. Lewis, were genuinely anti-Communist, and others, like Walter Reuther, at least publicly embraced anti-Communism. There was nothing surprising in that, Petro argued, because unions exist only in free societies. The American Federation of Labor (AFL) and the Congress of Industrial Organizations (CIO) thus had a vested interest in the anti-Communist battle.[29] But trade union anti-Communism gave Petro little comfort. He believed that "what counts is the real effect of present trade union thinking and action upon the real events and real life of America." And he was convinced that government-supported union power would gradually erode the foundations of American freedom.[30]

One cannot understand Petro's depiction of American society and its economy if one does not view it as distinct from the anti-Communist struggle led by Senator Joseph McCarthy and other conservatives. Petro's work represented a different kind of conservatism, one that stemmed from a conservative transatlantic crossing and came to the fore of American politics in the late 1950s precisely because McCarthyism had run its course, leaving the American Left debilitated, but statist liberalism intact and the free market none the better for it, or so it seemed from the libertarian standpoint. It is not surprising that Petro was active, along with William F. Buckley and Frank S. Meyer, in the foundation of the New York Conservative Party in 1962, which challenged the liberal wing of the GOP in that state and was in many ways the forerunner of the Draft Goldwater movement in New York. Still, more than Buckley's or Meyer's, Petro's support of that effort was primarily nourished by the influence of the Austrians, Mises and Hayek.[31]

It bears emphasizing that the libertarian-managerial network in which Petro began to play a significant role did not simply agitate for a return to rugged individualism. Beyond the tenets of the Austrian school of economics, what gave their effort to restore managerial rights a distinctive postwar tone was their ability to link it to America's long-standing antimonopoly tradition. Historically, the antimonopoly tradition was strongly linked to the American Left, particularly to the Progressive movement, but as Alan Brinkley demonstrated, the antimonopoly impulse gradually lost its impetus over the 1930s, making way for a Keynesian political economy. By the latter years of the 1950s, that order was under attack from the right. Petro's books came out in the midst of a rising gale of anti-union books and articles by conservative economists, jurists, and managers, who waged a campaign urging the public to see that labor organizations were inimical to the public good.[32] On one point Petro and the conservatives who now marshaled the antimonopoly argument agreed with the Progressives who had once controlled that agenda: monopolies led to corruption and threatened democracy.

The Fight Against Labor Monopolies and "Compulsory Unionism"

Unlike the conservative economists who focused on the impact of unions on general wages and argued that unions could only improve their share of the national income at the expense of the general public, Petro insisted that labor unions enjoyed no power that was not political in its origins. Indeed, it was the support of the state that made a monopoly unacceptable from the standpoint of the free market—Petro did not share Burnham's concern for large-scale organizations, because businessmen had no way of imposing their will on consumers who, by nature, are bent on resisting what others try to force on them. Hence he would not have challenged "natural" monopolies stemming from consumer choices, arguing that companies have no power to force consumers to buy a product, or even to prevent a businessman from setting up shop and competing for the consumers' choices. In the same fashion, Petro contended that should all the employees in an industry freely elect to join a union, they should in no way be prevented from doing so.[33]

Yet Petro argued that the unions that dominated the American industrial scene were not the product of "employee free choice." Claiming to speak in the name of the "silent" labor movement, he argued that "every union member was a serf"—not only did unions rely on the compulsory practices of the closed shop and stranger picketing (picketing by nonemployees), but they were top-down organizations in which the rank and file hardly expected to make decisions. For Petro, a long, bitter strike launched in 1954 by the United Auto Workers (UAW) against a Wisconsin-based plumbing fixture manufacturer, the Kohler Company, perfectly exemplified the problem. The strike began after two years of negotiations failed to produce a contract and it lasted eight years. The Kohler strike, Petro asserted, exemplified the authoritarian leadership of unions—since in that case, Walter Reuther, president of the UAW, claimed to have spent close to $10 million in a struggle in which no automobile worker was directly affected, turning the conflict into a war of attrition between unions and management. To Petro, the UAW's expenditure in no way reflected the wishes of the union's rank and file, and suggested that labor solidarity was not a social fact but a creation of undemocratic laws that allowed unions to politicize the workplace.[34]

Petro became involved in this protracted and violent conflict at the behest of Kohler officials. Having suffered several setbacks at the hands of the NLRB, they were looking for someone willing to expose the deficiencies of administrative law (as opposed to civil law). Kohler asked Petro to write about the Kohler struggle and promised to print two hundred thousand copies of Petro's resulting book for distribution by like-minded companies. Kohler managers—who saw themselves as ethical employers—had already spent vast sums of money in their campaign against the UAW. In engaging Petro they hoped for the support of an independent expert who could speak with authority about the broader issues involved in the conflict. The Henry Regnery Company, which was close to the John Birch Society, was a fitting publisher for the book—it was about to publish Barry Goldwater's *Conscience of a Conservative* as it became the leading conservative publishing house of the period.[35]

Published as *The Kohler Strike: Union Violence and Administrative Law*, and as summarized in various articles, Petro's effort was a relentless critique of the NLRB and administrative law—he berated its obscure and inconsistent procedures, and most importantly, its lack of fairness. Providing his own version of the theory of agency capture, he emphasized the corrupting nature of administrative law, arguing that the NLRB members were short-term appointees bowing to political pressure, even condoning violence and property violations. The NLRB's policy was so partial, Petro contended, that it might be summarized as the idea that unions—whatever may happen on the picket line—should never lose a strike. Making this argument, Petro's book provided an important counterpoint to the 1959 McClellan investigation into the dispute. While Senator Goldwater's inquiry had yielded no evidence that the UAW was responsible for the wave of violence that swept through the town of Sheboygan, Wisconsin, Petro sought to demonstrate that the strike was ill fated in the first place and that only the NLRB's intervention in the struggle had rescued the union leaders from their mistake. Hence Petro's forceful conclusion: the violence of union members against reluctant workers resulted from the undemocratic character of the strike and the support that the union received from the government.

As he put it in his 1959 book *Power Unlimited*—an account of the McClellan hearings—"Power grabbed by force and exercised subject to no pervasive structural or functional check is bound to corrupt."[36]

Petro's contention then was that Congress had forsaken constitutional principles, first by permitting labor contracts that made union membership compulsory through the closed shop, then by requiring companies to negotiate and sign collective bargaining contracts with unions, and finally by depriving the courts of their jurisdiction in labor disputes, which were now the province of administrative agencies such as the NLRB. To be sure, Congress had tried to reconcile the New Deal labor relations regime with the principles of the free market by outlawing many union compulsory practices in the Taft-Hartley Act, but as Petro argued in his *How the NLRB Repealed the Taft-Hartley Act*, the board had flouted congressional will in its interpretation of the law on issues such as stranger picketing or hot cargo contracts—clauses allowing employees not to handle goods that either came from a company dealing with a strike or were manufactured by a company placed on a union unfair list.[37]

Yet Petro did not argue that unions had no place in a free society. In Hartzian fashion, he argued that while workers had once been deprived of the right to organize in Great Britain, they had always enjoyed this right in America, "which became a nation at just that point in history when liberalism was most vigorously stimulating the minds of men."[38] In a liberal economy, he added, collective actions aimed at raising wages are indispensable to the free market, where labor is bought and sold. But the kind of unionism to which Petro was attracted bore no resemblance to the New Deal collective bargaining regime. Reviewing the nineteenth-century labor record, Petro found none of the judicial bias against unions that Felix Frankfurter and Nathan Greene had denounced in *The Labor Injunction*.[39] Rather he pointed to *Commonwealth v. Hunt* (1842) as the model of labor relations that was compatible with the unregulated economy he was calling for. In his famous opinion, Judge Lemuel Shaw had rested his defense of the right of journeymen to combine on the premise that unions were thoroughly compatible with the principles of the free market, and that associations of consumers or workers might play a role in maintaining a healthy, competitive economy.[40] Accordingly, Shaw ruled that workers had the right to organize as long as they did not combine to break a law. Following Shaw, Petro proposed to see unions as purely voluntary associations created to further the economic interests of their members in the marketplace, a notion thoroughly in tune with the rebirth of the Tocquevillian associative ideal in postwar America.⁴¹ Naturally, this endorsement of the right to organize left unions with little power—since all forms of compulsion were unacceptable to Petro. Free collective bargaining then would be no more than a modern version of an early nineteenth-century New England town hall meeting.

The Rise of a Libertarian Rights Talk

To understand the allure of *Commonwealth v. Hunt* to Petro, however, it is necessary to outline the legal battle that gradually developed out of this antimonopoly perspective. By invoking *Commonwealth*, Petro mostly wanted to recast the debate over unions in terms of freedom of association, as nineteenth century journeymen had done. But to Petro the overall framework of freedom of association was promising because it would allow conservatives to make a case for the freedom of individuals to dissent from or avoid membership in labor organizations, and more generally, it would make it easier to protect a number of "first class citizenship" rights deriving from property rights—the right to work, the right not to join a union and to remain free from union pressure, the right to set up alternative unions. It is important to note that Petro began to assemble his rights-based argument against union coercion at precisely the moment when the civil rights revolution was beginning to make "rights talk" more central than ever to American political discourse. Petro and his colleagues hoped to capitalize on this moment to drive their attack on government-supported union power.

Praxis: Ideas Have Consequences

By the 1960s, Petro had earned an authoritative voice in the libertarian community. He was cited by men like Hayek, and linked to efforts to propagate libertarian ideas. Beyond his role in the creation of the New York Conservative Party, Petro was active in the Philadelphia-based Intercollegiate Society of Individualists (ISI), an organization created in 1953 by Frank Chodorov after the model of the Intercollegiate Socialist Society to provide college students with the access to conservative literature and ideas that was necessary to challenge the reign of liberalism. The ISI organized seminars and lecturing tours where Petro rubbed shoulders with Meyer, Richard Weaver, and other leading conservative activists.[42]

Still, it remained difficult for Petro to determine how influential his ideas were. In 1961, back from a trip to Argentina where he had given lectures to and met with the anti-Peron forces, Petro commented to his publisher, Henry Regnery: "I've been working like a horse, traveling a lot, and trying to strike some blows for liberty. Whether the aforesaid liberty is gaining from all this is difficult to tell, but I know I'm pretty beat." Four years later, he expressed the same doubts in a letter to Friedrich Hayek, saying that in the United States, as in England, the "prospects for liberty" were "not very promising."[43] Not surprisingly, Petro viewed the Great Society as an enormous mistake. In his 1967 book *The Kingsport Strike*—which dealt with a publishing company located in a poor area of southern Appalachia in Tennessee—he lamented that people were oblivious to the fact that the Kingsport Press, the second largest employer in town, had been fighting a successful war on poverty for years and was about to fall prey to vicious union practices. Like Henry Simons two decades earlier, libertarians had to be content with producing heterodox ideas in the 1960s, hoping that one day they might find practical application, yet uncertain as to when that day might come.[44]

Thus, by the end of the 1960s, Petro turned his attention increasingly to trying to influence policy and the law. Although Petro's influence on the course of labor relations in the United States was marginal in the years before 1970, his greatest success, as a legal and policy entrepreneur, would come during the next two decades, when he became one of the nation's most vocal and effective critics of public sector unionism. By the 1960s, public sector unions had emerged as the fastest growing segment of the labor movement. Following the enactment of the first state law by Wisconsin in 1959 and the introduction of limited collective bargaining to the federal workforce in the 1960s, union membership and labor militancy spread on the local, state, and federal levels. For Petro, public sector union power epitomized all of the worst aspects of the state-union alliance that had emerged under the New Deal. The growth of collective bargaining in government, he feared, would accelerate Americans' loss of freedom, as public sector bargaining policies "brought to the public sector what national labor legislation previously brought to the private sector," a tragic triad of "conflict, disharmony, and waste."[45] If the new power of public sector unions was not repulsed, he believed, it would in time destroy constitutional government.

Moving South

Through a fortuitous set of circumstances, Petro had an opportunity to create his own labor research center just when an opening was emerging for the application of his ideas to the question of public sector unionism. In 1970, a former student of Petro's at the NYU Law School, Pasco M. Bowman II, was named dean of the Wake Forest University Law School. Bowman, a native Virginian who graduated from Bridgewater College in 1955, was a conservative libertarian whose inclinations were deeply influenced by Petro.[46] Bowman soon recruited Petro, who arrived in Winston-Salem, North Carolina, in 1973 and there established a new center, the Institute for Labor Policy Analysis.[47] The move to the more conservative Wake Forest, a university whose trustees were elected by the North Carolina Baptist State Convention, gave Petro a suitable institutional platform, and a more conducive political environment from which to advance his ideas in the 1970s. Petro soon recruited a newly minted Harvard Law School graduate, Edwin Vieira Jr., to serve as research director for his institute.[48]

It was a propitious time to establish a conservative legal redoubt in North Carolina. In 1972, Jesse Helms, the conservative gadfly made famous by his editorials on WRAL-TV in Raleigh, won election to the U.S. Senate from North Carolina. As a staunch "right-to-work" advocate, Helms proved a reliable ally in Petro's battle against the rise of public sector unions. North Carolina law banned collective bargaining by state or local government workers, and Helms championed this approach. Legislation to "compel sovereign governments to 'bargain' with unions as *equals*," Helms argued, would "compel public servants to accept unwanted unions as their only voice in dealing with their own government," would "permit crippling strikes," and "make public employees, administrators, and the public interest pawns of union organizers."[49]

For the National Right to Work Committee (NRTWC), 1973, the year that Petro arrived at Wake Forest, proved to be a watershed. Founded in 1955, the NRTWC had paid little attention to public sector unions before the late 1960s. But by 1973, this had changed. Right-to-work advocates viewed the rise of public sector labor militancy with alarm, and they had little faith in the Nixon administration's willingness to beat back this surging movement. They accused Nixon's secretary of labor, Peter J. Brennan, the former head of the New York City Building Trades Council, of "converting the Department of Labor into a Department of Labor Bosses,"[50] and charged the director of the Federal Mediation and Conciliation Service, William Usery, with "prostitut[ing] his post" to "assist union organizers."[51] Yet what most concerned the right-to-work movement was the National Public Employee Relations Act (NPERA), introduced by Congressman William L. Clay on June 14, 1973.[52] Clay's bill promised to extend to state and local government workers the same sort of labor protections that private sector workers had received under the Wagner Act: the right to organize and bargain collectively through exclusive union representation. The Clay bill would also set up a federal board to oversee government workers' rights, and would permit most state and local workers to strike. The NRTWC saw Clay's bill as "federal legislation that would authorize the forced unionization of public employees."[53] If successful, the bill would usher in "a new spoils system—with workers compelled to buy their jobs and other favors from union officials," fretted the NRTWC Newsletter.[54] Reed Larson of the NRTWC sounded a call to arms. "I want to call on all those who are truly concerned with the preservation of individual liberty in American to abandon the dangerous courtship with so-called 'political realities,'" he announced.[55] As it happened, Petro's Institute for Labor Policy Analysis was perfectly positioned to answer Larson's call. Over the next crucial decade, Petro's ideas would enable the opponents of public sector union power to argue that they were defending the very integrity of democracy itself.

Taking on Public Sector Unions

In response to the growing threat, the NRTWC sponsored a conference in Washington on the issue of public sector unions in 1973. At the conference Petro presented an early version of a lengthy law review article that would appear a year later in the Wake Forest Law Review as "Sovereignty and Compulsory Public Sector Bargaining." According to David Denholm, a right-to-work activist from California who attended the gathering, Petro's paper was "very controversial." Most right-to-work activists opposed "compulsory unionism" but in the case of public sector workers Petro took the anti-union logic a step further. He attacked the existence of collective bargaining in any form in the public sector. When unions bargained with the government, he argued, government sovereignty was inevitably compromised. This view was controversial, even among the NRTWC crowd.

According to Denholm, many said, "no, no, no. It's compulsory unionism that's the problem. Collective bargaining is not a problem." But Denholm and others soon came around to Petro's way of thinking.[56] The growing popularity of Petro's argument on the anti-union right in the years after 1973 represented an important departure.

Following the conference, the NRTWC increasingly incorporated Petro's arguments into its attacks on the Clay bill. NRTWC head Reed Larson echoed Petro's main theme. Those who supported collective bargaining in government "have declared that a sovereign government must negotiate, as an equal, with a labor union," Larson told a group of Indianapolis business owners.[57] Mainstream commentators like mediator Benjamin Aaron, who served as chair of a California legislative commission on public sector labor law, dismissed the sovereignty critique as "anachronistic."[58] But among conservatives the argument attracted a following.

In the aftermath of the NRTWC conference, a group of activists inspired by Petro's presentation decided to form a new organization specifically dedicated to combating public sector unionism, the Public Service Research Council (PSRC). In 1974, David Denholm moved to Washington to take charge of the PSRC. Within a year the new organization established an astonishing level of visibility. Its calling card was a widely circulated pamphlet published in 1974 and revised and reissued regularly thereafter. That pamphlet, *Public Sector Bargaining and Strikes*, dramatized a central contention of Petro's: that public sector collective bargaining itself, not just the threat of "compulsory unionism" in the public sector, was beginning to undermine government. The pamphlet, which prominently cited Petro's work, argued that the very extension of collective bargaining to state and local workers through legislation increased both unionization and strikes, rather than bringing labor peace as the advocates of such legislation promised. "In the overwhelming majority of cases," the pamphlet argued, "strike activity was notably higher in the period following legislation."[59] The PSRC also pointed out that political leaders rarely enforced the full range of penalties provided by laws outlawing government workers' strikes. Thus the pamphlet advanced themes central to Petro's thinking since the 1950s: union monopolies bred strikes; and union power corrupted government.

The publication of Petro's "Sovereignty and Compulsory Public Sector Bargaining" in the *Wake Forest Law Review* coincided with the formation of the PSRC. This 140-page article represented arguably the most ambitious critique yet formulated against public sector collective bargaining, and it became a primary reference point for the activist network that David Denholm began building.[60] Petro's article reviewed the liberalization of labor law since the 1950s, and advanced a detailed critique of public sector unionism that drew on ideas going back to Locke. Petro cleverly reformulated the right-to-work critique of "compulsory unionism," which had little resonance in the public sector where union security provisions were still uncommon in the early 1970s, into a critique of what he called "compulsory collective bargaining." In the public sector the problem was not primarily that workers were forced to join unions but that governments were increasingly being forced to negotiate with them. The introduction of "compulsory bargaining," he argued, represented an unconstitutional conferral of sovereignty from the people and their elected representatives on the nongovernmental entity of the union, and a "fatal threat to popular sovereignty."[61]

Drawing on the libertarian analysis of Mises and the same style of argument employed by Hayek in *The Road to Serfdom* (1944), Petro painted a relentlessly dark picture in which an expansive and coercive public sector union power led inevitably to tyranny. If government workers were to bargain with their employers, he argued, they would inevitably ask for and obtain the right to strike, otherwise bargaining would become "a sham." Strikes would in turn allow unions to press for "compulsory unionism." Nor would efforts to head off strikes through arbitration work. This approach would only accelerate government's loss of sovereignty to another group of nongovernmental agents and encourage unions to demand still more power. Petro's fears were most dramatically revealed in his comments on William Clay's National Public Employee Relations Act, which was then pending in Congress. If that bill passed, opening the floodgates to union organization at the state and local levels, he warned, it would be time "for us to take to the hills and the fields and the caves once more, as our ancestors have frequently had to do when integral—sovereign—government has broken down."[62]

Petro's shrill tone might have consigned him and the PSRC activists whom he inspired to the margins of debate in labor relations in the 1970s had not a confluence of events made his criticisms seem suddenly plausible beyond the confines of the right-to-work crowd's true believers. In 1975, the economy contracted, unemployment rose to 8.5 percent, and inflation reached a postwar high of 9.1 percent. Inflation and economic contraction strained government budgets even as unions fought hard to inflation-proof their wages and pensions. Public sector strikes jumped by 24 percent to a record 478 walkouts, the vast majority of which defied laws in the states where they took place. In New York City, Seattle, San Francisco, and the Commonwealth of Pennsylvania, Democratic officials once allied with the union movement came into bitter conflicts with striking unions. In response, union leaders loudly rattled their sabers, and the AFL-CIO called on Congress "to pass legislation to give all public employees the right to strike."[63] Such militant words worried conservatives all the more because the Watergate-influenced 1974 midterm elections gave Democrats a 291–144 majority in the House and a 61–39 advantage in the Senate, a margin that led one union strategist to predict the "certain passage" of William Clay's NPERA bill.[64]

These developments galvanized conservatives around Petro's ideas. In 1975 conservative writer Ralph de Toledano published *Let Our Cities Burn*, an attack on public sector union power and a warning against the passage of the Clay bill. The book drew inspiration from Sylvester Petro's "incisive essay on sovereignty," presenting it in simpler language, buttressed by dozens of lurid examples of alleged union abuses.[65] The book became a bestseller among conservatives. At the same time, the NRTWC increasingly identified itself with Petro's critique of public sector unions. In May 1975, when the NRTWC marked its twentieth anniversary, Petro was a featured guest along with William B. Ruggles, editor emeritus of the *Dallas Morning News*, whose famous 1941 Labor Day editorial calling for a constitutional amendment protecting the "right to work" was widely credited with having originated both the term and the movement.[66] By featuring the public sector union threat increasingly in its literature, the NRTWC began recruiting a record fifteen thousand new members per month in 1975, enough to convince its leaders that they would be heading the nation's "largest single-purpose citizens' organization" by 1976.[67] Members of Congress also embraced Petro's arguments. When a group of conservatives took to the floor of the House on July 17, 1975, to attack the Clay bill, they might as well have been quoting from Petro's works. The question raised by the NPERA legislation was "shall Government be sovereign or shall there be collective bargaining with Government?" according to Philip Crane (R-Ill.). "If government is to maintain its sovereignty," echoed John H. Rousselot (R-Cal.), it could not share "responsibility with a handful of professional union men who are not answerable to an electorate."[68] If Petro had felt like a voice crying in the wilderness when he testified before Congress in 1959, by 1975 he was hearing his ideas repeated by an increasing number of legislators and activists.

Petro's influence on the courts was marginal before the mid-1970s. Only twice between 1953 and 1974 did judges reference Petro's work in their opinions.[69] Yet in the mid-1970s Petro played an important role in two crucial legal battles that ended up before the Supreme Court, each of which brought decisive defeats to labor. The first of these, *National League of Cities v. Usery*, which declared unconstitutional an effort to extend the wage-and-hours provisions of the Fair Labor Standards Act (FLSA) to state and local employees, marked the most significant legal setback for public sector unions in the 1970s, one that also had a huge negative impact on chances for the passage of Clay's NPERA bill. In the second, *Abood v. Detroit Board of Education*, the Court's majority embraced Petro's employee "free choice" logic to rule that unions' use of compulsory dues to engage in political activity violated the First Amendment and furthermore that it was illegal to withhold from dissenters any union dues that exceeded the cost of collective bargaining.[70]

National League of Cities stemmed from a successful effort by organized labor to get Congress to extend minimum wage and overtime protections to state and local government workers in 1974. Both supporters and opponents saw the FLSA extension as an important prerequisite for the passage of the Clay bill. The extension, if granted by Congress and upheld by the courts, would deal a fatal blow to the arguments of those who contended that the NPERA constituted an unconstitutional breach of federalism that would allow the federal government to dictate to states and localities the terms of their labor relations policies. When Congress passed and President Richard M. Nixon signed the FLSA extension in 1974, NPERA advocates felt they had established an important precedent. If the federal government had the right to set minimum wages for state and local workers, then it should also have the power to protect their right to form unions and bargain collectively. If the Supreme Court upheld this extension, then passage of Clay's NPERA bill would become feasible. This worry led Petro to join the National League of Cities (NLC) in an effort to persuade the Supreme Court to overturn the FLSA extension, an effort that led to *National League of Cities v. Usery*.[71]

Petro well understood the importance of this case and prepared an amicus curiae brief on behalf of the PSRC. Petro was concerned that if the

PSRC did not submit its own brief, the NLC lawyers' "natural preoccupation with the issues which interest them most immediately will cause them, and hence this Court, to overlook the deeper, broader, and more ominous issues involved."[72] Petro wanted the Court to know that at stake was "the survival of the federal system and of representative government in the States and municipalities." Foremost in Petro's mind as well was the precedent the case would set for the NPERA. He warned the Court that if the FLSA extension was affirmed, it "would go far toward establishing the constitutionality also of federal laws imposing in the public sector the compulsory collective bargaining regime now prevailing in the private sector." Petro opened his argument by distinguishing between commerce and government. FLSA rules imposed on states and localities by Washington would amount to an unconstitutional regulation of state and local government, and could not be justified as a regulation of commerce among the several states, he argued. "Affirmance of the decision . . . will disintegrate the substance of constitutional federalism," he concluded, and lead to "the demise of the States and localities as independent, self-governing communities."[73]

With Petro's brief in their files, the justices of the Supreme Court heard oral arguments in *National League of Cities* on April 16, 1975. No decision came from this hearing and the case was held over for rehearing in the following term. In the meantime, the upsurge in public sector strikes in 1975 seemed to dramatize some of the points Petro had presented in his brief. By the time the Court heard arguments in the case again on March 2, 1976, Democratic governor Calvin L. Rampton of Utah, who argued on behalf of the National League of Cities, seemed to be channeling Petro's brief. "Right now there are pending before the Congress bills that would extend all provisions of the National Labor Relations Act to states, including . . . giving employees the right to strike," he warned, in a reference to Clay's NPERA bill, and its passage was being held up "only because of the pendency of this case." Like Petro, Rampton further argued that if the Court let the FLSA extension stand, then there would be "no logical stopping point" for the legislation that would follow. Similarly, Justice Lewis Powell wondered whether affirming the FLSA extension would give Congress permission to tell states "that they have no authority to outlaw strikes against the government."[74]

When the Court issued a 5–4 opinion overturning the FLSA extension several months later, Petro's influence seemed evident. The court majority could have overturned the extension merely by holding that the broad regulation of state and local government labor policies was not covered by the logic of precedents. Instead, the majority took a more aggressive approach, portraying the FLSA extension, in the manner of Petro, as a dangerous threat to federalism. Writing for the majority, Justice William Rehnquist invoked the Tenth Amendment, arguing that the Congress had overstepped its bounds and employed powers not expressly granted in the Constitution and thus "reserved to the States respectively, or to the people."[75]

Many legal observers were stunned by the Court's embrace of the Tenth Amendment argument in *National League of Cities*. "It has been 40 years since the Court used concepts of state sovereignty to strike down federal legislation," the editorial writers of the *Washington Post* observed. Since 1941, when Justice Harlan Fiske Stone had called it "but a truism" stating the obvious, that "all is retained which has not been surrendered," the amendment had seemingly disappeared from Supreme Court discourse.[76] When segregationists had tried to place Jim Crow statutes under the protection of the amendment, the courts rebuffed them. But after years of gathering dust, the amendment was again a viable tool of conservatives. Sylvester Petro and his allies could relish another outcome of the Court's decision: with the federal government's power to regulate the employment practices of state and local governments in constitutional doubt, William Clay's NPERA bill was abandoned by most of its backers and never brought to the House floor for a vote.[77]

The second crucial case in which Petro intervened in the mid-1970s was *Abood v. Detroit Board of Education*. This case saw the NRTWC's Legal Defense Foundation represent six hundred Detroit teachers who refused to join the union that represented their colleagues and who sought to avoid paying agency fees to that union on the grounds that it used their money to engage in political activity to which they objected, thus violating their First Amendment rights to freedom of speech. Since the early 1970s, the NRTWC had singled out teachers unions to emphasize the danger represented by public sector unions in general. Thus, the NRTWC argued that if the Clay bill passed, "union officials would control the . . . professional entrance requirements of school teachers."[78] Because it focused on teachers, right-to-work activists saw *Abood* as an ideal test case. It was natural that they turned to Petro to argue their case before the Supreme Court.

While in his *National League of Cities* brief Petro alluded to the threat posed by public sector strikes, in the *Abood* case Petro focused on the dangers inherent in a weapon even more vital to public sector unions than the strike: their ability to lobby and undertake political campaigns to advance the interests of their members. In making this point Petro joined two central strands of his thinking that dated back more than twenty-five years. He had long held that the role of government and the private sector were in no way analogous. He had also long based his critique of "compulsory unionism" on the First Amendment freedom of expression and association. He believed that no one should be compelled to join or support an organization whose policies one opposed, nor should such an organization wield a government-like taxing power over individuals in its jurisdiction, collecting dues or representation fees. *Abood* allowed Petro to weave these two strands of his thinking in a powerful synthesis. In the public sector, he argued, union activity was inseparable from politics. Endorsing political candidates, lobbying government employers, demanding a say in the policies of government agencies, virtually all of the things that government workers' unions did were inherently political acts. Thus any money paid to a union would inevitably be put to political uses. If a government worker was forced to pay a fee to a union, even if it was an "agency fee" supposedly paid only for the cost of the union's collective bargaining services, then that worker was inevitably paying the union to conduct political activities that the worker might find objectionable, and therefore such compulsion constituted a violation of the worker's constitutional rights. This was the argument that Petro placed before the Supreme Court in the only appearance he ever made as counsel in that chamber: the State of Michigan could not compel citizens to renounce their First Amendment rights to be eligible for public employment, and then require them to contribute financially to the suppression of their own political views.[79]

In the event, Petro's ideological zeal handicapped him in making an effective case before the Court. He burdened the justices with an overly long, professorial tome of a brief about which he was scolded by Chief Justice Warren Burger.[80] He also overstated elements of Justice Rehnquist's position in the *National League of Cities* case in an effort to co-opt that decision as a precedent for *Abood*, much to the consternation of Rehnquist, who sympathized with Petro's thinking in *Abood* but found his legal reasoning suspect.[81]

Nonetheless, Petro walked away with a qualified victory in *Abood*. When the Court announced its decision on May 23, 1977, the majority held that it is unconstitutional to require a public employee to join a labor union. This was largely a moot point, however, since no state or locality had adopted union-shop agreements. Moreover, the Court did not go so far as to hold that the payment of agency fees for collective bargaining services was an infringement on the constitutional right to freedom of association because all activities of public sector unions were inherently political, as Petro had argued. But, importantly, the majority did hold that a union's use of agency fees to pursue political activities was indeed an infringement on the First Amendment rights of those workers who objected to this use of their money. Furthermore, the Court held that workers who felt so aggrieved had a right to demand an accounting of the use of union funds and to receive a rebate for any portion of their fees that were used in political action.[82]

In *Abood*, Petro played a role in establishing an important constitutional principle with respect to freedom of association and collective bargaining, one that would be widened by subsequent decisions stemming from private sector labor law, such as *Communications Workers of America v. Beck*. In *Beck*, the Court held that exactions of agency fees or dues beyond those necessary to finance the collective-bargaining activities of unions in the private sector also violated dissenting workers' First Amendment rights as well as their rights to fair representation. It was no surprise that Petro's protégé, Edwin Vieira Jr., argued on behalf of the respondents in *Beck*, continuing the First Amendment attack against "compulsory unionism" that his mentor had begun waging decades earlier.[83]

As it turned out, the *Abood* case marked the pinnacle of Petro's influence. In the years after 1977, he receded from the front lines of the anti-union fight. Petro himself argued no more cases before the Supreme Court. In 1978, Dean Pasco Bowman left Wake Forest in a dispute, and the university severed formal ties with the Institute for Labor Policy Analysis. Yet as his personal prominence receded, Petro's ideas continued to animate an increasingly well-organized anti-public-employee-union movement. The PSRC, whose organization Petro had inspired, continued to espouse his theories. In 1978, the organization launched a biweekly newsletter, *The Government Union Report*, and in 1980 it added an academic journal, *Government Union Review*. The PSRC also created a lobbying organization called Americans Against Union Control of Government, and, with the help of a new breed of conservative direct-mail fund-aisers, such as Richard Viguerie, it built a sizable network of donors. And when President Ronald Reagan delivered a crushing blow to striking air traffic controllers in 1981, Petro had the satisfaction of seeing his arguments repeated by the only former union leader ever to occupy the Oval Office. It was wrong to "compare labor management relations in the private sector with government," Reagan argued, as he prepared to fire the Professional Air Traffic Controllers Organization (PATCO) strikers. "Government cannot close down the assembly line." Strikes by federal workers would not be tolerated, Reagan made clear.[84] "The President's stern response to the illegal air-controllers' strike has caused no outpouring of sympathy for the controllers who have been discharged," Petro gloated in 1982. "Fortunately, public esteem for all unions in this country is at an historic low."[85]

Petro himself could claim a small bit of credit for this turn, for his ideas had helped lay the groundwork for not only Ronald Reagan's breaking of the PATCO strike but for an increasingly successful attack on union power in the late twentieth century. While he had been a lonely legal crusader against union power in the 1950s, by the 1980s his views were no longer marginalized: while one protégé, Edwin Vieira, was successfully arguing the *Beck* case before the Supreme Court, another, Pasco Bowman, was a Reagan appointee to the U.S. Court of Appeals for the Eighth Circuit.[86]

Petro died in 2007. His influence lived on, however, in the anti-union struggles of the new century, carried on by followers like Howard Dickman, whom Petro had recruited into his intellectual movement in the late 1970s after Dickman received a PhD in history from the University of Michigan. Through the Liberty Fund, Petro provided the funding that brought Dickman's book *Industrial Democracy in America: Ideological Origins of National Labor Relations Policy* (1987) into print, where it remains the most intellectually respectable critical history of U.S. labor policy written from a libertarian perspective.[87] Dickman went on to a successful career as a popularizer of libertarian conservatism in the pages of *Reader's Digest* and as deputy editor of the *Wall Street Journal*'s editorial page, the most prominent anti-union platform in American journalism. The *Journal*'s editorials against the Employee Free Choice Act (EFCA), organized labor's bid to reform American labor law, helped rally enough opposition to the measure to prevent its passage after Barack Obama's election to the presidency. In those editorials and other critiques of EFCA, Petro's arguments against "compulsory unionism" continued to resonate. The anti-union movement had come a long way in the half century since Sylvester Petro came to Washington to testify before the McClellan Committee. History, it seemed, had turned his way.

Chapter 12

Wal-Mart, John Tate, and Their Anti-Union America

Nelson Lichtenstein

Corporate hostility to trade unionism has long represented both a highly ideological vision of what conservative elites have come to see as the proper structuring of the good society and a set of propagandistic initiatives and organizational techniques deployed within their own workplaces so as to repel an actual union effort to make inroads there. In few corporations have these two aims been so effectively combined as at Wal-Mart, the huge, controversial retailer whose dramatic growth in the last two decades of the twentieth century transformed a large slice of the U.S. economy,

"We have never had a union in Wal-Mart and don't need one now to represent our associates," founder Sam Walton told readers of *Wal-Mart World* in October 1989. "We resent outsiders coming in and saying things which aren't true and trying to change the Company that has meant so much to all of us."[1] That unionism and collective bargaining represented far more than a mechanism for adjusting wages and grievances became clear from the attitude of Larry English, one of Walton's best young managers, when he confronted unions questioning management's moral, paternal claim to speak and act on behalf of the work community. Of these organizations he said: "I hated them because they wanted to tell me how to take care of my people. I don't need someone to manage my store for me. I'll go to my grave believing that."[2]

Such sentiments flourished in mid-twentieth-century Arkansas, where trade unionism seemed a threat to a regional economy long structured around cheap labor, competitive enterprises, and a local elite anxious to preserve its social and economic hegemony. Here the fear of union organization united the plantation owners of the Mississippi delta, the Ozark branch plant managers whose only competitive advantage lay in cheap labor, and entrepreneurs of northwest Arkansas like John Tyson, J. B. Hunt, and Sam Walton who saw their booming firms as but an extension of their paternalism and fiercely defended autonomy. Led by the delta planters, who remembered well the biracial uprising led by the Southern Tenant Farmers Union in the 1930s, Arkansas was the first state to pass a "right-to-work" law—in 1944—which made illegal the union-shop contract. Such right-to-work laws weakened existing unions because they made dues collection much more difficult. But their greatest impact came in the realm of political symbolism and plebian ideology where, throughout the South and Mountain West, they were taken as a sign of government hostility to the very existence of trade unionism.[3]

But Wal-Mart, which was and is headquartered in the Ozark town of Bentonville, soon expanded beyond the rural South, where the absence of trade unionism seemed almost natural. If the company was to take its southern-born paternalism, low wages, and hostility to organized labor beyond northwest Arkansas, Wal-Mart would have to develop a more sophisticated, systematic, and ostensibly legal modus operandi. And this required a revolution in American labor law.

Employer Free Speech

When in 1935 Robert Wagner drafted the famous act that bears his name, he made sure that under its provisions employees in any given enterprise had the right to select "representatives of their own choosing" who could speak for them in collective negotiations with the management of the firm. To make sure this happened, he inserted a section that defined a set of "unfair labor practices" for which employers, but not unions, might be held accountable. When conservative critics of his law, and of the whole New Deal tilt toward organization of the working class, complained that the Wagner Act was one-sided, the New York senator replied that this was a "false equation." The kind of "unfair labor practices" in which workers might engage—physical or verbal intimidation of their workmates, punched noses and nasty threats—all that had been illegal for centuries, since the birth of the common law itself. But when it came to economic coercion, and economic coercion of the sort that shouted "You're fired if you mess with the union," well, that was almost exclusively an employer weapon, which Wagner and other labor partisans sought to proscribe.[4] The New Dealers whom President Franklin Roosevelt first appointed to the National Labor Relations Board (NLRB) interpreted the new Wagner Act so as to make the foreman and manager nonparticipants, mere bystanders, when the workers they supervised decided for or against forming a union. Indeed, the NLRB ruled that given the imbalance of power in an unorganized factory, mine, or mill, any kind of employer speech was inherently coercive and therefore an "unfair labor practice."[5]

Led by the National Association of Manufacturers and other employer organizations, most businessmen thought all this hateful, a personal insult, undemocratic, even socialistic. They wanted the unfettered right to talk to their employees, persuade them of their benevolence, and campaign against the unions, who seemed to deploy their money and their men with such potent effect. When the Republicans won the 1946 elections, it was therefore just a matter of time before resentful employers got the New Deal–era Wagner Act fixed to their liking. Executives running factories, warehouses, and offices wanted to call the workers together in a big meeting and lecture them on why joining a union would be a bad idea.

Sure enough, "free speech for employers" was soon enshrined in the new Taft-Hartley law. Particularly affected were the retail unions, which were making a major push in the late 1940s and early 1950s to organize chain supermarkets and department stores. At an educational conference held by the Retail Clerks in 1951, union organizers reported that "captive-audience speeches"—employer anti-union talks to workers who had been ordered to attend—were "beginning to grow by leaps and bounds" at larger stores, contributing to major union losses in NLRB elections. Initially, the Labor Board insisted that unions get equal time, on company property, if management held such compulsory meetings, but once the Republicans gained control of the NLRB after Dwight D. Eisenhower's election, employers got almost everything they wanted. As one of the conservative businessmen appointed to that board put it in his confirmation hearing, referencing one of his successful campaigns against unionism, " we 'free-speeched' them. . . . Now, you could say, if you like, in that instance I was a union buster."[6]

The labor law still held that employers could not retaliate against workers who voted for a union by threatening them with firing or plant closure. But this doctrine became increasingly formalistic. Thus in a dispute involving Chicopee Manufacturing, the NLRB enunciated a "prophecy doctrine" that permitted employers to state that voting for a union might result in a plant being moved. This employer advantage was further refined in the *Mt. Ida Footwear Company* case, where executives of an Arkansas-based shoemaker asserted that if employees signed union cards, "this can be fatal to a business such as Mt. Ida Footwear." The board ruled that such threats could be rendered permissible if an executive "sanitized" this kind of coercive and threatening speech by merely inserting a catch-phrase like "we are here to stay," which was the stratagem of Mt. Ida management. Meanwhile, in two rulings from the early 1950s the NLRB transformed employer free speech into an even more powerful managerial weapon. In *Livingston Shirt*, the board ruled that an employer "does not commit an unfair labor practice if he makes a pre-election speech on company time and premises and then denies the union's request for an opportunity to reply"; and in *Esquire* employers won the right to threaten that a pro-union vote would generate lengthy legal proceedings instead of the collective bargaining mandated by the original Wagner Act.[7]

John Tate and His America

Enter John Tate, the man who would sharpen these legal tools, stock them in Wal-Mart's arsenal, and deploy them in furious combat with the unions. A man of Sam Walton's generation, he was born in North Carolina in 1916, took a law degree from Wake Forest Law School, and became a bitter foe of trade unionism, all before he enlisted in the army. Tate acquired his bitter hostility to unionism in the labor wars of the late 1930s, when he crossed through a union picket line thrown up around the Reynolds Tobacco Company in Winston-Salem, his hometown. Aside from the cat-calls, Tate took a blow on the head that he would never forget. "I hate unions with a passion," he would later remark after he had established a pioneering law firm dedicated to what in the 1950s and 1960s was a newly aggressive "union avoidance" stratagem.[8]

Tate perfected his anti-union skills in Omaha. He landed there right after World War II when Nebraska and the rest of the northern plains states were an industrial frontier in which factories, warehouses, and packing sheds dotted the small-town landscape. Nebraska was a battleground state in which big, vigorous unions such as the Teamsters and the Packinghouse Workers sought to organize the firms that had just begun to flee high-cost Chicago, Minneapolis, and St. Louis. The ideological warfare became as intense as the strikes and bargaining sessions, and John Tate was right in the middle of the fight. In 1951 H. L. Hunt, the right-wing Texas oilman, paid him $10,000 a year to serve as the Omaha organizer of his Facts Forum, an organization that fought fluoridation of drinking water, supported the presidential ambitions of Douglas MacArthur, and demanded that the House Committee on Un-American Activities hold additional hearings throughout the Midwest.[9]

Tate traveled in right-wing political circles that linked a militant anti-unionism to a libertarian rejection of the welfare state, fair employment legislation, and regulatory oversight on the part of the federal government. This put him in league with the John Birch Society and the Christian Anti-Communist Crusade, as well as those who organized seminars and summer schools where the ideas of Friedrich Hayek and Ludwig von Mises were celebrated. When in the early 1960s the Federal Communications Commission sought to encourage Omaha's television stations to air more public interest programming, Tate denounced "faceless government bureaucrats," who thought of Midwesterners "as congenital incompetents who must be fooled and ruled by a special elite with some unspecified claim to superior wisdom and a lust for power."[10]

In 1956 Tate organized the Midwest Employers Council as a vehicle through which he could offer legal counsel to smaller companies seeking to avoid unionization. Today, every major city has at least one big law firm that specializes in an aggressive brand of union avoidance law. When corporate executives get wind of a union effort at one of their facilities, they pick up the phone, sign a contract, and let the outside legal experts take over their labor relations until the threat is eliminated. But in the 1950s, still just a couple of decades since the Wagner Act had become law, almost all "labor lawyers" were just that, pro-union advocates whose expertise and resources were often far greater than that commanded by Nebraska's entre-preneurial businessmen. Unions still won a majority of all the NLRB elections in which they participated, after which they quickly negotiated a first contract. Although most of the three hundred firms that paid dues to Tate's MEC were family-owned manufacturing firms, some of the most bitter battles came in the bakeries, department stores, and grocery chains, including their attendant warehouses, that the Teamsters and the Retail Clerks sought to organize.

Tate saw himself as a crusader for "freedom" who would rally the business class of Omaha and Lincoln in order to turn back this union invasion. He urged his clients to boycott unionized printing shops and buy as many meat products as possible from Wilson and Company during a long and divisive Packinghouse Workers strike. When a local chain of grocery stores sought to buck a strike early in 1963, Tate called for solidarity: "We do hope you care enough for freedom that if you are not buying some groceries from Shavers Stores—you might do so. Will free people like you and me help union coercion—or stop it—by good old honest methods of a free customer in a free market?" Tate sought to convince his clients that it was not enough to keep a union out of their shop alone; rather, a decline in union density and influence was essential to give businessmen a strong hand even if they were so unfortunate as to be stuck with an existing collective bargaining contract.[11]

But Tate was not just a propagandist. He was a pioneer in the nascent union avoidance industry, realizing that the fight against unionism had to be fought simultaneously on multiple fronts: before the NLRB and the courts, in the political arena, and most importantly, within the firm itself where Tate developed a whole repertoire of programs, techniques, and interventions designed to generate employee loyalty to management and hostility to "third-party" representation. "The issues that are most frequently cause of company-union disputes today are philosophical, not economic," asserted Tate in 1960. "The battle is for the minds of employees."[12] Backstopped by a phalanx of expert anti-labor law firms, this has become commonplace employer behavior in recent years, but in the 1950s and early 1960s it was so audacious, innovative, and, in the hands of John Tate, so successful that Nebraska unionists labeled the Midwest Employers Council, along with the John Birch Society, a "fascist trend" in the United States.[13]

Tate codified for his clientele all the key anti-union tactics that Wal-Mart and so many other firms would later deploy. Among these are profit-sharing schemes designed to give employees a stake in the productivity of the enterprise, NLRB election delays that demoralized union advocates, a tough negotiating posture that leaves the workforce in limbo and without a contract, and aggressive efforts to decertify unions already representing the workforce.[14] Employer "free speech" was the key element that made this strategy work, enabling executives to conduct compulsory meetings of the workforce, hold one-on-one interviews with employees, and imply—the courts had ruled that an outright threat would be illegal—that unionism would have disastrous consequences for the lives of all concerned.[15]

Tate's combativeness was manifest in the 1959 captive audience speech he prepared for a warehouse employer facing a Teamster organizing drive. After cataloguing the union's corruption, employment of violent thugs, and recent expulsion from the AFL-CIO, Tate put forward a message that would become standard fare for all his clients: "Remember this—*no union can guarantee you anything*! The law says that if you force us to deal with some outside third party—some union strangers, we have to bargain—but the law does not say we have *to agree to a single solitary thing*! If these union salesmen call you off of your jobs so you can't pay your bills—the law says we can go right out and hire someone else to take your place. If we never reach an agreement with the union, we never have to hire you back! We are not threatening—no—and please—don't misunderstand us. We just want you to understand some facts the unions usually fail to tell you."[16]

Against this picture of chronic acrimony, Tate counterpoised a friendly and informal community, or as he wrote in a talk for employees of another business client who sought to decertify an existing union, "You can do as you wish. It is, thank God, a free country. I do hope—and I don't mind telling you—that you vote *No Union*, and we can sit down together to work out any problems we have."[17]

Here was encapsulated the ideology that has since become operative in virtually every anti-union campaign of recent decades. On the one hand, Tate invokes the company as a source of community, solidarity, and even intimacy. But he also suggests that should workers violate this organic harmony by endorsing the union, management might well punish the workers in the most unpredictable and draconian fashion. As Kim Phillips-Fein has pointed out, such anti-union campaigns portrayed a vision of the world in which benevolent and powerful corporations would take care of their employees, but only if the latter offered the owners unconditional loyalty. Should the workers heed the call of a sly and self-interested group of "salesmen"—the union organizers—then the benevolent power of the corporation would suddenly turn sour.[18]

Tate's reputation as an effective union fighter spread throughout the Midwest, especially after he founded Omaha's largest labor relations law firm in 1967. Sam Walton called on him in 1972 when Wal-Mart faced union trouble at two stores in central Missouri. In truth, the St. Louis–based Retail Clerks local had not put on much of an organizing drive: it threw together informational picket lines at a couple of stores, but the union put few resources into organizing them, especially the small, thirty-four-employee store in Mexico, a farm town near Columbia, where Sam Walton had attended the state university. But Wal-Mart executives had made an embarrassing and illegal hash of their efforts to squash the union. As the NLRB would later note, Jack Shewmaker, one of Walton's rising stars, had been overheard telling store manager Robert Haines that "if he caught any employees with union cards, he should fire them even if he had to hire all new employees." Then, when Connie Kreyling, a young but highly competent office manager, began to talk up the union idea among her workmates, she had been summarily fired by Haines when she arrived for work on a Monday morning. The Retail Clerks took her firing to the NLRB. There Haines was shown to be a liar—he claimed that he had fired Kreyling for poor work habits rather than "protected" union activity—and Wal-Mart was ordered to rehire Kreyling and post in conspicuous places a "Notice to Employees" that asserted, "We will not discourage membership in or activities on behalf of Retail Store Employees' Union, Local No. 655 . . . by discharging, or in any other manner discriminating in regard to hire or tenure of employment of any of our employees because of their union activities."[19]

By this point Tate had visited the store where his well-tested anti-union spiel, plus the judicious transfer of Haines to another store, ended once and for all the union buzz. However, the incident worried Walton, who asked Tate what could be done, especially now that his chain was rapidly putting stores outside the Ozarks where rural poverty and Southern mores had made so many clerks grateful for a job with Mr. Sam. Tate told Walton, "You can hire me or someone like me to hold these people down, and fight them the rest of your life. Or you can decide to get them on your side." This was a script Tate had long rehearsed, made urgent by the legal war he was then waging against the Amalgamated Clothing Workers, whose strike at the slacks maker Farah Manufacturing deployed one of the union movement's earliest and most effective "corporate campaigns." Tate later remembered, "I won every [NLRB] election with Willie Farah in El Paso, we won every court case including a Supreme Court case, but we lost the war." That was because the Catholic archbishop of El Paso and the mainstream Protestant denominations sided with the union, prompting big retailers like Marshall Field's, Wanamaker's, and Macy's to heed the union boycott and drop the Farah line, thus forcing Farah to recognize the union.[20]

The defeat stuck in Tate's craw, and he was determined to apply the lessons at Wal-Mart. It was not enough to denounce trade unionism and intimidate its partisans. In addition, Wal-Mart needed a high-profile corporate campaign of its own that would convince both employees and the public that the company took care of its workers. Tate therefore proposed that Wal-Mart expand its profit-sharing plan, codify an open door policy, and give the employees access to much store-level information on sales, profits, and inventory shrinkage (chiefly employee theft and shoplifting). "Saying 'we care' isn't enough," Tate told a meeting of assembled store managers early in 1973. "If we can prove we care, then our people will care," adding that employees who feel a vested interest in the company won't be as likely to steal or shirk their duties.[21]

Sam Walton and his publicists would later attribute much of the impulse for this idea to his wife, Helen, who told her husband that unless the clerks and cashiers "were on board, the top people might not last long either."[22] But Wal-Mart's profit-sharing retirement plan also accorded with John Tate's ultraconservative vision of how workers could be made loyal to their employer. In the early 1970s almost all policymakers, corporate benefit managers, and trade unionists considered the very idea of such a stock-purchase scheme economically problematic and ideologically retrograde. Instead, most companies, unionized or not, offered their employees defined-benefit pension plans, which paid out a fixed monthly stipend at retirement, based on their salary and years of service. Social Security was a fixed-benefit plan, which the Nixon administration had just strengthened by indexing it to inflation. In 1974 came the Employee Retirement Income Security Act, designed to regulate private pension plans in order to make them a secure counterpart to Social Security. The individually controlled private retirement account—today ubiquitous as the 401(k)—would not come into legal existence until 1978 and did not become widely used until the mid-1980s.[23]

Profit-sharing plans were not unknown in the early 1970s, but they carried a distinctly right-wing inflection, especially when they substituted themselves for a traditional pension. In an era when security—national, social, union—was much valued, profit-sharing schemes shifted risk to the employee and linked his or her fortunes directly and exclusively to that of the firm for which he or she labored. In the 1960s Tate put together a number of such schemes for undercapitalized Nebraska firms determined to keep out the union, but on the cheap.[24] One of the most famous plans, with which John Tate must have been familiar, was that of Sears, Roebuck, then the greatest retailer in the land. With most of its assets invested in Sears stock, the plan paid out at least 10 percent of all profits, with long-service employees, largely male, enjoying the largest corporate contributions. Everyone watched the stock price, which Sears posted daily at every store and warehouse. The investment plan generated a sense of shared purpose and community; in the words of one executive, it was "the central unifying symbol around which the entire organization revolved." The plan and the ideology it embodied proved a bulwark against efforts by the Retail Clerks and the Teamsters to organize the company in the 1950s and early 1960s.[25]

Wal-Mart's scheme was a discount version of the Sears plan. It was not actually a profit-sharing plan per se. Rather, the company contributed about 6 percent of an employee's earnings to the plan dependent on the degree to which Wal-Mart hit certain predetermined earnings and profit targets. It required one year of service to kick in and required seven years to fully vest. By the turn of the millennium the corporate contribution had dropped to about 4 percent as Wal-Mart growth slowed. Thus only one Wal-Mart associate out of fifty ever accumulated $50,000 in stock.[26] Still, for those employees who remained with the company during the 1970s and 1980s, when the stock price soared, the profit-sharing plan reaped huge dividends. In 1990 *Wal-Mart World* bragged that ninety-three associates had retired in the past year with more than $100,000 in each of their accounts.[27]

But as Tate understood, the most important impact of the profit-sharing scheme was ideological, linking the employees to the fate of the company, but also justifying the self-exploitation that was integral to the

Wal-Mart culture. "Store associates are willing to work long years for modest pay and slim wage hikes," marveled *Discount Store News*, "content on knowing they will hold small fortunes in Wal-Mart stock upon retirement."[28] A company profit-sharing executive put it even more pointedly in 1990: "Your profit sharing account balance will depend upon how well you and every associate in our company does his or her job. There is no place for coasters or people just half-way doing their jobs—just as there is no place for shrinkage or other needless expenses. People who don't do their jobs take dollars out of your profit sharing just as theft and other factors that cause shrinkage in our company reduce profits and profit sharing."[29]

Using the Big Stick

Profit sharing was never going to be enough to keep Wal-Mart union free, so a stick always accompanied the carrots corporate management offered its "associates." When the Teamsters launched organizing drives at company distribution centers in both Bentonville and Searcy, Arkansas, in the early 1980s, Sam Walton responded with a combination of personal contrition and adroit institutional concessions, backstopped, of course, by an unrelenting, hard-nosed determination to rid the company of those workers whose union sentiment was not assuaged by company paternalism. "You'd think I'd learn, wouldn't you?" he asked the Searcy workers, shaking his head and apologizing for letting conditions get so bad. He asked for another chance: he'd accommodate worker grievances by making work shifts more predictable, cutting down on the overtime, and bringing conditions at Searcy in line with those at better-off Bentonville, where workers had just voted down the union. But Walton may have gone to the well one time to often with these blue collar men. The Teamsters seemed close to having the critical mass they need to win. Perhaps 300 out of 415 workers at the distribution center had signed cards asking the union to represent them.[30]

Wal-Mart executives therefore turned to the stick. An NLRB election was scheduled for February 1982, a month that remained in the ominous shadow cast by Ronald Reagan's destruction of the Professional Air Traffic Controllers Organization the previous August. When Walton and his brother Bud flew down to Searcy just before the election, the company founder assembled the workers to tell them he'd strip them of their profit sharing if they voted for the union. Walton told them he had 500 job applications on file, some from the evangelical, anti-union students at nearby Harding College. When one of the warehousemen asked Walton why they were getting paid $1.50 less an hour than those in a newly opened Texas facility, Sam replied forthrightly, "I can hire you for less in Arkansas."[31] And Walton offered his employees a threat that was then and is now an explicit violation of the labor law. "He told us that if the union got in, the warehouse would be closed," one of the workers recalled for Walton biographer Bob Ortega. "He said people could vote anyway they wanted, but he'd close her right up."[32]

Meanwhile, John Tate stirred the pot with a propaganda barrage that has since become a classic in the anti-union arsenal. Workers want justice, but not divisiveness. They seek harmony and cooperation, as well as dignity at work. They organize for a voice on the job, not a strike that puts them outside on the picket lines. Anti-union strategists like Tate had long been well aware of these social and psychological needs and how to turn them against the union impulse, promising violence, division, conflict, and an immediate strike if workers cast their lot with the union. Workers arriving at the Searcy distribution center one morning found Tate's rendition of this anti-union stratagem in the form of a ninety-foot-long bulletin board, covered with four decades worth of newspaper clippings describing every Teamster strike, violent incident, and allegation of criminality that Tate's researchers had been able to piece together. It was headlined "Walk the 90-Foot Wall of Teamster Shame," recalled Ronald Heath, who ran the organizing campaign for the Teamsters' local in Little Rock.[33]

Not unexpectedly, the Teamsters lost the election, after which Walton gloated in the company magazine, *Wal-Mart World*, "our good associates at our Searcy distribution center rejected the union by an overwhelming margin of over three to one. Bless them all. . . . We will never need a union in Wal-Mart if we work with and for one another and keep listening to each other."[34] It was a decisive, even a historic defeat. The Teamsters failed to contest the election and the hard-core unionists were soon eased out of the Searcy distribution center. The Arkansas labor movement, the Teamsters included, never renewed the struggle. That in turn sent a signal to the AFL-CIO in Washington that for the moment at least, Wal-Mart was too difficult to tackle and that company employees, in both the distribution centers and the stores, were too satisfied, complacent, or fearful to organize.[35]

Wal-Mart Versus Union America

Wal-Mart's militant anti-unionism seemed but a peculiarity of the rural South because, until the mid-1980s, Wal-Mart largely avoided putting its stores or distribution centers in metropolitan America. This was where trade unions had their greatest strength, in an archipelago of cities and suburbs that stretched from Boston to the District of Columbia, from New York to Minneapolis, and from Seattle to San Diego. In Missouri, for example, where trade unionists were strong enough to defeat a "right-to-work" referendum in 1978, Wal-Mart built scores of stores, but all were in small towns or in the exurban ring that skirted such union strongholds as St. Louis and Kansas City.[36] And this was the Wal-Mart pattern in other border or midwestern states: for more than a quarter century the company put its stores and its distribution centers largely beyond the easy reach of union influence. At the same time, trade unionism generally encountered an increasingly hostile political and social environment, first sent reeling by the deindustrialization of the old union strongholds and then slapped hard by Ronald Reagan and a generation of increasingly aggressive Republicans who saw the unions as a bar to U.S. international competitiveness and a financial prop for the Democrats.

Thus John Tate could brag in 1990 that Wal-Mart had not faced a single union petition for an NLRB election in almost a decade. But the battle was about to be joined. Tate quit his Omaha law firm to become an executive vice president and a member of the Wal-Mart Board of Directors in 1987, certainly an indication of the confidence in which Sam Walton held the union fighter. He retired in the mid-1990s, but Wal-Mart would continue to make use of his services, and showcase his sentiments, well into the new century, when many of the anti-union techniques and strategies he had developed decades before would form a rampart against a new wave of labor organizing.

Wal-Mart needed to be tough because the once-rural retailer was now putting its stores in states and regions that had long been friendly hosts to a vigorous trade union tradition. It was as if Lee's Army was once again moving across the Potomac and into Yankee territory. By the early 1990s the company had stores in Wisconsin, Minnesota, Michigan, Ohio, Pennsylvania, and California. Here it encountered the United Food and Commercial Workers (UFCW), a union of 1.3 million members that had organized supermarket chains that sold just over half of all groceries Americans bought. Union wages in this industry never approached those once paid in the muscular core of the old manufacturing economy, but they were enough to sustain a modest, recognizably middle-class standard of living. Most surveys put labor costs in the unionized grocery stores at about 30 percent above those paid by Wal-Mart. Wages were indeed higher, but the big, qualitative difference between Wal-Mart and its unionized competitors came in terms of those elements of the paycheck that made a real career possible: a full-time job, a defined-benefit pension, adequate family health insurance, and a seniority system that facilitated a worker's steady progression through a series of higher paying and more responsible jobs.[37]

The UFCW effort to organize Wal-Mart in the late 1990s and during the first years of the new century was therefore essentially a defensive one. Union organizing victories at a handful of scattered sites throughout the Wal-Mart empire were unlikely to result in anything that looked like effective collective bargaining. But the union hoped that the publicity generated by the campaign would force Wal-Mart to raise wages, improve its health insurance, and encourage the growth of union-community collaborations against the giant retailer. Even more important, the UFCW wanted to demonstrate that Wal-Mart's violation of the labor law was so widespread and so systematic that the NLRB should impose an "extraordinary nationwide remedy" against the company. In almost all unfair labor practice complaints issued by the board, the sanctions applied are narrowly local. But if an employer is caught using the same illegal tactics in various places, the NLRB can impose nationwide penalties, which if enforced in the federal courts can have a real impact on the way the company conducts its anti-union campaign. So the UFCW barraged the NLRB with allegations of unfair labor practices against Wal-Mart and it seemed just possible that the labor board might slap Wal-Mart with a serious company-wide penalty that would have personally fined Wal-Mart store managers themselves $10,000 for willful violations of the labor law. But Wal-Mart circumvented the entire process by appealing straight to the newly installed Bush administration. Just days before Wal-Mart was set to argue its case, in April 2001, Leonard Page, the union-friendly general counsel for the NLRB, took a phone call from the White House. Page held but a recess appointment, so he could be dismissed by the president at any time. And he was: he had thirty-six hours to clear out his office. Not unexpectedly, Page's more conservative successor decided against bringing a national complaint against Wal-Mart.[38]

Such overt help from a friendly administration was actually quite rare, for when it came to trade unionism, Wal-Mart and other firms seeking to stanch the threat from organized labor had the organizational and legal resources to fight on their own. They deployed multiple and overlapping lines of defense, like the intersecting lines of cannon fire that protected a well-constructed fortress. By the time the UFCW began its effort to organize Wal-Mart in the late 1990s, union avoidance strategies, at Wal-Mart and other corporations, had been well advanced since the days when John Tate and Sam Walton browbeat the Searcy warehousemen. An entire antiunion industry had grown up in the United States since the 1970s when the lawyers and consultants who orchestrated such work were thought to be just a step or two above ambulance chasers and bail bondsmen. But Ronald Reagan's celebration of the free market and the entrepreneur during his White House years legitimized an ideological and operational hostility to organized labor at just the moment when sharper competition at home and abroad had convinced many businessmen that the unionized workplace was both too expensive and too inflexible. So a flourishing set of consultants, law firms, personnel psychologists, and strike management firms peddled their services during an era when it was finally possible, in the North and West as well as the rural South, to promote what one consultant called the "morality of a union-free environment."[39]

Most companies outsource this dirty work. When executives get wind of a union organizing drive or some other indication of discontent, they hire an anti-union law firm to run, for all practical purposes, corporate personnel relations until the threat has passed. At a cost that often reaches several million dollars for a few months' work, these union busters deploy a well-tested set of stratagems to ensure that their new client is kept union free.[40] First, the lower-level supervisory staff is assembled and told that they are hereby drafted into the anti-union effort: any equivocation or desertion will result in instant dismissal, if only because these "managers" have no protection under existing interpretations of U.S. labor law. Then comes a barrage of leaflets, videos, personnel shifts, and meetings with individual employees, often climaxed with an on-site visit by top corporate executives. Captive audience assemblies become more frequent and more intimidating as the presumptive date of the NLRB election draws near. Should the union manage to eke out an election victory, then another round of delay and resistance begins, often continued by the same law firm which orchestrated the anti-union campaign in the first place. It's expensive but highly effective: union organizing efforts using traditional labor law procedures have virtually ground to a halt in the United States. Only about one union campaign in twenty ends with a signed collective bargaining contract.[41]

How Wal-Mart Wins

Wal-Mart does all this and more, in-house, with its own people taking on the key tasks, and thus making all the techniques and stratagems developed by the union avoidance experts an integral, organic part of the Wal-Mart culture. This begins with a forthright assertion that Wal-Mart is anti-union, codified for Wal-Mart managers in training manuals such as one entitled *A Manager's Toolbox to Remaining Union Free*. As Wal-Mart came under high levels of scrutiny in the 1990s, the company ritually announced, "We are not anti-union; we are pro-associate."[42] But company manuals for store and distribution center managers were otherwise far more explicit: "Staying union free is a full-time commitment," announced a 1991 version of a distribution center training manual designed to tutor and energize first-line managers in a region, central Indiana, where unionism had been historically robust. "No one in management is immune from carrying his or her 'own weight' . . . from the Chairperson of the 'Board' down to the frontline manager. . . . The entire management staff should fully comprehend and appreciate exactly what is expected of their individual efforts to meet the union free objective."[43]

Wal-Mart's Tom Coughlin, who in 2000 was number two in the corporate hierarchy, adopted the iron fist inside the velvet glove approach. In the 1980s Coughlin had been tutored by John Tate and a decade later he led the company effort to defeat the UFCW. He was uncompromising; "These union issues are going to get worse," he told a Bentonville staff meeting in March 2000, so managers should quickly identify the most "fertile ground for unions" among the Wal-Mart associates, and immediately report back to Bentonville. Then the regional vice presidents and district managers must ensure that all labor relations directives are "executed 100%! There is no room or tolerance for slippage."[44]

For Coughlin and all other Wal-Mart managers, unions were always referred to as "third-party representatives." This was a worldview driven home during a new employee's very first day on the payroll. A Wal-Mart training video, *You've Picked a Great Place to Work!*, makes the point with high effectiveness. Through a conversation among a human resources manager; two newly hired workers, one of whom was a former union member; and two current workers, of whom one also previously belonged to a union, the video pounds home Wal-Mart's disdain for trade unionism and the terrible consequences that befall workers and businesses that succumb to union blandishments. In just twenty-seven minutes the video encapsulates a generation of right-wing imagery and propaganda designed to demonize and marginalize the trade union idea. Absent is any denunciation of unions as Communist or radical; rather they are portrayed as essentially corrupt and parasitical institutions, marginal businesses—not unlike pawnbrokers or payday lenders—which are primarily concerned with the dues income generated by any set of naïve workers seduced by their promises.[45]

Wal-Mart's video portrays the unions as "political," spending dues money on campaigns for candidates that workers "don't even vote for," and "to pay union bigwigs and their lawyers." And the "politics" extends to the internal life of the workplace itself: work rules base promotions on "seniority or union politics," rather than merit; union procedures prohibit members from communicating directly with management and require workers "to go to your union steward," who will relay the message to management only "if he likes what you say." And most importantly, the union is ineffective or worse. Strikes—frequent, violent, and divisive—are certain to be lost, likewise "every benefit . . . could go on the negotiating table" and "unions will negotiate just about anything to get the right to have dues deducted from your paychecks." The video concludes with a newly minted Wal-Mart associate speaking directly into the camera. He asserts: "All of us every day, we see how our management listens and cares. . . . We see how many chances there are to move. There's no way we'd want a union to come in."

There's a racial subtext to this propaganda as well. The two most forceful and self-confident anti-unionists in the video are African Americans. The human resources manager who occupies the central role in the video is an attractive black women in her forties, who embodies the mature and kindly spirit of Mr. Sam. One of the former unionists, now a Wal-Mart associate who tells tales of union mendacity, is an African American man. And one of the naïve new hires, initially favorable to the union idea, is a young white man. That all of this completely inverts America's alignments on race, gender, and unionism is obvious and not lost on Wal-Mart, which has populated the executive ranks in its "People" division with numerous high-profile Latinos and African Americans.

Such indoctrination is hardly enough, so Wal-Mart keeps a close watch on what its workers think about their job, their boss, the company, and themselves. The "employee attitude survey" has long been a staple of the non-union workplace. Sears had perfected the system in the 1950s, when it employed skilled social scientists to identify patterns of discontent, and the employees who were most disloyal, before such sentiment could metastasize into a spreading union cancer.[46] Wal-Mart adopted a down-home approach, but hardly less effective. In the early 1970s Wal-Mart took the pulse of its workers by hosting an annual "grassroots" meeting for selected associates, during which top management heard complaints and exchanged ideas. Meetings were eventually held in every store. By 1994 they were replaced, in all but name, by a sixty-eight-question survey that dissected employee morale according to job, gender, ethnicity, age, length of service, and hours of work. The top five problems uncovered by the survey were always inadequate pay, the cost of health insurance, management favoritism, poor training, and the company policy that forced employees to relocate if they wanted a promotion into management ranks.[47]

Bentonville's computers also manipulated the data to generate something Wal-Mart called a "UPI," which originally stood for Union Probability Index, later renamed Unaddressed People Issues. About 20 percent of all Wal-Mart stores, most located outside the South, generate a UPI high enough to signal low morale, and therefore require the attention of company executives whose job it is to keep unionism at bay. "Maintaining high morale in a facility is crucial to remaining union free," is the way Wal-Mart's *Pipeline*, its intranet for store managers, put it in a confidential message to all store managers. "If a union organizer approaches an associate in a facility with low morale, the associate may believe the organizer's 'sales pitch.'"[48] Store managers who presided over a facility with a high UPI are vulnerable to transfer or demotion.

Indeed, Wal-Mart's own store managers and assistant managers are both the frontline troops and potential traitors in the battle against the unions. Like foremen in the factories and supervisors in the office, they are men and women in the middle, required to "execute 100 percent" the directives that come from above, but also tasked with the creation of a productive and harmonious workplace. Although they may be intensely hostile to "outside" union organizers, managers and assistant managers are enmeshed within a world of friendships and relationships that makes them unreliable union fighters. Thus, Brent Rummage, a former youth minister with the Church of God, who had been admitted to the Wal-Mart management training program, was supposed to report any union talk to his store manager. But when his own mother, who worked in the same Hillview, Kentucky, store to which he was assigned, ventured that unions might not be so bad, Rummage balked. "I wasn't going to report my mother," Rummage told a reporter. Likewise, Stan Fortune was managing a Wal-Mart in Weatherford, Texas, when his boss instructed him to fire an employee suspected of talking to the union. "I told him 'I'm not firing him,'" Fortune later recalled. "That's illegal.' . . . He got in my face and said 'You fire him or I'm going to fire you.'" A week later Fortune was gone.[49] Both Rummage and Fortune were later hired by the UFCW as part of the union's organizing drive at Wal-Mart.

Almost as troublesome to the company were those managers who took their hostility to unionism all too personally. In the late 1990s and early years of the twenty-first century, Wal-Mart faced hundreds of unfair labor practice charges filed by the UFCW and other unions. They were expensive, time consuming, and sometimes embarrassing to litigate, so Wal-Mart tried to teach lower-level managers to walk a fine line between militant but legal anti-unionism and those tactics that would generate an NLRB charge. This was the TIPS program, spelled out in Wal-Mart's *Manager's Toolbox to Remaining Union Free*: "Know your TIPS. As long as you do not Threaten, Interrogate, Promise, or Spy on your associates, Wal-Mart, through your efforts, will be able to share its views on unionization in an open, honest and legal manner."[50] Naturally, it proved impossible to adhere to such admonitions in practice. How could managers warn workers of the union danger if they did not implicitly threaten them on the one hand and promise a better future, either individually or collectively, on the other? And how were managers to know when they should pick up the Wal-Mart "union hotline" to Bentonville, unless they interrogated or spied on those who worked for them?

Thus trade unions lodged 288 unfair labor practice charges against Wal-Mart between 1998 and 2003. These included 41 charges claiming improper firings, 44 instances in which employees were threatened if they joined a union, 59 charges involving improper surveillance, and another 59 asserting that Wal-Mart illegally interrogated its associates to determine their views on sensitive labor-related issues. In all, 94 of these complaints were weighty enough to generate a formal NLRB complain against the corporation.[51]

When the union hotline did ring in Bentonville, Wal-Mart immediately put key members of its "labor team" on a corporate jet and dispatched them to the troubled store. At the height of the UFCW organizing campaign, about twenty midlevel Wal-Mart executives were assigned to this corporate office. Although some had a law degree, their function was not litigation. Instead, the labor team devoted itself exclusively to the "education" of store management and the associates who might have sparked the union drive or become subject to its siren song. Until the union drive was defeated, the labor team's skilled operatives sidelined local management and effectively took over the store, orchestrating the anti-union effort so as to stay on legally justifiable terrain. As a manager in Colorado told Human Rights Watch, "We have a union activity hotline. If you hear associates, you don't confront them. You or the store manager calls the hotline. Then higher-up management takes care of it."[52]

Blitzkrieg at Kingman

The labor team was extremely active during the first years of the twenty-first century when the UFCW organizing campaign was at its height. Typical was its intervention in a Wal-Mart store in Kingman, Arizona, where a group of young blue collar workers in the Tire and Lube Express (TLE) department got in touch with the UFCW, which on August 28, 2000, filed a petition with the nearby Phoenix office of the NLRB to represent as many as eighteen automotive service technicians.[53] The reaction from Wal-Mart top management was immediate, and little short of overwhelming. Within twenty-four hours more than twenty outside managers flooded the store, some to keep tabs on the mood of the associates via the Wal-Mart CBWA system, or "Coaching by Walking Around"; others to help out with the time-consuming annual inventory while the regular staff watched anti-union videos and attended near-daily captive audience meetings. At the TLE, Wal-Mart replaced the manager with a high-level personnel executive, untutored in changing oil or tires, but well versed in the corporation's union avoidance program. Wal-Mart's Loss Prevention department, the internal corporate police, got busy as well, training a new set of cameras on work areas in the tire and lube shop. "I had so many bosses around me, I couldn't believe it," remembered Larry Adams, a union supporter who worked in the TLE at that time. "They weren't there to help me. They were there to bug me. It was very intimidating."[54]

The key labor team figures who flew in from Bentonville were Vicky Dodson, a thirteen-year veteran in Wal-Mart's People division, and Kirk Williams, a young law school graduate from Chicago whom Wal-Mart had hired just a few months before. Dodson was a pro, a forceful and controlling "pistol," remembered one of the assistant managers who came under her authority; she was "an intelligent, articulate, sophisticated individual" in the more judicious words of an NLRB administrative law judge.[55] Williams, who had worked his way through Kent State as a Wal-Mart assistant store manager, including a stint in Loss Prevention, was a coldly ambitious functionary who would soon spend enormous amounts of time on the corporate jet putting out union fires throughout the company's retail empire.[56] Most people in the store, management and worker alike, called the Bentonville labor team the "union busters," or the "Nazi SS." Not unexpectedly, Dodson and Williams were contemptuous of the existing store management, whose maladroit handing of layoffs and scheduling issues they blamed for precipitating the union uprising. "They took us out of the store for a couple of days," remembered assistant manager Tony Kuc, "took us to a hotel, telling us how to handle the union, how to stop them from coming in . . . what to say, what not to say." Within a few weeks the store manager had been transferred and demoted, his two assistant managers marked for dismissal, and the TLE district manager fired outright.[57]

Within less than a week Dodson and her confederates met with 95 percent of all workers eligible to participate in the NLRB certification vote. Meanwhile, the labor team held daily meetings at 8 A.M. with all the salaried managers, as well as the hourly department heads, who they said were part of the store "management" and therefore ineligible to take part in an NLRB certification election. "We were basically spies, spies for the store, spies for the company," remembered a disenchanted associate. "We had to run our departments, do everything normally, and then be spies for them. The stress level was so high."[58] Unionists complained, at Kingman and elsewhere, that "Wal-Mart has tricked hourly department managers into thinking they were part of the management team and therefore obligated to report any signs of union activity," even though the NLRB ruled repeatedly against the company on the status of these hourly employees. Observed Michael Leonard, a UFCW official, "Wal-Mart's

M.O. is to test the limits of the law, and to only change its prepackaged anti-union program when it is forced to."[59]

The labor team screened one of five different anti-union videos every day. *Wal-Mart Under Attack* was a lurid depiction of union thuggishness and disruption directed toward a company that was portrayed as merely trying to provide inexpensive goods for ordinary working people. *Sign Now, Pay Later* urged Wal-Mart workers to resist the siren song of the union organizers, who would do and say anything to win another signature on a union card, all the while ensnaring the hapless retail worker in a world of burdensome dues and serf-like subservience to an alien, boss-ridden organization. These videos, always followed by a question-and-answer session with a member of the labor team, were highly effective. A worker later interviewed by Human Rights Watch remembered: "I actually had fears after seeing videos of Molotov cocktails and rocks, pelting rock, hurling bottles." Another said, "After those meetings, minds started changing" as one-time union supporters turned against the UFCW.[60]

Dodson, Williams, and regional executives from the Southwest stayed in Kingman for two solid months. This was the period during which the local NLRB held hearings to determine the size and composition of the TLE unit and in which both the UFCW and the Wal-Mart labor team marshaled their forces for the certification election itself. In minutely detailed reports back to Bentonville, labor team members described every instance of possible union talk, every wavering worker, and every meeting. Dodson kept track of the workers who wore union pins and the ones who took them off, what comments were made at the captive meetings, and the degree of union sentiment in various departments of the store. The labor team authorized raises for 85 percent of all workers, fixed the TLE cooling system, and repaired other equipment in that same department.[61] On October 9 Tom Coughlin jetted into Kingman to tell a group of TLE workers that the Wal-Mart "Open Door," not the UFCW, was the solution to their problems. "If you have any questions or problems," Coughlin told his grease-stained listeners, "don't hesitate to call me, and I will get you some results. I can override anybody."[62]

Given all this, it is hardly surprising that the UFCW organizing drive collapsed in inglorious defeat. Although the Labor Board ruled that the TLE was an appropriate bargaining unit, the union lost key supporters there within weeks of the labor team's arrival in town. Union partisans had virtually no opportunity to counter the propaganda barrage unleashed by the company. If they sought the telephone number of undecided associates, this violated Wal-Mart's "no solicitation" rule; if they distributed leaflets in the parking lot or break room in the store, managers immediately called Loss Prevention and then patrolled the facility to pick up any stray literature. And when UFCW organizers made evening house calls, Wal-Mart denounced this tactic as harassment and intimidation. So on October 24, UFCW lawyers filed a broad set of unfair labor practice complaints against Wal-Mart, thus postponing indefinitely the NLRB election scheduled for just a few days later. Working life for the remaining pro-union people in the Kingman store became increasingly intolerable. Within little more than a year virtually all would be fired, be forced to quit, or simply leave in disgust.

The Labor Board eventually ruled, at Kingman and elsewhere, that Wal-Mart had systematically harassed and spied on numerous workers, that it had threatened employees with a loss of benefits and raises if they supported the union, and that the company had fired outright key labor partisans. But none of this had any real impact on Wal-Mart's anti-union operation, if only because the penalties were so trivial: a few thousand dollars in back pay for a few unjustly fired employees, plus a formal notice briefly posted in the break room pledging to obey the labor law. In its authoritative report on Wal-Mart, *Discounting Rights: Wal-Mart's Violation of U.S. Workers' Rights to Freedom of Association*, Human Rights Watch concluded that the company "has translated its hostility towards union formation into an unabashed, sophisticated, and aggressive strategy to derail worker organizing at its US stores that violates workers' internationally recognized right to freedom of association."[63]

True enough, but John Tate deserves the last word. When in September 2004 Tom Coughlin introduced the eighty-seven-year-old union fighter to a large meeting of store managers and other Wal-Mart executives assembled in Dallas, Tate was in a valedictory, yet triumphant mood. The UFCW, decisively beaten in every store where it had managed to rear its head, had laid off its key organizers and abandoned any concerted effort to unionize Wal-Mart. "Most of you know that my chief interest has had to do with unions," Tate told the expectant crowd in a short speech captured on video. And then he hoarsely, but with calculated diction, asserted his credo, "Labor unions are nothing but blood-sucking parasites living off the productive labor of people who work for a living!" In a flash, hundreds of Wal-Mart managers jumped to their feet, cheering, shouting, and hooting. Fifty years ago union labor represented more than a third of the private sector workforce, Tate reminded his audience. "I am part of the reason that today they represent nine percent," he said to another standing ovation. "Sam would have been proud of you for that!" he added, to more sustained cheering. "The battle isn't yet won. I want to conclude by challenging you to reduce that percentage. You can do it and at the same time insure your own future."[64]

"All Deals Are Off": The Dunlop Commission and Employer Opposition to Labor Law Reform

John Logan

Congressional failure to enact the Employee Free Choice Act (EFCA) during the early years of the Obama presidency has demonstrated, yet again, that employer opposition is the greatest obstacle to the modernization of labor law. For the nation's major management associations, labor law reform is a life-and-death issue: nothing is more important than defeating revisions to the National Labor Relations Act (NLRA) intended to strengthen organizing and bargaining rights. The U.S. Chamber of Commerce, for example, described its campaign against EFCA as a "firestorm bordering on Armageddon."[1] In this respect, the campaign was a virtual replay of every attempt at labor law reform under Democratic presidents and Congresses since the Johnson administration. On each occasion, no-holds-barred employer opposition has undermined labor's effort to reform the law.

Prior to the Obama administration, the last effort to revise the NLRA took place early in the presidency of Bill Clinton when the Democrats held majorities in both houses of Congress. The Clinton administration had offered employers policies intended to encourage employee involvement and alternative dispute resolution in exchange for reform of organizing and bargaining rights. But nothing was important enough for the business community to trade in return for greater legal protection for workers seeking to form a trade union. After the sweeping Republican victories in the 1994 midterm elections, "all deals were off" and the administration's attempts at reform ended in defeat and disarray, a consistent theme in labor law campaigns of the past half century.

Origins of the Dunlop Commission

With the election of Bill Clinton in November 1992, labor law reform was once again on the legislative agenda. Clinton's victory provided labor an unexpected second chance to revise the NLRA after its narrow failure to do so under the Carter administration in 1978, when a five-week Republican filibuster finally killed a bill designed to facilitate organizing. Throughout the 1980s and early 1990s, hostile Republican administrations thwarted labor's legislative agenda. That changed with Bill Clinton's victory. During the presidential campaign, Clinton had announced his support for a bill outlawing permanent replacement workers, but he never got the opportunity to sign the striker replacement bill into law—an all-out employer campaign and then a Republican filibuster in the Senate defeated it in July 1994.[2]

But that battle did not stymie an even more ambitious effort to progressively reform the national labor law. In March 1993, Clinton's secretary of commerce, Ron Brown, and secretary of labor, Robert Reich, announced the formation of the Commission on the Future of Worker-Management Relations (or the Dunlop Commission). Reich wanted to transform workplace relations, move away from the adversarial model, and facilitate the diffusion of productivity-enhancing innovations—the "operative principle" behind the Dunlop Commission—in order to enable American firms to compete more effectively with their German and Japanese counterparts in an increasingly global economy. He believed that in the 90 percent of private sector workplaces where unions did not exist, and were not likely to do so for the near future, some form of works council or employee committee arrangement independent of collective bargaining was essential. Employee involvement was necessary if firms were to develop cooperative human resource strategies that took full advantage of workers' skills, empowered frontline workers, embraced win-win strategies, and created and maintained high-skill, high-wage jobs. The "jury was still out," Reich believed, on whether unions and collective bargaining would make the high-performance model work in practice.[3]

At the launch of the blue-ribbon presidential commission—whose ten members included former secretaries of labor and commerce and a nonpartisan group from business, labor, and academia—Brown announced that "labor and management must become . . . advocates for an entirely new way for American firms to compete and win in the global marketplace."[4] The commission's "mission statement" was to investigate the state of workplace relations and offer recommendations in three areas: First, what new methods should be encouraged to enhance productivity through labor-management cooperation and employee participation? Second, what changes should be made in the law and practices of collective bargaining to enhance cooperative behavior, improve productivity, and reduce conflict and delay? Third, what should be done to increase the resolution of workplace problems by the parties themselves, rather than through recourse to state and federal courts and government regulatory bodies? Political considerations demanded that these three main areas—employee participation, worker representation and collective bargaining, and regulation and litigation—be addressed simultaneously. The business community opposed reforms to facilitate organizing but favored employee participation and alternative dispute resolution (ADR). Unions, on the other hand, opposed relaxing the prohibition against company unions and had serious reservations about ADR, but sought reform of the NLRA's representation procedures.

The choice for the chair of the commission, Harvard professor and former secretary of labor John Dunlop, was of critical significance. Widely regarded as one of the nation's premier mediators, Dunlop enjoyed the trust of labor and management leaders and was considered to have the consensus-building skills necessary to prevent the debate over labor law reform from degenerating into the pitched battle of every previous campaign. If anyone could forge a consensus between unions and management on labor law reform, many observers believed, it was the politically realistic Dunlop.[5] At the inaugural meeting of the commission, Dunlop's first question was whether it was possible to develop a more consensual framework for labor-management relations or whether the parties involved were perpetually "doomed" to repeat the current level of discord.[6] Other key members of the commission included MIT professor Tom Kochan—a leading expert on high-performance work practices—and the commission's counsel, Harvard law professor Paul Weiler, who had written extensively on labor law and employer opposition to unionization in North America. The commission had two management representatives: Paul Allaire, chief executive officer of the unionized Xerox Corporation, a firm with cooperative labor-management relations, and Kathryn Turner, president of nonunion Standard Technology, a small high-tech firm.

After holding hearings in Washington, D.C., and around the nation, and considering written submissions from labor, management, and academic sources, the commission issued a "fact finding report" in May 1994, and published its final recommendations six months later. By the time the commission issued its final report, it had held twenty-one hearings, heard from 411 witnesses and working parties, and considered almost five thousand pages of transcript. But long before the publication of the final report—and before the Republican Party's 1994 election victories had rendered its policy recommendations irrelevant—it was clear that the commission had failed to reach consensus between labor and management on any major issue. The Dunlop Commission would not produce the much-hoped-for breakthrough on labor law reform. Therefore, employer organizations saw little reason to countenance comprehensive reform of the NLRA in the months before the midterm elections After the Republicans gained control of Congress, the only legislative change they supported was a bill repealing Section 8(a)(2)—the NLRA's prohibition of employer-dominated organizations—a proposal that the Dunlop Commission had explicitly rejected.[7]

A Historic Compromise?

The unions had once held high hopes for the Dunlop Commission, but they were never entirely sure about what they sought to include in the commission's final set of recommendations. If the midterm elections produced a poor result for the Democrats, thereby making labor law reform beyond reach, unions preferred that the commission restrict itself to broad recommendations rather than issue specific proposals for NLRA reform.[8] But if the election turned out well for Democrats, the unions wanted the commission to produce specific recommendations that would form the basis for a legislative campaign in 1995, if, as expected, the business community failed to endorse the initiative.[9] For his part Chairman Dunlop sought a report that stood a realistic chance of legislative success, even if he could not secure the business community's support. Dunlop favored recommendations that could be "sold" to the Clinton administration and to moderate Republicans and conservative Democrats. However, unless the commission was able to forge its own consensus between union and management commissioners, its recommendations would merely establish a starting point for future negotiations. Thus, unions warned that it was critical that the commission did not "trade away" too many recommendations to the business community early in the process.[10]

The commission could play a critical role by redefining the terms of the debate over labor law reform. If labor's allies in Congress promoted NLRA reform as a freestanding package designed to strengthen unions, it stood little chance of success. Instead, reform needed to be sold as an integral part of a program designed to make the law a force for encouraging workplace democracy, both for its own sake and as a means of improving the performance of American firms. Labor had to frame its labor law reform proposals in broad economic terms and explain why its proposals were "consistent with President Clinton's 'vision' of the U.S. economy and why organized employees enhance rather than detract from the competitive position of American business."[11] The early 1990s had witnessed a severe economic downturn and the central focus of the Clinton administration was on economic recovery, so the challenge was to reconnect labor law reform with the economic advancement of the American middle class.[12] The commission needed to rebut employers' charges that unions undermined firms' competitiveness in a global economy, thereby damaging the economic health of the nation. Labor law reform that strengthened the bargaining power of American workers was a necessary condition for economic recovery, as only then would gains in productivity and the pursuit of a high-performance workplace translate into higher wages. If the commission failed to make this argument, the Clinton administration would treat labor law reform as a peripheral issue of concern only to unions, and the business community, Republicans, and conservative Democrats would attack reform as "special interest" legislation.

When it came to specific remedies, labor's advocates argued that the commission could not merely condemn employer violations of the existing

collective bargaining law. The problem was far more profound and systematic, not the product of a minority set of "rogue" employers. Labor wanted
the commission to recommend enhanced remedies for discriminatory discharges to protect employees' right to form a union; especially these new
proposals would provide bargaining and arbitration rights, thereby ensuring that employers no longer benefited from routine violation of the labor
law. The existing weak remedies of the NLRA offered little incentive for
employers to comply with the law.[13] Weiler, the commission's counselor,
estimated that one in twenty union supporters were unlawfully discharged
during organizing campaigns, and the commission itself had documented
a significant increase in unfair management practices over the past three
decades.[14] However, the real problem was that the current system permitted
aggressive employer opposition that was entirely *within* the law but that
nevertheless effectively undermined employee free choice. Thus, the ultimate aim of NLRA reform was to make organizing less perilous, and this
could not be achieved by simply imposing harsher penalties on employers
who violated the law.[15] "Mere tinkering" with rules, procedures, and
remedies would "not suffice," argued AFL-CIO secretary-treasurer Tom
Donahue.[16]

If the principal shortcoming of the NLRA were its failure to punish
illegal conduct, the commission's task would be a straightforward one.
There was no mystery as to why employers violated the NLRA with such
regularity—most employers considered the law's paltry sanctions a small
price to pay to prevent unionization. The financial penalties for violating
the NLRA were significantly smaller than the penalties for violating other
federal and state employment laws.[17] Since the 1970s, employers had
increasingly appealed unfavorable NLRB decisions, correctly believing that
the federal courts were more likely than the labor board to grant them a
sympathetic hearing.[18] Organized labor, however, did not want the commission to dwell only on delays in the representation process or inadequate
remedies. The commission needed to go beyond the "easy issue" of
employer violations to deal with the heart of the problem: the implacable
hostility with which the vast majority of employers confronted efforts by
workers to form unions, normally by exploiting management's exclusive
control over employees at the workplace to thwart organizing campaigns.
So long as there existed a state-administered system for securing representation, employers would be free to make clear to employees that they opposed

unionization and that employees would suffer adverse consequences, individually and collectively, if they chose to organize. Thus, in order to loosen employers' stronghold over the representation system, NLRA reforms needed to reduce fear during organizing.

Unpacking Employer Opposition

What explained the intensity of employer hostility to unionization? The significant wage gap between union and non-union firms offers a partial explanation.[19] Unionization meant higher labor costs and—in a system of decentralized bargaining with low union density in most sectors– significant financial incentives for employers to fight organization.[20] The impact of the union wage premium was particularly significant in mature and highly organized industries, but actually less important in newer industries that unions were attempting to organize. However, the "control gap" remained of paramount managerial concern throughout all sectors of the economy. Absent a union, employers in the United States, unlike the situation in most other liberal democracies, enjoyed unilateral control of the workplace.[21] Indeed, American managers not only feared the competitive disadvantage associated with unionization—they feared for their own jobs. Managers whose plants were the target of successful union campaigns were four times more likely to lose their jobs than those who beat back the union.[22] Innovations in the structure of corporate governance since the 1970s—which had heightened pressures on top management to resist any changes that threatened the maximization of short-term shareholder value—had also intensified employer opposition to unionization.[23]

Corporate anti-unionism was also driven by ideology itself apart from any tough-minded evaluation of "bottom line" effects. This commitment to a union-free workplace had intensified since the 1970s, in tandem with the pressures generated by competitive product markets.[24] The major obstacle to workplace democracy was the "dominant management view in the US—as opposed to every other industrialized country—that worker organization is detrimental to the interests of the firm and that the desire of workers to organize represents a failure of management." Employer opposition to unionization in every other rich democracy paled in comparison with that found in the United States.[25] Thus, although anti-unionism among American employers was based on rational economic and job-control considerations,[26] it was bolstered by a powerful ideological commitment to a union-free environment. What was required to protect employee free choice, therefore, was nothing less than a comprehensive overhaul of the NLRA's representation procedures. Reform could not bring about a fundamental transformation in U.S. corporate culture and could not force employers to be more accepting of unionization. But it could make the organizing process less confrontational and fearful for employees, and this is what unions wanted.[27]

To reinforce this point, and disavow Dunlop of his "remedial mindset," labor provided "horror stories" that illustrated the often-insurmountable obstacles that confronted workers attempting to form unions, especially ones involving low-paid or minority workers. Employers used their control of the employment relationship to discourage unionization, and that fear and a sense of futility, argued labor, not a lack of desire for representation, stood in the way of workers forming unions. Richard Bensinger of the AFL-CIO told the commission that any employer "who expends maximum (and even not so maximum) effort to defeat a union can win, any time anywhere—without breaking the law. The potency of implied threats, the futility of winning first contracts, fear of retaliation, combined with exclusive access to the workforce . . . is virtually unbeatable. . . . What this means is that right now it is the boss, not the workers, who decides whether there will be a union."[28]

"Fact Finding Report"

In June 1994, the commission released its "Fact Finding Report," described by the *New York Times* as a "scrupulously balanced" document that had deliberately "sidestepped controversy."[29] Business and labor groups both issued statements of praise, with each group stressing those findings that best suited its constituents. Not all reactions to the report were positive, however. The Associated Builders and Contractors cautioned that the final report would likely recommend a comprehensive overhaul of the NLRA, thereby instigating the "mother of all wars" over labor law reform, and even those business leaders who welcomed the interim report remained unconvinced that the commission could broker a deal on reform.[30] Praise from labor sources was also far from universal. One labor attorney asserted that the "lukewarm" findings were designed not to offend unions, employers, "or anybody else who can influence an election."[31] Another labor activist called Dunlop's search for consensus a "fool's mission." The behavior of "virtually all" employers when confronted with attempts by their employees to form a union, he believed, indicated "how little support" existed within the business community for meaningful reform.[32] But Dunlop interpreted the generally favorable responses as an affirmation that he could negotiate a historic compromise.[33] Dunlop believed that he could convince the business community to adopt a tougher stance on employer violations. Consistent with this approach, the report focused on illegal discharges, thereby conveying the impression that a "few bad apples" were causing most of the problems in representation campaigns. But in stark contrast with this Dunlop perspective, labor leaders thought that the fundamental problem with the NLRA system was not the *number* of lawbreakers but the provisions of the law that enabled *all* employers to intimidate workers *without* violating the law.

Card Check and First-Contract Arbitration

Most unions believed that the highest reform priority ought to be card check certification. Although even the most pro-union member of the commission, former UAW president Doug Fraser, believed that card check was politically unattainable, unionists thought it indispensable to any reform quid pro quo. As a result of employers' sophisticated anti-union tactics, they argued, the NLRB election process was ineffective at revealing the true desires of workers.[34] Another system, which shielded workers from management intimidation, was essential if true employee free choice were to be rewon within a labor law framework.

But along with card check recognition, unions also wanted interest arbitration as a last resort in *all* first-contract cases. Employer aggression did not end with a union victory: one-third of newly certified unions failed to secure first contracts. Consultants advised employers that "you haven't lost until you sign a contract," and as a result, the NLRA was being undermined by "management attorneys who specialize in bargaining to impasse rather than on reaching agreement." First-contract arbitration would remove from employers the argument that organizing was futile and limit their ability to exploit employees' fears about losing existing wages and benefits.[35]

Labor leaders believed that the best way to protect employee free choice was to make organizing less perilous and more immediately beneficial for employees. First contract arbitration would do that if it were available in *all* cases as a last resort means of dispute resolution, not simply as a remedy for bad faith bargaining. However, commission chair Dunlop favored first-contract arbitration as a remedy only for bad faith bargaining, believing that if arbitration were available in all cases, the parties would seldom reach agreement because they would hold out for a better deal from the arbitrator. Arguing that difficulties in first-contract negotiations were the result of unrealistic promises unions had made during organizing campaigns, employer organizations rejected the arbitration idea. They maintained, with Dunlop, that the widespread deployment of such a dispute resolution mechanism would result in less incentive for unions and employers to reach agreement, not more.[36]

Section 8(a)(2) Reform

Almost all observers expected the commission to produce proposals to modify Section 8(a)(2)—the clause prohibiting employer-dominated labor organizations—for the purpose of encouraging employee participation. The Clinton administration had established the commission with the goal of promoting employee committees in nonunion workplaces. Employers argued that 8(a)(2) impeded the establishment of employee participation programs, especially after the NLRB's *Electromation* and *DuPont* decisions, which had ruled that certain participation committees violated the NLRA.[37] These decisions had created some degree of uncertainty about the legality of employee committees and provoked widespread calls for a change in the law to permit representation plans. Survey evidence demonstrated that employees favored greater workplace participation, and that participation improved quality and productivity, but firms worried that participation programs might be found to be in violation of the law. The case for encouraging employee participation, employers argued, was therefore compelling.[38]

The AFL-CIO had to tread carefully on 8(a)(2) reform, as any modification of the provision would likely provoke outrage among its affiliates. Some pro-union commentators believed that 8(a)(2) reform might lead to an expansion of employee voice. In addition to the performance benefits associated with employee participation, 8(a)(2) reform would provide some collective voice, albeit an imperfect form, for the 90 percent of private sector employees who currently had no workplace representation. Given that most of these employees were unlikely to gain independent representation anytime soon, it made little sense to insist that workers must be represented by bona fide unions or else go without representation. If the choice were independent representation or unilateral employer decision making, it would clearly mean the latter for the overwhelming majority of American workers. Employer-initiated employee committees—which unionists had labeled "company unionism" in decades past—might even lead to independent representation, as had happened with the steelworkers and communications workers in the 1930s. But most unionists rejected these speculations out of hand. Their major concern was not that employees would be duped by employer-dominated representation schemes, but that these workers would settle for a lesser form of workplace voice because of its easy accessibility in a system that exacted such a high price for real trade unionism. Thus, so long as employers could make independent representation so difficult to attain, union leaders argued, they should not be permitted to offer employee involvement as an alternative.[39]

What Did Employers Really, Really Want?

The commission appeared uncertain about what the business community wanted from labor law reform. Paul Allaire asked the National Association of Manufacturers (NAM) and Labor Policy Association (LPA) to clarify their positions on 8(a)(2) reform, and said that the commission was having "some degree of difficulty understanding exactly what management would advocate in this area."[40] Noting that several 8(a)(2) cases were pending before the NLRB, both organizations were content to adopt a "wait-and-see" approach and give the board an opportunity to remove the barriers to employee involvement erected by its *Electromation* and *DuPont* decisions.[41] But the "*Electromation* debate" was largely a red herring. The decision of the Bush-appointed NLRB concerned an old-fashioned company union, not work teams, quality circles, or other legitimate forms of employee involvement that employers alleged were under attack. Since the 1970s, the NLRB had decided on fewer than three 8(a)(2) cases per year and all but three of these had involved other kinds of employer unfair labor practices.[42]

For Dunlop, however, *Electromation* was a useful red herring, one he hoped to use in negotiations with employers in exchange for the reforms advocated by the trade unions.

The LPA and NAM also provided no concrete evidence that the existing law impeded employee involvement schemes.[43] Indeed, not one employer told the commission that 8(a)(2) repeal was essential for the operation of its participation program. On the contrary, employer representatives testifying before the commission had repeatedly stated that Taylorism was being replaced by participatory management, thereby refuting the notion that 8(a)(2) represented an obstacle to the diffusion of employer-controlled participation schemes. While stressing its commitment to employee involvement, for example, Toyota management acknowledged that nothing in the law had inhibited its team method of production at its pioneering facility in Georgetown, Kentucky. Certain employer-initiated participation committees that clearly violated 8(a)(2) had operated for decades without unfair labor practice complaints because of the absence of an aggrieved union, and survey evidence had demonstrated that employee participation programs were widespread and growing.[44] Thus, *Electromation* and *DuPont* notwithstanding, 8(a)(2) had provided employers with considerable latitude to involve their employees in production-related issues.[45] The fact that employers could point to "so many current, successful involvement programs" and were unable to provide evidence of any adverse 8(a)(2) decisions confirmed that the existing law was "*not* impeding legitimate employee involvement."[46] Thus, union leaders argued, the law did not prohibit the positive forms of participation that employees wanted, but it did prohibit the more autocratic forms of participation that some employers wanted. As the authors of the NLRA had intended, Section 8(a)(2) had prevented employers from using participation programs "as a vehicle to dominate or interfere with the formation or administration of a true, independent worker voice."[47]

While not of one mind on Section 8(a)(2), employer groups offered one consistent position on labor law reform: they dismissed any suggestion that they should accept reform of the NLRA's representation procedures as a quid pro quo for 8(a)(2) revision. Daniel Yager of LPA and Howard Knicely of TRW stressed the value of employee involvement and warned of the "dark cloud" cast by the *Electromation* decision.[48] But when questioned about the need for minimum standards if the law were relaxed to allow employee participation, Yager responded that such legal protections were unnecessary because these programs would flounder if they did not give employees a genuine voice. And when the commission suggested that employee free choice should be strengthened in return for relaxing the prohibition of employer-dominated organizations, Knicely responded that employees already enjoyed a full-fledged right to organize. If employers wanted 8(a)(2) reform, they did not want it badly enough that they were prepared to accept in return revision of the law's representation procedures. With 90 percent of the private sector workforce union free, reforms to facilitate organizing were simply too high a price for employers to pay in return for reforms to encourage greater employee participation. There was no bargain to be struck that would strengthen collective bargaining.

Employer groups wanted the Dunlop Commission to address other labor policy issues. The NAM stressed the need for government policy to reduce "nonproduction costs," such as regulatory compliance, litigation expenditures, and health-care provision. Like academic commentators, the NAM extolled the virtues of high-performance work systems and participatory management, but also suggested that nonunion companies were at the forefront of experimentation with employee involvement because of their "greater flexibility." Increased participation could reduce the extent and cost of government regulation of the employment relationship, the NAM concluded. The LPA repeated the same mantra celebrating workplace deregulation and high-performance work systems. The association saw little role for new federal mandates. "Worker empowerment" had spread, argued one employer representative, "without government mandates and without massive labor law reform."[49]

The business community also wanted employees to adjudicate employment discrimination claims through employer-created nonunion arbitration schemes. The commission considered recommending such reforms, providing it could ensure safeguards to assure fairness of the process. The current system adjudicating employees' civil rights through the courts had proven costly, which effectively priced many workers out of the system. But the existing claims procedure could also produce windfall recoveries for employees who made good witnesses and were lucky enough to get a sympathetic jury, which had a significant deterrent effect on illegal employer behavior. The business community's preference for nonunion arbitration therefore suggested that employers feared arbitrators' awards much less than those of a jury or judge. Indeed, civil rights and women's organizations would likely have resisted any recommendation to remove employment discrimination cases from the courts, as they had done on previous occasions, thereby making the entire issue a "nonstarter" for the Dunlop Commission.[50]

The Chamber of Commerce and National Federation of Independent Business (NFIB) also criticized government regulation for being too complex, costly, and burdensome, especially for their small business constituents. But the chamber and NFIB were more avowedly anti-union than the NAM and LPA, arguing that unions were no longer necessary because of extensive government mandates and employer benevolence. Unions harmed small businesses, they argued, and unions themselves bore responsibility for their decline in membership.[51] When former labor secretary Bill Usery asserted that employers should welcome reforms designed to vindicate the principles of the NLRA, the chamber responded that reform would prove disastrous for small businesses that "lacked the resources, knowledge and time it takes to defend against sophisticated union campaigns."[52] Standard Technology president Kathryn Turner, as noted earlier, one of the commission's two management representatives and the only one from a small nonunion firm, sympathized with attacks by the chamber and the NFIB on government regulations that "clearly failed" to "add value" to the employment relationship.

The militancy of the chamber and NFIB doomed any commission effort to achieve consensus on labor law reform. Even if some large employers endorsed its final report, the NFIB, chamber, and Business Roundtable would mobilize to defeat its recommendations that liberalized union organizing rights. Bitter battles over striker replacement legislation had illustrated how difficult it could be to enlist employer support for even the most minimal kind of reform. The AFL-CIO had failed to recruit a single corporate ally—even among firms that had cooperative labor relations—for its campaign to ban permanent replacements, even as the chamber, NFIB, NAM, and LPA mobilized thousands of companies to defeat the pro-labor bill.[53] Employer groups wanted to thwart labor's reform proposals because they saw no reason to alter the status quo. They were the overwhelming beneficiaries of the forty-year legislative stalemate that had stymied all efforts to reform American labor law. Dunlop proved myopic when it came to this reality. He had been encouraged that employers were interested in discussing employee participation and ADR, while labor wanted to debate worker representation. But contrasting agendas indicated that no common ground existed for meaningful discussion, not that there existed an opportunity for a historic accord that might break the decades old standoff on labor law reform.

No constituency existed for the commission's recommendations among the business community because 8(a)(2) reform was simply not that important to employers.[54] As a system designed to motivate workers, Taylorism may have been discredited among some top manufacturers, but it was still practiced by the vast majority of employers, especially in retail and services.[55] While celebrated within the academy, participatory management remained the exception rather than the rule in the American workplace. Many employers claimed that they desired a high-involvement, high-commitment, high-skill workforce, but they were clearly unwilling to cede authority over the terms and conditions of employment. Instead, they wanted to strengthen and rationalize their own unilateral control of the workplace by maintaining or restoring a union-free environment. The current legal regime had gone a long way to delivering that goal. The congressional impasse on labor law reform that had existed since the 1940s served the interests of nonunion employers, and thus, it was unlikely that they would support recommendations on 8(a)(2) revision, ADR, or anything else if the price they had to pay would be greater protection for organizing and bargaining rights. And whatever slim prospects did exist for a deal abruptly ended with the Republicans' victory in the 1994 midterm elections. Immediately afterward LPA president Jeff McGuiness asserted that "all deals are off, all swaps; whatever deals there might have been are now off. . . . ADR is not worth the swap."[56]

"Labor Law Deformed"

Indeed, rather than entertain prospects for a grand social compromise, the U.S. business community used the platform provided by the Dunlop Commission to sharpen and advertise its increasingly militant anti-union ideology. To coordinate employer opposition to reform, a coalition of trade and professional associations, corporate organizations, and business groups

formed the "Voice for the American Workplace" (VAW), whose "sole purpose" was to "monitor the activities of the Dunlop Commission." Warning
that labor was seeking to "Europeanize" U.S. labor law, VAW warned that
if the Democrats maintained legislative power after 1994, the "prospects for
union-style labor law reform are good in the next Congress." VAW executive director Francis Coleman believed that the composition of the commission should give employers "cause for grave concern," and stressed the
need to "balance" its record through the submission of employer testimony. Coleman feared that the final report would serve as a "stalking horse
for labor law reform AFL-CIO style," but warned that VAW would "take
off the gloves" to defeat pro-union proposals.[57]

Before the commission itself, most employer spokesmen and -women
denied that there was any problem with American labor law, blaming the
unions themselves for the persistent decline in their fortunes. Employer
associations dismissed instances of no-holds-barred anti-union campaigns
as anecdotal and unrepresentative.[58] Homer Deakins, cofounder of one of
the nation's largest management law firms, Ogletree-Deakins, argued that
unions were losing NLRB elections because workers no longer wanted or
needed them, and because unions could no longer represent their interests
in the new American workplace. Structural changes favoring nonunion
employment and rising job satisfaction levels among nonunion employees
resulting from new methods of work organization and sophisticated human
resource policies best explained union decline over the previous two decades, Deakins argued.[59] Tom Kochan accused Deakins of replaying the
political battles of the 1970s and refusing to acknowledge the legitimate
public interest in curbing illegal employer conduct. But when Kochan suggested that unions could add value to the employment relationship if
employers cooperated with them, Deakins expressed deep skepticism.
Meanwhile, Edward Miller, the former chairman of the Nixon-era NLRB,
disparaged the idea, common in liberal circles, of a "labor law deformed,"
thus questioning the need for an expansion of "union power."[60] The Associated Builders and Contractors found also "no empirical evidence" of
problems with NLRB procedures, asserting that the public was "generally
satisfied" with the status quo.[61]

Other employer representatives repeated the same anti-union themes.
Unions were pursuing outdated, antagonistic relationships and stood as
impediments to employee involvement, insisted Clifford Ehrlich, senior
vice president for human resources for Marriott International. Relying on

an employer-commissioned opinion poll, Ehrlich suggested that workers themselves no longer wanted unions, and argued that discriminatory dismissals were "self-defeating" because they had the "opposite effect of galvanizing the remaining workers against the company."[62] Likewise, former solicitor of labor William Kilberg told the commission that unions were seeking reform because they were unable to win representation elections. Union losses were not due to higher levels of employer coercion than existed during periods when they were more successful, he argued, and existing legal remedies for unfair practices were adequate and expeditious. Moreover, employer illegalities were the result of employers who had not been counseled, not inadequate laws, and excluding employers and consultants from the representation process would lead to uninformed choices by employees.[63]

When Kochan asked what might be done to reduce the significant resources spent on resisting unionism and high levels of antagonism in organizing campaigns that diminished trust between labor and management, these employer representatives had no suggestions. Dunlop asked for empirical evidence demonstrating that employers who failed to hire outside law firms committed most unfair labor practices, but in response Kilberg argued that the fact that unions won more elections in smaller units supported his theory because these employers were more likely to lack counsel and commit unfair practices, thereby turning workers against them. Rather than greater regulation, Kilberg's solution was more guidance to ensure that employers knew what was and was not permissible behavior during organizing campaigns.[64] Both Kilberg and Ehrlich dismissed the need for NLRA revisions designed to protect employee choice.

Aftermath

When the commission issued its final report in January 1995, the AFL-CIO lamented that the document fell "far short" of what was required to protect employee free choice. It had four main criticisms. First, although the commission had found substantial evidence of employer interference, it proposed no new penalties for violators. Second, despite finding fault with the current representation process, the commission did not recommend card certification, establish firm deadlines for representation elections, or recommend allowing union organizers into the workplace,[65] and instead limited itself to authorizing prehearing elections and recommending that elections be conducted "promptly." Third, it failed to recommend expanding the subjects for bargaining, increasing the penalties for bad faith bargaining, or balancing the economic weapons available to parties should they be unable to reach agreement. Finally, despite finding a significant expansion of contingent work that had contributed to workplace insecurity and income inequality, the commission failed to minimize the incentives for employers to shift to temporary, part-time, or contract employees.[66]

In stark contrast to generally favorable comments on the fact finding report six months earlier, the commission's final set of recommendations, reported the *Washington Post*, provoked "immediate condemnation from both business and labor—for entirely different reasons. What labor liked, business called 'disappointing' and 'flawed.' What business liked was generally condemned by labor."[67] *Industry Week* believed that the final report had "offended everyone."[68] The NAM called the commission's proposal for a limited version of first-contract arbitration the "death knell of democratic collective bargaining," while the LPA lamented a "lost opportunity" to tackle the real obstacles to enhancing workplace competitiveness.[69] The chamber expressed its "bitter disappointment," while another employer group believed that the commission had attempted to split the business community by "angling" for the support of those employers adversely affected by the *Electromation* and *DuPont* decisions. But it was confident that employers would see through this transparent ploy and reject the "limited fix" on employee participation and "unhelpful thoughts" on ADR.[70] Unions were equally critical. Service Employees International Union president John Sweeney lambasted the recommendation for revision of 8(a)(2) as a "grave step backward," while Communications Workers of America president Morton Bahr regretted the failure to tackle "widespread worker fear and employer intimidation."[71]

Dunlop acknowledged that the interested parties might deem the recommendations "below their expectations," but remained hopeful that they would find "something that they liked" and use the report as a starting point for further dialogue.[72] Media interest in the recommendations focused almost exclusively on the proposal for clarifying 8(a)(2).[73] In the conservative political climate of 1995, it was inevitable that the recommendations on employee participation would dominate coverage of the final report, while those on representation and collective bargaining received short shrift. After the November elections, the AFL-CIO had anticipated that labor's adversaries would seize upon any 8(a)(2) recommendation to advance their anti-union agenda and disregard those recommendations they disliked. With anti-union Republicans controlling the Congress, the commission could not prevent the report from being misused, no matter how much it protested that its recommendations must be treated as a package.[74] Commission members seemed dismayed by the reaction to the final report. Tom Kochan warned against piecemeal reform: "Any effort to pick and choose only those changes in the law that suits one party's narrow self-determined interest will intensify the polarization that the full set of recommendations is designed to reduce." Kochan concluded that only when public opinion demanded reform would we see a breakthrough in the paralysis that had blocked every attempt to modernize the country's antiquated labor laws for three decades.[75]

Try, Try Again

After the debacle of the Dunlop Commission, the turn to the right after the 1994 midterms, and the election of reformer John Sweeney to the presidency of the AFL-CIO in 1995—which resulted in a greater emphasis on organizing and less on national legislative campaigns—NLRA reform was a dead letter for the rest of the decade. But organizing under NLRB elections remained extraordinarily difficult, with the number of workers gaining union recognition through official channels reduced to a trickle. Thus, in the late 1990s, senior AFL-CIO officials drew up legislation that formed the basis of the Employee Free Choice Act, introduced in Congress in 2003. After its disastrous experience with an open-ended presidential commission (i.e., one with a mandate asking it what to do about labor policy) in the 1990s, labor was determined that, next time round, it would have a bill ready to go if and when reform became politically possible again. Following the 2006 midterm elections—which produced Democratic majorities in the House and Senate—EFCA won majority support in both chambers in 2007, though well short of the supermajority of sixty required to force an up-or-down vote in the Senate. With the election of a pro-union president and substantial Democratic majorities in Congress in 2008, labor believed that NLRA reform might finally be within reach. By early 2010, however, its hopes had been dashed. While the immediate cause of labor's defeat was its inability to win sixty votes in the Senate, the underlying cause, once again, was determined and cohesive opposition from the business community. In the decade that began in 2010, the prospects for reform are worse than they were during the Clinton era, as there is now absolutely nothing that employers would trade in return for stronger organizing rights. And as the erosion in union membership and economic leverage continues, labor's capacity to mount the sort of national legislative campaign necessary to reform the labor law diminishes apace. Private sector union density is now below 7 percent, and in 2009 and 2010 public sector union members—themselves facing ferocious political attacks in 2011—outnumbered their private sector counterparts for the first time in U.S. history. While no one in the labor community will say so, it appears that NLRA reform is a dead letter for the foreseeable future.

Chapter 14

Is Democracy in the Cards? A Democratic Defense of the Employee Free Choice Act

Susan Orr

Labor law reform has always been politically divisive, and efforts to pass the Employee Free Choice Act (EFCA), the latest attempt to update a legal framework largely unchanged since the late 1950s, have been no exception. While virtually all Republicans have opposed the bill, Democrats have struggled to maintain support for the legislation among their conservative members. First introduced in 2003, EFCA passed the House on the third attempt in 2006, but it failed in the Senate when opponents threatened a filibuster. Things looked more promising after the Obama victory, but even with something approaching a filibuster-proof sixty-seat supermajority in the Senate, EFCA languished. As with every other attempt to pass labor law reform, not all Democrats offered support. Meanwhile, President Barack Obama, despite championing EFCA during the campaign, exerted scant political pressure on Congress to enact the legislation.[1] Even before the 2010 midterm elections, the labor-liberal effort to enact EFCA was effectively dead. Yet leaders of organized labor, accustomed to long struggles to win favorable legislation, have made it clear that it is a policy proposal they intend to resurrect.

The struggle over EFCA raises important questions about the very concept of democracy. This is hardly new. The idea of "industrial democracy" has influenced U.S. labor law since before the passage of the National Labor Relations Act (NLRA). Just as Senator Robert Wagner and the labor movement campaigned for the NLRA on the grounds that it would bring much needed democracy to despotic workplaces, so little more than a decade later, did Wagner's conservative adversaries and business leaders insist that the NLRA needed reforms that would protect democratic rights of workers and employers from "authoritarian" union bosses.

More than half a century later, the concept of democracy remains central to the attempt to pass EFCA. A key provision of the bill mandates that a union be certified as the exclusive representative of a group of workers in an appropriate unit once a majority sign authorization cards.[2] This would provide an alternative to the current process of union certification through a secret ballot election administered by the National Labor Relations Board (NLRB).[3] Presently, employees can form unions by signing cards, but employers are not obliged to bargain with unions formed in this way, nor do such unions gain the benefits of NLRB certification.[4] Thus it is an effective route to collective bargaining only when an employer voluntarily cooperates. Although mandatory recognition based on majority sign-up is only one part of EFCA—the bill also increases penalties for employer unfair labor practices and allows for mandatory arbitration of first contracts if unions and employers fail to reach agreement within 120 days—it is the provision that generates the most controversy. Opponents of the proposed reform have framed the bill as both un-American and antidemocratic, while proponents counter that it would afford workers "free choice" over whether to form a union in ways that the current NLRB election process cannot. They present majority sign-up as preferable to the present secret ballot process that seems democratic but which, in reality, subjects workers to undue management pressure to vote against the union.

Historians and legal scholars chronicle and debate the central role the concept of democracy has played in shaping U.S. labor law and industrial relations.[5] Some explicitly question the veracity of the analogy frequently drawn between union representation elections and political elections.[6] Thus, political scientist Gordon Lafer argues that the legal framework governing union representation elections does not meet the democratic standards we expect in elections for political representatives in the United States, or indeed, other democratic nations.[7] But few EFCA advocates, in the academy or out, have provided a positive argument for why majority sign-up is an appropriate democratic mechanism for certifying a union.

This essay draws on the history and theory of American democracy to argue both that the current system of secret ballot elections for forming unions falls short compared to democratic standards for political elections and that, in the context of a union certification process, the use of authorization cards closely approximates democratic ideals. Three points are central to the argument. First, opponents of majority sign-up tacitly and mistakenly assume that union certification elections are analogous to elections for political representatives. In fact, a union certification election is a process of group formation. Workers in certification elections determine whether or not they wish to form a collective for purposes of bargaining with their employer. They decide whether to establish a system to represent their shared interests in the workplace. Therefore, mechanisms for certifying unions are better compared with those used in constitution making in the formation of political societies. Second, parties to current debates accord a questionable centrality to secret ballot elections. While secret ballots are used in many democratic processes, they are just one among many institutional mechanisms that can be, and are, used for purposes of democratic decision making. Finally, whether secrecy and publicity facilitate or thwart democratic decision making depends on context. While secrecy—in the form of secret ballots—protects voters in political elections from undue influence and coercion, it is ineffectual in union representation elections. Many of the threats made in union representation campaigns are not leveled against particular individuals. Rather, they are directed toward the potential group as a whole. A secret ballot offers no protection against group threats. In contrast, the process of majority sign-up allows prospective group members to use secrecy to protect themselves against such group threats. These factors combine to form a positive argument for the democratic nature of the majority sign-up proposed in EFCA.

"Democracy" Frames the Debate

Although multiple groups have rallied to the anti-EFCA cause, they maintain a consistent message. Focusing almost exclusively on the majority sign-up provision of the bill, they relentlessly and creatively portray the legislation as "undemocratic." While there are variations on this theme, the central, simplistic message EFCA's foes present to the public is that the bill eliminates the secret ballot from the union certification process, and because a secret ballot is the "cornerstone" of democracy, EFCA therefore lacks democratic credentials.

The Center for Union Facts, a conservative advocacy group, produced a series of advertisements along these lines. One accused unions of "shredding democracy," complete with an illustration of a ballot box turned paper shredder. Another put a photo of Bruce Raynor, a prominent union leader, alongside similar portraits of Idi Amin and Mahmoud Ahmadinejad above the caption " 'There's no need to subject workers to an election'—who said it?" A third spot featured school children dressed as mobsters in muscle shirts and sunglasses. It asked viewers to imagine what might happen if "union bosses" ran class elections. A distressed and apparently coerced teacher shook her head in the background as a student declared, "there ain't gonna be no secret vote, just sign these cards showing who you like best and my campaign committee will count the votes." The video then panned to the campaign committee, a trio of young "enforcers," as the voice-over declared, "union bosses have a new scheme to do away with secret ballot elections."[8]

The mobster theme featured prominently in an aggressive $20 million print, broadcast, and direct-mail campaign that ran during the 2008 election season in states with close Senate races. Sponsored by the Coalition for a Democratic Workplace, whose members include the U.S. Chamber of Commerce and National Association of Manufacturers, the campaign starred actor Vince Curatola (who played the mob boss Johnny "Sack" Sacramoni on *The Sopranos*). The ads' central motif was that candidates supportive of EFCA were allied with union henchmen (depicted by Curatola) seeking to "eliminate the secret ballot for workers." Those opposed to the EFCA were described as heroic individuals attempting to save the secret ballot for working people.[9]

Former senator George McGovern, the Democratic presidential nominee in 1972, also joined the anti-EFCA forces. He appeared in television advertisements aired by the Employee Freedom Action Committee, another corporate-backed group. In one McGovern echoed an op-ed piece he wrote for the *Wall Street Journal*,[10] asserting, "It's hard to believe that any politician would agree to a law denying millions of employees the right to a private vote. . . . I have always been a champion of labor unions. But I fear that today's union leaders are turning their backs on democratic workplace elections."[11] Evidently, McGovern's "large D" democratic credentials lent credibility to his "small d" claims.

Following the 2008 election, the Chamber of Commerce and its allies ran advertisements exhorting President Obama: "You were elected by secret ballot. Don't take that right away from millions of American workers."[12] Americans for Job Security ran television spots featuring images of Democratic congressional leaders Harry Reid, Nancy Pelosi, Charles Schumer, and Dick Durbin. The voice-over first said, "Democrats met in Washington recently to elect their leaders and they cast their votes in the American tradition, by secret ballot," and then claimed that at the same time elected officials sought to deny workers the same protection. This, the announcer asserted, was "no change," just a "payback to union bosses."[13]

In a similar vein, Republican Party leaders framed Democratic support for EFCA as a politically motivated subversion of American democratic values, a repayment for union support. In an op-ed piece, then House minority leader John Boehner wrote of EFCA: "Big Labor allies are pushing hard for speedy votes in Congress on this decidedly undemocratic bill. . . . It will be received warmly at the White House. . . . The irony should not be lost on anyone, of course, that President Obama resides in the White House because of a secret-ballot election—just as all 535 members of the United States Congress hold their offices thanks to the secret ballot. . . . This legislation is not about workers' rights. It's about meeting the demands of special-interest allies who helped Democrats take control of Washington."[14] The uniformity in the message of those opposed to EFCA is impressive, but perhaps unsurprising given the vehemence with which they oppose labor law reform. "I have never seen the business community so focused and coalesced on one issue and ready to go to the mat on it," said Rhonda Bentz, spokesperson for the five hundred corporate groups in the Coalition for a Democratic Workplace.[15]

Rather than respond directly to their opponents' claims that EFCA violated American democratic values, proponents of the legislation focus on the role unions play in reducing inequality, improving pay and working conditions, and making the entire economy more robust. Early on, John Sweeney, then AFL-CIO president, captured the tone of the proponents' message in the *New York Times*: "We really need fundamental change to counterbalance corporate power and reverse the decline of the middle class . . . and that's why we support the Employee Free Choice Act."[16] After the Democrats failed to secure sixty Senate seats during the 2008 election, Tom Woodruff, director of strategic organizing for the Change to Win union federation, remained hopeful that the economic message would have an impact: "There are a number of Republicans who, in order to save our economy, can be brought around to supporting the act," he predicted.[17] Richard Trumka, Sweeney's successor as AFL-CIO president, reiterated this theme, declaring in a 2010 National Press Club address, "We must pass the Employee Free Choice Act so that workers can have the chance to turn bad jobs into good jobs, and so we can reduce the inequality which is undermining our prospects for stable economic growth."[18] Likewise, American Rights at Work, a pro-labor advocacy group, made the economic benefits of increased union membership central to its EFCA campaign. To business claims that majority sign-up (or card check) is undemocratic, a spokesman replied, "We're not trying to respond to their misleading message frames. . . . They've crafted their message to be about secret ballots and intimidation. . . . Those images of intimidation strike a nerve, regardless of the fact that it has nothing to do with this issue. We're trying to switch focus to what unions can do for you in making a better life."[19] Framing EFCA on the basis of its economic benefits instead of in terms of fairness and democracy proved ineffectual for its proponents.

Conservatives regularly claim that any legislation strengthening unions leads to job loss and lower economic growth. What was new in this debate was the business claim that the legislative reform was undemocratic on its face. Opponents of the Employee Free Choice Act had a clear message: the bill, pushed by hypocritical politicians elected by the very secret ballots they wished to deny workers, violates American democratic practices. They insisted too that the EFCA campaign was funded by undemocratic union bosses who were demanding the bill as "payback" and were only interested in fleecing workers of their dues.

Such hyperbole plays on the public's limited knowledge of the bill and panders to popular stereotypes of unions. It invokes a superficial analogy between common practices in political elections and those that adversaries of the bill suggest are embodied in current labor law. Undoubtedly such language appeals to poorly articulated yet popular visions of democracy. But as former labor secretary Robert Reich argued when discussing EFCA with then president Andy Stern of the Service Employees International Union, "We are talking about public perceptions. . . . One of the perceptions people have is that this is about getting rid of secret ballots as opposed to . . . getting rid of coercion on the part of employers."[20] This is the crucial point.

The anti-EFCA campaign exemplifies what philosopher Robert Nozick outlines in an essay titled "How to Do Things with Principles."[21] Nozick contends that we use principles to group actions, and thus to provide arguments and justifications for why we should treat some new situation or phenomenon in the same manner as a situation or phenomenon we have encountered in the past. Nozick argues that principles operate akin to precedent in legal cases. Faced with a new situation or phenomenon, we use principles to depict it as "the same" as some earlier occurrence and as unlike others. Having done so, we then are warranted by our principles to approach the new setting as we have approached those in the past. In this way we can use principles to convince others that our position or judgment is correct. A principle deemed fitting in one circumstance should be adopted in a new case. If those we seek to convince accept the principle in the first instance, we need only demonstrate how the new situation is like the first in order to persuade others that the same principle should apply. In Nozick's view, this is an effective argumentative strategy: "Justification by general principles is convincing in two ways: by the face appeal of the principles and by recruiting other already accepted cases to support a proposed position in this case."[22]

This is what opponents of the EFCA have done with the principle of democracy—using the general attractiveness of "democracy" to garner support for their position. In doing so, they implicitly, and sometimes explicitly, assume that union certification elections are analogous to elections for political representatives. If they can persuade others to see union certification votes in such a manner, it follows that a secret ballot is essential to union certification. For added effect, they deploy what might be called the "Hoffa effect," evoking historical stereotypes of union organizers as coercive thugs. The clear implication is that current union leaders have similarly undemocratic intentions. This argument suffers from two weaknesses. First, union representation elections are not equivalent to political elections. In short, EFCA's foes draw on a flawed analogy. Second, commitment to democracy does not entail commitment in all instances to the secret ballot. Those who equate the two are using the "principle of democracy" simplistically.[23] In fact, the secret ballot was introduced relatively late in the development of democracy to redress a problem arising from the extension of the franchise, namely the potential for powerful interests to coerce or bribe voters to cast their ballots in a specific way.[24] Secret balloting was contentious when it was introduced and is not used in all settings. This is because the extent to which secrecy furthers democratic ideals is contingent on the context in which it is used. In union certification elections, secret ballots do not protect workers from coercion or bribery as they may protect voters in political elections. Consequently, one can marshal democratic ideals to *justify* passage of the EFCA and majority sign-up rather than concede that the bill is antidemocratic.

Union Representation Elections and Political Elections: A Flawed Analogy

Political actors of all partisan persuasions have long invoked democratic values when debating the legal framework for workplace governance. Indeed, much NLRA prehistory was shaped by appeals for "industrial democracy" as the United States was fighting for political democracy in World War I.[25] Recognizing the political expediency of such appeals, Senator Robert Wagner and his allies appropriated the democratic ideas to legitimize the 1935 Wagner Act.[26] Yet the NLRA itself did not require a secret ballot election to certify a union in any given workplace. It allowed the National Labor Relations Board, the agency established to administer the Wagner Act, to use a secret ballot election or "any other suitable means" to determine majority support and thus certify the union. Until 1939, the NLRB regularly did so, authorizing unions based on signed cards, petitions, or other indicators of worker sentiment.

Only in the face of intense political pressure and employer resistance to NLRB certifications did the board change policy and mandate a secret ballot election to determine majority support before certifying a union.[27] The passage of the Taft-Hartley Act in 1947 transformed such elections from NLRB policy into a statutory requirement. In discussions over Taft-Hartley, Senator Carl Hatch drew on the political analogy, arguing, "this is merely an extension of our general voting practices to the field of labor relations"[28] Once Wagner set it in motion, the call to bring democracy to the workplace was difficult to control. Adversaries of organized labor and collective bargaining used it as effectively as did their champions.

Over time, the principle of "democracy" was narrowed to the point that "industrial democracy" became synonymous with a union certification election. David Brody sums up the situation well: "The representation election once in, was in. The democratic resonance was too great. Wagner, indeed, exploited it in just that way, pumping up the industrial democracy rhetoric on behalf of his bill to great effect."[29] Eight decades after Wagner, contemporary opponents of EFCA are "pumping up" the democracy rhetoric and deploying the same kind of "principled" argument as Wagner. They are relying on the "democratic resonance" of union certification by secret ballot to make their case. In order to counter this appeal to democracy, proponents of the bill should be asking: is the parallel drawn between union certification elections and political elections appropriate? The answer is no.

This point is not new. Scholars of labor law, federal judges, members of the NLRB, and prominent unionists all have questioned the analogy. This can be traced at least as far back as the debate over Wagner's original legislation. In the hearings regarding Wagner's bill, the question of whether an employer should be considered "party" to certification elections was fiercely debated. Wagner and his allies thought employer wishes should have no bearing on employee decisions regarding representation. They illustrated their claim with a metaphor from "international relations." Recognizing employers as "party" to the employee's selection of representatives would be akin to allowing one state a voice in selecting another nation's negotiators in an international dispute.[30] Decades later, labor lawyer Paul Weiler rejected equating union representation and political elections in similar terms. He argued that the employer in a union election is akin to a foreign government in an American election; while a foreign government has an interest in our electoral outcomes, it surely is not entitled to participate in our election.[31]

Thinking about representation uncovers additional flaws in the analogy between union certification and political elections. One fundamental difference is that unlike most political elections, a union certification process does not actually select an individual representative. Instead, workers decide whether in fact they wish to be represented collectively. Moreover, if a union is certified, neither that institution nor its officers gain the right to *govern* the workplace. Instead, if certified, a union simply wins the right to represent workers in negotiations with employers. Thus, in reality, there are no candidates in union certification elections, in contrast to most political contests.[32] Depicting unions and employers as opposed parties in an election is therefore problematic. This critical distinction between the two processes also means that union certification elections are not held on a regular schedule like political elections, nor are there designated constituencies to be represented, or publicly available lists of voters.

The Wagner Act remained silent as to whether employers should be viewed as a "party" in union certification elections, leaving the issue open to interpretation by the NLRB. While the board initially prohibited employers from campaigning, it granted them standing in representation cases, for example, when management challenged the scope of a bargaining unit or the eligibility of particular voters.[33] This has enabled employers to delay elections and thereby dampen support for unionization primarily by challenging the composition of the bargaining unit. Such a tactic distinguishes the process from most political elections, where stalling strategies are simply not available to candidates.[34]

The early NLRB was clear that employers had little role to play in representation elections. The board held that employers were not candidates and therefore did not appear on the ballot or have the right to vote. More importantly, the NLRB argued that the economic dependence of employees made employer speech inherently coercive, asserting in the *American Tube* case that "it was impossible for the employees to distinguish between the [employer] qua candidate, and the [employer] qua employer."[35] By interpreting the NLRA this way, the board sought to preserve for workers the right to "self-organization" free from employer interference or coercion.

In the long term this attempt by the NLRB to grant employers standing in proceedings surrounding questions of representation while denying them standing in the election process became untenable. The Taft-Hartley reforms exacerbated this difficulty. They not only made an election mandatory for union certification but also included an employer "free speech amendment." This amendment asserted that employer speech did not violate employees' rights to self-organization so long as "such expression contains no threat of reprisal or force or promise of benefit."[36] In effect, Taft-Hartley used the political analogy to elevate employers to the status of equal parties, or candidates, in union elections. Architects of the bill recognized that employers were *not* candidates and were *not* included on the ballot. Nevertheless, they justified management engagement in certification campaigns on grounds that employees needed to be "fully informed"; the employer served as proxy for the choice of self- (or individual) representation, as opposed to the union. In addition, proponents of the employer speech amendments argued that prohibiting employer speech violated employers' First Amendment rights.

In the years following Taft-Hartley, the NLRB sought to limit the prospect that employer speech would unduly influence election processes. It conjured a new analogy for union representation elections. In the *General Shoe* case, the board argued that a certification process should be considered a "laboratory experiment" aimed at determining the "uninhibited desires of workers."[37] By substituting the "laboratory experiment" for the "political election" analogy, NLRB members hoped to highlight the fact that unlike in the electoral arena, wherein candidates have roughly equal status, workers in representation elections are economically dependent on employers. Thus while Taft-Hartley's "free speech" provision precluded regulating speech that did not involve direct threats or promises, framing the representation election as an experiment allowed the NLRB to scrutinize the *conditions* under which the experiment was conducted. Under this new doctrine, the NLRB ruled that any employer speech that "tainted" employees' decisions about or prevented their "untrammeled" choice regarding representation could afford grounds for overturning an election result.[38] After all, scientists can, and frequently do, repeat experiments performed under less than ideal conditions. In contrast, and underscoring the consequential shift in analogy, elections even when conducted in less than ideal circumstances are rarely rerun.

The NLRB's decision in *General Shoe* remains good law, but the laboratory metaphor lacks the resonance attached to the political election analogy in wider debates surrounding labor law reform. This may in part be due to the fact that trying to effectively delineate what constitutes a violation of "laboratory conditions" has proven difficult. Initially the NLRB suggested the location or timing of employer speech—either in a place of "authority" in the workplace, or in the employee's home, or immediately prior to the election—might contaminate the proceedings. However, as the partisan composition of the NLRB changed, the interpretation of what kinds of conditions might preclude workers' choice shifted. Business-dominated boards did not overturn the "laboratory conditions" doctrine. Instead, they interpreted the circumstances under which employer speech might violate experimental conditions in limited ways. They held that compelling employees to listen to anti-union speeches during work time (so-called captive audience meetings), precluding union organizers or pro-union workers from speaking at such meetings, or dismissing employees for leaving them does not violate workers' rights.[39] Clearly, there are no correlates to this sort of campaign speech in political elections; no matter how much candidates might wish they could compel voters to listen to them, they have no mechanism by which to do so.

The Supreme Court has used the political analogy in contradictory ways when adjudicating cases involving union representation. In a 1945 case, *Thomas v. Collins*, the Court argued that employer and employee speech should be given equal protection under the First Amendment. This decision traded on the idea that, like democratic discussion in political campaigns, union representation elections require a "marketplace of ideas." Justice Robert Jackson stressed this view in a concurring opinion, arguing that "the necessity for choosing collective bargaining representatives brings the same nature of problem to groups of organizing workmen that our representative democratic processes bring to the nation."[40] Legal scholars have challenged the use of the "marketplace of ideas" metaphor in the workplace setting, suggesting that the Court's concern with the importance of the "free exchange" of ideas has been inconsistent. Too often, they argue, equity in speech has been sacrificed to employers' property rights or workplace control. The former has justified prohibiting union organizers or pro-union workers from presenting their views on company property even though it is often the location where the election takes place. The latter facilitates captive audience meetings with workers wherein competing viewpoints cannot be articulated and where workers cannot simply leave.

The Court itself also has voiced reservations about equating employer speech in union campaigns with that of candidates in political settings. In *NLRB v. Gissel Packing Co.*, it held that while the First Amendment protects employer speech, the protection is not absolute. Rather, it must be balanced against the employees' right to associate. Due to their "economic dependence" on their employer, the Court noted, workers may attend more to employer speech and its "intended implications" than voters would to campaign rhetoric in political elections.[41] Further, the political analogy was flawed, the justices concluded, because "what is basically at stake [in a certification election] is the establishment of a nonpermanent, limited relationship between the employer, his economically dependent employee and his union agent, not the election of legislators or the enactment of legislation."[42] The *Gissel* decision upheld the NLRB's right, in situations where employers' coercive behavior made a fair election impossible, to order a company to bargain with a union based on signed cards as evidence of majority support (this has become known as a "*Gissel* order"). However, the same ruling made clear that secret ballots are the preferred method of certifying a union. The NLRB subsequently has rarely issued "*Gissel* orders." In many respects, adopting EFCA would make such orders the norm rather than the exception.

Craig Becker, whom President Obama named to the NLRB in a recess appointment, acknowledges that majority sign-up is sometimes useful, but ultimately rejects it. Instead, he argues that certification decisions should be made by secret ballot, albeit under an amended legal framework. This is not because Becker endorses the political analogy.[43] In a 1993 essay, he proposed that employers be stripped of "party" status in certification proceedings in order to both foreclose their delaying tactics and prevent them from exerting their economic influence in subsequent certification campaigns. Becker held that union representation proceedings are "constitutive" of collective representation that is binding on all workers. Thus, because the "majority rules," the convention of using an election to determine the will of the majority should apply.[44]

Others have also highlighted the constitutive nature of union representation processes to *endorse* the majority sign-up proposal in EFCA. Political scientist Gordon Lafer argues that union representation elections are attempts to "change the form of government in the workplace from one party rule to something slightly more democratic." He illustrates this point with two alternative analogies. Unionization, he proposes, is similar to the formation of new political parties, or the creation of a nation-state. To highlight the notion that publicity rather than secrecy is sometimes crucial to foundational processes, and so support majority sign-up, Lafer compares union formation with the signing of the Declaration of Independence. A public declaration of commitment to the cause was essential to the process, he contends, because, "unlike voting for representatives, this foundational act was not simply a statement of political beliefs. It was a declaration of confidence, commitment, and courage of exactly the type necessary to rally rebellion against an entrenched power."[45]

These arguments are persuasive, but in suggesting alternatives to the political election analogy, Becker and Lafer do not push far enough. They correctly suggest that union certification processes are formative moments, enabling workers to decide whether they wish to form a collective entity through which they henceforth will bargain with their employer. In this sense union certification resembles forming a new political party in an authoritarian state. Where this analogy falls short is that, unlike political parties, labor unions once formed are not purely voluntary organizations. Unions bargain on behalf of all the workers, even those who choose not to join (and in states with "right-to-work" laws, even those who do not contribute to the cost of bargaining or maintaining the union).

While it is true that even once certified, a union does not become the "government of the workplace," it becomes *more* than a representative of employees in negotiations with their employer. When a majority of workers vote for collective representation, the workers essentially *become* a union. They form a collective organization that regulates members' rights and privileges, and that, ideally, is governed by its members. It is here that those concerned with workers' rights to secret ballots should direct their attention. In the workplace setting, the closest analogy to elections for political office is elections for union representatives once a union has been formed.

This "constitutive" nature of the union certification process suggests that a more appropriate analogy is to a constitutional convention. Just as societies are created and existing governmental systems are altered in constitutional moments, so a union is formed and the workplace regime altered following a successful union certification. If we depict union certification elections as "constitutional moments," we highlight the *collective* nature of the enterprise. Any threats that those who oppose forming the group (or union) make are addressed not to individuals serially but to members of the group as a whole, as a consequence of its formation. The American Constitutional Convention, for example, took place behind closed doors, because secrecy allowed discussion to transpire in a democratic way between similarly situated participants. Secrecy, it was argued, would allow delegates to speak freely, engage in honest discourse, and change their mind if they saw fit. As James Madison explained, "No Constitution would ever have been adopted by the Convention if the debates had been made public."[46] Deliberations at the convention were kept secret, not only to improve the quality of debate but also to avoid potential threats from those opposed to such a constitutional event. This is how majority sign-up could work in union certification procedures. It would enable workers—at least in the initial stage of organization—to use privacy to avoid potentially coercive efforts of their employer and engage in the process of self-organization in ways that better approximate democratic ideals.

Democracy Is More Than a Secret Ballot

What follows from shifting analogies, and suggesting that union certification processes are closer to constitutional moments than to elections for representatives within an existing polity? It does not mean that union certification should not be conducted under conditions that approximate democratic ideals. Instead, it means that determining just what those conditions might be is complicated, and that they may differ from those we commonly associate with elections for political office. Opponents of EFCA who equate democracy with a secret ballot offer an impoverished view of what democracy requires even in a political election. Yet they have been strategically astute to frame the bill in this simplistic way. For as political theorist Ian Shapiro insists, "the democratic idea is close to non-negotiable in today's world."[47] Thus, even authoritarian leaders profess to be democrats to legitimize their rule. How can proponents of majority sign-up counter this compelling frame?

While we might all be democrats in principle, we disagree on precisely what the principle requires. In fact, the "principle of democracy" is multifaceted and contested; no consensus exists regarding precisely what the ideal entails. When they insist that the secret ballot is essential to democracy, opponents of EFCA fail to distinguish between determining what democracy demands in the ideal sense and deciding what set of institutions would best facilitate those ideals in a given context. In fact, not only is the secret ballot insufficient to render a decision-making process democratic, it is not even necessary to that purpose. This is true not just of the secret ballot but of any specific institution. Indeed it is doubtful whether any set of institutional arrangements fully realizes the "ideal" of democracy. As John Dewey argues, "The idea of democracy is a wider and fuller idea than can be exemplified in the state even at its best. To be realized it must affect all modes of human association, the family, the school, industry, religion. And even as far as political arrangements are concerned, government institutions are but a mechanism for securing to an idea channels of effective operation. . . . What the faithful insist upon, however, is that the idea and its external organs and structures are not to be identified."[48] Proponents of EFCA should find Dewey's observation useful. Democratic ideals, he insists, do not require any particular set of institutions. Rather, he recommends that we see institutions—the secret ballot included—as contingent mechanisms we use to best approximate the ideal. And Dewey does this, it should be noted, while endorsing the notion—one that all sides of the dispute over labor law reform tacitly support—that there is a legitimate place for democracy in industry.

A common feature of any institutional configuration that meets the requirements of a "representative democracy" is that it involves both voting and arguing.[49] Of course, not just any voting and arguing will suffice; both must be conducted under conditions of approximate freedom and equality—circumstances that facilitate the ability of individuals to make decisions free from domination. Democratic theorists frequently study these mechanisms in isolation. Some focus on voting, and seek to determine the optimal way to aggregate preferences according to democratic ideals. Others devote their energy to the prior process of preference formation, attempting to uncover the conditions under which political discussion best approximates democratic standards. Yet this division of labor is not useful when considering empirical American democracy because "modern democratic institutions do not break down easily along a deliberative-aggregative divide. . . . Neither mechanism alone affords a sufficient basis for arriving at political decisions within a democratic framework."[50] Not unexpectedly, opponents of EFCA parse democratic institutions in a way that isolates voting from the discussion that precedes it. Their claims that a secret ballot is essential to democracy focus exclusively on the process by which workers register their preference for unionization. Not only do they fail to ask if the secret ballot operates effectively in the workplace. They also fail to ask if discussion and debate about unionization prior to the certification vote— the process through which workers form their preferences—occurs under democratic conditions.

This is a significant oversight insofar as discussion and the processes through which preferences are formed are vital components of representative democracy in the American tradition. James Madison promoted the Constitution because it proposed "a republic . . . a government in which a scheme of representation takes place." He did so at least in part because such a scheme "would refine and enlarge the public views by passing them through the medium of a chosen body of citizens."[51] Representation, for Madison, was desirable because it facilitated discussion and argument. Likewise, Dewey emphasized that "the ballot is, as is often said, a substitute for bullets. But what is more significant is that counting of heads compels prior recourse to methods of discussion, consultation and persuasion."[52] That the "trial of debate" has been an "essential feature of representative govern-ment from its origins through today is a commonplace among democratic theorists."[53] So, if representative government is the proper model of democ-racy, then opponents of EFCA are excluding a crucial element, that of arguing or discussing, when they propose that democracy is all about voting or casting ballots.

The Secret Ballot—What Is It Good For?

The secret ballot has a problematic history as a mechanism for ensuring democratic outcomes. It was introduced toward the end of the nineteenth century, initially in Australia and subsequently in other representative democracies including the United States. In North America the rise of polit-ical party machines proved a catalyst for the state-by-state enactment of secret ballot procedures in the 1880s and 1890s.[54] Reformers condemned "party bosses" who could bribe poor urban voters with promised rewards or coerce them with threatened punishment if they voted in accord with or opposition to party dictates. While the secret ballot may have been an appropriate remedy for such practices, it also served to disenfranchise many illiterate poor and immigrant voters who could no longer effectively cast their vote. In the South, after the end of Reconstruction, elites found the secret ballot served the "American democratic tradition" by disenfranchis-ing black voters who had difficulty reading the often deliberately complex ballots.[55]

The secret ballot, then, was introduced as a historical contingency that in some cases served to subvert as much as to advance democratic ideals. Voting in secret was designed to redress the problem of individuals with power and resources threatening weaker citizens with harm or promising them a benefit if they voted in a certain way. But no less a champion of representative government than John Stuart Mill denounced it. Mill believed secrecy could protect voters from coercion, but he thought that public balloting would ward off a greater threat, namely the propensity of voters to subordinate the public good to their own self-regarding interests.[56] Clearly, any assessment of the secret ballot is contingent on the type of threat that looms in a given context. Mill also suggested that the democratic consequences of secrecy, and its converse publicity, may depend on whether we are considering mechanisms to authorize representatives or hold them to account.

If the relationship between the secret ballot and democracy has been contingent historically, then how precisely does secrecy work to protect voters? The answer is quite simple. The secret ballot ensures that no voter can verify how he cast his ballot. Lacking the ability to prove how he voted, the voter cannot "sell" his vote for profit or benefit. Conversely, the voter is freed from any potential blackmail by those who may seek to coerce him to vote according to their wishes. As Thomas Schelling argues, "Powerless to prove whether or not he complied with the threat, he knows—and so do those who would threaten him—that any punishment would be unrelated to the way he actually voted."[57] This mechanism may work effectively in political elections wherein an individual voter is selecting a representative, but what about in the union certification setting?

The Secret Ballot in the Workplace—Is It Working?

Once we see union certification elections as analogous to constitution making, the kinds of threats and bribes that workers might face appear different from those that citizens may encounter when electing representatives in two ways. First, the potential threats workers confront typically are directed not at individuals but at the workers as a group, in the event they formally become a group by forming a union. Second, employers typically issue such threats during discussions that take place prior to the election. These characteristics converge to undermine the usefulness of the secret ballot as a way of protecting workers. A brief consideration of the "threats" workers face during union certification demonstrates why this is so.[58]

Employers use multiple tactics to deter union formation.[59] In over 85 percent of cases, employers hold captive audience meetings on work time at which executives offer workers "predictions" about the consequences of forming a union. These "predictions" are thinly veiled threats or bribes that skirt the legal prohibition against employers making "threat[s] of reprisal or force or promise of benefit" during certification. Managers commonly predict that they anticipate having to close or relocate the plant should workers vote to form a union. This occurs in more than 57 percent of campaigns.[60] Employers issue such threats most often in manufacturing industries where capital is mobile (71 percent of campaigns), but they also do so regularly in what we think of as "nonmobile" sectors such as retail (58 percent of campaigns) and hospitality (33 percent of campaigns).

Plant closing threats cause workers as a group to fear they will lose their livelihood entirely. Other common union avoidance tactics involve predictions that working conditions will deteriorate should workers form a union. These predictions incorporate a variety of claims—that organizing efforts create a hostile relationship with management that will persist if the union prevails; that collective bargaining will mean that workers may lose current pay levels and benefits; and that if it is formed the union will force workers to strike and collect hefty union dues.[61] None of these threats are directed at individuals. They are leveled at workers as a group. They are actions or consequences that employers predict will follow if employees vote to unionize and that will negatively affect all the workers, not as a consequence of the actions of any identifiable individual but because of a decision of the majority.

The secret ballot is ineffective in the face of such threats. That is because casting a ballot in secret works to protect individuals from retaliation for their vote choices by preventing them from credibly revealing how they voted, thereby foreclosing the ability of others to find out. However, in the case of union certification, it is irrelevant how any particular individual votes if the majority votes for collective bargaining. If employers' threats are carried out, all workers bear the consequences regardless of their individual vote choice. The purpose of predicting plant closing and other dire eventualities is to dampen support for the union and intimidate workers in a manner that the secret ballot does nothing to prevent.

Another common tactic used to thwart unionization is for employers to "promise" to raise wages or improve working conditions so as to undermine the necessity for collective bargaining. This may well occur in half or more of all campaigns.[62] Again the secret ballot is ineffectual in combating this kind of "bribe" because it is directed at employees generally rather than at specific individuals. Employers are not "buying" selected individual votes, but rather seeking to diminish enthusiasm for unionization among workers generally.

Another somewhat less common action that employers take to deter support for unionization is to unlawfully dismiss workers who are involved in organizing efforts. Researchers document illegal firings in 26 percent to 34 percent of all union organizing campaigns.[63] While this act primarily affects an individual employee, it is one that also aims to send a chilling message to employees as a group.[64] In either case the secret ballot does not shield employees from this kind of intimidation. If employers want to deter union formation by illegally firing pro-union workers, they must do so before the election. The secret ballot is irrelevant, if only because just 3 percent of dismissed workers are reinstated prior to a vote.[65] A further frequently deployed union avoidance strategy is for supervisors to conduct "one-on-one" meetings with their employees. Such meetings take place in more than three-quarters of all campaigns.[66] Supervisors are instructed to question workers during these meetings about their views on possible unionization. Of course, the secret ballot in no way thwarts this kind of intrusive and coercive interrogation.

If the secret ballot is ineffectual against employer intimidation, does it nevertheless protect anti-union workers from intimidation by union organizers and fellow workers? The fact that union organizers and colleagues have little or no formal power over workers prior to unionization limits their ability to coerce or bribe them during the certification process. It is difficult to imagine a plausible way that union organizers or fellow workers could make threats against workers as a group, and it is questionable how they could coerce individual workers to vote in accordance to their dictates. Remember, secrecy works to protect individuals because it undercuts the utility of threats directed toward them prior to voting, because they cannot, after the fact, reveal how they voted. This raises the question of how fellow workers and union organizers might punish workers for their votes if, in the absence of a secret ballot, they could determine how they voted.

If the union is successful, organizers and union officials do gain some power over workers and in theory could threaten to penalize those who did not support the union. However, any contract that the union negotiates through collective bargaining covers all workers regardless of their stance in the certification process. Further, union staffers have incentives and a legal obligation to represent all workers fairly, especially if workers have effective means to hold their elected representatives to account. Workers can do this in several ways. In right-to-work states they can simply refuse to pay their dues. In every state they can initiate decertification proceedings that require signed cards from just 30 percent of all workers. Alternatively, individual workers can appeal to the NLRB or the courts if they think the union is not representing them fairly. Finally, workers can vote union representatives out of office, replacing them with others who will better promote their interests.

This last matter—accountability—is where proponents of workers' rights and advocates of the secret ballot ought to be directing their energies. Why? Because once the union has formed, an entrenched officialdom does have potential coercive power over its constituents, and a secret ballot, combined with an open and contested election process, can facilitate accountability of representatives to the rank and file. Unlike in union certification processes, the threats workers may face when electing union officers are often individual-level threats against which the secret ballot does offer some protection. Indeed, the 1959 Landrum-Griffin Act that oversees union governance mandates a secret ballot election for almost all posts. Whether this provides adequate accountability is a question for another time.[67]

If union organizers have few credible ways to threaten workers in anticipation of a union victory, what if they anticipate a loss? In such cases the power of organizers and union partisans is virtually nil. They could threaten to physically harm or harass workers who voted "no" to the union—but such threats would be both illegal and costly to carry out. Indeed, what incentive would organizers have to physically intimidate or harass those who voted against unionization once the campaign has failed? Union organizers, even those of beefy stature and quick temper, simply leave town.

Of course, even if opponents of EFCA conceded that the secret ballot does not function to democratize the union certification process, they might still question whether majority sign-up offers any improvement. Opponents of EFCA claim that it exposes workers to potential intimidation by union organizers and peers who might coerce them into signing a card indicating support for the union. But empirical studies of majority sign-up procedures find little if any evidence of coercion by organizers or peers. By their own account, opponents of majority sign-up can document only forty-two cases of intimidation in more than sixty years. As a point of comparison, in 2005 alone the NLRB awarded thirty thousand workers back pay because of antiunion discrimination by employers.[68]

A study that compared employees' experiences under voluntary majority sign-up and NLRB secret ballot campaigns reinforces this conclusion. In each kind of campaign, researchers found that "management's pressure on workers to oppose unionization was significantly greater than pressure from co-workers or organizers to support the union." More important, they found that "union representatives were not more likely to exert undue pressure on workers under card check regimes. . . . 94% of workers who signed cards in the presence of union representatives . . . did not report feeling pressured into signing the card."[69] In sum, majority sign-up seems not to invite intimidation in the ways its opponents allege; even if it did, the NLRB retains the power to establish procedures whereby a neutral arbiter verifies the fairness of the card signing campaign.

Majority Sign-Up Works to Enhance Democratic Debate

Once we set aside concerns about coercion, it becomes apparent that a great virtue of majority sign-up is that it facilitates a more democratic context within which workers can form preferences about unionization. When workers certify a union by signing authorization cards, it allows them, at least in the initial stages of the process, to refrain from disclosing their efforts to their employer. In this way, the mechanism of secrecy can be used to protect workers while they are discussing and arguing about the merits of collective organization.

Democratic theorists differ about the conditions under which genuinely democratic discussion can best take place. They also disagree about the types of argument that are permissible and the ultimate purpose of debate in democratic decision making.[70] However, there is near universal agreement that, in the ideal, democratic discussion should take place between equals. That is, democratic discussion presupposes circumstances where every individual is given equal respect and opportunity to express his or her views and present arguments that might persuade others to adopt that position. In such circumstances, genuine debate can ensue because theorists identify the absence of coercive power as the criterion that most clearly distinguishes democratic debate from other kinds of rhetorical exchange. Such debate demands that "participants should not try to change others' behavior through the threat of sanction or the use of force."[71]

Theorists also converge on the basic requirements that participants in democratic discussions should provide reasons that support their perspective, be willing to consider the arguments of other participants, and be open to the possibility of changing their views. In this way, the process is one that involves information sharing and exchange, not simply rhetorical posturing. There is some debate among democratic theorists about the role that secrecy and publicity play in facilitating this kind of discussion. Publicity, some suggest, pushes participants to provide reasons and arguments as to why they hold the preferences they do. And it also serves to ensure that they adopt alternatives that are aimed toward a greater public good rather than being merely self-serving. But secrecy also has some virtues. It shields participants from broad public view and the pressures that such visibility often entails; it enhances discussion because participants are more willing to change their views in the face of a compelling argument; and it discourages posturing, pandering, and demagoguery.[72]

All this helps illuminate why majority sign-up is preferable to the status quo. A brief look at the kinds of discussion and debate that characterize the current process will demonstrate why.[73] Under the Wagner Act, as currently enforced, employers have much more opportunity to make appeals to workers than do union organizers. Employers frequently hold captive audience meetings, screen anti-union videos, and hold one-on-one sessions where they offer dire predictions about the consequences of unionization to their enterprise. In each case the power inequities between management and dependent employees are readily apparent. Indeed, union representatives are barred from the workplace and workers can discuss the organizing campaign only in restricted areas and at limited times. They cannot challenge, question, or respond to employer propaganda. This kind of asymmetrical "dialogue" hardly approximates democratic debate.

In this context, neither secrecy nor publicity promotes democratic discussion. The public nature of captive audience meetings perhaps encourages employers to couch their arguments against collective bargaining with claims of concern for the common good. Yet to employees, denied the ability to probe and challenge employers' arguments, such concern simply appears as rationalization. The relative privacy under which one-on-one meetings are held does not mean that the worker and her supervisor engage in a free discussion. Any supervisors who might be convinced of the need for unionization would be subject to instant dismissal, since their employment is not protected by the National Labor Relations Act.

The possibility for democratic debate is much greater when considering majority sign-up. This is because it enables workers to keep their efforts to unionize secret from their employer, and allows for a genuine exchange of views between similarly situated workers and union organizers. To gain employees' signatures endorsing the union, pro-union workers and union organizers must convince their colleagues through argument and debate that collective bargaining would indeed be beneficial. The relatively equal standing of the parties makes it plausible for skeptical workers to raise their concerns and objections and assess any response before making a decision. Thus they benefit from public discussion about the merits of unionization but are shielded from the potential of coercive speech from their employers. Empirical studies demonstrate that the majority sign-up process does work in precisely this way: limiting the coercive speech of employers, but enhancing the flow of information and genuine debate among the workers themselves.[74]

Conclusion

Although the Employee Free Choice Act is unlikely to be enacted in the near future, its demise is hardly a consequence of its presumptive violation of democratic norms. Instead, the controversial but necessary majority sign-up provisions in the act advance union formation, in an analogous fashion to the "constitutional moments" that created democratic polities in this nation's past. Shifting the analogy from political elections to constitutive events draws attention to the fact that the major threats in union certification campaigns are directed toward workers as a group, as a consequence of their desire to form a union. The secret ballot, which opponents of EFCA mistakenly champion as fundamental to democracy, affords no protection from such threats. Conversely, the majority sign-up process enhances the democratic nature of union formation by allowing workers to deliberate democratically and minimizes the opportunity for employers to engage in coercive speech.

Notes

Introduction

1. Thomas Frank, "It's Time to Give Voters the Liberalism They Want," *Wall Street Journal*, November 19, 2008, A19; Michael Mishak, "Ensign Finds an Ace in Senate Election Hole: Fear of Unions," *Las Vegas Sun*, July 27, 2008.

2. "The Workforce Freedom Airlifts," www.uschamber.com/wfi/airlift.htm, accessed July 21, 2010.

3. Bradley Blackburn, "Christie Calls Union Leaders 'Political Thugs,'" *ABC News*, April 6, 2011.

4. Scott Walker, "Striking the Right Bargain in Wisconsin," *Washington Post*, March 16, 2011.

5. "Wisconsin Governor to AWOL Senate Democrats: Come Home and Get Back to Work," *On the Record with Greta Van Susteren*, Fox News, February 17, 2011.

6. Leo P. Ribuffo, "Why Is There So Much Conservatism in the United States and Why Do So Few Historians Know Anything About It?" *American Historical Review*, 99:2 (April 1994), 438.

7. Daniel Bell, ed., *The Radical Right: The New American Right, Expanded and Updated* (Garden City, N.Y.: Doubleday, 1964); Sam Tanenhaus, *Whittaker Chambers: A Biography* (New York: Random House, 1997); Robert Goldberg, *Barry Goldwater* (New Haven: Yale University Press, 1995); Dan T. Carter, *The Politics of Rage: George Wallace, the Origins of the New Conservatism, and the Transformation of American Politics* (New York: Simon & Schuster, 1995); Jennifer Burns, *Goddess of the Market: Ayn Rand and the American Right* (Oxford: Oxford University Press, 2009); Donald T. Critchlow, *Phyllis Schlafly and Grassroots Conservatism: A Woman's Crusade* (Princeton: Princeton University Press, 2007); David Witwer, *Shadow of the Racketeer: Scandal in Organized Labor* (Urbana: University of Illinois Press, 2009); Alan Brinkley, *Voices of Protest: Huey Long, Father Coughlin, and the Great Depression* (New York: Alfred A. Knopf, 1982).

8. Michael Kazin, "The Grass-Roots Right: New Histories of U.S. Conservatism in the Twentieth Century," *American Historical Review*, 97:1 (February 1992), 136.

9. Nancy K. MacLean, *"Behind the Mask of Chivalry": The Making of the Second Ku Klux Klan* (Oxford: Oxford University Press, 1995); Lisa McGirr, *Suburban Warriors: The Origins of the New American Right* (Princeton: Princeton University Press 2001); Thomas J. Sugrue, *Origins of the Urban Crisis: Race and Inequality in Postwar Detroit* (Princeton: Princeton University Press, 1996).

10. Kim Phillips-Fein, *Invisible Hands: The Making of the Conservative Movement from the New Deal to Reagan* (New York: W. W. Norton, 2009).

11. Howard Brick, *Transcending Capitalism: Visions of a New Society in Modern American Thought* (Ithaca: Cornell University Press, 2006), 162–164; Richard Parker, *John Kenneth Galbraith: His Life, His Politics, His Economics* (New York: Farrar, Straus and Giroux, 2005), 435–451; Paddy Riley, "Clark Kerr: From the Industrial to the Knowledge Economy," in Nelson Lichtenstein, ed., *American Capitalism: Social Thought and Political Economy in the Twentieth Century* (Philadelphia: University of Pennsylvania Press, 2006), 71–87.

12. Kerr quoted in John T. Dunlop, Frederick H. Harbison, Clark Kerr, and Charles A. Myers, *Industrialism and Industrial Man: The Problems of Labor and Management in Economic Growth* (Cambridge: Harvard University Press, 1960), 293; Kempton quoted in Judith Stein, *Pivotal Decade: How the United States Traded Factories for Finance in the Seventies* (New Haven: Yale University Press, 2010), 15.

13. See, for example, David Renshaw, *American Labor and Consensus Capitalism, 1935–1990* (Jackson: University Press of Mississippi, 1991); and Paul Buhle, *Taking Care of Business: Samuel Gompers, George Meany, Lane Kirkland, and the Tragedy of American Labor* (New York: Monthly Review Press, 1999).

14. Gerald Zahavi, "Passionate Commitments: Race, Sex, and Communism at Schenectady General Electric, 1932–1954," *Journal of American History* (September 1996), 514–548; Phillips-Fein, *Invisible Hands*, 87–114; Timothy Minchin, *What Do We Need a Union For? The TWUA in the South, 1945–1955* (Chapel Hill: University of North Carolina Press, 1997); Daniel Clark, *Like Night and Day: Unionization in a Southern Mill Town* (Chapel Hill: University of North Carolina Press, 1997); Marc Linder, *Wars of Attrition: Vietnam, the Business Roundtable, and the Decline of Construction Unions* (Iowa City, Iowa: Fanpihua Press, 1999).

15. Taylor Dark, *The Unions and the Democrats: An Enduring Alliance* (Ithaca: Cornell University Press, 1999), 61; for a contrary interpretation, see Nelson Lichtenstein, "Labor, Liberalism, and the Democratic Party: A Vexed Alliance," *Industrial Relations Quarterly Review* 66 (Fall 2011), 512–534.

16. Nelson Lichtenstein, *State of the Union: A Century of American Labor* (Princeton: Princeton University Press, 2002); Stein, *Pivotal Decade*; John Logan, "The Clinton Administration and Labor Law: Was Comprehensive Reform Ever a Realistic Possibility?" *Journal of Labor Research*, 28 (2007), 609–628.

17. Jefferson Cowie, *Capital Moves: RCA's Seventy-Year Quest for Cheap Labor* (New York: New Press, 2001); Eric Schlosser, *Fast Food Nation: The Dark Side of the All-American Meal* (New York: Houghton Mifflin, 2001); Nelson Lichtenstein, *The Retail Revolution: How Wal-Mart Created a Brave New World of Business* (New York: Metropolitan Books, 2009).

18. Thomas Geoghegan, *Which Side Are You On? Trying to Be for Labor When Labor Is Flat on Its Back* (New York: Farrar, Straus and Giroux, 1991); Michael Zweig, *The Working Class Majority: America's Best Kept Secret* (Ithaca: Cornell University Press, 2000); Bruce Nissan, ed., *Which Direction for Organized Labor? Essays on Organizing, Outreach, and Internal Transformations* (Detroit: Wayne State University Press, 1998); Michael Yates, *Why Unions Matter* (New York: Monthly Review Press, 1998); Bill Fletcher Jr. and Fernando Gaspin, *Solidarity Divided: The Crisis in Organized Labor and a New Path Toward Social Justice* (Berkeley: University of California Press, 2009).

19. Phillips-Fein, *Invisible Hands*, 166–184; Alice O'Connor, "Financing the Counterrevolution," in Bruce Schulman and Julian Zelizer, eds., *Rightward Bound: Making America Conservative in the 1970s* (Cambridge: Harvard University Press, 2008), 148–168.

20. Charles McCormick, *Seeing Reds: Federal Surveillance of Radicals in the Pittsburgh Mill District, 1917–1921* (Pittsburgh: University of Pittsburgh Press, 2003); Gwendolyn Mink, *Old Labor and New Immigrants in American Political Development: Union, Party, and State, 1875–1920* (Ithaca: Cornell University Press, 1990); Daniel Walkowitz, *Working with Class: Social Workers and the Politics of Middle-Class Identity* (Chapel Hill: University of North Carolina Press, 1999).

21. Two excellent studies of union corruption are Witwer, *Shadow of the Racketeer*; and Andrew Wender Cohen, *The Racketeer's Progress: Chicago and the Struggle for the Modern American Economy, 1900–1940* (New York: Cambridge University Press, 2004).

22. On the labor-management accord argument, see Lichtenstein, *State of the Union*, 98–140; on managerial "exceptionalism," see Sanford Jacoby, "American Exceptionalism Revisited: The Importance of Management," in Jacoby, ed., *Masters to Managers: Historical and Comparative Perspectives on American Employers* (New York: Columbia University Press, 1991), 173–200; and David Vogel, "Why Businessmen Distrust Their State: The Political Consciousness of American Corporate Executives," *British Journal of Political Science*, 8 (January 1978), 45–78.

Chapter 1. Unions, Modernity, and the Decline of American Economic Nationalism

1. Andrew Wender Cohen, *The Racketeer's Progress: Chicago and the Struggle for the Modern American Economy* (New York: Cambridge University Press, 2004).

2. These critiques are described beautifully in Thomas Geoghegan's *Which Side Are You On? Trying to Be for Labor When It's Flat on Its Back* (New York: Farrar, Straus and Giroux, 1991); Barry Bluestone and Irving Bluestone, *Negotiating the Future: A Labor Perspective on American Business* (New York: Basic Books, 1992).

3. See, for example, editorial, "Unlabor Days," *Washington Times*, September 4, 1992, F2; Clifford Krauss, "House Passes Bill to Ban Replacement of Strikers," *New York Times*, June 6, 1993, A23; "Enraged Union Leaders Say They Won't Forget, Will Get Revenge at Polls," *Boston Globe*, November 19, 1993, 85.

4. David Montgomery, *Beyond Equality: Labor and the Radical Republicans, 1862–1872* (New York: Knopf, 1967), 24, 46, 64, 65, 84, 86–88, 247, 343–345, 430; Dana Frank, *Buy American: The Untold Story of Economic Nationalism* (Boston: Beacon, 1999), 33–55.

5. Melvyn Dubofsky, *The State and Labor in Modern America* (Chapel Hill: University of North Carolina Press, 1994), 6, 22, 84; Frank, *Buy American*, 56–101, 158; Matthew Frye Jacobson, *Barbarian Virtues: The U.S. Encounters Foreign Peoples at Home and Abroad, 1876–1917* (New York: Hill and Wang, 2001), 82; Kathy Peiss, *Cheap Amusements: Working Women and Leisure in Turn-of-the-Century New York* (Philadelphia: Temple University Press, 1987); Eric Rauchway, *Blessed Among Nations: How the World Made America* (New York: Hill and Wang, 2007), 155–160.

6. David Nasaw, *Andrew Carnegie* (New York: Penguin, 2006), 376.

7. Henry Clay, speech of September 1842, quoted in Jonathan A. Glickstein, *American Exceptionalism, American Anxiety: Wages, Competition, and Degraded Labor in the Antebellum United States* (Charlottesville: University of Virginia Press, 2002), 192; Montgomery, *Beyond Equality*, 86–87, 344–345; Eric Foner, *Free Soil, Free Labor, and Free Men* (New York: Oxford University Press, 1967), 21.

8. William D. Kelley, *Speech of Hon. William D. Kelley of Pennsylvania on Protection to American Labor Delivered in the House of Representatives, January 31, 1866* (Washington, D.C.: Congressional Globe Office, 1866), 24.

9. Joanne Reitano, *The Tariff Question in the Gilded Age: The Great Debate of 1888* (University Park: Penn State University Press, 1994), 23–25, Frank, *Buy American*, 36–37.

10. John Shovlin, *The Political Economy of Virtue: Luxury, Patriotism, and the Origins of the French Revolution* (Ithaca: Cornell University Press, 2006), 118–151; T. H. Breen, *The Marketplace of Revolution: How Consumer Politics Shaped American Independence* (New York: Oxford University Press, 2004); Robert Remini, *Henry Clay: Statesman for the Union* (New York: W. W. Norton, 1991), 53.

11. "Report of the Secretary of the Treasury," *American Review* 26 (February 1850): 123.

12. George Thompson, *"Venus in Boston" and Other Tales of Nineteenth-Century City Life*, ed. David S. Reynolds and Kimberly R. Gladman (Amherst: University of Massachusetts Press, 2002), 4–104, esp., 103–104.

13. "The One Cure for Smuggling," *St. Lawrence Plain Dealer*, August 29, 1878, n.p.; Andrew Wender Cohen, "Smuggling, Globalization, and America's Outward State, 1870–1909," *Journal of American History* 97:2 (September 2010): 371–398.

14. Burton Spivak, *Jefferson's English Crisis* (Charlottesville: University Press of Virginia, 1979), 224–225; Lafayette C. Baker, *History of the United States Secret Service*

(Philadelphia: L. C. Baker, 1867), 71–92; Benjamin Butler, *Speech of Benjamin Butler of Massachusetts upon the Frauds of the Revenues of the Government* (Washington, D.C.: Government Printing Office, 1874), 4–5; Andrew Wender Cohen, *Sweet Land of Contraband: Smuggling and the Birth of the American Century* (New York: W. W. Norton, forthcoming).

15. "The Influence of Manufactures and the Protective System," *American Whig Review* 82 (October 1851): 269; *Testimonials to Henry C. Carey Esq. Dinner at the LaPierre House. Philadelphia, April 27, 1859* (Philadelphia: Collins, 1859), 50–51; Foner, *Free Soil*, 36; Nasaw, *Andrew Carnegie*, 375; Reitano, *Tariff Question*, 74–86.

16. Bruce Laurie, *Beyond Garrison: Antislavery and Social Reform* (New York: Cambridge University Press, 2005), 15, 52–53, 71.

17. Richard S. West, Jr., *Lincoln's Scapegoat General: A Life of Benjamin F. Butler, 1818–1893* (Boston: Houghton Mifflin, 1965), 30; John R. Mulkern, *The Know-Nothing Party in Massachusetts: The Rise and Fall of a People's Movement* (Boston: Northeastern University Press, 1990), 31; George A. Stevens, *New York Typographical Union No. 6* (Albany: J. B. Lyons, 1913), 527; William H. Sylvis, *The Life, Speeches, Labors and Essays of William H. Sylvis: Late President of The Iron-Moulders' International Union; and Also of the National Labor Union* (Philadelphia: Claxton, Remsen & Haffelfinger, 1872), 292–293; John Jarrett, "The Story of the Iron Workers," in George E. McNeill, ed., *The Labor Movement: the Problem of To-day. . .* (Boston: A.M. Bridgman, 1886), 275; E. Benjamin Andrews, "A History of the Last Quarter Century in the United States," *Scribner's Magazine* July 1895, 86.

18. Dubofsky, *State and Labor*, 1–37; William Forbath, *Law and the Shaping of the American Labor Movement* (Cambridge: Harvard University Press, 1991); Michele Landis Dauber, "Judicial Review and the Power of the Purse," *Law and History Review* 23:2 (Summer 2005): 451–58; Robert P. Reeder, "The Constitutionality of Protective Tariffs," *University of Pennsylvania Law Review* 76:8 (June 1928): 974–979.

19. Montgomery, *Beyond Equality*, 202–205, 246–247; Michael Holt, *The Rise and Fall of the American Whig Party* (New York: Oxford University Press, 2003), 184; Foner, *Free Soil*, 2, 5, 18, 21, 36, 151, 168, 169, 173, 175, 182; John R. Commons, "Tariff Revision and Protection for American Labor," *Annals of the American Academy of Political and Social Science* 32 (September 1908): 52.

20. Henry Adams, "Art II. The Session," *North American Review* 111:228 (July 1870): 45.

21. "Patriotism Protects our Home Industries," editorial, *Clay County Enterprise*, September 14, 1922, quoted in *American Economist* 70:13 (September 1922): 122; Andrew Neather, "Labor Republicanism, Race, and Popular Patriotism in the Era of Empire," in John Bodnar, ed., *Bonds of Affection: Americans Define Their Patriotism* (Princeton: Princeton University Press, 1996), 93–100.

22. James Woodburn, *The Life of Thaddeus Stevens* (Indianapolis: Bobbs-Merrill, 1913), 114–115, 150–151; George Francis Dawson, *Republican Campaign Text Book, 1888* (New York: Brentano's, 1888), 90–91; Reginald H. Williams, "One Effect of Free

Trade," *New York Times* October 4, 1903, 14; Charles Postel, *The Populist Vision* (New York: Oxford University Press, 2007), 19, 152; Irwin Unger, *The Greenback Era* (Princeton: Princeton University Press, 1964), 210–212; Elizabeth Wallace, *Goldwin Smith: Victorian Liberal* (Toronto: University of Toronto Press, 1957), 102, 264, 268, 274; Quentin R. Skrabec, *William McKinley, Apostle of Protectionism* (New York: Algora, 2007), 79; Andrew Gyory, *Closing the Gate: Race, Politics, and the Chinese Exclusion Act* (Chapel Hill: University of North Carolina Press, 1998), 50; Matthew Hild, *Greenbackers, Knights of Labor, and Populists: Farmer-Labor Insurgency in the South* (Athens: University of Georgia Press, 2007), 125; George Frisbie Hoar, *Autobiography of Seventy Years* (New York: Scribners, 1905), 1: 134, 251, 278; Walter LaFeber, *The New Empire* (Ithaca: Cornell University Press, 1963), 102–149; Emily Rosenberg, *Spreading the American Dream* (New York: Hill and Wang, 1982), 52–55.

23. Douglas Irwin, *Against the Tide: An Intellectual History of Free Trade* (Princeton: Princeton University Press, 1996); Theda Skocpol, *Protecting Soldiers and Mothers: The Political Origins of Social Policy in the United States* (Cambridge: Harvard University Press, 1995); Montgomery, *Beyond Equality*, 247–249.

24. Laurie, *Beyond Garrison*, 71–73; Frank, *Buy American*, 45, 49–51; Democratic Party National Committee, *The Campaign Text Book of the Democratic Party of the United States for the Presidential Election of 1888* (New York: Brentano's, 1888), 369; Reitano, *The Tariff Question*, 86.

25. Samuel Gompers, editorial, *American Federationist* 20:7 (July 1913): 530; Lyle W. Cooper, "The Tariff and Organized Labor," *American Economic Review* 20:2 (June 1930): 210–225; Daniel J. B. Mitchell, *Essays on Labor and International Trade* (Berkeley: Institute of Industrial Relations, University of California, 1970), 49; "Tariff Compromise Spurned by Wilson," *New York Times*, May 16, 1913, 2.

26. *Hearings Before a Subcommittee of the Committee on Judiciary: United States Senate. Maintenance of a Lobby to Influence Legislation*, vol. 4, *Appendix* (Washington, D.C.: General Printing Office, 1913); Karen Schnietz, "Democrats' 1916 Tariff Commission: Responding to Dumping Fears and Illustrating the Consumer Costs of Protectionism," *Business History Review* 72:1 (Spring 1998): 20; "American Federation of Labor's Legislative Committee's Report," *Pattern Makers' Journal* 26:4 (April 1915): 12.

27. *Tariff Act of 1930, Copy of Public Law # 361*, House Document 476, 71st Cong., 2nd Sess. (Washington, D.C.: General Printing Office, 1930).

28. Walter LaFeber, "The Constitution and United States Foreign Policy: An Interpretation," Journal of American History 74: 3 (December 1987): 710–714.

29. Michael Anthony Butler, *Cautious Visionary: Cordell Hull and Trade Reform, 1933–1937* (Kent: Kent State University Press, 1998), 179–182.

30. Nelson Lichtenstein, *Labor's War at Home: The CIO in World War II* (New York: Cambridge University Press, 1987); Nelson Lichtenstein, *Walter Reuther: The Most Dangerous Man in Detroit* (Chicago: University of Illinois Press, 1997), 171, 289–290; Cohen, *The Racketeer's Progress*, 265–295.

31. Bluestone and Bluestone, *Negotiating the Future*, 19–20.

32. Robert J. Samuelson, " 'Fair Trade' Foolishness," *Washington Post*, November 30, 2006, A23; Sebastian Mallaby, "Capitalism: The Remix," *Washington Post*, December 4, 2008, A21; Thomas L. Friedman, "We Are All French Now?" *New York Times*, June 24, 2005, 23; Joe Klein, "The Temptation of Howard Dean," *Time*, September 15, 2003, 31.

33. Steven E. Landsburg, "On My Mind: Xenophobia and Politics," *Forbes Magazine*, March 28, 2005, 46; Nelson Lichtenstein, *The Retail Revolution: How Wal-Mart Created a Brave New World of Business* (New York: Macmillan, 2009), 30, 249–250; Laura Rowley, *On Target: How the World's Hottest Retailer Hit a Bull's-Eye* (Hoboken, N.J.: John Wiley & Sons, 2003), 1–3.

Chapter 2. The American Legion and Striking Workers During the Interwar Period

1. Contemporary historians have proven little better at teasing apart this puzzle. William Pencak chronicles Legion vigilantism and strikebreaking but does not delve significantly into its deeper ideological basis for justifying such actions. M. J. Heale lumps the American Legion in with other interwar antiradicals like the Ku Klux Klan, fundamentalist Protestant ministers, Father Charles Coughlin and his followers, pro-Nazi anti-Semites, and isolationist xenophobes like the Liberty League as a parochial reaction against the cosmopolitan and centralizing forces afoot in 1920s and '30s America, an aggregation that does little justice to the Legion's particular conservative ideology and rejection of religious bigotry. Pencak, *For God and Country: The American Legion, 1919–1941* (Boston: Northeastern University Press, 1989); Heale, *American Anticommunism: Combating the Enemy Within, 1830–1970* (Baltimore: Johns Hopkins University Press, 1990), 80–81, 100–112.

2. Steve Fraser, "The 'Labor Question,' " in Fraser and Gary Gerstle, eds., *The Rise and Fall of the New Deal Order, 1930–1980* (Princeton: Princeton University Press, 1989), 55–78.

3. Alvin M. Owsley, "The Spirit of America's Warriors," *Texas Legionnaire*, November 1920, 28–29. Owsley's last name is erroneously spelled "Ousley" and his middle initial is noted as "N" in this article's byline.

4. *The Legionaire* (North Dakota), March 1921, 14.

5. George S. Wheat, *The Story of the American Legion* (New York: G. P. Putnam's Sons, 1919), 184.

6. Theodore Roosevelt Jr. to Eleanor Butler Alexander Roosevelt, January 21, 1919, Theodore Roosevelt Jr. Papers, box 8—Family Correspondence, Library of Congress (hereafter LoC); Eric Fisher Wood, "The American Legion: Keep Alive the Spirit of the Great War," *Forum*, August 19, 1919, 220.

7. *Boston Globe*, September 13, 1919, 2, September 17, 1919, 5, September 18, 1919, 12.

8. Fred Robertson to Henry J. Allen, November 29, 1919, box B-38—Gubernatorial Papers, Henry J. Allen Papers, LoC.

9. Richard J. Loosbrock, *The History of the Kansas Department of the American Legion* (Topeka: Kansas Department of the American Legion, 1968), 42–43; Allen to Byron Blair, December 24, 1919, W. A. Phares to Allen, December 5, 1919, George H. Hamilton to Allen, November 26, 1919, Allen Papers; Pencack, *For God and Country*, 212–213.

10. George Adriance to Allen, November 28, 1919, Allen Papers; Pencak, *For God and Country*, 213.

11. Gaston Druart to Allen, November 27, 1919, Allen Papers; petition entitled "Ex-service Men of Arma, Kansas," December 2, 1919, Allen Papers; Loosbrock, *History of the Kansas Department*, 43–44.

12. *New York Times,* May 2, 1920, RE2; Walter Wilson, "Labor Fights the American Legion," *American Mercury* 34:133 (January 1935) 5–6; American Legion, *Fourth Annual Report of National Officers of the American Legion and Legion Publishing Corporation, 1922* (New York: Legion Publishing, 1922), 5, 7; 1920 membership figure from American Legion, *Third Annual Report of National Officers of the American Legion and Legion Publishing Corporation, 1921"* (New York: Legion Publishing, 1921), 5.

13. Jennifer D. Keene, *Doughboys, the Great War, and the Remaking of America* (Baltimore: Johns Hopkins University Press, 2001), 18–21, 169; Pencak, *For God and Country*, 51, 80, 339.

14. "Progress Report of Organization Division, American Legion," National Recreation Association, Howard Braucher Collection, series 5, box 16—American Legion—folder 1, National Recreation and Park Association, Joseph Lee Memorial Library and Archives, Ashburn, Va.; Pencak *For God and Country*, 81–85. For a useful point of comparison for the Legion with other like-minded civic and professional organizations of the interwar era, see Jeffrey A. Charles, *Service Clubs in American Society: Rotary, Kiwanis, and Lions* (Urbana: University of Illinois Press, 1993).

15. Lemuel Bolles to H. M. Payne, January 13, 1920, quoted in Pencak, *For God and Country*, 208.

16. Christopher Capozzola, *Uncle Sam Wants You: World War I and the Making of the Modern American Citizen* (New York: Oxford University Press, 2008). For discussion of the American Legion specifically, see 210–212.

17. Wood, "The American Legion," 220.

18. John W. Inzer and Mark T. McKee, memorandum to Community Service, Inc., "Excerpts from Committee Reports of the American Legion of Special Interest to Community Service," n.d., Braucher Collection.

19. Minutes, National Americanism Commission, January 19, 1920, National Americanism Commission—minutes, n.p., American Legion National Headquarters and Archives, Indianapolis, Ind.

20. Pencak, *For God and Country*, 214–216; *The Legionaire* (North Dakota), January 1922, 13, 27, 29; William Green, "The Why of Trade Unionism," *American Legion Monthly*, September 1926, 6; *Pacific Legion*, June 1923.

21. *Proceedings of the Twelfth Annual Convention of the American Legion, Boston, Massachusetts, October 6–9, 1930* (Washington, D.C.: Government Printing Office, 1931), 139.

22. "Colmery Outlines Legion Program at Convention of Labor Federation," *Minnesota Legionnaire*, December 9, 1936, 3, "Legion Greets Labor of U.S. at Convention," December 26, 1936, 3.

23. Pencak, *For God and Country*, 222–229; Bruce Nelson, *Workers on the Waterfront: Seamen, Longshoremen, and Unionism in the 1930s* (Urbana: University of Illinois Press, 1988), 147–149.

24. Carl Parker, memorandum to American Civil Liberties Union, Mena, Arkansas. Aug 25, 1934, reel 114, vol. 764, ACLU; *Nation*, September 19, 1934, reel 111, vol. 730, 49, ACLU.

25. Kevin Starr, *Endangered Dreams: The Great Depression in California* (New York: Oxford University Press, 1996), 157–159; James Gray, *The American Civil Liberties Union of Southern California and Imperial Valley Agricultural Labor Disturbances: 1930, 1934* (San Francisco: R&E Research Associates, 1977); United States Senate Subcommittee of the Committee on Education and Labor, "Violations of Free Speech and Rights of Labor," 74th Cong., 3rd Sess., part 55, January 16, 1940, 20140–20142.

26. Gray, *American Civil Liberties Union*, 29–35; "Facts Regarding Alleged Legion Participation in Imperial Co. Riots," *California Legionnaire* March 1934, 1, 5; "The Imperial Valley Trouble," *California Legionnaire*, March 1934, 4.

27. Pencak, *For God and Country*, 224–249. For a history of strikebreaking at auto plants perpetrated by others, see Stephen H. Norwood, *Strikebreaking and Intimidation: Mercenaries and Masculinity in Twentieth-Century America* (Chapel Hill: University of North Carolina Press, 2002).

28. Pencak, *For God and Country*, 228–229.

29. Ibid., 238–239; "Investigation of Un-American Propaganda Activities in the United States," House Un-American Activities Committee (hereafter Dies Committee), part 2, October 13, 1938, Federal Building, Detroit, Mich. 75th Cong., 3rd Sess. 1339–1353.

30. Dies Committee, 1334–1335.

31. Pencak, *For God and Country*, 223–224; Walter Wilson, *The American Legion and Civil Liberty* (New York: American Civil Liberties Union, 1936), 24–25; "2 Posts Suspended in Legion Picketing," *New York Times*, May 1, 1936, letter to the editor from Lambert Fairchild, *New York Post*, May 23, 1936, reel 133, vol. 906, 36, ACLU; "Vigilante Group Is Repudiated by Legion Body," *Daily Worker*, December 4, 1935, reel 119, vol. 801, 42, ACLU.

32. Wilson, *The American Legion and Civil Liberty*, 2, 32.

33. Cyrus LeRoy Baldridge, *Americanism: What Is It?* (New York: Farrar & Rinehart, 1936), n.p.

34. My work clearly owes a heavy debt to that of historians exploring the other ideological side of this story—how workers and liberals fashioned a new Americanism

during the New Deal: Gary Gerstle, *Working-Class Americanism: The Politics of Labor in a Textile City, 1914–1960* (1989; rpt. Princeton: Princeton University Press, 2002), and *American Crucible: Race and Nation in the Twentieth Century* (Princeton: Princeton University Press, 2001); Lizabeth Cohen, *Making a New Deal: Industrial Workers in Chicago, 1919–1939* (New York: Cambridge University Press, 1990).

Chapter 3. Democracy or Seduction?

1. Richard Trahair, *The Humanist Temper: The Life and Work of Elton Mayo* (New Brunswick, N.J.: Transaction, 1984); Richard Gillespie, *Manufacturing Knowledge: A History of the Hawthorne Experiments* (Cambridge: Cambridge University Press, 1991); Ellen O'Connor, "The Politics of Management Thought: A Case Study of the Harvard Business School and the Human Relations School," *Academy of Management Review* 241 (1999): 117–131; Ellen O'Connor, "Minding the Workers: The Meaning of 'Human' and 'Human Relations' in Elton Mayo," *Organization* 62 (1999): 223–246; James Hoopes, *False Prophets: The Gurus Who Created Modern Management and Why Their Ideas Are Bad for Business Today* (Cambridge, Mass.: Perseus, 2003).

2. Hindy Schachter, *Frederick Taylor and the Public Administration Community: A Re-Evaluation* (Albany: State University of New York Press, 1989); Chris Nyland, *Reduced Worktime and the Management of Production* (Cambridge: Cambridge University Press, 1989); Chris Nyland, "Taylorism and the Mutual-Gains Strategy," *Industrial Relations* 37 (1998): 519–542; Steven Fraser, *Labor Will Rule: Sidney Hillman and the Rise of American Labor* (Ithaca: Cornell University Press, 1991); Mark Barenberg, "The Political Economy of the Wagner Act: Power, Symbol, and Workplace Cooperation," *Harvard Law Review* 106 (1993): 1381; Chris Nyland, "An Early Account of Scientific Management as Applied to Women's Work with Comment from Frederick W. Taylor," *Journal of Management History* 6, no. 4 (2000); Kyle Bruce and Chris Nyland, "Scientific Management, Institutionalism and Business Stabilization: 1903–1923," *Journal of Economic Issues* 35 (2001): 955–978; Di Kelly, "Marxist Manager Amidst the Progressives: Walter N. Polakov and the Taylor Society," *Journal of Industrial History* 6(2) (2003): 61–75; Chris Nyland and Tom Heenan, "Mary Van Kleeck, Taylorism, and the Control of Management Knowledge," *Management Decision* 43 (2005): 1358–1374; Chris Nyland and Andrea. McLeod, "The Scientific Management of the Consumer Interest," *Business History* 49 (2007): 717–735.

3. O'Connor, "The Politics of Management Thought" and "Minding the Workers."

4. Elton Mayo, *Democracy and Freedom: An Essay in Social Logic* (Melbourne: Macmillan, 1919), 59.

5. Carole Pateman, *Participation and Democratic Theory* (Cambridge: Cambridge University Press, 1970).

6. Mayo, *Democracy and Freedom*, 57, 59.

7. O'Connor, "Minding the Workers," 224, 238.

8. Ibid.

9. Nyland, "Taylorism and the Mutual-Gains Strategy."

10. Samuel Haber, *Efficiency and Uplift: Scientific Management in the Progressive Era, 1890–1920* (Chicago: University of Chicago Press, 1964).

11. Edwin Layton, *The Revolt of the Engineers: Social Responsibility and the American Engineering Profession* (Cleveland: Press of Case Western Reserve University, 1971).

12. Nyland, "Taylorism and the Mutual-Gains Strategy."

13. Nyland and McLeod, "The Scientific Management."

14. John Kenneth Galbraith, *A Life in Our Times* (Boston: Houghton Mifflin, 1981); Kyle Bruce, "Conflict and Conversion: Henry S. Dennison and the Shaping of J. K. Galbraith's Economic Thought," *Journal of Economic Issues* 34 (2000): 949–967.

15. Nyland, "Taylorism and the Mutual-Gains Strategy."

16. Frederick W. Taylor, letter to Louis D. Brandeis, 1913, Frederick Taylor Papers, Stevens Institute Archives, http://stevens.cdmhost.com/cdm4/item_viewer .php?cisoroot = /p4100coll1&cisoptr = 558&cisobox = 1&rec = 5.

17. Nyland, "Taylorism and the Mutual-Gains Strategy."

18. Frederick W. Taylor, *Industrial Relations: Final Report and Testimony Submitted to Congress* (Washington, D.C.: Government Printing Office, 1916), 810.

19. Frederick W. Taylor, "Scientific Management and Labor Unions," *Bulletin of the Society to Promote the Science of Management* 1, no. 1 (1914), 3.

20. Morris Llewellyn Cooke, preface to Morris Llewellyn Cooke, Samuel Gompers, and Fred J. Miller, eds., *Labor, Management and Production*, spec. ed. of *Annals of the American Academy of Political and Social Science* 91 (1920), vii, emphasis in original.

21. Sanford Jacoby, *Employing Bureaucracy: Managers, Unions, and the Transformation of Work in American Industry, 1900–1945* (New York: Columbia University Press, 1985), 103.

22. Harlow S. Person, "The Manager, the Workman, and the Social Scientist," *Bulletin of the Taylor Society* 3, no. 2 (1917): 1–7. See also Taylor Society, "Discussion of the Manager, the Workman and the Social Scientist," *Bulletin of the Taylor Society* 3, no. 6 (1917): 1–18.

23. Person, "The Manager, the Workman, and the Social Scientist," 3.

24. Ibid., 1.

25. Ibid., 4.

26. Ibid., 5.

27. Ibid.

28. Elton Mayo, "The Basis of Industrial Psychology," *Bulletin of the Taylor Society* 9 (1924): 249–259.

29. Daniel A. Wren, *White Collar Hobo: The Travels of Whiting Williams* (Ames: Iowa State University Press, 1987).

30. Mayo "The Basis of Industrial Psychology."

31. Elton Mayo "The Great Stupidity," *Harper's Monthly Magazine*, May 1925, 151, 226.

32. Ibid., 228.

33. Ibid., 229.

34. Ibid.

35. Robert W. Bruere, "The Great Obsession: A Challenge to Management Engineers and Industrial Psychologists to Join in Establishing a Circular Response Between Employers and Trade Unions," *Bulletin of the Taylor Society* 10, no. 5 (1925), 221.

36. Ibid., 222.

37. Elton Mayo, "A Supplement to 'The Great Stupidity,'" *Bulletin of the Taylor Society* 10, no. 5 (1925), 25.

38. Nyland, *Reduced Worktime*; Bruce and Nyland, "Scientific Management"; Nyland and McLeod, "The Scientific Management."

39. O'Connor, "The Politics of Management Thought"; O'Connor, "Minding the Workers"; Ellen O'Connor, "Industrial Democracy v. Democratic Realism: Early 20th-Century Debates on the Moral Purpose of the Firm," best paper, *Proceedings*, Academy of Management annual meeting, Chicago, 1999.

40. Bruce Kaufman, *The Global Evolution of Industrial Relations: Events, Ideas, and the IIRA* (Geneva: International Labour Office, 2004).

41. Herbert Gitelman, *Legacy of the Ludlow Massacre: A Chapter in American Industrial Relations* (Philadelphia: University of Pennsylvania Press, 1988); Jonathan Rees, *Representation and Rebellion: Employee Representation at the Colorado Fuel and Iron Company, 1914–1942* (Boulder: University of Colorado Press, 2010).

42. Donald Fisher, *Fundamental Development of the Social Sciences: Rockefeller Philanthropy and the United States Social Science Research Council* (Ann Arbor: University of Michigan Press, 1993).

43. Rees, *Rockefeller's Cross*; Daphne Taras, "Voice in the North American Workplace: From Employee Representation to Employee Involvement" in Bruce E. Kaufman; Richard A. Beaumont; Roy B. Helfgott, eds., *Industrial Relations to Human Resources and Beyond: The Evolving Process of Employee Relations Management* (Armonk, N.Y.: M. E. Sharpe, 2000); Kaufman, "The Case for the Company Union," *Labor History* 413 (2000): 321–350; Kaufman, *Managing the Human Factor: The Early Years of HRM in American Industry* (Ithaca, N.Y.: ILR Press, 2008).

44. Elton Mayo to Willits, 1923, Mayo Papers, box 1c, f. 75, Baker Library, Harvard Business School.

45. Elton Mayo, "A New Way of Statecraft" (1924), Laura Spelman Rockefeller Memorial papers, box 53, folder 572, Rockefeller Archive Center.

46. Charles Harvey, "John D. Rockefeller Jr., Herbert Hoover, and President Wilson's industrial conferences of 1919–1920" in J. E. Brown *and* P. D. Reagan, *eds., Voluntarism, Planning and the State: The American Planning Experience 1914–1946* (New York: Greenwood, 1988); Brody, "Why No Shop Committees" (2001); Greg Patmore, "Employee Representation Plans at the Minnequa Steelworks Pueblo Colorado 1915–1942," *Business History* 496 (2007): 844–867.

47. Charles Mills to George J. Anderson, 1923, RFA Friends and Services Series, box 62, folder 469, RAC; italics added.

48. Ibid.

49. Raymond Fosdick to John D. Rockefeller Jr., March 22, 1934, RFA Economic Interest Series, box 16, folder 127, RAC.

50. Rockefeller to Fosdick.

51. Gitelman, *Legacy of the Ludlow Massacre*; Kaufman, "The Case for the Company Union"; Kaufman, *Managing the Human Factor*.

52. Stephen Scheinberg, *The Development of Corporation Labor Policy 1900–1940*. (PhD diss., University of Wisconsin, 1966); Harris "Industrial Democracy and Liberal Capitalism, 1890–1925," in Nelson Lichtenstein and Howell J. Harris, eds., *Industrial Democracy in America: The Ambiguous Promise* (Cambridge Cambridge University Press, 1993); ; McCartin, *Labor's Great War* (1997); Kaufman, *Managing the Human Factor*.

53. Trahair, *The Humanist Temper*, 208.

54. David Hammack and Stanton Wheeler *Social Science in the Making: Essays on the Russell Sage Foundation, 1907–1972* (New York: Russell Sage Foundation, 1994), 50.

55. Ben M. Selekman and Mary Van Kleeck, *Employees' Representation in the Coal Mines: A Study of the Industrial Representation Plan of the Colorado Fuel and Iron Company* (New York: Russell Sage Foundation, 1924), 385.

56. Julie K. Kimmel, "Creating 'A Real Science of Human Relations': Personnel Management and the Politics of Professionalism, 1910–1940" (Ph.D. diss., Johns Hopkins University, 2000), 233.

57. Kimmel, "Creating 'A Real Science,'" 240.

58. Ibid.

59. Ibid.

60. Trahair, *The Humanist Temper*; John H. Smith, "Elton Mayo and the Hidden Hawthorne," *Work, Employment, and Society* 11 (1987): 107–120; Gillespie, *Manufacturing Knowledge*.

61. Ordway Tead, "Trends in Industrial Psychology," *Annals of the American Academy of Political and Social Science* 149 (1930): 110–119.

62. Bruce and Nyland, "Scientific Management," 955.

63. Henry C. Melcalf, ed., introduction to *Democratic Influences in Industry*, Proceeding of the First Annual Conference of Industrial Experimenters Associated, May 26, 1932 (New York: Henry C. Metcalf, Director, Bureau of Personnel Administration, 1932), 6.

64. Galbraith, *A Life*.

65. Bruce, "Conflict and Conversion."

66. Mark Barenburg, "The Political Economy of the Wagner Act: Power, Symbol, and Workplace Cooperation," *Harvard Law Review* 7 (1993): 1379–1496.

67. Ordway Tead and Henry C. Metcalf, *Personnel Administration*, 3rd ed. (New York: McGraw-Hill, 1932).

68. Elton Mayo, *The Human Problems of an Industrial Civilization* (New York: Macmillan, 1933), 138.

69. Ibid., 168.

70. Ibid., 174.

71. Gillespie, *Manufacturing Knowledge*, 189–190.

72. Cabot Papers, box c. 5, f. 169, Baker Library, Harvard Business School.

73. Fritz J. Roethlisberger, *The Elusive Phenomena* (Cambridge: Harvard Business School Press, 1977), 86–87.

74. Mayo Papers, c. 2, f. 2; Baker Library, Harvard Business School.

75. Elton Mayo, (1949), cited in Gillespie 1991, *Manufacturing Knowledge*, 246.

76. Elton Mayo, 1935, "The Blind Spot in Scientific Management," in *Sixth International Congress for Scientific Management* (London: P. S. King, 1935), 214.

77. Ibid., 217.

78. Thomas N. Whitehead, *Leadership in a Free Society* (London: Oxford University Press, 1936), 209.

79. Robert S. Lynd, review of Thomas N. Whitehead, *Leadership in a Free Society*, *Political Science Quarterly* 52, no. 4 (1937), 590.

80. Ibid., 591.

81. Charles D. Wrege and Ronald G. Greenwood, "Mary B. Gilson—A Historical Study of the Neglected Accomplishments of a Woman who Pioneered in Personnel Management," *Business and Economic History* 11 (1982), 37.

82. Mary B. Gilson, *What's Past Is Prologue* (New York: Harper, 1940), 295.

83. Ibid., 100.

84. Ibid., 101.

85. Fraser, *Labor Will Rule*.

86. William J. Breen, "Social Science and State Policy in World War II: Human Relations, Pedagogy, and Industrial Training 1940–1945," *Business History Review* 76, no. 2 (2002): 233–266.

87. Trahair, *The Humanist Temper*.

88. Fritz J. Roethlisberger, review of Morris Cooke and Philip Murray, *Organized Labor and Production*, *Annals of the American Academy of Political and Social Science* (1940), 211, 230.

89. International Labour Office, *Labour-Management Co-operation in United States War Production* (Montreal: International Labour Office, 1948). See also Sanford Jacoby. "Union-Management Cooperation in the United States During the Second World War," in Melvyn Dubofsky, ed., *Technological Change and Worker's Movements* (Beverly Hills, Calif.: Sage, 1985), 100–129.

90. Jacoby, *Employing Bureaucracy*, 274.

91. Ordway Tead, "Employee Counseling: A New Personnel Assignment—Its Status and Its Standards," *Advanced Management* 8 (1943), 103.

92. Crauford D. Goodwin, "The Patrons of Economics in a Time of Transformation," in Mary S. Morgan and Malcolm Rutherford, eds., *From Interwar Pluralism to Postwar Neoclassicism* (Durham: Duke University Press, 1998), 53–81.

93. Ibid., 60–61.

94. Ibid.

Chapter 4. Capital Flight, "States' Rights," and the Anti-Labor Offensive

1. On the rise of modern conservatism, see Dan T. Carter, *The Politics of Rage: George Wallace, the Origins of the New Conservatism, and the Transformation of American Politics* (Baton Rouge: Louisiana State University Press, 1995); Lisa McGirr, *Suburban Warriors: The Origins of the New American Right* (Princeton: Princeton University Press, 2001); Jonathan M. Schoenwald, *A Time for Choosing: The Rise of Modern American Conservatism* (New York: Oxford University Press, 2001); Tom Wicker, "Lyndon Johnson and the Roots of Contemporary Conservatism," in Alexander Bloom, ed., *Long Time Gone: Sixties America Then and Now* (New York: Oxford University Press, 2001), 99–121; and Donald T. Critchlow, *The Conservative Ascendancy: How the GOP Right Made Political History* (Cambridge, Mass.: Harvard University Press, 2007). For the impact of capital flight on U.S. unionism, see Tami J. Friedman, "Exploiting the North-South Differential: Corporate Power, Southern Politics, and the Decline of Organized Labor After World War II," *Journal of American History* 95, no. 2 (September 2008), 323–348.

2. For "backlash" against 1960s activism, see Kevin P. Phillips, *The Emerging Republican Majority* (1969; Garden City, N.Y.: Anchor Books/Doubleday, 1970), 32–33, 37; Thomas Byrne Edsall with Mary D. Edsall, *Chain Reaction: The Impact of Race, Rights, and Taxes on American Politics* (New York: W. W. Norton, 1992); and Wicker, "Roots of Contemporary Conservatism." For the postwar "social contract," see Barry Bluestone and Bennett Harrison, *The Deindustrialization of America: Plant Closings, Community Abandonment, and the Dismantling of Basic Industry* (New York: Basic Books, 1982), 133–139; William Greider, "The Future Is Now," *Nation*, June 26, 2006, 23–26; and Thomas Kochan, "Wages and the Social Contract," *American Prospect*, 18 (May 2007), A22–A23. A recent study that does show how business interests shaped modern conservatism is Kim Phillips-Fein, *Invisible Hands: The Making of the Conservative Movement from the New Deal to Reagan* (New York: W. W. Norton, 2009). See also Elizabeth Tandy Shermer, "Origins of the Conservative Ascendancy: Barry Goldwater's Early Senate Career and the De-legitimization of Organized Labor," *Journal of American History* 95, no. 3 (December 2008), 678–709.

3. Some early studies of the Right pay almost no attention to southern segregationists; see Daniel Bell, ed., *The Radical Right: The New American Right*, expanded and updated (Garden City, N.Y.: Doubleday, 1963); and relevant essays in Richard Hofstadter, *The Paranoid Style in American Politics and Other Essays* (New York: Alfred A. Knopf, 1965). For white supremacy as anomalous, see Critchlow, *Conservative*

Ascendancy, 86. For the "southern strategy," see Phillips, *Emerging Republican Major-ity*; Joseph A. Aistrup, *The Southern Strategy Revisited: Republican Top-Down Advance-ment in the South* (Lexington: University Press of Kentucky, 1996); Edsall with Edsall, *Chain Reaction*; Wicker, "Roots of Contemporary Conservatism"; and Carter, *Politics of Rage*. For newer studies that do emphasize southerners' active role in shaping mod-ern conservatism, see Kari Frederickson, *The Dixiecrat Revolt and the End of the Solid South, 1932–1968* (Chapel Hill: University of North Carolina Press, 2001); Kevin M. Kruse, *White Flight: Atlanta and the Making of Modern Conservatism* (Princeton: Princeton University Press, 2005); Matthew D. Lassiter, *The Silent Majority: Suburban Politics in the Sunbelt South* (Princeton: Princeton University Press, 2006); Joseph Crespino, *In Search of Another Country: Mississippi and the Conservative Counterrevolu-tion* (Princeton: Princeton University Press, 2007); Joseph E. Lowndes, *From the New Deal to the New Right: Race and the Southern Origins of Modern Conservatism* (New Haven: Yale University Press, 2008); and Nancy MacLean, "Southern Dominance in Borrowed Language: The Regional Origins of American Neoliberalism," in *New Land-scapes of Inequality: Neoliberalism and the Erosion of Democracy in America*, ed. Jane L. Collins, Micaela di Leonardo, and Brett Williams (Santa Fe, N. Mex.: School for Advanced Research Press, 2008), 21–37.

4. Daniel Nelson, "The Other New Deal and Labor: The Regulatory State and the Unions, 1933–1940," *Journal of Policy History*, 13, no. 3 (2001), 388 (n. 21); Phillips-Fein, *Invisible Hands*, 14–15; Colin Gordon, *New Deals: Business, Labor, and Politics in America, 1920–1935* (Cambridge, U.K.: Cambridge University Press, 1994), 261–279; "Statement of Henry I. Harriman, President, United States Chamber of Commerce," U.S. Congress, Senate, Committee on Finance, *Economic Security Act: Hearings . . .* , 74th Cong., 1st Sess., February 14, 1935, 916–917, http://www.ssa.gov/history/reports/ 35senate.html; Bruce J. Schulman, *From Cotton Belt to Sunbelt: Federal Policy, Eco-nomic Development, and the Transformation of the South, 1938–1980* (New York: Oxford University Press, 1991), 59. For Republicans' actions, see Melvyn Dubofsky, *The State and Labor in Modern America* (Chapel Hill: University of North Carolina Press, 1994), 112, 146–147; and Phillips-Fein, *Invisible Hands*, 20–21.

5. For union membership data, see Howell John Harris, *The Right to Manage: Industrial Relations Policies of American Business in the 1940s* (Madison: University of Wisconsin Press, 1982), 43; and David Brody, *Workers in Industrial America: Essays on the Twentieth Century Struggle* (New York: Oxford University Press, 1980), 173.

6. For the postwar strike wave, see Dubofsky, *State and Labor in Modern America*, 193. For workers' gains, see Brody, *Workers in Industrial America*, 184, 186, 191–192; and Seth Wigderson, "How the CIO Saved Social Security," *Labor History* 44 (Novem-ber 2003), 502–503.

7. For the Employment Act of 1946, see Robert H. Zieger and Gilbert J. Gall, *American Workers, American Unions: The Twentieth Century* (Baltimore: Johns Hop-kins University Press, 2002), 165; Kevin Boyle, *The UAW and the Heyday of American Liberalism, 1945–1968* (Ithaca: Cornell University Press, 1995), 47; Dubofsky, *State*

and Labor in Modern America, 197–198; and Felix Belair Jr., "Employment Bill Signed by Truman," *New York Times*, February 21, 1946, 11. For unions' political activities, see Zieger and Gall, *American Workers, American Unions*, 159–160; and Brody, *Workers in Industrial America*, 221.

8. For postwar anti-labor strategies, see Sanford M. Jacoby, *Modern Manors: Welfare Capitalism Since the New Deal* (Princeton: Princeton University Press, 1997); Elizabeth A. Fones-Wolf, *Selling Free Enterprise: The Business Assault on Labor and Liberalism, 1945–60* (Urbana: University of Illinois Press, 1994); Brody, *Workers in Industrial America*, 173–214; Nelson Lichtenstein, "From Corporatism to Collective Bargaining: Organized Labor and the Eclipse of Social Democracy in the Postwar Era," in *The Rise and Fall of the New Deal Order, 1930–1980*, ed. Steve Fraser and Gary Gerstle (Princeton: Princeton University Press, 1989), 122–152; and Lichtenstein, *State of the Union*, 98–140. "Renovation in NAM," *Fortune*, July 1948, esp. 166. For Republican gains, see Kim McQuaid, *Uneasy Partners: Big Business in American Politics, 1945–1990* (Baltimore: Johns Hopkins University Press, 1994), 22.

9. William F. Hartford, *Where Is Our Responsibility? Unions and Economic Change in the New England Textile Industry, 1870–1960* (Amherst: University of Massachusetts Press, 1996); "Capital's Flight: The Apparel Industry Moves South," *NACLA's Latin America and Empire Report*, March 1977, 2–33; Thomas J. Sugrue, *The Origins of the Urban Crisis: Race and Inequality in Postwar Detroit* (Princeton: Princeton University Press, 1996), 127–129; Jefferson Cowie, *Capital Moves: RCA's Seventy-Year Quest for Cheap Labor* (Ithaca: Cornell University Press, 1999); Ronald Schatz, *The Electrical Workers: A History of Labor at General Electric and Westinghouse, 1923–60* (Urbana: University of Illinois Press, 1983), 233–234; Jane D. Poulsen, "An Uneasy Stability: 'Unpacking' the Postwar Labor-Management Accord," *Labor Studies Journal*, 34 (December 2009), 554. For the Alexander Smith story, see Herbert J. "Jack" Potts interview by author, Fair Hope, Ala., March 2, 1996, audiotape, in author's possession, side 2; and Friedman, "Exploiting the North-South Differential." For Royal Little, see Hartford, *Where Is Our Responsibility?* 92, 119, 156–157. For Robert E. Wood, see Schulman, *From Cotton Belt to Sunbelt*, 91; Robert E. Wood, "The Gulf Coast—Our New Frontier," *Reader's Digest*, September 1948, 17–20, esp. 17 and 18; and Jacoby, *Modern Manors*, 95–142.

10. "Chamber Fetes Carpet Mill on Its Centennial," *Yonkers Herald-Statesman*, October 17, 1945, esp. 2; Patricia Ewing Richter interview by author, New York, September 28, 1995, audiotape, in author's possession, side 2; F. E. Masland Jr., "The Welfare State—and What It Means," *The News*, April 19, 1950, 5, "Employers Files 1943–1952 Alexander-Smith General (1949–1950)" folder, box 4, series B, file 4B, MSS 129A, Textile Workers Union of America (TWUA) Records, Wisconsin Historical Society, Madison. For Royal Little, see "Investment Bankers Take a Crack at Bonds for Plants," *Mississippi Magic: The BAWI Bulletin*, December 1951 (Mississippi Department of Archives and History (MDAH), Jackson. For Robert E. Wood, see Jacoby,

Modern Manors, 232–233; "Robert E. Wood, Who Built Sears, Roebuck Into a Retailing Giant, Dies at 90," *New York Times*, November 7, 1969, 35; Rick Perlstein, *Before the Storm: Barry Goldwater and the Unmaking of the American Consensus* (2001; rpt., New York: Nation Books, 2009), 6–11; and Phillips-Fein, *Invisible Hands*, 83. For Birch affiliations, see "Pamphlet Listing Birch Society Council Is Released," *New York Times*, April 1, 1961, 5.

11. Schulman, *From Cotton Belt to Sunbelt*, 21–26, 32–34, 54–60; Ira Katznelson, *When Affirmative Action Was White: An Untold History of Racial Inequality in Twentieth-Century America* (New York: W. W. Norton, 2005), 42–48; Sean Farhang and Ira Katznelson, "The Southern Imposition: Congress and Labor in the New Deal and Fair Deal," *Studies in American Political Development*, 19 (Spring 2005), 11–15. Ira Katznelson and his colleagues show that the New Deal-era "conservative coalition" of Republicans and southern Democrats was limited to labor legislation; see Ira Katznelson, Kim Geiger, and Daniel Kryder, "Limiting Liberalism: The Southern Veto in Congress, 1933–1950," *Political Science Quarterly* 108 (1993), 283–306.

12. Calculations of union membership data by region draw on data in Leo Troy, *Distribution of Union Membership Among the States, 1939 and 1953* (New York: National Bureau of Economic Research, 1957), 4–5, table 1, and 18–19, table 4. See also Ernest J. Hopkins, *Mississippi's BAWI Plan: An Experiment in Industrial Subsidization* (Atlanta: Federal Reserve Bank of Atlanta, 1944), 43–44; and Donald Crumpton Mosley, "A History of Labor Unions in Mississippi" (Ph.D. diss., University of Alabama, 1965), 133–137. For southern union membership data from 1938 and 1948, see Katznelson, *When Affirmative Action was White*, 69–70.

13. Hopkins, *Mississippi's BAWI Plan*; James C. Cobb, *The Selling of the South: The Southern Crusade for Industrial Development, 1936–1990* (Urbana: University of Illinois Press, 1993), 5–36; Kendrick Lee, "Labor Organization in the South," *Editorial Research Reports*, May 29, 1946, 375–387, "Southern Legacy: 'Economic Dominion'" folder, box 47, Hodding and Betty Werlein Carter Papers, Special Collections Department, Mitchell Memorial Library, Mississippi State University, Starkville; Friedman, "Exploiting the North-South Differential."

14. "The Text of President Truman's Message on Civil Rights," *New York Times*, February 3, 1948, 22; Lee, "Labor Organization in the South," esp. 385.

15. Delta Council Executive Committee meeting minutes, July 7, 1948, esp. 1, 2, and 12, "Correspondence and Papers (9)" folder, Mississippi Economic Council (MEC) Papers, 1948–1949, MDAH; Walter Sillers to Hodding Carter, April 25, 1950, "HC: Correspondence: 1950: S (March-May)" folder, "Correspondence: 1950: S-Telegrams" box, Carter Papers.

16. For Fantus's initial review of locations, see initial survey, attached to Leonard C. Yaseen to William F. C. Ewing, June 22, 1950, in author's possession, courtesy Deloitte, Chicago. For Leonard C. Yaseen's comments about nonunion operations, see Yaseen to Ewing, June 22, 1950, 1–2, attached to Mississippi survey, in author's possession, courtesy Deloitte. For "fewer restrictions," wage differences, and "prevailing custom," see "Conclusion," in Mississippi survey. For information from Greenville

leaders, see Yaseen to Ewing, August 2, 1950, 4–5, esp. 5, attached to Greenville, Miss., survey, copy in author's possession, courtesy Deloitte. For "Survey of White Labor" results, see "Statistical Analysis of Greenville, Mississippi," in Greenville, Miss., survey. For Smith's labor costs, see Alexander Smith and Sons Carpet Company, *Annual Report, 1950*, 11, chart, "Industries—Alexander Smith Inc." folder, Yonkers Vertical Files, Yonkers Public Library, Yonkers, N.Y. For factors motivating industry to move to the South, see Cobb, *Selling of the South*, 98–99, 209–217.

17. Potts interview, March 3, 1996, sides 1 and 2, tape 1; John W. "Jack" Baskin, interview by author, Greenville, Miss., January 18, 1996, audiotape, in author's possession, side 2, tape 1; William E. Blundell, "Dixie vs. the Unions," *Wall Street Journal*, July 12, 1962, 1, "Union File" folder, Greenville Area Chamber of Commerce (GACOC) Records, Greenville Area Chamber of Commerce, Greenville, Miss.

18. "Top Ten to Be Elected C of C Directors from 20," *Delta Democrat-Times*, November 15, 1953, 1; "Seven Washington Countians on MEC Committees to Meet," *Delta Democrat-Times*, May 12, 1954, p. 16; Potts interview, March 3, 1996, side 2, tape 1; "Mr. and Mrs. H. J. Potts Give Informal Party at Local Country Club," *Delta Democrat-Times*, April 15, 1953, 5; "Miss Jackie Potts is Honoree at Country Club Luncheon on Tuesday," *Delta Democrat-Times*, August 27, 1953, 3; "Greenville Mills Group Have Luncheon Tuesday at Local Country Club," *Delta Democrat-Times*, May 13, 1954, 3; "Olin Taylor Joins Baxter Laboratories," *Mississippi Magic: The BAWI Bulletin*, July 1949; "Carpet Firm's Head Praises Greenville," *Delta Democrat-Times*, January 24, 1951, 1, 2l; Baskin interview, side 2, tape 1.

19. For Rice-Stix, see Jack Edward Prince, "History and Development of the Mississippi Balance Agriculture with Industry Program, 1936–1958" (Ph.D. diss., Ohio State University, 1961), 34 (n. 46), 155–156, and Mosley, "History of Labor Unions in Mississippi," 149–151. For Westinghouse, see Cobb, *Selling of the South*, 49; and "Governor Signs Enabling Bill for Plant Here," *Vicksburg Evening Post*, February 7, 1952, series 958, Governors' Records, RG 27, MDAH.

20. For the differences in unemployment insurance and workers' compensation benefits, see "Diversity of State Unemployment Insurance Benefits," in Mississippi survey; and "The States Compared," ibid. For low turnover rates, see "Conclusion," ibid. For Virginia laws, see Leonard C. Yaseen to Harold C. Zulauf, January 5, 1951, 1, attached to Chilhowie, Va., survey, copy in author's possession, courtesy Deloitte). For Greenville's industrial waste policy, see Yaseen to Ewing, August 2, 1950, esp. 4, attached to Greenville, Miss., survey.

21. Dubofsky, *State and Labor in Modern America*, 202–208; Gilbert J. Gall, *The Politics of Right to Work: The Labor Federations as Special Interests, 1943–1979* (New York: Greenwood Press, 1988), 33–43. Calculations of southerners' support for the Taft-Hartley Act and the veto override draw on data in "House Vote on Labor Bill," *New York Times*, April 18, 1947, p. 6; "Senate Vote on Passage of Labor-Control Bill," *New York Times*, May 14, 1947, 3; and Neal R. Peirce, ed., *Congress and the Nation, 1945–1964: A Review of Government and Politics in the Postwar Years* (Washington:

Congressional Quarterly Service, 1965), 46a–47a, chart 1, and 44a, chart 1. *Proceedings of the Twenty-Ninth Annual Session of the Mississippi State Federation of Labor, Held at Jackson, Mississippi, September 15–16–17, 1947*, esp. 8 and 29–30. Sean Farhang and Ira Katznelson identify the passage of Taft-Hartley as a key moment in southern Democrats' shift away from support for New Deal labor policies; see Farhang and Katznelson, "Southern Imposition," 16–18.

22. Gall, *Politics of Right to Work*, 19, 34, 13–14; Delta Council, *Annual Report, 1947–1948*, 7, MDAH; Mississippi Economic Council Board of Directors minutes, April 28, 1949, 6, "Correspondence and Papers [2]" folder, MEC Papers; remarks of Edmund Taylor in Delta Council Executive Committee minutes, July 7, 1948, 1; "Judiciary Committee Kills Anti-Labor Bills," *Mississippi Labor Federationist*, April 2, 1950, 1–2, Holt E. Ross Papers, Special Collections Department, Mitchell Memorial Library; "Mississippi Solons Study 'Right to Work' Bill," *Delta Democrat-Times*, October 25, 1953, 1; "Governor Signs 'Right to Work' Bill Outlawing Closed and Union Shops," *Jackson Daily News*, February 24, 1954, "Right to Work Laws, 1951–1959" folder, box 2220, "Subject Files, 1947–1986" series, Mississippi State AFL-CIO Records, Southern Labor Archives, Special Collections and Archives, Georgia State University, Atlanta; "Industrial Survey of Greenville, Mississippi" (1960), "M Thru Z Industrial Prospects Transfer" box, GACOC Records; William A. Mosow, interview by author, Greenville, Miss., December 23, 1995, audiotape, in author's possession, side 1, tape 1. For Ralph J. Cordiner, see "Atomic Energy: The Powerhouse," *Time*, January 12, 1959, 84–85, 86; and "Cordiner Backs Work Laws," *New York Times*, October 10, 1958, 25.

23. On the effort to raise the minimum wage, see "Raise in Minimum Wage," *Congressional Quarterly*, 11 (1955), 321–322; Richard Amper, "Harriman Seeks Basic Pay Backing," *New York Times*, January 18, 1955, esp. 28; Richard Amper, "Harriman Assails Eisenhower Plans," *New York Times*, Jan. 13, 1955, esp. 21; "Eisenhower Hears Union Wage Plea," *New York Times*, March 8, 1955, 21; A. H. Raskin, "Clothing Makers for $1.25 Base Pay," *New York Times*, Jan. 19, 1955, 16; C. P. Trussell, "Vote Postponed on U.S. Pay Base," *New York Times*, July 20, 1955, 14; and "House Roll-Call on Wage," *New York Times*, July 21, 1955, 16. For the unemployment insurance debate, see Iwan W. Morgan, *Eisenhower Versus "The Spenders": The Eisenhower Administration, the Democrats, and the Budget, 1953–60* (London: Pinter, 1990), 114–117; "Statement by Marion Williamson, Director, Employment Security Agency, Georgia Department of Labor, Before the Committee on Finance, United States Senate, on Proposed Federal Additions to Benefits Under Existing State Job Insurance Laws, May 14, 1958," 4, "Temporary Unemployment Compensation Hearings 1958" folder, box 27, New York State Department of Labor, Division of Employment, Executive Director's Subject Files, 15382–90, New York State Archives, Albany; and "Statement by Richard C. Brockway, Executive Director, New York State Division of Employment, Before the Senate Committee on Finance on Temporary Extension of Unemployment Benefits, HR 12065, May 16, 1958," 16–17, "Temporary Unemployment Compensation Hearings 1958" folder.

24. For Textron, see Hartford, *Where Is Our Responsibility?* 120, 156–157, 176–181; "New England Wages War on the South," *Mississippi Magic: The BAWI Bulletin*, January 1952; Walter Murtagh, "Textron South Mills Project Strikes Snag," *Manchester, N.H., Sunday News*, November 25, 1951, "Steel Allocations for Textile Mills, 1951" folder, box 21, series A, file 10A, MSS 129A, TWUA Records; and *Anderson Independent* editorial, "CIO Anti-South Attitude Seen in New Plant Fight," reprinted in *Greenville, S.C., Observer*, October 26, 1951, *Greenville, S.C., Observer*. Alden Whitman, "Charles E. Wilson of GE Dies," *New York Times*, January 4, 1972, 1, 37; "Atomic Energy," 85–86; "Plant Dispersal Urged by Wilson," *New York Times*, August 17, 1951, 25; "New North-South Scrap over Textiles," *Delta Democrat-Times*, March 21, 1952, 1; editorial, "Parties of the Concerned," *Delta Democrat-Times*, [June 1953], 1953–1954 Scrapbook, George F. Archer Papers, William Alexander Percy Memorial Library, Greenville, Miss.

25. Delta Council Executive Committee meeting minutes, July 7, 1948, esp. 2; Ann Waldron, *Hodding Carter: The Reconstruction of a Racist* (Chapel Hill: Algonquin Books of Chapel Hill, 1993), 215; Frederickson, *Dixiecrat Revolt*, 130–131, 135–136, 168, 153–154, 157, 140–141, esp. 174–175.

26. On political changes in the South and Eisenhower's campaigns, see Hodding Carter, "The Hegira of Alexander Smith," *Sales Management*, February 15, 1956, esp. 38; Pete Daniel, *Standing at the Crossroads: Southern Life Since 1900* (New York: Hill & Wang, 1986), 159; advertisement, "Eisenhower Rally *Tonight!*" *Delta Democrat-Times*, September 22, 1952, 3; "Big Ike Rally Throws Doubt on Coalition," *Delta Democrat-Times*, September 23, 1952, 1; Frederickson, *Dixiecrat Revolt*, 229; and Numan V. Bartley, *The Rise of Massive Resistance: Race and Politics in the South During the 1950s* (Baton Rouge: Louisiana State University Press, 1969), 116–121, esp. 121, 290–291. For 1952 and 1956 election data, see Neal R. Peirce, ed., *Politics in America, 1945–1964* (Washington, D.C.: Congressional Quarterly Service, 1965), 94–95, table.

27. For Barry Goldwater, see Shermer, "Origins of the Conservative Ascendancy"; and Mary C. Brennan, "Winning the War/Losing the Battle: The Goldwater Presidential Campaign and Its Effects on the Evolution of Modern Conservatism," in *The Conservative Sixties*, ed. David Farber and Jeff Roche (New York: Peter Lang, 2003), 63–78. For Goldwater's supporters, see David R. Jones, "H. L. Hunt: Magnate with a Mission," *New York Times*, August 17, 1964, 16; Perlstein, *Before the Storm*, 441; and Robert O. May to Barry Goldwater, November 8, 1963, "1964, A-Z, General files" box, GACOC Records. For 1964 election data, see Peirce, *Politics in America*, 96, table.

28. For the impact of capital flight on northern communities, see Tami J. Friedman, "'A Trail of Ghost Towns across Our Land': The Decline of Manufacturing in Yonkers, New York," in *Beyond the Ruins: The Meanings of Deindustrialization*, ed. Jefferson Cowie and Joseph Heathcott (Ithaca: Cornell University Press, 2003), 19–43.

29. Gall, *Politics of Right to Work*, 45–46; 137–138, 162–183; "'Right to Work' Repeal Defeated by Filibuster," *Congressional Quarterly* 21 (1965), 818–831, esp. 826.

Chapter 5. Orval Faubus and the Rise of Anti-Labor Populism in Northwestern Arkansas

1. *United Mine Workers of America et al. v. Coronado Coal Company,* 259 U.S. 344 (1922), quotation on 399; Stephen H. Norwood, *Strikebreaking and Intimidation: Mercenaries and Masculinity in Twentieth Century America* (Chapel Hill: University of North Carolina Press, 2002), 154–163; Samuel A. Sizer, "'This Is a Union Man's Country': Sebastian County 1914," *Arkansas Historical Quarterly* 27 (Winter 1968), 306–329.

2. James R. Green, *Grass-Roots Socialism: Radical Movements in the Southwest, 1895–1943* (Baton Rouge: Louisiana State University Press, 1978); Cedric Belfrage, *South of God* (New York: Modern Age Books, 1941); Melvyn Dubofsky, *We Shall Be All: A History of the Industrial Workers of the World,* abridged ed. (Urbana: University of Illinois Press, 2000), 43–51; Michael Pierce, "Great Women All, Serving a Glorious Cause: Freda Hogan Ameringer's Reminiscences of Socialism in Arkansas," *Arkansas Historical Quarterly* 69 (Winter 2010), 293–324; William H. Cobb, Radical Education in the Rural South: Commonwealth College, 1922–1940 (Detroit: Wayne State University Press, 2000).

3. Raymond Arsenault, *The Wild Ass of the Ozarks: Jeff Davis and the Social Bases of Southern Politics* (1984; rpt., Knoxville: University of Tennessee Press, 1988), 89–90; Elizabeth Sanders, *Roots of Reform: Farmers, Workers, and the American State, 1877–1917* (Chicago: University of Chicago Press, 1999), 286.

4. Nelson Lichtenstein, *The Retail Revolution: How Wal-Mart Created a Brave New World of Business* (New York: Metropolitan Books, 2009), 118–148; Bethany Moreton, *To Serve God and Wal-Mart: The Making of Christian Free Enterprise* (Cambridge: Harvard University Press, 2009); Steve Striffler, *Chicken: The Dangerous Transformation of America's Favorite Food* (New Haven: Yale University Press, 2005), 74–79.

5. Brooks Blevins, *Hill Folks: A History of Arkansas Ozarkers and Their Image* (Chapel Hill: University of North Carolina Press, 2002), 9–69; Margaret Jones Bolsterli, *During Wind and Rain: The Jones Family Farm in the Arkansas Delta, 1848–2006* (Fayetteville: University of Arkansas Press, 2008), 1–20; Carolyn Earle Billingsley, *Communities of Kinship: Antebellum Families and the Settlement of the Cotton Frontier* (Athens: University of Georgia Press, 2004); Albert Webb Bishop, *Loyalty on the Frontier; or, Sketches of Union Men of the Southwest* (1863; rpt., Fayetteville: University of Arkansas Press, 2003); Andrew Roy, *Recollections of a Prisoner of War,* 2nd ed. (Columbus, Ohio: Trauger, 1909), quotation on 106.

6. Kenneth C. Barnes, *Who Killed John Clayton? Political Violence and the Emergence of the New South, 1861–1893* (Durham: Duke University Press, 1998); J. Morgan Kousser, *The Shaping of Southern Politics: Suffrage Restriction and the Establishment of the One-party South, 1890–1910* (New Haven: Yale University Press, 1974); Michael Perman, *Struggle for Mastery: Disfranchisement in the South, 1888–1908* (Chapel Hill: University of North Carolina Press, 2001), 48–69.

7. Jacqueline Froelich and David Zimmerman, "Total Eclipse: The Destruction of the African American Community of Harrison, Arkansas, in 1905 and 1909," *Arkansas Historical Quarterly* 58 (Summer 1998), 131–159; Guy Lancaster, " 'They Are Not Wanted': The Extirpation of African Americans from Baxter County, Arkansas," *Arkansas Historical Quarterly* 69 (Spring 2010), 28–44; Kimberly Harper, *"White Man's Heaven": Lynching and the Expulsion of Blacks in the Southern Ozarks, 1894–1909* (Fayetteville: University of Arkansas Press, 2010); James W. Loewen, *Sundown Towns: A Hidden Dimension of American Racism* (New York: New Press, 2005).

8. Calvin R. Ledbetter, Jr., *Carpenter from Conway: George Washington Donaghey as Governor of Arkansas* (Fayetteville: University of Arkansas Press, 1993), 130–131; Arsenault, *Wild Ass of the Ozarks*, 214.

9. Alvin Arthur Steel, *Coal Mining in Arkansas* (Little Rock: Democrat Printing and Lithographing, 1910), 122–123; Arsenault, *Wild Ass of the Ozarks*, quotation on 214; Cobb, *Radical Education in the Rural South.*

10. Roy Reed, *Faubus: The Life and Times of an American Prodigal* (Fayetteville: University of Arkansas Press, 1997), 3–72, 92–113; Green, *Grass-Roots Socialism*, 414; Historical Census Browser, University of Virginia Library, *fisher.lib.virginia.edu/collections/stats/histcensus*, accessed August 23, 2009.

11. Donald H. Grubbs, *Cry from the Cotton: The Southern Tenant Farmers' Union and the New Deal* (1971; reprint, Fayetteville: University of Arkansas Press, 2000); H. L. Mitchell, *Mean Things Happening in This Land: The Life and Times of H. L. Mitchell, Cofounder of the Southern Tenant Farmers Union* (Montclair, N.J.: Allanheld Osum, 1979); H. L. Mitchell, *Roll the Union On: A Pictorial History of the Southern Tenant Farmers' Union* (Chicago: Charles H. Kerr, 1987).

12. Gilbert J. Gall, "Southern Industrial Workers and Anti-Union Sentiment: Arkansas and Florida in 1944," in *Organized Labor and the South in the Twentieth Century*, ed. Robert H. Zieger (Knoxville: University of Tennessee Press, 1991), 223–249; C. Calvin Smith, *War and Wartime Changes: The Transformation of Arkansas, 1940–1945* (Fayetteville: University of Arkansas Press, 1986), 109–118.

13. "Proceedings of the Annual Convention of the Arkansas State Federation of Labor, 1945," typescript, Special Collections, University of Arkansas Libraries, Fayetteville; "Proceedings of the Annual Convention of the Arkansas State Federation of Labor, 1946," typescript, Special Collections, University of Arkansas Libraries.

14. The Arkansas labor movement's relationship with McMath is detailed in Michael Pierce, "John McClellan, the Teamsters, and Biracial Labor Politics in Arkansas, 1947–1959," in *Life and Labor in the New New South: Essays in Southern Labor History Since 1950*, ed. Robert H. Zieger (Gainesville: University Press of Florida, forthcoming).

15. Harry S. Ashmore, "McMath Enlarges His Beachhead," *Reporter*, April 25, 1950, 22–24; Jim Lester, *A Man for Arkansas: Sid McMath and the Southern Reform Tradition* (Little Rock: Rose, 1976), 98–99; Daisy Bates, *The Long Shadow of Little Rock: A Memoir* (1962; rpt., Fayetteville: University of Arkansas Press, 2007), 79.

16. "Has John McClellan Represented the People of Arkansas in the Senate?" (Little Rock: Arkansas Industrial Union Council, 1954); Henry Woods, interview by T. Harri Baker, December 8, 1972, 15, Eisenhower Administration Project, Oral History Research Office, Columbia University, New York; "Voting Record of John McClellan, 1943–1952," in Arkansas State Industrial Union Council-CIO, "Arkansas Legislative Manual, 1953," box 1, folder 9, CIO PAC Collection, Walter Reuther Library, Wayne State University, Detroit; "Statement of James L. McDevitt, National Director, Labor's League for Political Education, on Voting Record of John L. McClellan," box 5, folder 9, Sidney S. McMath Papers, Special Collections, University of Arkansas Libraries.

17. Tildford E. Dudley to Roy Reuther, November 15, 1955, box 1, folder 9, CIO PAC Collection; Dan Powell to James L. McDevitt, November 11, 1959, box 2, folder 29, Daniel Augustus Powell Papers, Southern Historical Collection, University of North Carolina, Chapel Hill; McMath to Chuck Bannister, February 6, 1958, box 3, folder 2, McMath Papers; minutes of the Executive Board meeting, Arkansas State Federated Labor Council, May 6, 1956, Arkansas AFL-CIO, Little Rock.

18. Don Ellinger to Jack Kroll, March 19, 1953, box 1, folder 10, CIO PAC Collection; Ellinger to Kroll, April 22, 1953, CIO PAC Collection; Tilford E. Dudley to Phil Weightman, March 12, 1953, box 1, folder 5, Philip Weightman Papers, Tamiment Library, New York University.

19. Wiley A. Branton to Phil Weightman, May 27, 1953, box 1, folder 4, Weightman Papers; Jackie Shropshire to Weightman, May 26, 1953, box 1, folder 4, Weightman Papers; Shropshire to Weightman, May 28, 1953, box 1, folder 4, Weightman Papers; I. S. McClinton to Weightman, September 20, 1953, box 1, folder 4, Weightman Papers; "Minutes of Meeting of Poll Tax Campaign Committee, June 2, 1953," box 1, folder 4, Weightman Papers; Weightman to William Dawson, telegram, August 31, 1953, in box 1, folder 4, Weightman Papers; Charles Catton to Kroll, January 4, 1954, box 1, folder 6, Weightman Papers; Catton to Weightman, January 4, 1954, box 1, folder 6, Weightman Papers; Weightman and James E. Turner, "Report on Minority Group Vote, 1954 Elections," box 8, folder 11, Weightman Papers; Catton to Kroll, May 21, 1953, box 1, file 10, CIO PAC Collection.

20. Woods, interview by Baker, 6–9; Sidney McMath, interview by John Luter, December 30, 1970, 4–6, Eisenhower Administration Project; James Woods, *Era of Sidney McMath Arkansas Political Leader, 1946–1954: A Look at an Arkansas Progressive in Light of the Political Tradition of the New South* (n.p.: n.p., 1975), 66; Truman Baker to Orval Faubus, July 6, 1953, box 44, file 4, Orval Eugene Faubus Papers, Special Collections, University of Arkansas Libraries; Reed, *Faubus*, 83–85; Victor K. Ray, "The Role of the Labor Union," in *Arkansas: Colony and State*, ed. Leland DuVall (Little Rock: Rose, 1973), 102.

21. *Merger Convention of the Arkansas State Federated Labor Council, AFL-CIO, March 20–21, 1956, Little Rock* (Little Rock: Arkansas State AFL-CIO), 84.

22. Woods, interview by Baker, 10; Report of the Arkansas Industrial Union Council Legislative and PAC Committee, January 15–16, 1955, box 1, folder 9, CIO PAC Collection; Reed, *Faubus*, 88–116; Bates, *Long Shadow of Little Rock*, 81.

23. Ellinger to Kroll and McDevitt, January 22, 1956, box 2, folder 29, Powell Papers. See also Ellinger to Powell, December 31, 1955, box 2, folder 29, Powell Papers.

24. Pegler's syndicated column appeared in hundreds of papers; see, e.g., *San Antonio Light*, January 4, 1955.

25. Ellinger to Kroll, January 19, 1955, box 1, file 9, CIO PAC Collection; "Report of the Arkansas Industrial Union Council Legislative and PAC Committee, January 15–16, 1955," box 1, file 9, CIO PAC Collection; "Phases of CIO PAC Activity in Arkansas, January 1955," in box 1, file 9, CIO PAC Collection; Catton to Kroll, October 15, 1954, box 1, file 9, CIO PAC Collection; Ellinger to Kroll, October 14, 1954, box 1, file 9, CIO PAC Collection; minutes of Arkansas Labor's League for Political Education meeting, November 11, 1954, Arkansas AFL-CIO Papers.

26. "Governor Calls for Decent Wages," *Arkansas Democrat*, January 15, 1955, 1; Ellinger to Kroll, January 19, 1955; minutes of Arkansas Labor's League for Political Education meeting, January 29, 1956, Arkansas AFL-CIO.

27. Ellinger to Kroll, March 30, 1955, box 1, file 9, CIO PAC Collection; Kroll to Orval Faubus, March 30, 1955, box 1, file 9, CIO PAC Collection.

28. Ethel B. Dawson to Weightman, March 3, 1955, box 1, folder 4, Weightman Papers; Weightman to Dawson, June 6, 1956, box 1, folder 4, Weightman Papers; Dawson to Weightman, June 8, 1955, box 1, folder 4, Weightman Papers; "Pay Your Poll Tax Now, before Oct. 1, 1955," broadside in box 1, folder 4, Weightman Papers; Kroll to A. F. Hartung, September 12, 1955, box 1, folder 9, CIO PAC Collection.

29. *Merger Convention of the Arkansas State Federated Labor Council*, quotation on 12.

30. "Has Arkansas Gone Liberal?" *Chicago Defender*, May 7, 1955, cited in Neil R. McMillen, "The White Citizens' Council and Resistance to School Desegregation in Arkansas," *Arkansas Historical Quarterly* 66 (Summer 2007), 125–144.

31. "A Morally Right Decision," *Life*, July 25, 1955, 29–31; Elizabeth Jacoway, *Turn Away Thy Son: Little Rock, the Crisis That Shocked the Nation* (New York: Free Press, 2007), 28–45; Reed, *Faubus*, 172–176.

32. *Merger Convention of the Arkansas State Federated Labor Council*; minutes of Arkansas State Federated Labor Council Executive Board meeting, August 25, 1956, Arkansas AFL-CIO; "Recommendations of Committee on Political Education on Constitutional Amendments and Initiated Acts," Arkansas AFL-CIO.

33. Catton to Kroll, October 15, 1954; Ellinger to Kroll, October 14, 1954; Reed, *Faubus*, 169–193.

34. "Don't be Fooled! Know the Facts!" broadside in box 3, file 42, Powell Papers; minutes of Arkansas State Federated Labor Council Executive Board Meeting, August 25, 1956; A. M. Judge, "Negro Political Heads Take Hands Off While Many Uncle Toms Grab Cash," *Arkansas State Press*, July 27, 1956; 1; "Mr. Faubus Was Right . . . We Were Wrong . . . We Apologize," *Arkansas State Press*, August 10, 1956, 1.

35. Minutes of Arkansas State Federated Labor Council Executive Board Meeting, August 25, 1956; "Recommendations of Committee on Political Education on Constitutional Amendments and Initiated Acts," Arkansas AFL-CIO.

36. Powell to Kroll and McDevitt, September 10, 1956, box 3, file 42, Powell Papers; minutes of Arkansas State Federated Labor Council Executive Board meeting, August 25, 1956.

37. Wayne Glenn, interview by author, Nashville, September 5, 2007; Jacoway, *Turn Away Thy Son*, 111–112.

38. Benjamin Fine, "Little Rock Sets Integration Date: Board, in Wake of U.S. Court Ruling, to Admit Negroes to High School Tuesday," *New York Times*, September 1, 1957, 35.

39. Minutes of Arkansas COPE convention, May 24, 1958, Arkansas AFL-CIO; E. L. Weeks to Faubus, May 25, 1958, box 54, folder 6, Faubus Papers; "COPE Raps Faubus but Refuses to Endorse Finkbeiner," *Union Labor Bulletin*, May 30, 1958, 1; "Labor Council Refuses to Support Faubus," *Arkansas Gazette*, May 25, 1958, 1; "Faubus Looks for Support From Labor; Governor Disputes Committee's Charge of Breach of Faith," *Arkansas Gazette*, May 27, 1958, 1.

40. "Mr. Faubus and the Labor Unions," *Arkansas Gazette*, July 3, 1958, 4A.

41. Ray Moseley, "Faubus: Organization and Confidence," *Arkansas Gazette*, July 27, 1958, 4A.

42. Mrs. John D. McBurnett, "A Defense of Faubus on the Labor Issue," *Arkansas Gazette*, May 29, 1958, 4A.

43. By 1958, several school districts in northwestern Arkansas—Fayetteville, Van Buren, Fort Smith, Bentonville, Lincoln, Ozark, Charleston—had begun at least token integration. Other than Hoxie, no schools on the other side of the state had done so; John A. Kirk, "Not Quite Black and White: School Desegregation in Arkansas, 1954–1966," *Arkansas Historical Quarterly* 70 (Autumn 2011), 225–257.

44. Ray Moseley, "Outsiders Interefering in Campaign, Faubus Tells Springdale Audience," *Arkansas Gazette*, July 2, 1958, 1B; George Douthit, "Faubus to Challenge Opponents," *Arkansas Democrat*, July 2, 1958, 3.

45. "Faubus Names 3 as 'Quislings,'" *Arkansas Democrat*, July 3, 1958, 3; campaign speech, box 54, folder 9, Faubus Papers; "Governor Faubus and the Truth," *Union Labor Bulletin*, July 11, 1958, 1; "McMath Replies to Faubus 'Fabrications' on Labor Outsiders," *Union Labor Bulletin*, July 18, 1958, 1.

46. Ray Moseley, "Faubus Charges Union Teams Undermine Him; Governor Visions Violence Worse Than CHS Strife," *Arkansas Gazette*, July 5, 1958, 1; "Labor Official, Negro Leader Answer Faubus," *Arkansas Gazette*, July 6, 1958; George Douthit, "Faubus Says He'll Get Union Vote," *Arkansas Democrat*, July 7, 1958, 2.

47. David Witwer, *Corruption and Reform in the Teamsters Union* (Urbana: University of Illinois Press, 2003), esp. 183–184; "McClellan Talks At Park With Cherry, Johnson," *Arkansas Gazette*, July 27, 1954, 1; Reed, *Faubus*, 116.

48. "Faubus and Labor," *Arkansas Gazette*, July 9, 1958, 4A; "Those 'Union Teams.'"*Arkansas Gazette*, July 14, 1958, 4A; "Laney on TV Panel Against Faubus Bid," *Arkansas Gazette*, July 25, 1958, 1; "Labor Has More Questions for Faubus," *Arkansas Gazette*, July 26, 1958, 4A; "Laney Scores Faubus Tactics," *Arkansas Gazette*,

July 27, 1958, 1; telecast, Little Rock, Ark., July 25, 1958, transcript, box 54, folder 8, Faubus Papers; C. R. Thornbrough to Faubus, July 18, 1958, box 54, folder 8, Faubus Papers; AFL-CIO COPE news release, August 30, 1958, box 3, folder 81, Weightman Papers.

49. Glenn interview; "Wayne E. Glenn Beats Veazey In Race for AFLCIO Helm,"- *Arkansas Gazette*, November 20, 1958, 1; Donald Slaiman, "Summary Report on Arkansas, November 25, 1958," box 322, folder 63, Jewish Labor Committee Papers, Tamiment Library. Glenn opposed Faubus's actions during the Little Rock crisis, but as an official in the United Paperworkers International Union, he worked to keep blacks relegated to low-paying jobs in the paper industry; see Timothy J. Minchin, *The Color of Work: The Struggle for Civil Rights in the Southern Paper Industry, 1945–1960* (Chapel Hill: University of North Carolina Press, 2000), 28, 78–80.

50. George Ellison to Weightman, July 17, 1961, box 3, folder 32, Weightman Papers; J. Bill Becker, interview by Jack Bass and Walter De Vries, June 13, 1974, 9, 15, Southern Oral History Project, University of North Carolina, Chapel Hill; Becker, interview by John Luter, August 16, 1971, Oral History Research Office, Columbia University.

51. Becker, interview by Luter; Alan Draper, *Conflict of Interest: Organized Labor and the Civil Rights Movement in the South, 1954–1968* (Ithaca, N.Y.: ILR Press, 1994), 60; Victor Ray, interview by author, June 13, 2007, Little Rock, Ark.

52. Draper, *Conflict of Interest*, 94–95. The association of the labor movement with the civil rights movement increased in the 1960s when the state's two most prominent African American civil rights activists—Daisy Bates and Wiley Branton—went to work for union-funded projects; see Grif Stockley, *Daisy Bates: Civil Rights Crusader from Arkansas* (Jackson: University Press of Mississippi, 2005), 251; Judith Kilpatrick, *There When We Needed Him: Wiley Austin Branton, Civil Rights Crusader* (Fayetteville: University of Arkansas Press, 2007).

53. Lichtenstein, *Retail Revolution*; Moreton, *To Serve God and Wal-Mart*; Brent E. Riffel, "Feathered Kingdom: Tyson Foods and the Transformation of American Land, Labor, and Law, 1930–2005" (Ph.D. diss., University of Arkansas, 2008).

Chapter 6. "Is Freedom of the Individual Un-American?"

1. Frederic Meyers, *"Right to Work" in Practice* (New York: Fund for the Republic, 1959); Gilbert J. Gall, *The Politics of Right to Work: The Labor Federations as Special Interests, 1943–1979* (Westport, Conn.: Greenwood Press, 1988); David T. Ellwood and Glenn Fine, "The Impact of Right-to-Work Laws on Union Organizing," *Journal of Political Economy* 95 (1987), 250–273; William J. Moore, "The Determinants and Effects of Right-to-Work Laws: A Review of Recent Literature," *Journal of Labor Research* 19 (1998), 445–469; Elizabeth A. Fones-Wolf, *Selling Free Enterprise: The Business Assault on Labor and Liberalism, 1945–60* (Urbana: University of Illinois Press, 1994), 261, 262, 274, 278.

2. Carl Abbott, *The New Urban America: Growth and Politics in Sunbelt Cities* (Chapel Hill: University of North Carolina Press, 1987); Amy Bridges, "Politics and Growth in Sunbelt Cities," in Raymond A. Mohl, ed., *Searching for the Sunbelt: Historical Perspectives on a Region* (Knoxville: University of Tennessee Press," 85–103; Bruce J. Schulman, *From Cotton Belt to Sunbelt: Federal Policy, Economic Development, and the Transformation of the South, 1938–1990* (New York: Oxford University Press, 1991), esp. 162–164; Gavin Wright, *Old South, New South: Revolutions in the Southern Economy Since the Civil War* (New York: Basic Books, 1986), quotation on 257; Neil Foley, *The White Scourge: Mexicans, Blacks, and Poor Whites in Texas Cotton Culture* (Berkeley: University of California Press, 1997); Nayan Shah, *Contagious Divides: Epidemics and Race in San Francisco's Chinatown* (Berkeley: University of California Press, 2001); James C. Cobb, *The Selling of the South: The Southern Crusade for Industrial Development, 1936–1990* (Urbana: University of Illinois Press, 1993); Matthew Lassiter, *The Silent Majority: Suburban Politics in the Sunbelt South* (Princeton, N.J.: Princeton University Press, 2006).

3. Gerald D. Nash, *The American West in the Twentieth Century: A Short History of an Urban Oasis* (Albuquerque: University of New Mexico Press, 1977), and *The Federal Landscape: An Economic History of the Twentieth-Century West* (Tucson: University of Arizona Press, 1999).

4. Nelson Lichtenstein, *Labor's War at Home: The CIO in World War II, with a New Introduction* (Philadelphia: Temple University Press, 2003), 71–81, quotation on 81.

5. William S. Collins, *The New Deal in Arizona* (Phoenix: Arizona State Parks Board, 1999), 20–25; Mary Ellen Glass, *Nevada's Turbulent '50s: Decade of Political and Economic Change* (Reno: University of Nevada Press, 1981), 93, 4.

6. Union density is very difficult to calculate. The most trusted source, and the one Gall used, is Leo Troy and Neil Sheflin's study of union statistics. See Gall, *The Politics of Right to Work*, 235; Leo Troy and Neil Sheflin, *U.S. Union Sourcebook: Membership, Finances, Structure, Directory* (West Orange, N.J.: Industrial Relations Data and Information Services, 1985), 7–3 and 7–4 (tables on these pages also show union growth for all fifty states); Glass, *Nevada's Turbulent '50s*, 73; Robert Kern, ed., *Labor in New Mexico: Unions, Strikes, and Social History Since 1881* (Albuquerque: University of New Mexico Press, 1983), 13; Charles A. Esser, "Pay Hike Request Renewed," November 25, 1946, unattributed newspaper clipping, frame 145, City of Phoenix Scrapbook October 10–November 28, 1946, scrapbook CD 2, Personal and Political Papers of Barry M. Goldwater, Arizona Historical Foundation, Tempe (hereafter Goldwater Papers); "Cops Encounter Union 'Trouble,'" unattributed newspaper clipping, frame 122, City of Phoenix Scrapbook; "Phoenix Firemen Get Wage Boost," unattributed newspaper clipping, frame 110, City of Phoenix Scrapbook; "City Firemen Get Salary Hike," *Arizona Labor Journal* n.p., n.d., frame 113, City of Phoenix Scrapbook; Amy Bridges, *Morning Glories: Municipal Reform in the Southwest* (Princeton, N. J.:

Princeton University Press, 1997), 107; Michael S. Wade, *The Bitter Issue: The Right to Work Law in Arizona* (Tucson: Arizona Historical Society, 1976), 36–41.

7. Donald Garnel, *The Rise of Teamster Power in the West* (Berkeley: University of California Press, 1972), 279–291; Becky M. Nicolaides, *My Blue Heaven: Life and Politics in the Working-Class Suburbs of Los Angeles, 1920–1965* (Chicago: University of Chicago Press, 2002), 79–83; Ruth Milkman, *L.A. Story: Immigrant Workers and the Future of the U.S. Labor Movement* (New York: Russell Sage Foundation, 2006); George Lipsitz, *Rainbow at Midnight: Labor and Culture in the 1940s* (Urbana: University of Illinois Press, 1994), 148–152; Glass, *Nevada's Turbulent '50s*, 12–13; James J. Lorence, *The Suppression of* Salt of the Earth: *How Hollywood, Big Labor, and Politicians Blacklisted a Movie in Cold War America* (Albuquerque: University of New Mexico Press, 1999).

8. Glass, *Nevada's Turbulent '50s*, 41; Barry M. Goldwater, "A Fireside Chat with Mr. Roosevelt," *Phoenix Gazette*, June 23, 1938, n.p., frame 94, scrapbook CD 1, Goldwater Papers; George O. Ford to Barry M. Goldwater, June 24, 1938, frame 90, scrapbook CD 1; Bradford Luckingham, *The Urban Southwest: A Profile History of Albuquerque, El Paso, Phoenix, and Tucson* (El Paso: Texas Western Press, 1982), 83–89.

9. On early right-to-work campaigns, see John G. Shott, *How "Right-to-Work" Laws Are Passed: Florida Sets the Pattern* (Washington, D.C.: Public Affairs Institute, 1956), 2; Ray Stannard Baker, "The Right to Work: The Story of the Non-Striking Miners," in Ellen Fitzpatrick, ed., *Muckraking: Three Landmark Articles* (Boston: Bedford/St. Martin's, 1994). On the incredible continuity in arguments against labor, see Fones-Wolf, *Selling Free Enterprise*; Lawrence G. Richards Jr., "'Union Free and Proud:' America's Anti-Union Culture and the Decline of Organized Labor" (Ph.D. diss., University of Virginia, 2004).

10. For the origins of the National Right to Work Committee (NRTWC), see National Right to Work Committee, sec. 4—special #12, "Facts About: the National Right to Work Committee," December 13, 1962, 5–6. For the nature of the Christian American Association, see Thomas Becnel, *Labor, Church, and the Sugar Establishment: Louisiana, 1887–1976* (Baton Rouge, Louisiana State University Press, 1980), 21–22, 180; Barbara S. Griffith, *Crisis of American Labor: Operation Dixie and the Defeat of the CIO* (Philadelphia: Temple University Press, 1988), 113–115.

11. Darryl Holter, "Labor Law and the Road to Taft-Hartley: Wisconsin's 'Little Wagner Act,' 1935–1945," in *Labor Studies Journal* 15 (Summer 1990), 20–47; "Senate Bill No. 70: Labor Peace Act—Union Security Elections," Labor Peace Act—Amendments 1957, box 22, Colorado Labor Council Collection, Archives of the University of Colorado at Boulder Libraries, Boulder (hereafter Colorado Labor Collection); E. Merrick Dodd, "Some State Legislatures Go to War—on Labor Unions," *Iowa Law Review* 29 (1944), 148–175. For more on state-level efforts to curb union power before 1947, see Charles W. Baird, "Right to Work Before and After 14(b)," *Journal of Labor Research* 19 (1998), 471–493.

12. There is a fourth type of union security agreement, the agency or "fair-share" shop. Under such an agreement, nonmembers have to pay a percentage of union dues. This type of contract negotiation really did not become pertinent until after the 1950s, with the NRTWC pushing to overturn such agreements made in right-to-work states like Texas, which led to a 1963 Supreme Court decision that stipulated that the agency shop was implicitly banned in states that had passed right-to-work laws; see Baird, "Right to Work before and After 14(b)." In the two southern states, the new regulations passed with 55 percent supporting. See Gall, *The Politics of Right to Work*, 234; Philip Taft, *Labor Politics American Style: The California State Federation of Labor* (Cambridge, Mass., 1968), 233. For example, the Arizona right-to-work supporters directly drafted their initiative from the Florida statute; see Wade, *The Bitter Issue*, 36–41.

13. James C. Cobb, *The Most Southern Place on Earth: The Mississippi Delta and the Roots of Regional Identity* (New York: Oxford University Press, 1992), quotation on 227; Cobb, *The Selling of the South*, 96–102; Griffith, *Crisis of American Labor*; Michael Honey, "Industrial Unionism and Racial Justice in Memphis," in Robert Zieger, ed., *Organized Labor in the Twentieth-Century South* (Knoxville: University of Tennessee Press, 1991), 135–147; Thomas A. Scott, "Winning World War II in an Atlanta Suburb: Local Boosters and the Recruitment of Bell Bomber," in Philip Scranton, ed., *The Second Wave: Southern Industrialization from the 1940s to the 1970s* (Athens: University of Georgia Press, 2001), 1–23.

14. Cobb, *The Selling of the South*, 108, and *The Most Southern Place on Earth*, 212; Shott, *How "Right-to-Work" Laws Are Passed*, quotation on 31; Gilbert Gall, "Southern Industrial Workers and Anti-Union Sentiment: Arkansas and Florida in 1944," in Zieger, *Organized Labor in the Twentieth-Century South*, 234.

15. Bernard A. Cook and James R. Watson, *Louisiana Labor: From Slavery to "Right-to-Work"* (Lanham, Md.: University Press of America, 1985), 251–285; Becnel, *Labor, Church, and the Sugar Establishment*, 184–186; J. R. Dempsey, *The Operation of the Right-to-Work Laws: A Comparison Between What the State Legislatures Say About the Meaning of the Laws and How State Court Judges Have Applied These Laws* (Milwaukee: Marquette University Press, 1961), 16; William Canak and Berkeley Miller, "Gumbo Politics: Unions, Business, and Louisiana Right-to-Work Legislation," *Industrial and Labor Relations Review* 43 (1990), 258–271.

16. "New Legislators' List," *Your Legislative Voice*, November 1952, p. 1, Other Chambers of Commerce, 1951–1952, box 67, Governor's Files, Arizona State Library, Archives and Public Records, Phoenix, Ariz. (hereafter Arizona Governor's Files); Wade, *The Bitter Issue*, 40–41; Gladwin Hill, "Labor Showdown Looms in Nevada," *New York Times*, November 10, 1950, folder 11, box 15, Committee on Political Education, Research Division Files, 1944–1979, George Meany Memorial Archives, Silver Spring, Md. (hereafter Research Division Files); Russell R. Elliott, *History of Nevada* (Lincoln: University of Nebraska Press, 1973), 351; James J. Miller, "A History of the

Enactment of the Arizona Right to Work Law" (M.A. thesis, Arizona State University, 1970), 30.

17. G. O. Arnold to Georgia L. Lusk, April 15, 1947, folder 39, box 1, Georgia L. Lusk Papers, New Mexico Commission of Public Records, State Records Center and Archive, Santa Fe (hereafter Lusk Papers).

18. Robert Valdez to Antonio Fernandez, June 16, 1947, folder 39, box 1, Lusk Papers; J. D. Trainor to Lusk, June 17, 1947, folder 39, box 1, Lusk Papers; Anna M. Gemmell to Senator [Carl] Hayden, March 25, 1949, folder 13, box 33, Carl Hayden Papers, Department of Archives and Special Collections, Arizona State University Libraries, Tempe (hereafter Hayden Papers); W. A. Pray to P. T. McCarran, March 2, 1949, no folder or box number, Patrick McCarran Papers, Nevada Historical Society, Reno, Nev. (hereafter McCarran Papers).

19. "1956 Utah Republican State Platform," 4–6, folder 14, box 23, Research Division Files; Mrs. Parker Dunn to Lusk, January 10, 1947, folder 39, box 1, Lusk Papers; E. V. Silverthorne to Hayden, February 28, 1948, folder 13, box 33, Hayden Papers; Colorado and New Mexico Coal Operators Association to Lusk, April 14, 1947, folder 39, box 1, Lusk Papers; Lusk to Erna Fergusson, June 12, 1947, folder 39, box 1, Lusk Papers.

20. Wade, *The Bitter Issue*, 10–17, 36–41; Robert Alan Goldberg, *Barry Goldwater* (New Haven: Yale University Press, 1995), quotation on 69.

21. David Witwer, "Westbrook Pegler and the Anti-Union Movement," *Journal of American History* 92 (September 2005), 540.

22. Lusk to G. F. Coope, April 22, 1947, folder 39, box 1, Lusk Papers; Margaret B. Saloman to McCarran, March 1, 1949, no folder or box number, McCarran Papers.

23. Nevada Citizens Committee, "Did He Used to Say 'Good Morning?'" *Reese River Reveille*, October 23, 1954, "Right to Work Issue," Clipping Files, Nevada Historical Society, Reno.

24. Ibid.

25. For information on the bureaucratization of the labor movement, see Lichtenstein, *Labor's War at Home*; "Reporter's Transcript of Hearing Before Senate Judiciary Committee on Senate Bills Nos. 6 and 61 and House Bill 25 (So-Called 'Right to Work' bills), Held Feb. 8, 1945," p. 71, vol. 5, box 1, Legislative Files, Arizona State Library, Archives and Public Records, Phoenix; E. W. Duhame to Hayden, January 28, 1949, folder 10, box 33, Hayden Papers; "Reporter's Transcript of Hearing," 46–47; Dove Riggins to Sidney P. Osborn, December 29, 1946, p. 1–2, Legislative Matters and General Correspondence, 1939–1948, box 32, Arizona Governor's Files.

26. Jack [Kroll] to George B., n.d., letter likely written between 1951 and 1952, as writer mentions that CIO-PAC had been formed and the run-up to the 1952 election, folder 1, box 22, Research Division Files; Clarence L. Palmer to Mary Goddard, July 14, 1950, folder 11, box 23, Research Division Files; Members United Labor Legislative Committee to All Locals and Central Bodies, n.d., right to work boxes, AFL-CIO, Nevada Collection, Nevada Historical Society, Reno (hereafter

Nevada AFL-CIO Collection), (collection is unprocessed, with materials loose in one of two boxes, with no identifying information to differentiate them); Glass, *Nevada's Turbulent '50s*, 82; Glen Slaughter to James L. McDevitt, "Address Before Arizona State Federation of Labor LLPE [Labor's League for Political Education] Session, Phoenix, Arizona, April 18, 1952," April 30, 1952, 1–2, folder 1, box 22, Research Division Files.

27. Reno Central Trades and Labor Council, "You Were Born with the Right to Work," 1952, right to work boxes, Nevada AFL-CIO Collection; C. C. Day, secretary-treasurer, Central Labor Council, to Lusk, April 14, 1957, folder 39, box 1, Lusk Papers; C. E. Driscoll to Lusk, telegram, May 31, 1947, folder 39, box 1, Lusk Papers.

28. Angus Cauble, chairman, Reno Central Trades and Labor Council, to Washoe County voter, October 1952, right to work boxes, Nevada AFL-CIO Collection; F. G. Broome, Clint Jencks, and L. F. Grinsdale to Lusk, telegram, May 19, 1947, folder 39, box 1, Lusk Papers; "Special Meeting of the New Mexico State Federation of Labor," December 22, 1946, typescript, p. 2, folder 11, box 226, AFL-CIO Collection, Department of Archives and Special Collections, Arizona State University Libraries, Tempe (collection still unprocessed in September 2005).

29. Taft, *Labor Politics American Style*, 234.

30. Mario T. García, *Memories of Chicano History: The Life and Narrative of Bert Corona* (Berkeley: University of California Press, 1994), 169; Jennie Milosivich to Lusk, April 13, 1947, folder 39, box 1, Lusk Papers.

31. Jencks to the brothers and sisters, members and families of Mine-Mill Local 890, February 10, 1954, folder 21, box 27, Clinton Jencks Collection, Archives of the University of Colorado at Boulder Libraries (hereafter Jencks Collection); Adolfo Barela, financial secretary of Local 890 to all local unions, International Union of Mine, Mill and Smelter Workers, March 10, 1952, folder 21, box 27, Jencks Collection.

32. Fones-Wolf, *Selling Free Enterprise*, 262; Robert Kern, "Right to Work Again," *Century*, January 20, 1982, p. 17, folder 21, box 6, Dorothy Cline Papers, Center for Southwest Research, University Libraries, University of New Mexico, Albuquerque; Archbishop of Santa Fe Robert Sanchez, "Statement by Archbishop Sanchez on 'Right to Work,'" typescript, undated, folder 40, box 23, Frank I. Sanchez Papers, Center for Southwest Research, University Libraries, University of New Mexico, Albuquerque.

33. For voting statistics, see Gall, *The Politics of Right to Work*, 234. There was a drawback in Arizona: drafters had failed to outline the consequences for violating the law. Although the legislature passed and the governor signed a 1947 bill designed to rectify the problem, the Arizona labor movement had already mobilized members to get a measure repealing the law placed on the ballot for the 1948 election. See Miller, "History of the Enactment," 1–2. Arizona voters dealt labor another blow in 1948 when citizens voted against repealing the statute. Union density had increased to 24.1 percent (about 41,000 workers), but the number favoring right to work climbed to over 86,000, roughly 59 percent of the vote. See Gall, *The Politics of Right to Work*, 45. The number of citizens voting for right to work increased throughout the 1950s in Nevada as well. As noted, in 1952 the measure barely passed, with just 38,823 votes in

favor. The percentage in favor stayed the same in 1954, even though 1,700 fewer Nevadans cast their ballots. The major jump in support was in 1956, with almost 50,000 citizens supporting the union shop ban and only 42,337 opposing, making the percentages fluctuate to 54 percent and 46 percent, respectively. See Gall, *The Politics of Right to Work*, 234. The 1956 election also included a proposition to amend Nevada's constitution to prohibit right-to-work laws. This measure went down to even greater defeat than the effort to repeal the statute, with 56 percent of Nevada voters opposing such a change. See Glass, *Nevada's Turbulent '50s*, 82. In 1958 anti-union forces crafted a ballot initiative designed to make it almost impossible to bring any more referenda before voters. A twenty-five-person committee in Reno spearheaded the effort, desiring to "prevent the same question being put on the ballot again and again, after its defeat." See Glass, *Nevada's Turbulent '50s*, 83. The Nevada statute required petitioners to not only obtain 10 percent of the electorate's signatures but also acquire consent from 10 percent in thirteen of Nevada's seventeen counties. No longer could unionists rely on finding support solely in the well-unionized Clark County. Even during the push to get the petition referendum on the ballot, unionists were unable to get enough signatures for a fourth union- or open-shop election. It was clear from political advertisements that the 1958 referendum was designed to end the debate. Nevadans supported the measure overwhelmingly, with 61 percent favoring the reform measure, a margin of over 14,000 votes. See Elliott, *History of Nevada*, 355–356, n. 8.

34. Gall, *The Politics of Right to Work*, 231.

35. Fones-Wolf, *Selling Free Enterprise*, 262.

36. Alan Draper, *A Rope of Sand: The AFL-CIO Committee on Political Education, 1955–1967* (New York: Praeger, 1989), 28–30; Sub-Committee of the Executive Council Dealing with Right-to-Work Laws to the Executive Council, April 16,1958, typescript, 1–3 and appendage, folder 7, box 2, Office of the Secretary-Treasurer, Secretary-Treasurer's Files, William F. Schnitzler, 1952–1980, Meany Archives, (hereafter Schnitzler Files); National Right to Work Committee, "Constitution and By-Laws: National Right to Work Committee" (Washington, D.C., June 21, 1958), box 1, National Right to Work Committee Collection, Hoover Institution Archives, Stanford, Calif. (hereafter NRTWC Collection); National Right to Work Committee, *The Right to Work National Newsletter*, February 21, 1955, p. 1, loose in box 4, NRTWC Collection.

37. American Federation of Labor and Congress of Industrial Organizations, *Facts vs. Propaganda: The Truth About "Right to Work" Laws* (Washington, D.C.: American Federation of Labor and Congress of Industrial Organizations, 1958); National Right to Work Committee, "The Economics of Right to Work" (Washington, D.C.: National Right to Work Committee, June 21, 1960), box 1, NRTWC Collection.

38. Cobb, *The Selling of the South*, 254; Canak and Miller, "Gumbo Politics," 265–267; Cook and Watson, *Louisiana Labor*, 293–299.

39. "Arizona Builders for Right to Work," *Right to Work National Newsletter*, September–October 1956, p. 4, loose in box 4, NRTWC Collection; "Shades of Carrie

Nation! Quick Henry—the Arnica!" November 1956, *Right to Work National Newsletter*, p. 1, loose in box 4, NRTWC Collection; Lafayette A. Hoose, "Why I'm For Right-to-Work," reprint from *National Review*, June 17, 1961, box 2, NRTWC Collection.

40. National Council for Industrial Peace, news release, n.d., folder 7, box 2, Schnitzler Files.

41. National Council for Industrial Peace, "Responsible Business Leaders Oppose the So-Called 'Right to Work' Law" (Washington, D.C., n.d.), right to work boxes, Nevada AFL-CIO Collection.

42. Note that my discussion of labor's claims about industrial peace is not meant to imply that there was a postwar labor-management accord, an argument that gained popularity briefly in the 1980s. These claims of an "industrial peace" corroborate Nelson Lichtenstein's assertions that any claims of an agreement or peace between labor and management actually represent labor's concession to a vigorous and potent anti-unionism within American business. See Nelson Lichtenstein, *State of the Union: A Century of American Labor* (Princeton: Princeton University Press, 2002), 98–140.

43. Senate investigations of corruption in the labor movement also made right to work an important issue that year. In 1957 the Senate created the Senate Select Committee on Improper Activities in the Labor or Management Field (also known as the McClellan Committee or Rackets Committee) after various scandals erupted that seemed to tie organized labor to organized crime. The investigations showed the underbelly of labor and were, arguably, a serious blow to labor's legitimacy. See Anthony V. Baltakis, "Agendas of Investigation: The McClellan Committee, 1957–1958" (Ph.D. diss., University of Akron, 1997); David Witwer, *Corruption and Reform in the Teamsters Union* (Urbana: University of Illinois Press, 2003), 157–211.

44. AFL-CIO Right-to-Work Campaign, summary statement of expenses as of October 3, 1958, typescript, p. 1, folder 8, box 2, Schnitzler Files; "Breakdown of Use of Films and Spots," November 7, 1958, typescript, 1–4, folder 8, box 2, Schnitzler Files; George A. Cavender to Jack Kroll and James McDevitt, November 8, 1956, p. 1, folder 2, box 9, Colorado Labor Collection; Carpenters Local 2243, meeting, August 8, 1958, n.p., minute book of Local Union no. 2243, Durango, Colo., February 1, 1955 to May 22, 1959, box 1, L. U. #2243 Durango, United Brotherhood of Carpenters and Joiners of America Local Unions Collection, Archives of the University of Colorado at Boulder Libraries.

45. "*This* Happened in a 'Right-to-Work' State: It Could Happen Here!" 1958, folder 1, box 3, Research Division Files; Robert O. Self, *American Babylon: Race and the Struggle for Postwar Oakland* (Princeton: Princeton University Press, 2003), 87–95, esp. 88.

46. Cavender to Joseph T. Zamora, August 21, 1958, in Compulsory Open Shop—Joe Zamora, box 25, 2nd accession, Colorado Labor Collection; Zamora to Cavender, August 29, 1958, Compulsory Open Shop—Joe Zamora, box 25, 2nd accession, Colorado Labor Collection; Zamora to Cavender, September 23, 1958, Compulsory Open Shop—Joe Zamora, box 25, 2nd accession, Colorado Labor Collection.

47. National Council for Industrial Peace, "Sample Speech for Study Groups and Speakers' Bureau," p. 10, loose papers, box 24, Colorado Labor Collection; Colorado CC, n.d., folder 16, box 2, Morris S. Novik Papers, 1940–1989, Meany Archives.

48. Zamora to Cavender, November 6, 1958, Compulsory Open Shop—Joe Zamora, box 25, 2nd accession, Colorado Labor Collection; Gall, *The Politics of Right to Work*, 234; "Labor Took Farming Communities in Fight Against Proposition 18, Victory Margin 990,862 Votes," *California Labor Federation, AFL-CIO Weekly News Letter*, January 2, 1959, p. 1, folder 23, box 2, Schnitzler Papers; Lisa McGirr, *Suburban Warriors: The Origins of the New American Right* (Princeton: Princeton University Press 2001), 67.

49. McGirr, *Suburban Warriors*, 115. In her dissertation, Kim Phillips-Fein extends McGirr's arguments to other conservative campaigns across the country; see Phillips-Fein, "Top-Down Revolution: Businessmen, Intellectuals and Politicians Against the New Deal" (Ph.D. diss., Columbia University, 2005), 366.

Chapter 7. Singing "The Right-to-Work Blues"

For Victor Marchioro.

Catherine Powell of the California Labor Archives and Research Center at San Francisco State University and Chuck Marcus of the library at the University of California, Hastings College of the Law, were particularly helpful to me as I researched and wrote this essay. My thanks to them. Dean Frank Wu, Dean Nell Newton, Dean Shauna Marshall, and Dean Evan Lee, as well as the Chip Robertson Fund, provided much needed financial support for this project. Charles Belle and Kate Feng were both first-rate research assistants. Finally, I'd like to thank Nelson Lichtenstein, Elizabeth Tandy Shermer, and the other participants in the American Right and Labor Conference at the University of California, Santa Barbara, for their valuable thoughts and comments.

1. "Right to Work Blues," Papers of the Central Labor Council of Alameda County (hereafter CLCAC), Labor Archives and Research Center, San Francisco State University (hereafter LARC), box 36, folder 24.

2. Under the NLRA, a bargaining unit is a group of workers who share common interests to such a degree that it is appropriate for a union to negotiate a single collective bargaining agreement on their behalf.

3. California Proposition 18, section 5 (1958).

4. For information about the politics of the right-to-work movement in the decade following the passage of Taft-Hartley, see Gilbert J. Gall, *The Politics of Right to Work: The Labor Federations as Special Interests, 1943–1979* (Westport, Conn.: Greenwood Press, 1988),18–128; Paul Sultan, *Right-to-Work Laws: A Study in Conflict* (Los Angeles: Institute of Industrial Relations, 1958), 43–62; Joseph Richard Dempsey, *The Operation of the Right-to-Work Laws* (Milwaukee: Marquette University Press, 1961), 15–28.

5. See Kurt Schuparra, *The Triumph of the Right: The Rise of the California Conservative Movement, 1945–1966* (Armonk, N.Y.: M. E. Sharpe, 1998), 30, 32–35, 38; "Workers Rights on Trial in California," LARC Ephemera Collection, "Right-to-Work—Prop. 18" folder; "Who's Who? Behind Little Front Men of Compulsory Open Shop Are Big Boys with Billions," LARC Ephemera Collection, "Right-to-Work—Prop. 18" folder; Daniel V. Flanagan, "Big Fight in California," *AFL-CIO American Federationist* (June 1958), 6–8.

6. For detailed descriptions of the 1958 gubernatorial campaign, see Schuparra, *Triumph of the Right*, 27–41; Gayle B. Montogomery and James W. Johnson, *One Step From the White House: The Rise and Fall of William F. Knowland* (Berkeley: University of California Press, 1998), 228–254; Gladwin Hill, *The Dancing Bear: An Inside Look at California Politics* (Cleveland: World, 1968), 139–162; Herbert L. Phillips, *Big Wayward Girl: An Informal Political History of California* (Garden City, N.Y.: Doubleday, 1968), 177–186; David Halberstam, *The Powers That Be* (New York: Knopf, 1979), 262–266; Robert Gottlieb and Irene Wolt, *Thinking Big: The Story of The Los Angeles Times, Its Publishers, and Their Influence on Southern California* (New York: Putnam, 1977), 280–285; Royce D. Delmatier, Clarence F. McIntosh, and Earl G. Waters, *The Rumble of California Politics, 1848–1970* (New York: John Wiley & Sons, 1970), 337–353; Robert O. Self, *American Babylon: Race and the Struggle for Postwar Oakland* (Princeton: Princeton University Press, 2003), 87–95; Kevin Starr, *Golden Dreams: California in an Age of Abundance, 1950–1963* (New York: Oxford University Press, 2009), 212–216.

7. Hill, *The Dancing Bear*, 144.

8. Delmatier, McIntosh, and Waters, *The Rumble of California Politics*, 339. For descriptions of Knight's term as governor as well as the moderate California Republicanism of the 1940s and 1950s in general, see Starr, *Golden Dreams*, 191–216; Delmatier, *The Rumble of California Politics*, 300–36; Hill, *The Dancing Bear*, 91–107, 142–43.

9. Delmatier, McIntosh, and Waters, *The Rumble of California Politics*, 341.

10. Gall, *The Politics of Right to Work*, 118.

11. Delmatier, McIntosh, and Waters, *The Rumble of California Politics*, 341.

12. Quoted in Hill, *The Dancing Bear*, 159.

13. Schuparra, *The Triumph of the Right*; Lisa McGirr, *Suburban Warriors: The Origins of the New American Right* (Princeton: Princeton University Press, 2001).

14. Office of the Secretary of State, State of California, "Proposed Amendments to Constitution Propositions and Proposed Laws Together With Arguments" (Sacramento, 1958), 26.

15. Louis Ets-Hokin, "Prop. 18—Yes or No?" *San Francisco Examiner*, October 24, 1958, sec. 2, p. 2.

16. Ibid.

17. "With or Without a Union Card," *Los Angeles Times*, October 9, 1958, pt. 3, p. 4. The *San Francisco Chronicle*'s editorial sounded the same theme ("Individual Rights Hinge on Prop. 18," *San Francisco Chronicle*, October 29, 1958, p. 32), as did

Knowland himself (William Knowland, "Why Not a Bill of Rights for Labor?" *Reader's Digest*, May 1958, 78).

18. Self, *American Babylon*, 90.

19. See, e.g., advertisement, *Los Angeles Times*, September 21, 1958, pt. 1, p.12. See also advertisement, *San Francisco Examiner*, October 29, 1958, sec. 1, p. 12.

20. Cartoon, David F. Selvin Papers, LARC, box 27, folder 2.

21. Cartoon, *Los Angeles Times*, October 16, 1958, pt. 3, p. 6.

22. See, for example, "Hoodlum-Union Links Assailed by Knowland," *Los Angeles Times*, September 1, 1958, pt. 1, p. 15; "Knowland Sees Reuther, Hoffa Plot to Win U.S.," *Los Angeles Times*, September 22, 1958, pt. 1, p 25; "Need for Union Reforms Cited by Knowland," *Los Angeles Times*, September 23, 1958, pt. 1, p. 18.

23. Mrs. William F. Knowland, "At Stake in California: Why Knowland Backs the Right to Work," reprinted from *Human Events,* September 29, 1958, Selvin Collection, box 27, folder 9.

24. Advertisement, "Why Are the Promoters of Proposition 18 So Afraid to Tell the Truth?" *Los Angeles Times*, October 19, 1958, pt. 1A, p. 10.

25. Ibid.

26. Advertisement, "Look Who's Coming to the Rescue!" *San Francisco Examiner*, October 28, 1958, sec. 1, p. 16.

27. "WHO ARE THEY?" Poster Collection, LARC. This poster ran as an advertisement in California newspapers. See *Oakland Tribune*, October 22, 1958, p. 18.

28. "Save Our State from the Compulsory Open Shop," p. 30, LARC Ephemera, "Right-to-Work—Prop. 18" folder.

29. "WHO ARE THEY?" See also advertisement, "Prop. 18 Backed by Big Money Interests," *Los Angeles Times*, October 5, 1958, pt. 1, p. 22.

30. Self, *American Babylon*, 89.

31. "Attitude Survey," September 29, 1958, CLCAC, box 31, folder 6, 2, 12.

32. *Alameda County Tribunal*, n.d., p. 1, CLCAC, box 36, folder 12.

33. Office of the Secretary of State, State of California, "Proposed Amendments to Constitution Propositions and Proposed Laws Together With Arguments", 25–26 (Sacramento, 1958).

34. CLCAC, box 33, folder 4.

35. *California Voter Guide*, 26.

36. See the pro-18 ad in the *Los Angeles Times,* above, as well as Mrs. Knowland, "At Stake in California."

37. Mrs. Knowland, "At Stake in California," 2.

38. Ibid.

39. For a nice summary of the arguments used in a large number of these campaigns, see Sultan, *Right-to-Work Laws*, 43–74.

40. Memorandum from Lester Bailey to all directors, September 10, 1958, CLCAC, box 33, folder 10.

41. See below, n. 67.

42. Quoted in Sultan, *Right-to-Work Laws*, 80.

43. Stanley Robertson, "Some Interesting Right to Work Slants," *Los Angeles Sentinel*, October 23, 1958, p. C1.

44. Joseph V. Baker, "The Negro and His Right to Work," 2, pamphlet in the possession of author.

45. Ibid., 4–5.

46. Ibid., 6.

47. Ibid., 9; emphasis in original.

48. Ibid., 9–10; emphasis in original.

49. For the NAACP's "Don't Buy Budweiser" campaign in Los Angeles, see "What the Branches Are Doing," *The Crisis*, August–September 1958, 416. For the history of discriminatory craft unions in the Bay Area, see Charles Wollenberg, "James v. Marinship: Trouble on the New Black Frontier," in Daniel Cornford, ed., *Working People of California* (Berkeley: University of California Press, 1995), 159–179.

50. Baker, "The Negro and His Right to Work," 3.

51. Ibid. 6–7.

52. "Proposition 18 Proponents Rap NAACP," *Los Angeles Sentinel*, October 30, 1958, p. A16; letter, Maurice A. Dawkins to Claude V. Worrell, May 31, 1958, in John Bracey, Jr., Sharon Harley, and August Meier, eds., *Papers of the NAACP*, part 13 (*NAACP and Labor*), series B (Cooperation with Organized Labor), supplement, 1956–1965, reel 14, frame 9 (hereafter "NAACP Labor Papers"). Worrell's stump speech seems to have directly lifted phrases from Baker's flyer. See "Attorney Flays Practices of Labor Bosses," *Los Angeles Sentinel*, October 16, 1958, p. 12.

53. "Both Sides of California's Controversial Initiative," *San Francisco Sun-Reporter*, May 3, 1958, p. 3, May 10, 1958, p. 5, May 17, 1958, p. 13, and May 24, 1958, p. 3.

54. "Both Sides," May 24.

55. "Both Sides," May 3.

56. Ibid.

57. Ray Marshall, *The Negro and Organized Labor* (New York: John Wiley & Sons, 1965), 89–132; Robert H. Zieger, *For Jobs and Freedom: Race and Labor in America Since 1865* (Lexington: University Press of Kentucky, 2007), 139–174.

58. Herbert Hill, "The Right to Work Laws and the Negro Worker," *The Crisis* (June–July 1958), 332.

59. Ibid.

60. Zieger, *For Jobs and Freedom*, 168; Paul D. Moreno, *Black Americans and Organized Labor: A New History* (Baton Rouge: Louisiana State University Press, 2006), 232–233.

61. Clarence Mitchell, "NAACP Statement Before Senate Committee on Labor and Public Welfare," February 18, 1947, "NAACP, 1946–47" folder, box 149, CIO Office of the Secretary-Treasurer Records Walter P. Reuther Library, Wayne State University, Detroit, Michigan. My thanks to Sophia Lee for bringing this source to my attention.

62. Franklin Williams and C. L. Dellums to all NAACP presidents, area and regional officers, California, n.d., LARC, Papers of the California Labor Federation, box 36, folder 12; "'Right-to-Work' Laws," *The Crisis*, November 1958, 567; "Right to Work," *The Crisis*, December 1958, 620.

63. Hill's article lays out the NAACP's position in the most detail. Hill, "'Right to Work' Laws and the Negro Worker," 327–332.

64. See, for example, the records of Alameda County Labor Council representatives sent to speak at local NAACP branches, CLCAC Papers, box 32, folder 9. For records of radio advertising purchases and the script of an ad mentioning fair employment practices and Proposition 18, see CLCAC Papers, box 33, folders 2, and 11, respectively. For records of other meetings, literature distributions, and a list of African American leaders to be contacted about Proposition 18, see "Daily Activities Report, Tuesday August 5th," CLCAC Papers, box 34, folder 18; "East Bay Personalities for Citizens' Committee Against Prop. 18," CLCAC, box 35, folder 10; "Resume of Activities and Accomplishments," CLCAC Papers, box 31, folder 6. For International Longshore Workers' Union President Harry Bridges on Proposition 18 and union discrimination, see International Longshore Workers' Union news release, October 29, 1958, 6–7, LARC, California Labor Federation Papers, box 36, folder 11. For San Francisco Labor Council publicist and labor journalist David Selvin's notes and speeches on the same subject, see "Notes on the Record of Labor in San Francisco on Civil Rights and Equal Practices" and "The Unpleasant Facts," in Selvin Papers, box 28, folder 2. For anti-18 ads in African American newspapers, see *San Francisco Sun-Reporter*, September 27, 1958, 11; October 4, 1958, 4; October 11, 1958, 8; October 25, 1958, 5; November 1, 1958, 7. Also see *Los Angeles Sentinel*, October 23, 1958, A5; October 30, 1958, A18, C3.

65. Williams to all NAACP staff members, etc., August 6, 1958, NAACP Labor Papers, frame 31.

66. J. Francis Pohlhaus to Herbert Hill, March 18, 1958, NAACP Labor Papers, frame 4.

67. "Keep Mississippi out of California," CLCAC Papers, box 36, folder 20.

68. "This Happened in a Right-to-Work State!" LARC Ephemera Collection, "Right-to-Work—Prop. 18" folder.

69. For letters in which Wilkins provides union leaders with the language that appeared in the pamphlet, see Roy Wilkins to Boris Shishkin, September 19, 1958, NAACP Labor Papers, frames 45–46; Wilkins to Emery F. Bacon, August 29, 1958, NAACP Labor Papers, frame 33.

70. "NAACP Condemns So-Called 'Right to Work' Laws," LARC, California Labor Federation Papers, box 36, folder 12.

71. For an unexpurgated copy of the letter, see "Right-to-work 1950s-1960s Folder," Freedom Center Ephemera File, University Archives and Special Collections Unit, Pollak Library, California State University, Fullerton.

72. "The Brown-Powers Team," *Los Angeles Sentinel*, October 23, 1958, A6.

73. Editorial, "Stop Dixie Labor Relations from Being Saddled on California," *San Francisco Sun-Reporter*, October 25, 1958, supplement, 1.

74. Ibid.

75. "Negroes and the 'Right-to-Work,'" *San Francisco Sun-Reporter* April 5, 1958, 14.

76. Ibid.

77. "Speaking Engagement," record of talk given by CLCAC at Berkeley NAACP branch on August 28, 1958, CLCAC Papers, box 23, folder 9.

78. "East Bay Personalities for Citizens' Committee Against Prop. 18," CLCAC Papers, box 35, folder 10.

79. For Worrell's trials and tribulations, see Dawkins to Worrell, May 31; "Attorney Flays Practices of Labor Bosses," *Los Angeles Sentinel*, October 16, 1958, B12. For the testy exchange of letters and telegrams between Marcus and Wilkins, see NAACP Labor Papers, frames 10–23.

80. Wilkins to James E. McCann, July 13, 1958, NAACP Labor Papers, frame 25.

81. George Beavers to Wilkins, November 17, 1958, NAACP Labor Papers, frame, 90–91. For biographical information on Beavers, see http://www.blackpast.org/?q = aaw/ beavers-jr-george-1892–1989 (accessed December 9, 2008).

82. Wilkins to James McDevitt, December 16, 1958, NAACP Labor Papers, frame 76.

83. I generated this information from the data from this poll, available at http:// arc.irss.unc.edu/dvn/dv/odvn/faces/study/StudyPage.jsp?studyId = 2407 (accessed December 8, 2008).

84. For contemporary reporting of African American votes, see "Responsibilities of Victory," *San Francisco Sun-Reporter*, November 8, 1958, 10; Self, *American Babylon*, 91. My own empirical work confirms that African Americans voted against Proposition 18 in overwhelming numbers. Only 19 percent of voters in the census tracts that made up the Western Addition voted for the proposition. The California census tracts with the highest percentage of African Americans were all in Los Angeles County, particularly in South Central Los Angeles. Each of these tracts was at least 96 percent African American. In the electoral precincts that most closely overlapped with these tracts, Proposition 18 received only 10 percent of the vote. For census data from 1960, see   http://www.socialexplorer.com/pub/maps/map3.aspx?g = 0&mapi = 1960   Census Tract (public ed.)&themei = 1(accessed September 3, 2009). Precinct-by-precinct voting returns are available at the California State Archives. Many thanks to Chuck Marcus and Michael Salerno for helping me assemble this data.

85. "Responsibilities of Victory," *San Francisco Sun-Reporter*, November 8, 1958, 10.

86. For the failure of liberalism to satisfactorily address issues of fair employment practices and the African American response to that fact, see Nancy MacLean, *Freedom Is Not Enough: The Opening of the American Workplace* (Cambridge: Harvard University Press, 2006); Judith Stein, *Running Steel, Running America: Race, Economic Policy,*

and the Decline of Liberalism (Chapel Hill: University of North Carolina Press, 1998); Thomas J. Sugrue, *Sweet Land of Liberty: The Forgotten Struggle for Civil Rights in the North* (New York: Random House, 2008), 266–279, 357–367, 411–412.

Chapter 8. Whose Rights?

This work benefited from comments by my colleagues at the University of Pennsylvania Law School and the audience and commentators at the 2010 Policy History Conference, the American Society for Legal History's 2008 Annual Conference, and the 2008 Legal History Consortium Conference. I thank also Reuel Schiller for delivering the paper on my behalf at the American Right and U.S. Labor: Politics, Ideology, and Imagination Conference. I am particularly indebted to Daniel Ernst, Sarah Gordon, Howard Lesnick, Nelson Lichtenstein, Elizabeth Tandy Shermer, and Michael Wachter for their helpful suggestions and to the American Historical Association's Littleton-Griswold Prize for its support of this research.

1. National Right to Work Legal Defense Foundation, "We're Working to Protect Human and Civil Rights for America's Wage Earners," n.d. [1972], mailer, folder 8, box 25, United Auto Workers Washington Office, Steve Schlossberg Collection, Archives of Labor and Urban Affairs (ALUA), Wayne State University, Detroit.

2. The outstanding works that tie the rise of postwar conservatism to America's history of racial subordination are too numerous to cite. Exemplary texts include Dan T. Carter, *The Politics of Rage: George Wallace, the Origins of New Conservatism, and the Transformation of American Politics* (New York: Simon & Schuster, 1995); Joseph Crespino, *In Search of Another Country: Mississippi and the Conservative Counterrevolution* (Princeton: Princeton University Press, 2007); Kevin M. Kruse, *White Flight: Atlanta and the Making of Modern Conservatism* (Princeton: Princeton University Press, 2007); Matthew D. Lassiter, *The Silent Majority: Suburban Politics in the Sunbelt South* (Princeton: Princeton University Press, 2007). Classic treatments of racial backlash among the white working class include Ronald Formisano, *Boston Against Busing: Race, Class, and Ethnicity in the 1960s and 1970s* (Chapel Hill: University of North Carolina Press, 1991); Jonathon Rieder, *Canarsie: The Jews and Italians of Brooklyn Against Liberalism* (Cambridge: Harvard University Press, 1985). Excellent histories of conservatives' anti-union mobilization, which argue that, at least outside the South, pro-business, anti –New Deal politics, not race, were the best explanation, include Elizabeth Fones-Wolf's *Selling Free Enterprise: The Business Assault on Labor and Liberalism: 1945–1960* (Urbana: University of Illinois Press, 1994) and Kim Phillips-Fein's *Invisible Hands: The Making of the Conservative Movement from the New Deal to Reagan* (New York: W. W. Norton, 2009). Elizabeth Tandy Shermer, "Counter-Organizing the Sunbelt: Right-to-Work Campaigns and Anti-Union Conservatism, 1943–1958," *Pacific Historical Review* 78 (February 2009): 81–118, places this mobilization at the center of the rise of the Right in the 1940s and 1950s. Lisa McGirr, *Suburban Warriors: The Origins of the New American Right* (Princeton: Princeton University Press, 2001), argues that antigovernment politics rather than race also drove the grassroots conservatism of the late 1950s and 1960s.

3. National Labor Relations (Wagner) Act, §1, ch. 395, 74 Stat. 450 (1935); Railway Labor Act, ch. 691, 48 Stat. 1185 (1934). Exemplary histories of the CIO include Nelson Lichtenstein, *Labor's War at Home: The CIO in World War II* (New York: Cambridge University Press, 1982); Steven Fraser, *Labor Will Rule: Sidney Hillman and the Rise of American Labor* (Ithaca: Cornell University Press, 1991); Robert H. Zieger, *The CIO, 1935–1955* (Chapel Hill: University of North Carolina Press, 1995). Despite labor's apparent strength in the 1950s, many historians argue that its promise had already passed, whether due to the labor laws' bureaucratizing effect, the labor movement's failure to adequately address racism or organize the South, anti-Communism's corrosive effect, or anti–New Deal, pro-business activism. See, for example, Nelson Lichtenstein, *State of the Union: A Century of American Labor* (Princeton: Princeton University Press, 2002); Christopher L. Tomlins, *The State and the Unions: Labor Relations, Law, and the Organized Labor Movement in America, 1880–1960* (New York: Cambridge University Press, 1985); Paul Frymer, *Black and Blue: African Americans, the Labor Movement, and the Decline of the Democratic Party* (Princeton: Princeton University Press, 2007); Robert Rodgers Korstad, *Civil Rights Unionism: Tobacco Workers and the Struggle for Democracy in the Mid-Twentieth Century South* (Chapel Hill: University of North Carolina Press, 2003); Ellen Schrecker, *Many Are the Crimes: McCarthyism in America* (Boston: Little, Brown, 1998); Fones-Wolf, *Selling Free Enterprise*; Jennifer Klein, *For All These Rights: Business, Labor, and the Shaping of America's Public-Private Welfare State* (Princeton: Princeton University Press, 2003). Those who attribute labor's eventual decline to later events include Kevin Boyle, *The UAW and the Heyday of American Liberalism, 1945–1968* (Ithaca: Cornell University Press, 1995); Judith Stein, *Running Steel, Running America: Race, Economic Policy, and the Decline of Liberalism* (Chapel Hill: University of North Carolina Press, 1998); Reuel E. Schiller, "From Group Rights to Individual Liberties: Post-War Labor Law, Liberalism, and the Waning of Union Strength," *Berkeley Journal of Employment and Labor Law* 20 (1999): 1.

4. Daniel R. Ernst, *Lawyers Against Labor: From Individual Rights to Corporate Liberalism* (Champaign: University of Illinois Press, 1995); Chad Pearson, "'Organize and Fight': Communities, Employers and Open-Shop Movements, 1890–1920" (Ph.D. diss., University of Albany, State University of New York, 2008); Donald R. Richberg, *Labor Union Monopoly: A Clear and Present Danger* (Chicago: Henry Regnery, 1957), v–vii; Phillips-Fein, *Invisible Hands*, 90–97, 117–124.

5. Friedrich A. Hayek, *The Constitution of Liberty* (Chicago: University of Chicago Press, 1960), 269; see also Sylvester Petro, *The Labor Policy of the Free Society* (New York: Ronald Press, 1957), 97–99,107–109; Edward A. Keller, *The Case for Right-to-Work Laws: A Defense of Voluntary Unionism* (Chicago: Heritage Foundation Press, 1956), 37–45. I thank Howard Lesnick for pointing out that unions had also long contended that open shops left unionized workers vulnerable to employer discrimination.

6. William B. Ruggles, "The Genesis of Right to Work: How the Name for Laws Prohibiting Compulsory Unionism Originated in 1941," excerpts from speech, September 29, 1966, box 1, National Right to Work Committee (NRWC) Papers, Hoover Institution Archives, Stanford, Calif.; Fones-Wolf, *Selling Free Enterprise*, 261; The Labor Management Relations (Taft-Hartley) Act of 1947, Pub. L. No. 120–101, 61 Stat. 136. Under Taft-Hartley, unions also could not enforce union-shop provisions against employees who were denied or terminated from union membership for any reason other than nonpayment of dues. On state right-to-work campaigns in the 1940s and 1950s, see Fones-Wolf, *Selling Free Enterprise*, ch. 9; Gilbert Gall, *The Politics of Right to Work: The Labor Federations as Special Interest, 1943–1979* (Westport, Conn.: Greenwood Press, 1988); Shermer, "Counter-Organizing the Sunbelt." Unions adopted agency-shop agreements to work around state right-to-work laws; see Charles W. Baird, "The Right to Work Before and After 14(b)," *Journal of Labor Research* 19 (1998): 471–493.

7. Ernst, *Lawyers Against Labor*. On the turn to rights in the 1940s, see Alan Brinkley, *The End of Reform: New Deal Liberalism in Recession and War* (New York: Alfred A. Knopf, 1995).

8. *DeMille v. American Federation of Radio Artists*, 31 Cal. 2d 139 (Cal. 1947), aff'd 175 P.2d 851 (Cal. Ct. App. 1946); "Union Levy of $1 on DeMille Upheld," *New York Times*, January 25, 1945.

9. 64 Stat. 1238, §2, 11 (1951).

10. Note, "The New Union Shop Provision in the Railway Labor Act," *Indiana Law Journal* 31, no. 1 (1955): 148–159, quote on 158; National Committee for Union Shop Abolition, "Its Background, Origin and Plan of Action," n.d. [1952–54], pamphlet, box 1, NRWC Papers. A number of railroad unionists turned right-to-work activists were also members of a failed industrial union, the United Railroad Operating Crafts. See Lafayette Hooser, "The Meaning of 'Laborism' and How to Stop It," n.d. [late 1950s], box 1, NRWC Papers; George R. Horton and Ellsworth H. Steele, "The Unity Issues Among Railroad Engineers and Firemen," *Industrial and Labor Relations Review* 10, no. 1 (October 1956): 48–69, 66–68.

11. *Hanson v. Union Pacific Railroad Co.*, 160 Neb. 669, 695–700 (Neb. 1955).

12. George C. Leef, *Free Choice for Workers: A History of the Right to Work Movement* (Ottawa, Ill.: Jameson Books, 2005), 43–44; Shermer, "Counter-Organizing the Sunbelt," 115; NRWC, "Constitution and By-Laws," pamphlet, June 21, 1958, box 1, NRWC Papers.

13. Fones-Wolf, *Selling Free Enterprise*, 262. See also Kimberly Phillips-Fein, "'As Great an Issue as Slavery or Abolition': Economic Populism, the Conservative Movement and the Right-to-Work Campaigns of 1958," *Journal of Policy History* (forthcoming); Shermer, "Counter-Organizing the Sunbelt."

14. Report of the Subcommittee on RTW laws to the Executive Council, April 16, 1958, AFL-CIO, Office of the Secretary-Treasurer, William F. Schnitzler, 1952–1980, Reference Files (Schnitzler Papers), 1954–1967, folder 7, box 2, series 1, RG 2–007,

George Meany Memorial Archives, Silver Spring, Md.; Report of Staff Committee on Restrictive Legislation, August 14, 1958, Schnitzler Papers, folder 7, box 2, series 1, RG 2–007; "Films and Spots," November 7, 1958, Schnitzler Papers, folder 8, box 2, series 1, RG 2–007; Clarence Mitchell, NAACP Statement Before Senate Committee on Labor and Public Welfare," February 18, 1947, "NAACP, 1946–47" Folder, box 149, CIO Secretary-Treasurer's Office Collection, ALUA, p. 5; Gilbert J. Gall, "Thoughts on Defeating Right-to-Work: Reflections on Two Referendum Campaigns," in *Organized Labor and American Politics, 1894–1994: The Labor-Liberal Alliance*, ed. Kevin Boyle (Albany: State University of New York Press, 1998); Reuel Schiller, Chapter 7 in this volume.

15. NRWC, "The National Labor Relations Act (NLRA): Enemy of Employee Rights," n.d. [1960], pamphlet, box 1, NRWC Papers; Jerry Norton, "A Fighter for Freedom," *Conservative Digest*, November 1975, folder 14, box 29, UAW Washington Office, Schlossberg Collection; Gall, *The Politics of Right to Work*, 115–117, 144.

16. "The Right to Work Laws: A Pro-Con Discussion with Rebuttals," Joseph F. Wagner, Inc., 1958, pamphlet, folder 28, box 1, Edward A. Keller Papers, University of Notre Dame Archives, Notre Dame, Ind.; Keller, *The Case for Right-to-Work Laws*; Barry Goldwater to Edward Keller, February 5, 1958, folder 18, box 1, Keller Papers; Keller to Clyde E. Broussard, December 26, 1956, folder 12, box 1, Keller Papers.

17. *Railway Employes' Department v. Hanson*, 351 U.S. 225, 232, 238 (1956); *Street v. International Association of Machinists*, 367 U.S. 740 (1961).

18. *Street*, 367 U.S. 740.

19. NRWC, "Area of Increase in 1962 Program," n.d. [1962], box 1, NRWC Papers.

20. Baird, "Right to Work," 489–490; NRWC, "The Right to Refrain: How and Why the Advocates of Compulsory Unionism Were Beaten," report, March 1, 1966, box 2, NRWC Papers; Everett McKinley Dirksen, "Individual Freedom Versus Compulsory Unionism: A Constitutional Problem," *De Paul Law Review* 15, no. 2 (1966), reprint, box 1, NRWC Papers; Ralph de Toledano, "The Case for Right to Work," *Politics* 4, no. 10 (March 19, 1969), reprint, box 1, NRWC Papers. Labor, having just lost its fight to repeal the closed-shop ban, assessed NWRC's congressional support quite differently.

21. John Kilcullen, "Background on Legal Challenges of Compulsory Unionism," October 1, 1967, speech, box 2, NRWC Papers. On the growth of individual rights during this period and their adverse potential for labor, see Schiller, "From Group Rights to Individual Liberties."

22. "With Honesty and Courage: Defending America's Working Men and Women; A History of the National Right to Work Legal Defense Foundation," enclosed in Ray Bowie to Reed Larson, Rex Reed, Edith Hakola, and Duke Cadwallader, October 17, 1979, memo, folder 1, box 25, John Davenport Papers, Hoover Institution Archives, Stanford University.

23. Ibid.

24. Ibid.; Thomas J. Harris to Roy Horton, November 29, 1971, folder 8, box 24, Schlossberg Collection; Tom Nelson, "Compulsory Union Payments Are Challenged," *Dickinson Press*, December 30, 1971, 1, folder 12, box 24, Schlossberg Collection; NRWLDF, "Civil Rights of Workers Protected by Legal Victories," May 6, n.d. [1972] news release, folder 2, box 25, Davenport Papers; Reed Larson, "A Place to Turn," National Right to Work News Service, June 14, 1973, box 1, NRWC Papers; "The Right-to-Work Issue: Sleeping but Not Dead," *Industry Week*, June 16, 1975, folder 5, box 25, Schlossberg Collection; Bowie to Larson et al., October 17, 1979; Reed Larson, "Legal Defense Program," May 1, 1986, report, folder 8, box 25, Davenport Papers.

25. Reed Larson, "An Important First Step," National Right to Work News Service, March 8, 1973, box 1, NRWC Papers.

26. Ibid.; Reed Larson, "Supreme Court Raises Questions," National Right to Work News Service, December 23, 1976, box 1, NRWC Papers.

27. U.S. Const., amends. I, V, and XIV.

28. New Deal economic regulation was hardly unprecedented; see Morton Keller, *Regulating a New Economy: Public Policy and Economic Change in America, 1900–1933* (Cambridge: Harvard University Press, 1990); William Novak, *The People's Welfare: Law and Regulation in Nineteenth-Century America* (Chapel Hill: University of North Carolina Press, 1996). However, the New Deal transformed the scope and depth of economic regulation.

29. *Lochner v. New York*, 198 U.S. 45, 63 (1905); *Hammer v. Dagenhart*, 247 U.S. 251 (1918); *Adair v. United States*, 208 U.S. 161, 178 (1908). On why courts embraced substantive due process, compare William Forbath, "The Ambiguities of Free Labor," *Wisconsin Law Review* (1985): 786–800, with Robert C. Post, "Defending the Lifeworld: Substantive Due Process in the Taft Court Era," *Boston University Law Review* 78 (1998): 1489. Historians who argue that courts were not as antipathetic toward regulation as the standard narrative suggests include Michael Willrich, "The Case for Courts: Law and Political Development in the Progressive Era," in *The Democratic Experiment: New Directions in American Political History*, ed. Meg Jacobs et al. (Princeton: Princeton University Press, 2003), 198–221; Melvin I. Urofsky, "State Courts and Protective Legislation During the Progressive Era: A Reevalution," *Journal of American History* 72 (1985): 63–91. Risa L. Goluboff, in "Deaths Greatly Exaggerated," *Law and History Review* 24 (Spring 2006): 201–208, argues that the New Deal did not extinguish substantive due process.

30. Shermer, "Counter-Organizing the Sunbelt," 90–103; McGirr, *Suburban Warriors*, chs. 1–2, especially 103–107; Walter L. Scratch, "Douglas Employes File Suit," *Santa Monica Evening Outlook*, August 21, 1962, reprint, box 1, NRWC Papers; "29 Workers File Suit Against Douglas, IAM in Legal Challenge to Compulsory Unionism," *Free Choice*, October 1967, box 3, NRWC Papers; "In Memorium, George Seay, 1907–1971," *Free Choice*, July–August 1971, folder 7, box 25, Schlossberg Collection.

31. On public worker unionization, see Joseph A. McCartin, "'A Wagner Act for Public Employees': Labor's Deferred Dream and the Rise of Conservatism, 1970–

1976," *Journal of American History* 95:1 (June 2008): 123–48; *Warczak v. Detroit Board of Education*, Case No. 145080, Mich. Cir. Ct., County of Wayne, November 7, 1969, complaint, folder 6, box 24, Schlossberg Collection; *Abood v. Detroit Board of Education*, 431 U.S. 209, 234 (1976); "Court Decision Boosts Worker-Led Assault on Use of Compulsory Dues for Politics," *Free Choice*, July–August 1970, box 3, NRWC Papers; Reed Larson, "Surrender Unto Cesar?" National Right to Work News Service, May 18, 1979, box 1, NRWC Papers. On the United Farm Workers in California, see Richard Griswold del Castillo and Richard A. Garcia, *Cesar Chavez: A Triumph of Spirit* (University of Oklahoma Press, 1995); Craig Scharlin and Lilia V. Villanueva, *Philip Vera Cruz: A Personal History of Filipino Immigrants and the Farmworkers Movement* (Los Angeles: UCLA Workers Center, 1992); Craig Jenkins, *The Politics of Insurgency: The Farm Worker Movement in the 1960s* (New York: Columbia University Press, 1985).

32. National Right to Work Legal Defense Foundation, "Foundation Aims for Supreme Court," *Foundation Action in the Courts*, n.d. [1970], folder 8, box 25, Schlossberg Collection.

33. Herbert Hill, *Black Labor and the American Legal System: Race, Work, and the Law* (Madison: University of Wisconsin Press, 1977), 107; *Steele v. Louisville & Nashville R. Co.*, 323 U.S. 192 (1944). The Court did not rule that the Constitution *directly* bound labor agencies or unions, instead reasoning that the labor statute would be unconstitutional unless it was interpreted to *implicitly* impose the duty of fair representation. For a nuanced history of *Steele*, see Deborah C. Malamud, "The Story of *Steele v. Louisville & Nashville Railroad*: White Unions, Black Unions, and the Struggle for Racial Justice on the Rails," in *Labor Law Stories*, ed. Laura J. Cooper and Catherine L. Fisk (New York: Foundation Press, 2005); see generally Risa L. Goluboff, *The Lost Promise of Civil Rights* (Cambridge: Harvard University Press, 2007); Sophia Z. Lee, "Hotspots in a Cold War: The NAACP's Postwar Workplace Constitutionalism, 1948–1964," *Law and History Review* 26:2 (Summer 2008): 327–378.

34. J. C. Gibson, "The Legal and Moral Basis of Right to Work Laws," speech to the Section of Labor Relations Law, American Bar Association, reprinted in NRWC, pamphlet, n.d. [1956–1960], box 1, NRWC Papers, 11–12.

35. J. A. McClain, Jr., "The Union Shop Amendment: Compulsory 'Freedom' to Join a Union," *American Bar Association Journal* August 1956, 3, reprint, box 5, NRWC Papers.

36. Ibid., 5. The states involved in *Brown v. Board of Education*, 347 U.S. 483 (1954), argued that their segregation statutes promoted the public welfare.

37. Keller, *The Case for Right-to-Work Laws*; Edward A. Keller, "Right to Work Laws: Just and Beneficial," October 1957, *Homiletic and Pastoral Review*, reprint, folder 28, box 1, Keller Papers; Reed Larson, "Voluntary," *Point at Issue*, January 31, 1962, box 1, NRWC Papers. On the 1950s right-to-work movement's ties to Catholicism and to intra-Catholic and intra-Christian divisions over Communism and labor, see Fones-Wolf, *Selling Free Enterprise*, ch. 8, 262–266. On the threat of socialism, see "Progress Memo," 1959, pamphlet, box 1, NRWC Papers; "The Right to Work," n.d.

[1958–1959], pamphlet, box 1, NRWC Papers. On the religious and patriotic themes of Cold War–era conservatism, see McGirr, *Suburban Warriors*. Shermer does not find evidence of anti-Communism in early Sunbelt conservatives' right-to-work activism; instead, she finds antiracketeering and support of free enterprise to be the dominant tropes. Shermer "Counter-Organizing the Sunbelt," 97, 101–103.

38. "With Honesty and Courage," folder 1, box 25, Davenport Papers; Ralph de Toledano, "Right to Work Under Assault," *Free Choice*, April 12, 1976, box 3, NRWC Papers.

39. Eve to Steve [Schlossberg], July 10, 1974, memo, folder 5, box 25, Schlossberg Collection; NRWC Legal Foundation, July 16, 1975, pamphlet, folder 34, box 13, Schlossberg Collection; de Toledano, "Right to Work Under Assault." On southern states' harassment of the NAACP, see Mark Tushnet, *Making Civil Rights Law: Thurgood Marshall and the Supreme Court, 1936–1961* (New York: Oxford University Press, 1994), chs. 19–20; August Meier and John H. Bracey, Jr., "The NAACP as a Reform Movement, 1909–1965: 'To Reach the Conscience of America,'" *Journal of Southern History* 59 (February 1993): 3, 25.

40. Complaint, *Marker v. Connally*, Case No. [2486–71], U.S. District Court, District of Columbia, January 3, 1972, folder 6, box 24, Schlossberg Collection, "We're Working to Protect Human and Civil Rights." For the NAACP's tax-exempt schools cases' complicated racial, religious, and political implications, see Joseph Crespino, "Civil Rights and the Religious Right," in *Rightward Bound*, ed. Bruce J. Schulman and Julian E. Zelizer (Cambridge: Harvard University Press, 2008).

41. "With Honesty and Courage," October 17, 1979; NRWLDF, "We're Working to Protect Human and Civil Rights."

42. See n. 14 above; Ray Marshall, *The Negro and Organized Labor* (New York: John Wiley & Sons, 1965), 49; Reed Larson, "Two Court Cases," National Right to Work News Service, January 9, 1975, box 1, NRWC Papers. Although unions' racial practices were more complicated and varied than David Bernstein captures, he documents how unions used the law to African American workers' disadvantage in the early twentieth century. Bernstein, *Only One Place of Redress: African Americans, Labor Regulations, and the Courts from Reconstruction to the New Deal* (Durham: Duke University Press, 2001). For a nuanced account of African Americans' varying approaches to unionization in this period, see Eric Arnesen, *Brotherhoods of Color: Black Railroad Workers and the Struggle for Equality* (Cambridge: Harvard University Press, 2001).

43. Reed Larson, "Compulsory Unionism . . . A Major Obstacle to Full Employment Opportunities," February 17, 1967, pamphlet, box 1, NRWC Papers. On the convergence of race and right-to-work politics in California at this time see Reuel Schiller, *Forging Rivals: Race, Class, and the Postwar Legal Order* (Cambridge: Cambridge University Press, forthcoming).

44. John Chamberlain, "Black Power and Right to Work," *Tulsa Tribune*, September 6, 1967, reprinted in *Free Choice*, September 1967, box 3, NRWC Papers; W. Earl

Douglas, "Unions Like 'Massah,'" *Charleston Post*, November 1, 1976, reprinted in *Free Choice*, December 13, 1976, box 3, NRWC Papers.

45. "CORE Chapter Votes to Endorse Right to Work," *Free Choice*, January 1969, box 3, NRWC Papers; "New Missouri Board Member Tough Battler for Voluntarism," *Free Choice*, May 1969, box 3, NRWC Papers; Ruth Johnson, letter to the editor, *Ebony*, June 1973, reprinted in "She's no Patsy. . . ," *Free Choice*, August 17, 1973, box 3, NRWC Papers.

46. "Catalog of Educational Materials," August 1977, pamphlet, box 1, NRWC Papers; Stan Evans, interview of Reed Larson, January 15, 1976, transcript (1 of 2), box 2, NRWC Papers, 26–28; Reed Larson, "Blacks and Compulsory Unionism: 'The Classic Double Bind,'" National Right to Work News Service, November 3, 1980, box 1, NRWC Papers.

47. "Aroused Public Workers Fight Compulsion," *Free Choice*, June 1969, box 3, NRWC Papers; "*Free Choice*: Another Area of Civil Rights That Jim Nixon Deeply Believes In," *Free Choice*, May–June 1972, box 3, NRWC Papers.

48. "Nineteen Wage-Earners Honored for Right to Work Leadership," *Free Choice*, June 14, 1973, box 3, NRWC Papers; "Minority Union Favors Right to Work, Opposes Big Labor," *Free Choice*, December 20, 1977, box 3, NRWC Papers.

49. Evans, interview; Walter Mossberg, "20-Year Fight: Right to Work Drive: A Friend to Workers or a Menace to Them?" *Wall Street Journal*, April 22, 1975, 1; Jerry Flint, "Reed Larson vs. the Union Shop," *New York Times Magazine*, December 4, 1977, 1.

50. Reed Larson, "Is Monopoly in the American Tradition? The Elimination of Forced Union Membership," *Vital Speeches of the Day*, June 15, 1973, pamphlet, box 1, NRWC Papers; Lee Edwards and Associates, interview with Reed Larson, July 9, 1975, transcript, box 2, NRWC Papers; Evans, interview, 12–15.

51. "Reuther Makes Big Show in Alabama but Denies Rights of UAW Members," *Free Choice*, April 1965, box 3, NRWC Papers; "Wider Legal Assault Against Compulsion and Award for Employee Leaders Approved by Board," *Free Choice*, February 1968, box 3, NRWC Papers; *National Right to Work Newsletter*, May 25, 1973, folder 35, box 13, Schlossberg Collection; "Court Says First Amendment Guarantees Radio, TV News Analysts Right to Work," *Free Choice*, February 28, 1973, box 3, NRWC Papers; "Wisconsin Public Employees Rebel Against Compulsory Unionism," *Free Choice*, June 26, 1973, box 3, NRWC Papers.

52. "Nineteen Wage-Earners Honored"; "Phillip Wallace: Forced Unionism Abruptly Shatters American Dream," *Free Choice*, November–December 1979, box 3, NRWC Papers; "Minority Union Favors Right to Work, Opposes Big Labor," *Free Choice*, December 20, 1977, box 3, NRWC Papers.

53. Flint, "Reed Larson vs. the Union Shop"; Gertrude L. Wood, "(Civil) Right to Work," letter to the editor, *New York Times*, February, 15, 1972, 32; Joseph Rauh to Plato E. Papps, February 4, 1976, folder 11, box 25, Schlossberg Collection.

54. Reed Larson, "Is Monopoly in the American Tradition?"; *National Right to Work Newsletter*, July 25, 1973, folder 35, box 13, Schlossberg Collection. Larson thought the Republican Party was also corrupted by union dollars and riddled with supporters of big government, big business, and big labor. Edwards Associates, interview.

55. On the labor–civil rights alliance and its raveling, see, for example, Steve Fraser and Gary Gerstle, *The Rise and Fall of the New Deal Order, 1930–1980* (Princeton: Princeton University Press, 1989); Lichtenstein, *State of the Union*; Stein, *Running Steel*; Larson, "Blacks and Compulsory Unionism."

56. Steven M. Teles, *The Rise of the Conservative Legal Movement* (Princeton: Princeton University Press, 2008), 239. See also Reva B. Siegel, "The Right's Reasons: Constitutional Conflict and the Spread of Woman-Protective Antiabortion Argument," *Duke Law Journal* 57 (2008): 1641.

Chapter 9. "Such Power Spells Tyranny"

Nancy MacLean provided extensive comments on various incarnations of this essay. I thank her especially for her patience and encouragement. For advice on later drafts, I thank Anthony S. Chen, Nelson Lichtenstein, Elizabeth Tandy Shermer, Michael Sherry, and David Sellers Smith. I also thank commentators at the Right and Labor Conference at the University of California, Santa Barbara, the 2009 Annual Meeting of the Labor and Working-Class History Association, and the history department dissertators' workshop at Northwestern University.

1. Laurence H. Silberman, "Will Lawyering Strangle Democratic Capitalism?" *Regulation* 2, no. 2 (March 1978), 15–44.

2. See for example Nathan Glazer, "Towards an Imperial Judiciary?" *Public Interest*, no. 41 (Fall 1975), 104–123; Jeremy Rabkin, "The Judiciary in the Administrative State," *Public Interest*, no. 71 (Spring 1983), 62–84. For an overview of the longstanding intellectual controversy surrounding "legal liberalism," see Laura Kalman, *The Strange Career of Legal Liberalism* (New Haven: Yale University Press, 1996). On the complementary roles of business lobbyists and media institutions in stoking fears of "litigiousness," see William Haltom and Michael McCann, *Distorting the Law: Politics, Media, and the Litigation Crisis* (Chicago: University of Chicago Press, 2004).

3. John Fabian Witt, *The Accidental Republic: Crippled Workingmen, Destitute Widows, and the Remaking of American Law* (Cambridge: Harvard University Press, 2004), 196–197; John Fabian Witt, "Speedy Fred Taylor and the Ironies of Enterprise Liability," *Columbia Law Review* 103, no. 1 (January 2003), 627–657. On this phenomenon more broadly, see Robert A. Kagan, *Adversarial Legalism: The American Way of Law* (Cambridge: Harvard University Press, 2001); Thomas Geoghegan, *See You in Court: How the Right Made America a Lawsuit Nation* (New York: New Press, 2007).

4. Illinois was the last northern state to create an FEPC. On the proliferation of state FEPCs, see Anthony S. Chen, "The Party of Lincoln and the Politics of State Fair Employment Practices Legislation in the North, 1945–1964," *American Journal of*

Sociology 112, no. 6 (May 2007), 1713–1774. On political culture in Illinois during this period, see Arnold Hirsch, *Making the Second Ghetto: Race and Housing in Chicago, 1940–1960* (Chicago: University of Chicago Press, 1983); Andrew Edmund Kersten, *Race, Jobs, and the War: The FEPC in the Midwest, 1941–1946* (Urbana: University of Illinois Press, 2000); Milton Derber, *Labor in Illinois: The Affluent Years* (Urbana: University of Illinois Press, 1999); Jonathan Bell, "The Changing Dynamics of American Liberalism: Paul Douglas and the Elections of 1948," *Journal of the Illinois State Historical Society* 96, no. 4 (Winter 2003–2004), 368–393.

5. Anthony S. Chen, *The Fifth Freedom: Jobs, Politics, and Civil Rights in the United States: 1941–1972* (Princeton: Princeton University Press, 2009), 23.

6. Sylvester Petro, *The Kohler Strike: Union Violence and Administrative Law* (Chicago: Henry Regnery, 1961), 106.

7. On "racial conservatism" in the postwar era, see any number of works, including Thomas J. Sugrue, *The Origins of the Urban Crisis: Race and Inequality in Postwar Detroit* (Princeton: Princeton University Press, 1996); Kevin Kruse, *White Flight: Atlanta and the Making of Modern Conservatism* (Prinecton: Princeton University Press, 2005); Nancy MacLean, *Freedom Is Not Enough: The Opening of the American Workplace* (New York and Cambridge: Russell Sage Foundation and Harvard University Press, 2006); James Wolfinger, *Philadelphia Divided: Race and Politics in the City of Brotherly Love* (Chapel Hill: University of North Carolina Press, 2007). On business conservatism and the "right to manage," see Howell John Harris, *The Right to Manage: Industrial Relations Policies of American Business in the 1940s* (Madison: University of Wisconsin Press, 1982); Elizabeth Fones-Wolf, *Selling Free-Enterprise: The Business Assault on Labor and Liberalism, 1945–1960* (Urbana: University of Illinois Press, 1994); Sanford Jacoby, *Modern Manors: Welfare Capitalism Since the New Deal* (Princeton: Princeton University Press, 1997); Nelson Lichtenstein, *State of the Union: A Century of American Labor* (Princeton: Princeton University Press, 2002), 98–140; Elizabeth Tandy Shermer, "Origins of the Conservative Ascendency: Barry Goldwater's Early Senate Career and the De-Legitimization of Organized Labor," *Journal of American History* 95, No. 3 (December 2008), 678–709; Kim Phillips-Fein, *Invisible Hands: The Conservative Movement from the New Deal to Reagan* (New York: W. W. Norton, 2009).

8. "Pass the State FEPC Measure Now," *Chicago Defender*, May 19, 1945.

9. Thomas Sugrue, "The Tangled Roots of Affirmative Action," *American Behavioral Scientist* 41, no. 7 (April 1998), 886–897, esp. 889.

10. Landis quoted in Morton J. Horwitz, *The Transformation of American Law, 1870–1960: The Crisis of Legal Orthodoxy* (New York: Oxford University Press, 1992), 214. On the development of legal realism and administrative law, see 169–246.

11. On this faith in administrative expertise, see Stephen Skowronek, *Building a New American State: The Expansion of National Administrative Capacities, 1877–1920* (Princeton: Princeton University Press, 1982), 165–176; Sidney Milkis, *The President and the Parties: The Transformation of the American Party System Since the New Deal*

(New York: Oxford University Press, 1994). On black intellectuals and lawyers' views of administrative governance, see Kenneth W. Mack, "Rethinking Civil Rights Lawyering and Politics in the Era Before *Brown*," *Yale Law Journal* 115 (2005), 256–354; Sophia Z. Lee, "Hotspots in a Cold War: The NAACP's Postwar Workplace Constitutionalism, 1948–1964," *Law and History Review* 26, no. 2 (Summer 2008), 328–377.

12. See Eileen Boris, "The Right to Work Is the Right to Live! Fair Employment and the Quest for Social Citizenship," in *Two Cultures of Rights: The Quest for Inclusion and Participation in Modern America and Germany*, ed. Manfred Berg and Martin H. Geyer (Cambridge: Cambridge University Press, 2000).

13. Illinois Fair Employment Practices Committee, *Fair Employment Practices Commission (FEPC) Fact Book, 1951* (Chicago: Illinois Fair Employment Practices Committee, 1951).

14. Ibid.

15. "Questions and Answers about S. 101 and H.B. 2232 the Permanent FEPC Bill," part 13, series B, reel 13, *Papers of the NAACP*, ed. John H. Bracey, Jr., Sharon Harley, and August Meier (Bethesda, Md.: University Publications of America, 2000).

16. Erik Gellman, "Carthage Must Be Destroyed: Race, City Politics, and the Campaign to Integrate Chicago Transportation Employment, 1929–1943," *Labor: Studies in Working-Class History of the Americas* 2 (Summer 2005), 81–114. On Randolph and the BSCP, see Beth Tompkins Bates, *Pullman Porters and the Rise of Protest Politics in Black America, 1925–1945* (Chapel Hill: University of North Carolina Press, 2001); Eric Arnesen, *Brotherhoods of Color: Black Railroad Workers and the Struggle for Equality* (Cambridge: Harvard University Press, 2001).

17. Kersten, *Race, Jobs, and the War*, 24–28.

18. Lichtenstein, *State of the Union*, 85. On the wartime FEPC, see Merl E. Reed, *Seedtime for the Modern Civil Rights Movement: The President's Committee on Fair Employment Practices* (Baton Rouge: Louisiana State University Press, 1991).

19. Kersten, *Race, Jobs, and the War*, 51–54. The percentage of blacks in the Chicago workforce rose from 8.6 percent in 1941 to 13.1 percent in 1944. At International Harvester, the percentage of total employees who were black rose from 4.5 percent in 1940 to 11.7 percent in 1945. See Jennifer Delton, "Good Business: Nondiscrimination Policies and Labor-Management Relations, 1945–1964," *Journal of the Historical Society* 6, no. 3 (September 2006), 359. On the UPWA and fair employment, see Rick Halpern, *Down on the Killing Floor: Black and White Workers in Chicago's Packinghouses, 1904–1954* (Urbana: University of Illinois Press, 1997), 214–215.

20. Kersten, *Race, Jobs, and the War*, 47–59.

21. Hirsch, *Making the Second Ghetto*, 177. On the 1943 Detroit race riot, see Sugrue, *The Origins of the Urban Crisis*, 29–31.

22. Lionel Kimble, Jr., "Combating the City of Neighborhoods: Housing, Employment, and Civil Rights in Chicago, 1935–1955" (PhD diss., University of Iowa, 2004), 294–295.

23. Illinois Fair Employment Practices Committee, *Fair Employment Practices*. Russell Ballard, "Statement By Russell Ballard in Support of Fair Employment Practices Act," April 14, 1945, *Urban Experience in Chicago: Hull-House and its Neighborhoods, 1889–1963*, ed. Rima Lunin Schultz, http://www.uic.edu/jaddams/hull/urban exp/ (Accessed May 26, 2008).

24. Illinois Council for a State Fair Employment Practices Law, "Preliminary Draft," November 26, 1946, part 13, series B, reel 14, *Papers of the NAACP*.

25. "Senate Group Votes Against FEPC Measure," *Chicago Tribune*, May 17, 1945.

26. "Pass the State FEPC Measure Now."

27. Lizabeth Cohen, *Making a New Deal: Industrial Workers in Chicago, 1919–1939* (Cambridge: Cambridge University Press, 1990), 182.

28. Meeting of the Board of Directors of the Illinois Manufacturers Association, March 9, 1945, box 12, folder 18, Records of the Illinois Manufacturers Association, Chicago History Museum (hereafter IMA Records); "Senate Group Votes Against FEPC Measure"; "Committee in House Puts FEPC Bill on Shelf," *Chicago Tribune*, May 24, 1945. Business organizations testifying against the FEPC bill included the IMA, the Illinois State Chamber of Commerce, the Associated Employers of Illinois, the Peoria Manufacturers Association, the Chicago Association of Commerce, the East Side Manufacturers Association of Granite City, and the Illinois Federation of Retail Associations, among others.

29. Meeting of the Board of Directors of the Illinois Manufacturers Association, June 8, 1945, box 12, folder 18, IMA Records.

30. "Pass the State FEPC Measure Now."

31. Delton, "Good Business," 370. On the role of UAW Local 6, in Melrose Park, Ill., in facilitating the continued success of this policy at International Harvester, see Derber, *Labor in Illinois*, 108–126, esp. 118.

32. Marshall Field to Walter White, June 20, 1945, part 13, series B, reel 19, *Papers of the NAACP*.

33. Many contemporary commentators pointed to resistance from downstate business leaders to explain the opposition to fair employment legislation from organized business associations, but the regional disparity in business outlook was not always clear-cut. The Illinois Federation of Retail Associations, according to one FEPC advocate, was in reality "financed almost totally by the multi-million dollar department store industry centering on State Street in Chicago." Gilbert Gordon, "A New Birth of Freedom in Illinois," April 26, 1949, box 100, folder 14, Adlai Stevenson II Papers, Abraham Lincoln Presidential Library, Springfield, Ill. (hereafter Stevenson Papers), 4–5.

34. Jacoby, *Modern Manors*, 114–115.

35. "FDR Accused of Aiding CIO in Ward's Strike," *Chicago Tribune*, April 20, 1944.

36. Display ad 20, "Montgomery Ward's Reply to the President of the United States," *Chicago Tribune*, April 26, 1944.

37. On the AFL's conflicts with the NLRB, see Christopher L. Tomlins, *The State and the Unions: Labor Relations, Law, and the Organized Labor Movement in America, 1880–1960* (Cambridge: Cambridge University Press, 1985), 148–196.

38. "Exhibit C," addendum to minutes of the Meeting of the Board of Directors of the Illinois Manufacturers Association, February 12, 1943, box 11, folder 2, IMA Records.

39. The American Bar Association and former Harvard Law School dean Roscoe Pound had begun waging an attack on New Deal administrative agencies in 1938, securing passage of a bill in 1940 that placed far-reaching limits on administrative discretion by requiring courts to review agency findings of both fact and law. The legislation was vetoed by Roosevelt, but for the remainder of the decade New Dealers fought a rearguard battle against attempts to place nearly all actions of administrative agencies under judicial supervision. "For a time," argues legal historian Morton Horwitz, "the battle over administrative procedure was nothing less than a struggle over the legitimating premises of the New Deal." Horwitz, *Transformation of American Law*, 217–233, quotes on 227 and 231. See also Reuel E. Schiller, "The Era of Deference: Courts, Expertise, and the Emergence of New Deal Administrative Law," *Michigan Law Review* 106, no. 3 (December 2007), 399–441, esp. 421–429.

40. "Administrative Law in Illinois," *Chicago Tribune*, June 13, 1946.

41. Administrative Review Act, (Ill. 1945). Congress passed a similar law, the Administrative Procedure Act, in 1946.

42. Harry G. Fins, *Illinois Administrative Review Act, Annotated* (Chicago: Current Law, 1946).

43. "Administrative Law in Illinois."

44. Ibid.; "Pass the State FEP Measure Now."

45. "Address by Charles F. Hough, Counsel, Before the Senate Judiciary Committee, May 8, 1945, in Opposition to S.B. 254 and 255 (Bills for Fair Employment Practices Act)," box 100, folder 14, Stevenson Papers.

46. Horwitz, *Transformation of American Law*, 230–233; Nelson Lichtenstein, "From Corporatism to Collective Bargaining: Organized Labor and the Eclipse of Social Democracy in the Postwar Era," in *The Rise and Fall of the New Deal Order, 1930–1980*, ed. Steve Fraser and Gary Gerstle (Princeton: Princeton University Press, 1989), 122–152.

47. Gordon, "New Birth of Freedom," 1–9.

48. Ibid., 5; Derber, *Labor in Illinois*, 175–183; Wesley W. South to Adlai Stevenson, November 29, 1948, box 100, folder 14, Stevenson Papers. On IFL conflict with the NLRB, see William Bromage, "Federation Hits National Labor Relations Law," *Chicago Tribune*, September 22, 1937. On the black swing vote in the North, see Thomas J. Sugrue, *Sweet Land of Liberty: The Forgotten Struggle for Civil Rights in the North* (New York: Random House, 2008), 87–130.

49. Gordon, "New Birth of Freedom," 6–9.

50. In 1947, four different Illinois FEPC bills stalled in the Senate and House Judiciary Committees. Johnson Kanady, "FEPC Dead This Session, Backers Decide," *Chicago Tribune*, April 23, 1947.

51. "Fair Practices Bill Explained by Stevenson," *Chicago Tribune*, February 2, 1949.

52. "House Bill No. 163," February 16, 1949, box 100, folder 14, Stevenson Papers; "Illinois FEPC Bills Introduced in Both House and Senate," *Chicago Tribune*, February 17, 1949.

53. Jerome Finkle to Walter V. Schaefer, February 10, 1949, box 100, folder 14, Stevenson Papers.

54. "Resolution on Proposed Illinois State FEPC Bill," February 9, 1949, box 100, folder 14, Stevenson Papers.

55. "Fair Practices Bill Explained by Stevenson."

56. "House Bill No. 163."

57. "No Employer FEPC Guide Is Proposed," *Chicago Tribune*, February 3, 1949; Illinois State Chamber of Commerce, "Fair Employment Practice Laws," April 1949, box 100, folder 14, Stevenson Papers.

58. Illinois State Chamber of Commerce, "Fair Employment Practice Laws" (italics in original).

59. R. M. Westcott to Stevenson, January 5, 1949, box 123, folder 13, Stevenson Papers.

60. Frank Koch to Stevenson, March 21, 1949, box 100, folder 14, Stevenson Papers.

61. Floyd E. Thompson, "Address in Opposition to So-Called Fair Employment Practices Commission Bills (S.B. 145 and H.B. 163) Before the House Executive Committee," March 22, 1949, box 100, folder 14, Stevenson Papers; Johnson Kanady, "Illinois House Group Votes FEPC, 20–6," *Chicago Tribune*, March 23, 1949.

62. Illinois State Chamber of Commerce, "Fair Employment Practice Laws"; Meeting of the Board of Directors of the Illinois Manufacturers Association, February 11, 1949, box 13, folder 4, IMA Records.

63. Of course, the vast majority of business leaders were not constitutional law scholars, and their invocation of a constitutional right to manage was at best antiquated in the wake of the Supreme Court's validation of New Deal legislation in the years following 1937. In June 1945, the U.S. Supreme Court determined in *Railway Mail Association v. Corsi* that New York's FEPC law did not violate employers' property rights or employees' liberty to contract. Nevertheless, as Risa Goluboff points out, the particular meaning of "civil rights" was highly uncertain during the 1940s and early 1950s, and it is not surprising that businessmen would attempt to shape public discourse about rights and influence the development of civil rights doctrine to serve their own interests. Risa L. Goluboff, *The Lost Promise of Civil Rights* (Cambridge: Harvard University Press, 2007), 16–50, 231–232; *Railway Mail Association v. Corsi* 326 U.S. 88 (1945).

64. Fox River Valley Manufacturers Association, Memo Re: FEPC legislation, March 16, 1949, box 100, folder 14, Stevenson Papers.

65. Clarence Mark Jr. to Stevenson, March 21, 1949, box 100, folder 14, Stevenson Papers.

66. Earl Kribben to Stevenson, May 31, 1949, box 100, folder 14, Stevenson Papers.

67. Associated Employers of Illinois, "Summary Fair Employment Practices Commission Bills S.B. 145 and H.B 163," n.d., box 100, folder 14, Stevenson Papers.

68. Kribben to Stevenson.

69. Gordon, "New Birth of Freedom."

70. Albert J. Weiss to Schaefer, April 12, 1949, box 100, folder 14, Stevenson Papers.

71. "Label FEPC Bill Herald of Tyranny," *Chicago Tribune*, June 2, 1949.

72. "Senate Votes Amendment of FEPC Bill," *Chicago Tribune*, June 15, 1949.

73. "FEPC: Some State Legislatures Knuckle Under to Threats and Intimidations," unattributed newspaper clipping, handwritten date September 1949, box 100, folder 14, Stevenson Papers; "FEPC Is Beaten in State Senate," *Chicago Tribune*, June 17, 1949.

74. A. L. Foster, "The NAACP Fight for Equal Job Opportunity: A Report on the FEPC Campaign," 1953, part 13, series B, reel 14, *Papers of the NAACP*; Derber, *Labor in Illinois*, 384.

75. George Tagge, "FEPC Measure Defeated in State Senate," *Chicago Tribune*, May 15, 1957.

76. "The Fair Employment Bill," *Chicago Tribune*, April 12, 1961.

77. "FEPC in Springfield," *Chicago Tribune*, May 25, 1959.

78. Joseph Minsky, "FEPC in Illinois: Four Stormy Years," *Notre Dame Lawyer* 41 (1964), 152–181, quote on 155.

79. "Senate Group Stalls on State FEPC," *Chicago Tribune*, May 11, 1961.

80. "GOP Wavers in Fight over Illinois FEPC," *Chicago Tribune*, March 21, 1961.

81. "NAACP Hits FEPC Bill in State Senate," *Chicago Tribune*, May 18, 1961.

82. Minsky, "FEPC in Illinois," 155–158.

83. Krock quoted in Judith Stein, *Running Steel, Running America: Race, Economic Policy, and the Decline of Liberalism* (Chapel Hill: University of North Carolina Press, 1998), 83. For details of the Motorola case, see Minsky, "FEPC in Illinois," 161–171.

84. James L. Donnelly, "IMA Law Digest: Title VII of Civil Rights Act of 1964," July 1964, box 199, folder 3, IMA Records.

85. On Dirksen's close relationship with the IMA, see correspondence between Dirksen and IMA vice president James L. Donnelly and president Merle R. Yontz, box 78, folder 1, IMA Records; Presentation to the Honorable Everett McKinley Dirksen by the Board of Directors of the Illinois Manufacturers Association, December 17, 1959, box 78, folder 1, IMA Records.

86. Hugh Davis Graham, *The Civil Rights Era: Origins and Development of National Policy, 1960–1972* (New York: Oxford University Press, 1990), 146.

87. Chen, *Fifth Freedom*, 182–190; Sean Farhang, "The Political Development of Job Discrimination Litigation, 1963–1976," *Studies in American Political Development* 23 (April 2009), 31–40.

88. Donnelly, "IMA Law Digest."

89. Farhang, "Political Development," 23.

90. On class actions and affirmative action, see Maclean, *Freedom Is Not Enough.* On due process and welfare rights, see Martha F. Davis, *Brutal Need: Lawyers and the Welfare Rights Movement, 1960–1973* (New Haven: Yale University Press, 1993), 81–98; Morton Horwitz, *The Warren Court and the Pursuit of Justice* (New York: Hill and Wang, 1998), 88–91.

91. Steven M. Teles, *The Rise of the Conservative Legal Movement* (Princeton: Princeton University Press, 2008), 2.

92. For the shift as a result of ideology and "rights consciousness," see Mary Ann Glendon, *Rights Talk: The Impoverishment of Political Discourse* (New York: Free Press, 1991), 1–17; Lichtenstein, *State of the Union*, 178–211. As tactical evolution, see MacLean, *Freedom Is Not Enough.*

93. William J. Collins, "The Political Economy of State-Level Fair Employment Laws, 1940–1960," *Explorations in Economic History* 40, no. 1 (January 2003), 24–51.

94. See "Assessing the Legacy of Herbert Hill," symposium essays by Nancy MacLean, Clarence E. Walker, Nelson Lichtenstein, and Alex Lichtenstein, in *Labor: Studies in Working-Class History of the Americas* 3, no. 2 (Summer 2006), 11–39.

95. Jaffe quoted in Horwitz, *Transformation of American Law*, 240.

96. Horwitz, *Transformation of American Law*, 246.

97. Paul Frymer, *Black and Blue: African Americans, the Labor Movement, and the Decline of the Democratic Party* (Princeton: Princeton University Press, 2008), 70–97.

98. Ibid., 78.

Chapter 10. Pattern for Partnership

1. U.S. Senate, Select Committee on Improper Activities in the Labor or Management Field, *Investigation of Improper Activities in the Labor or Management Field*, 85'h Cong., 1st Sess., April 16, 17, 18, and 29, 1957 (Washington, D.C.: U.S. Government Printing Office, 1957), part 6, 1783–90 (hereafter McClellan Committee Hearings).

2. See, for example, Bernard D. Nossiter, "Union Terror Charged," *Washington Post*, April 17, 1957, 1; and "Unions Face Inquiry on Terrorism," *Los Angeles Times*, April 14, 1957, 1; magazine stories include "The Ungentle Art," *Time*, April 29, 1957, 20–21; "Strong Arm Tactics in Unions: Case History of a City," *U.S. News & World Report*, April 26, 1957, 80–87; "The Investigation," *Newsweek*, April 29, 1957, 33; "Labor Violence on the Local Level," *Life*, April 29, 1957, 30–35, photo on 32.

3. Paul Healy, "Probe to Hear Scranton Teamster Terror Story," *New York Daily News*, April 11, 1957, all in Microfilm Newsclips, 1956–1959, Working Files, Robert F.

Kennedy's Pre-Administration Papers, 1937–1960, John F. Kennedy Library, Boston (hereafter RFK Clipping File).

4. "Strong Arm Tactics in Unions."

5. "Goons at Work," *Washington Star*, April 21, 1957, RFK Clipping File.

6. "Labor: Curbing the Unions," *Newsweek*, May 6, 1957, RFK Clipping File.

7. "What Eisenhower Said About Labor Rackets," *U.S. News & World Report*, May 3, 1957, 104.

8. "Pattern for Partnership," *Time*, May 6, 1957.

9. "Labor Rackets: 48-State Survey," *Newsweek*, ril 29, 1957, 31–33.

10. "1956 Public Relations Program for NAM Campaign Against Labor Monopoly," February 1956, 2, accession number 1411, box 851.1, folder 2, National Association of Manufacturers Papers, Hagley Museum and Library, Wilmington, Del. For more on NAM's leadership role in the postwar anti-union movement, see Elizabeth-Fones Wolf, *Selling Free Enterprise: The Business Assault on Labor and Liberalism, 1945–1960* (Chicago: University of Illinois Press, 1994), esp. 24–44, 50–57; and Kim Phillips-Fein, *Invisible Hands: The Making of the Conservative Movement from the New Deal to Reagan* (New York: W.W. Norton, 2009), who describes the role of anti-unionism in the postwar mobilization of a conservative movement among business elites, 87–114.

11. "1956 Public Relations Program," 3, 11–12.

12. "Labor Gets a Close-Up of Some High-Flying 'Leaders,'" *Saturday Evening Post*, April 3, 1957, RFK News Clipping File.

13. "Labor Rackets."

14. Victor Riesel, "The Night That Changed My Life," *Saturday Evening Post*, September 15, 1956, 32, 98.

15. Untitled editorial, "Acid Attack," news clipping, *Des Moines Register*, May 7, 1956, Clippings Folder, April–June 1956, box 5, Victor Riesel Papers, Robert F. Wagner Labor Archives, Tamiment Library, New York University.

16. "Victor Riesel, Labor Columnist," *Meet the Press*, June 3, 1956, CD recording of broadcast, Jerry Haendiges Productions, Whittier, Calif., 2008.

17. "Why the New Move to Investigate Racketeering in Labor Unions," *U.S. News & World Report*, June 15, 1956, 124; "Employer Scored in Labor Rackets," *New York Times*, July 2, 1956, 11; Victor Riesel, "Aims Typewriter at Mobs," *Hollywood (California) Citizen News*, June 1, 1956, in RFK Clipping Files; quote from "Ives Urges Inquiry Into Union Rackets," *New York Times*, July 6, 1956, 35.

18. Interview of Robert F. Kennedy by Kenneth Brodney, Newhouse Newspaper Features Syndicate, July 2, 1957, attached to Brodney to Kennedy, July 4, 1957, box 40, RFK Pre-Administration Working Files; "Labor—Kennedy Operation," rough draft *Fortune* magazine article, enclosed with Daniel Seligman to Kennedy, May 1, 1957, box 51, RFK Pre-Administration Working Files. From RFK Clipping File: Victor Riesel, "Even Dave Beck Lives in Fear," *Hollywood Citizen News*, May 24, 1956; Clark Mollenhoff, "New Labor Probe Will Reach City," *Minneapolis Morning Tribune*, December 5, 1956; Clark Mollenhoff, "Charging Teamster Scheme to Hide Evidence,"

Des Moines Register, January 18, 1957; Victor Riesel, "That Acid Attack Started Broad Scale Drive on Mobs," *Philadelphia Inquirer,* September 18, 1956; Willard Edwards, "Senate Groups Clash on Labor Rackets Probe," *Chicago Tribune,* January 8, 1957.

19. From RFK Clipping File: "Sensational"; Edwards, "Senate Groups Clash."

20. Robert McFadden, "Clark Mollenhoff Is Dead at 69," *New York Times,* March 3, 1991, 43; Clark Mollenhoff, untitled chronology, [August 1958?], box 67, folder 8, Teamsters General, Clark Mollenhoff Papers, Wisconsin State Historical Society, Madison.

21. "Committee Rebels Against Hoffman," *New York Times,* July 15, 1953, 10.

22. William Wilson to Karl E. Mundt, June 3, 1953, box 67, folder 10, Teamsters Research, Mollenhoff Papers; quotes from Wilson to W. J. McGill, January 9, 1954, box 67, folder 9, Teamsters General, Mollenhoff Papers.

23. This is a second chronology in Mollenhoff's papers; its heading bears the handwritten notation "To Ned McGuire," October 17, 1957, box 67, folder 8, Teamsters General, Mollenhoff Papers.

24. Mollenhoff, chronology dated August 1958.

25. Clark R. Mollenhoff, *Tentacles of Power: The Story of Jimmy Hoffa* (Cleveland: World, 1965), 12.

26. "The Cowles World," *Time,* December 8, 1958; "John Cowles, Sr., Minneapolis Newspaper Publisher, Is Dead at 84," *New York Times,* February 26, 1983, 11; "Gardner Cowles Jr., Is Dead at 82," *New York Times,* July 9, 1985, B6.

27. Reference to Wilson's case is in Sam [Romer] to Clark [Mollenoff], February 19, 1953, box 67, folder 9, Teamster Research Material, Mollenhoff Papers; reference to collusion, Mollenhoff, chronology dated October 17, 1957, box 67, folder 8, Teamsters General; Wilson to Mundt.

28. Mollenhoff, *Tentacles of Power,* 20.

29. Untitled wire service copy, November 10, 1955, box 52, folder 2, Wire Service Copy, 1953–1955, Mollenhoff Papers.

30. Clark Mollenhoff, "How Labor Bosses Get Rich," *Look,* (March 9, 1954, 38–45, quote on 45.

31. David Witwer, *Shadow of the Racketeer: Scandal in Organized Labor* (Chicago: University of Illinois Press, 2009), 182–188, 192–204; David Witwer, "The Racketeer Menace and Antiunionism in the Mid-Twentieth Century US," *International Labor and Working-Class History* 74 (Fall 2008), 124–147, quote on 128.

32. Witwer, "The Racketeer Menace," 132.

33. Seymour Martin Lipset and William Schneider, *The Confidence Gap: Business, Labor, and Government in the Public Mind* (New York: Free Press, 1983), 41–44, 215–220.

34. William J. Puette, *Through Jaundiced Eyes: How the Media View Organized Labor* (Ithaca, N.Y.: ILR Press, 1992), 83.

35. Westbrook Pegler, "Fair Enough," February 10, 1943, box 121, James Westbrook Pegler Papers, Herbert Hoover Presidential Library, West Branch, Iowa.

36. Phillips-Fein, *Invisible Hands*, 106; Fones-Wolf, *Selling Free Enterprise*, 271; William H. Miernyk, *Trade Unions in the Age of Affluence* (New York: Random House, 1962), 112–123; Joseph Loftus, "Unions at a Low in Poll Victories," *New York Times*, May 5, 1957, 62; Grace Palladino, *Skilled Hands, Strong Spirits: A Century of Building Trades History* (Ithaca: Cornell University Press, 2005), 150–151; Shane Hamilton, *Trucking Country: The Road to America's Wal-Mart Economy* (Princeton: Princeton University Press, 2008), 133–134, 180; Marc Linder, *Wars of Attrition: Vietnam, the Business Roundtable, and the Decline of Construction Unions* (Iowa City, Iowa: Fanpihua Press, 2000), 34–35.

37. Mollenhoff, *Tentacles of Power*, 28–29.

38. Edwin Guthman, *We Band of Brothers* (New York: Harper & Row, 1971), 3.

39. Louis J. Kramp to Clark Mollenhoff, December 7, 1955, box 67, folder 9, Teamsters General, Mollenhoff Papers.

40. Guthman, *We Band of Brothers*, 4.

41. Ibid., 10.

42. Wallace Turner and William Lambert, "Hearings Set on Teamsters in Portland," *Portland Oregonian*, December 6, 1956, RFK Clipping Files.

43. Westbrook Pegler, "Big Union Dinner Honors 4 Felons," *New York Journal American*, September 18, 1956, RFK Clipping Files.

44. In August 1958, Pegler sent a harsh letter to McClellan asserting that his "Committee's investigation of union rackets has been a hoax." McClellan's handwritten notation on the letter reads: "Keep on file in my office. This nut should not be dignified with a reply." File 24, drawer E, Labor Committee Out of State Folder, John L. McClellan Papers, Ouchita Baptist University, Arkadelphia, Ark.

45. J. Harold Brislin, "Relates Why Story Told to Tribune," *Scranton Tribune*, June 1, 1955, 1.

46. J. Harold Brislin to Kennedy, January 15, 1957, serial No. 18–48–1, and Brislin to Kennedy, June 6, 1957, serial No. 18–48–86, both in case file 18–48, Records of the Select Committee on Improper Activities in the Labor or Management Field (hereafter Scranton Hearings), Record Group 46, Center for Legislative Archives, National Archives and Records Administration, Washington, D.C.; "Labor—Kennedy Operation."

47. "'Goon Tactics' in Scranton Probed," *Washington Post*, April 14, 1957, A2.

48. Edward F. Woods, "Senators Look into Employer's Reported Bribes to Union Agent," *St. Louis Post-Dispatch*, April 18, 1957, 1.

49. Herbert Foster, "Probe Challenges Labor's Pledge," *New York World-Telegraph & Sun*, April 17, 1957, RFK Clipping Files.

50. John A. Grimes, "Probe Preview: Senators Set to Expose Violence, Rigged Votes, Bribes in Many Unions," *Wall Street Journal*, April 10, 1957, 1.

51. McClellan Committee Hearings, part 6, 1736.

52. Interview of Paul Bradshaw by L. J. Duffy, February 6, 1957, 30–33, quote on 30, case file 18–48, Scranton Hearings, serial no. 18–48–3, Record Group 46, Center for Legislative Archives.

53. For other examples of the McClellan Committee's tendency to absolve employers for their involvement in corruption, see David Witwer, *Corruption and Reform in the Teamsters Union* (Chicago: University of Illinois Press, 2003), 188–191; Sanford M. Jacoby, *Modern Manors: Welfare Capitalism Since the New Deal* (Princeton: Princeton University Press, 1997), 130–138, 140–141.

54. L. J. Duffy to Kennedy, Re: Outline and Summary of the Case Relating to Labor Racketeering in Scranton, Pennsylvania, March 8, 1957, 4, serial no. 18–48–9, case file 18–48, Record Group 46, Center for Legislative Archives.

55. "Fraud on U.S. Laid to House Member," *New York Times*, December 15, 1956, 18.

56. "Two Independents Win Union Jobs," *Scranton Times*, February 9, 1959, envelope, Drivers & Helpers Union, No. 14, 1959, *Scranton Times Tribune* library.

57. Lawrence Richards, *Union-Free America: Workers and Antiunion Culture* (Chicago: University of Illinois Press, 2008), 7–88.

58. Witwer, "The Racketeer Menace."

59. Brodney interview; Robert F. Kennedy, *The Enemy Within* (New York: Harper and Brothers, 1960), 160–161.

60. "Labor Racket Probe Will Be Expanded," *Fresno Bee*, March 28, 1957, 1, RFK Clipping Files.

61. Fones-Wolf, *Selling Free Enterprise*, 257–261, quote on 257.

62. Witwer, "Racketeer Menace," 141–142.

63. James Reston, "G.O.P.–Labor Feud," *New York Times*, February 20, 1959, 17.

64. Elizabeth Tandy Shermer, "Origins of the Conservative Ascendancy: Barry Goldwater's Early Senate Career and the De-legitimization of Organized Labor," *Journal of American History*, 95 (December 2008), 703–709.

65. Kennedy to John Siegenthaler, July 29, 1958, box 44, RFK Pre-Administration Working Files.

66. Guthman, *We Band of Brothers*, 58.

67. Ed Guthman to Kennedy, June 28, 1957, box 40, RFK Pre-Administration Working Files.

68. Wendy Kozol, *Life's America: Family and Nation in Postwar Photojournalism* (Philadelphia: Temple University Press, 1994), 35; "News of Advertising and Marketing," *New York Times*, May 16, 1956, 47; "Advertising News from Magazine Industry," *New York Times*, March 20, 1957, 56; "Time, Inc., Raised Its Earnings on Record Revenues Last Year," *New York Times*, March 30, 1961, 36.

69. Kennedy to Hugh Moffett, May 8, 1959, and Moffett to Kennedy, May 9, 1959, both in box 48, RFK Pre-Administration Working Files; "A National Threat: Hoffa's Teamsters," *Life*, May 18, 1959, 30–41.

70. Duffy to Kennedy, 4–19.

71. Witwer, *Corruption and Reform in the Teamsters Union*, 186–187; see also Anthony V. Baltakis, "Agendas of Investigation: The McClellan Committee, 1957–1958" (Ph.D. diss., University of Akron, 1997).

72. John Siegenthaler Oral History, interview by William A. Geoghegan, July 22, 1964, 1–2, 10–11; quotes from John Siegenthaler, Address to American Society of Newspaper Editors, 1963, enclosed in same file with Oral History, Southern Oral History Program Collection, University of North Carolina, Chapel Hill, North Carolina.

Chapter 11. "Compulsory Unionism"

1. Sylvester Petro, *Labor Policy of a Free Society* (New York: Ronald Press, 1957); *Hearings Before the Select Committee on Improper Activities in the Labor or Management Field*, 85th Cong., 1st Sess., 1957; 85th Cong., 2nd Sess., 1958; and 86th Cong., 1st Sess., 1959, undated, 19884–19900.

2. The hearings were held during one of the longest strikes in American history, which pitted the United Auto Workers against the Kohler Company in Wisconsin from 1954 to 1963. See Kim Phillips-Fein, *Invisible Hands: The Making of the Modern Conservative Movement from the New Deal to Reagan* (New York: W. W. Norton, 2009).

3. Christopher Tomlins, *The State and the Unions: Labor Relations, Law, and the Organized Labor Movement in America* (New York: Cambridge University Press, 1985); Howell Harris and Nelson Lichtenstein, eds., *Industrial Democracy in America: The Ambiguous Promise* (New York: Cambridge University Press,1993); Elizabeth Fones-Wolf, *Selling Free Enterprise: The Business Assault on Labor and Liberalism, 1945–60* (Urbana: University of Illinois Press,1994); Sanford Jacoby, *Modern Manors* (Princeton: Princeton University Press, 1998); Phillips-Fein, *Invisible Hands*.

4. Henry C. Simons, "Some Reflections on Syndicalism," *Journal of Political Economy*, 52:1 (March 1944), 1–25.

5. Raymond Moley, "Interpreting the News," *Troy (New York) Record*, June 22, 1957, 22. See John Chamberlain's preface to the 1944 edition of Friedrich von Hayek, *The Road to Serfdom* in Bruce Caldwell, ed., *The Road To Serfdom: Texts and Documents* (Chicago: University of Chicago Press, 2008), 253–254.

6. On the contribution of white ethnic workers to the rise of the New Deal Order, see Lizabeth Cohen, *Making a New Deal: Industrial Workers in Chicago, 1919–39* (Chicago: University Press of Chicago, 1990), particularly, 291–321. Petro's past as a unionist is explained in his testimony in favor of S 3671, 91st Cong. (1970), box 60, folder 1, John Davenport Papers, Hoover Institution Archives, Stanford University.

7. In regard to anti-union violence particularly in steel, see Ruth Needleman, *Black Freedom Fighters in Steel* (Ithaca, N.Y.: ILR Press, 2003), 42–44. For Petro's quote, see Sylvester Petro, *The Kingsport Strike* (New Rochelle, N.Y.: Arlington House, 1967), back cover.

8. Petro, *The Kingsport Strike*, viii.

9. Joel Seidman et al., *How the Worker Views His Union*, quoted in Cohen, *Making a New Deal*, 319. On Westbrook Pegler, see David Witwer, "Westbrook Pegler and the Anti-Union Movement," *Journal of American History* 92:2 (September 2005): 527–552. Too much, of course, should not be made of these individual trajectories. As the

historian Gerald Friedman recently reminded us, strike activity peaks occur infrequently, and union expansion is a phenomenon that occurs only during those peaks, when a communitarian interest arises among workers. See Gerald Friedman, *Reigniting the Labor Movement* (New York: Routledge, 2007).

10. Aaron Director was an erstwhile leftist, who had once taught labor history. At the time, the ideological gap between the law school and the economics department was wide. See E. W. Kitch, "The Fire of Truth: A Remembrance of Law and Economics at Chicago, 1932–1970," *Journal of Law and Economics*, 26 (1983), 163–234.

11. William Crosskey, *Power and Politics in the History of the United States* (Chicago: University of Chicago Press, 1953); Sylvester Petro, "Crosskey and the Constitution: A Reply to Goebel," *Michigan Law Review*, 53:2 (December 1954), 312–349, esp. 316.

12. It bears remembering that these federal agencies were premised on the theory that Congress could delegate some of its powers to them. See the classic analysis offered by Theodore Lowi in *The End of Liberalism: The Second Republic of the United States* (New York: W. W. Norton, 1963). Petro's reading of the role of the courts in labor relations was again premised on the work of Crosskey, who argued that the Supreme Court's preemption doctrine was contrary to the original meanings of the framers of the Constitution.

13. See William KixMiller's two books, *Can Business Build a Great Age?* (New York: Macmillan, 1933) and *We Can Have Prosperity* (New York: Foundation Press, 1935). On the Labor Policy Association, see David Jacobs, "Labor and Social Legislation in the United States: Business Obstructionism and Accommodation," *Labor Studies Journal* 23:2 (Summer 1998): 52–73. The Tower Bill, S. 3671, was sponsored by—among others—Senators John Tower, Goldwater, and Strom Thurmond, but it lacked the support of the Nixon administration, particularly the Department of Justice, let alone the support of the Democratic-controlled Congress.

14. The importance of Mises and Hayek to postwar American thought was noted as early as 1976 by George Nash in his *The Conservative Intellectual Movement in America Since 1945* (New York: Basic Books, 1976).

15. Our understanding of neoclassical economics and of the role of the Austrian school is based on William Tabb, *Reconstructing Political Economy: The Great Divide in Economic Thought* (London: Routledge, 1999); Frank Stilwell, *Political Economy: The Contest of Economic Ideas* (New York: Oxford University Press, 2006); Peter Boettke and Peter Leeson, "The Austrian School of Economics, 1950–2000," in Jeff Biddle and Warren Samuels, eds., *Blackwell Companion to the History of Economic Thought* (Oxford: Basil Blackwell, 2002).

16. Phillips-Fein, *Invisible Hands*.

17. Phillips-Fein, *Invisible Hands*, 41–51; Petro largely acknowledged the influence of Mises in the introduction to his *Labor Policy of a Free Society*.

18. Petro, *Labor Policy of a Free Society*, 12. "The Communists have not been able to raise the standard of living of the Russian people over that which prevailed under

the relatively primitive and medieval economic system of the czars," Petro wrote. See Sylvester Petro, *Power Unlimited: The Corruption of Union Leadership; A Report on the McClellan Committee Hearings* (New York: Ronald Press, 1959), 274.

19. Petro, *Labor Policy of a Free Society*, 104.

20. See for example, Russell Kirk, "Humane Political Economy," *Modern Age*, 3:3 (Summer 1959), 226. The *National Review* gave a statement of principles entitled "Our Mission Statement" in the November 19, 1955, issue of the journal. On Ayn Rand, see Jennifer Burns, "Godless Capitalism: Ayn Rand and the Conservative Movement," in Nelson Lichtenstein, ed., *American Capitalism: Social Thought and Political Economy in the Twentieth Century* (Philadelphia: University of Pennsylvania Press, 2009), 271–290.

21. Petro, *Labor Policy of a Free Society*, 3–4.

22. Ibid., 11, 12. See also 61: "Government personnel are simply not godlike. They are not omniscient, not omnipotent." Such indeed was the message that Hayek had conveyed in the *The Road to Serfdom*, which Max Eastman serially published in his *Reader's Digest*. See Friedrich Hayek, *The Road to Serfdom* (Chicago: University of Chicago Press, 1944).

23. See Ludwig von Mises, *Human Action: A Treatise on Economics* (New Haven: Yale University Press, 1949), ch. 8.

24. Petro, *Labor Policy of a Free Society,* 68; Edward Chamberlin, "The Monopoly Power of Labor," in David McCord Wright, *The Impact of the Union* (New York: Harcourt and Brace, 1951), 168–187; Milton Friedman, "Some Comments on the Significance of Labor Unions for Economic Policy," in Wright,*The Impact of the Union,* 204–234.

25. Petro, *Labor Policy of a Free Society*, 68–69, 104–111.

26. By contrast, most neoclassical scholars used mathematical models, and it was in this vein that Jevons created his *homo economicus.*

27. Tellingly, at that time the National Science Foundation sought to promote behaviorism as an "American science," while in Congress the Reece Commission investigated nonprofit foundations and castigated them for neglecting theoretical and ethical perspectives. James Miller, *National Support for Behavioral Science* (Washington, D.C.: Government Printing Office, 1958), as quoted in Romain Huret, *La fin de la Pauvreté?* (Paris: EHSS, 2008).

28. On this history, see Nelson Lichtenstein, *State of the Union: A Century of American Labor* (Princeton: Princeton University Press, 2002), 114–117.

29. Petro, *Labor Policy of a Free Society*, 99.

30. Petro, *Power Unlimited,* 276. Petro nonetheless had harsh words for Communists; see 276–277.

31. Niels Bjerre Poulsen, *Right Face: Organizing the American Conservative Movement, 1945–65* (New York: Museum Tusculanum Press, 2002), 142–150; George J. Martin, *Fighting the Good Fight* (South Bend, Ind.: St. Augustine Press, 2002), 42.

32. Edward Chamberlin "Can Union Power Be Curbed?" *Atlantic Monthly,* June 1959, 46–50; Lemuel Boulware et al., *Monopoly Power as Exercised by Labor Unions: A*

Problem for Every Citizen (New York: National Association of Manufacturers, 1957); Donald Richberg, *Labor Monopoly: A Clear and Present Danger* (Chicago: Henry Regnery, 1957); Philip D. Bradley, Edward H. Chamberlin, Gerard D. Reilly, and Roscoe Pound, *Labor Unions and Public Policy* (Washington, D.C.: American Enterprise Institute, 1958).

33. Petro, *Labor Policy of a Free Society*, 241. This was a thread throughout his career; see his "The Economic-Power Syndrome," in Friedrich Hayek, Henry Hazzlit, Leonrad R. Read, Gustavo Velasco, and F.A. Harper, eds., *Toward Liberty: Essays in Honor of Ludwig von Mises on the Occasion of His 90th Birthday* (Menlo Park: Institute for Humane Studies, 1971).

34. See Petro, *Labor Policy of a Free Society*, 112–113, and *Power Unlimited*, 262–263. On Reuther and the Kohler strike, see *Power Unlimited*, 149; Sylvester Petro, *The Kohler Strike: Union Violence and Administrative Law* (Chicago: Henry Regnery, 1961).

35. Roger Reynolds to Henry Regnery, October 19, 1960, Henry Regnery Archives, box 60, folder 19, Hoover Institution. On the Kohler strike, see Phillips-Fein, *Invisible Hands*, 120, 126; "The Almost Sinful Strike: Four Years and Stubbornness Have Torn a Town," *Time*, March 17, 1958; available at http://www.time.com/time/magazine/article/0,9171,863137,00.html (last accessed October 2, 2011); "The Golden Handshake," *Time*, December 24, 1965, available at http://www.time.com/time/magazine/article/0,9171,834841,00.html (last accessed October 2, 2011).

36. Petro, *The Kohler Strike*; "Law Professor Says: No Justice for Kohler," *Lima (Ohio) News Sunday*, April 30, 1961, A6; "Reward the Guilty," *Barron's*, December 21, 1964, 1. On Senator Barry Goldwater's decision to investigate the Kohler dispute, see Phillips-Fein, *Invisible Hands*, 125–126.

37. Sylvester Petro, *How The NLRB Repealed Taft-Hartley* (Washington, D.C.: Labor Policy Association, 1958).

38. Petro, *Labor Policy of a Free Society*, 191

39. Felix Frankfurter and Nathan Greene, *The Labor Injunction* (New York: Macmillan, 1930).

40. *Commonwealth v. Hunt*, 4 Metcalf Reports III (1842), Massachusetts Historical Society, 122–129.

41. See Richard Pells, *The Liberal Mind in a Conservative Age: An Intellectual History of the 1940s and 1950s* (New York: Harper and Row, 1985), 141.

42. Stanton Evans, *Revolt on the Campus* (Chicago: Henry Regnery, 1961), 66–68.

43. Sylvester Petro to Regnery, June 20, 1961, box 60, folder 19, Henry Regnery Archives; Petro to Friedrich Hayek, May 10, 1965, box 43, folder 15, Friedrich Hayek Papers, Hoover Institution.

44. Petro believed that the main reason for the strike was not the workers' discontent—the union leaders mostly wanted to bridge the gap between working conditions and wages at Kingsport Press and those at the main competitors. Petro, *The Kingsport Strike*, 62–66.

45. Sylvester Petro, "Public Sector Bargaining: An Assessment," *Government Union Review*, 3:1 (Winter 1982), 30.

46. *Outstanding Young Men of America* (Montgomery, Ala.: Junior Chamber of Commerce, 1967), 57.

47. Stephen Wermiel and Gerald F. Seib, "With Bork Rejected, Reagan Pores over Lists to Pick Next High Court Nominee," *Wall Street Journal*, October 26, 1987, 1; Edward Walsh and Ruth Marcus, "Bork Rejected for High Court; Senate's 58-to-42 Vote Sets Record for Margin of Defeat," *Washington Post*, October 24, 1987, A1.

48. Vieira had a most unusual background, having received a Ph.D. in Chemistry from Harvard in 1969. See Edwin Vieira, Jr., "Tetrodotoxin: A Synthetic Approach" (Ph.D. diss., Harvard University, 1969).

49. See Jesse Helms, foreword to Ralph De Toledano, *Let Our Cities Burn* (New Rochelle, N.Y.: Arlington House, 1975), 8.

50. "Union Bosses Continue 'Labor' Takeover," *National Right to Work Newsletter*, April 25, 1973, 7.

51. "U.S. 'Mediation' Service Continues to Function as Union Organizing Tool," *National Right to Work Newsletter*, October 20, 1973, 7.

52. *Government Employee Relations Report*, June 25, 1973, B-2.

53. "Public Employees Warned of Forced Membership Drive," *National Right to Work Newsletter*, November 24, 1972, 5.

54. "Compulsory Unionism Number One Goal of Public Employee Union Bosses," *National Right to Work Newsletter*, March 26, 1973, 6–7.

55. "'Political Realists' Ignore Moral Issue," *National Right to Work Newsletter*, October 20, 1973, 7.

56. David Denholm interviewed by Joseph A. McCartin, Vienna, Virginia, January 28, 2004 (tape in possession of coauthor).

57. "Union Militants Eye Government Control," *National Right to Work Newsletter*, July 25, 1973, 5.

58. Benjamin Aaron et al., *Final Report and Proposed Statute of the California Assembly Advisory Council on Public Employee Relations, March 15, 1973* (Sacramento: California State Assembly, 1973), 198–205.

59. Denholm interview; [Public Service Research Council], *Public Sector Bargaining and Strikes* (Vienna, Va.: Public Service Research Council, 1974); quote from [Public Service Research Council], *Public Sector Bargaining and Strikes*, 6th ed. (Vienna, Va.: Public Service Research Council, 1982), 16.

60. Prior critiques of public sector unionism included Harry Wellington and Ralph K. Winter, "The Limits of Collective Bargaining in Public Employment," *Yale Law Journal* 78:7 (June 1969), 1107–1127.

61. Sylvester Petro, "Sovereignty and Compulsory Public Sector Bargaining," *Wake Forest Law Review*, 10 (March 1974): 25–165, quote on 165.

62. Ibid., 28.

63. *Proceedings of the Eleventh Constitutional Convention of the AFL-CIO* (Washington, D.C.: AFL-CIO, 1975), 489, 499; "Political Action, Bargaining Rights Are Key to Full Union Strength, Kirkland Tells AFGE," *Government Employee Relations Report*, November 3, 1975, A9.

64. The view of Ralph Flynn of AFSCME reported in "A Many-Sided Squeeze," *Time*, December 16, 1974, 31.

65. De Toledano, *Let Our Cities Burn*, 216.

66. Other prominent guests included Shelby Collum Davis, then U.S. ambassador to Switzerland; Richard DeMille, son of the famed film director Cecil B. DeMille; and a dozen members of Congress. "Right to Work Committee Marks its 20th Anniversary," *National Right to Work Newsletter*, May 28, 1975, 4.

67. Membership growth cited in "Letter from Reed Larson," *National Right to Work Newsletter*, July 28, 1975, 2.

68. *Congressional Record*, 94th Cong., 1st Sess., July 17, 1975, 23267–23274, quotes on 23268–23269.

69. The two cases were *Blue Boar Cafeteria Co. v. Hotel & Restaurant Employees & Bartenders International Union*, 254 S.W.2d 335; 1952 Ky.; and *Winston-Salem/Forsyth County Unit of North Carolina Assoc. of Educators v. Phillips*, 381 F. Supp. 644 (1974).

70. *Abood v. Detroit Board of Education*, 431 U.S. 209 (1977).

71. For a full account of the history of this case, see Joseph A. McCartin, "A Wagner Act for Public Employees: Labor's Deferred Dream and the Rise of Conservatism, 1970–76," *Journal of American History*, 95:1 (June 2008), 123–148.

72. Sylvester Petro, "Brief of the Public Service Research Council as Amicus Curiae, National League of Cities, et al., v. Hon. Peter J. Brennan," October Term 1974, 2.

73. Petro, "Brief of the Public Service Research Council," 4, 5, 12, 113, 22, 23, 32.

74. "FLSA Extension to State and Local Employees Re-argued Before United States Supreme Court," *Government Employee Relations Report*, March 8, 1976, B7–13; quotes from "National League of Cities v. Usery–Oral Reargument," audio file, *Oyez U.S. Supreme Court Media*, http://www.oyez.org/cases/1970–1979/1974/1974_74_878/reargument/ (Rampton at 13:20).

75. The Tenth Amendment reads: "The powers not delegated to the United States by the Constitution, nor prohibited by it to the States, are reserved to the States respectively, or to the people." U.S. Const., amend. X.

76. "The Revival of States Rights," *Washington Post*, July 2, 1976, A22; Stone quote from *United States v. Darby*, 312 U.S., 100, 124 (1941).

77. In *Garcia v. San Antonio Metropolitan Transit Authority et al.*, 469 U.S. 528, 531 (1985), 5–4 majority of the court substantially reversed key elements of *Usery*, admitting in effect that aspects of the 1976 decision had been "inconsistent with established principles of federalism." See 469 U.S. 531 (1985).

78. "Union Bosses Move Ahead with Efforts to Control Machinery of Government," *National Right to Work Newsletter*, April 25, 1973, 3. See also Russell Kirk,

"'Agency Shop' Threatens Academic Freedom," *National Right to Work Newsletter*, May 25, 1973, 3; "Key to Teacher Strikes Is Compulsory Unionism," *National Right to Work Newsletter*, October 29, 1973, 4.

79. For evidence of his early thinking about the irreconcilable incompatibility of public and private sectors, see Sylvester Petro, "Trade-Unionism and the 'Public Sector,'" in Helmut Schoeck and James W. Wiggins, eds., *The New Argument in Economics: The Public Versus the Private Sector* (Princeton, N.J.: Van Nostrand, 1963); and on the dangers of union "taxing power," see Sylvester Petro, "The External Significance of Internal Union Affairs," *Fourth Annual NYU Conference on Labor* (New York: New York University, 1951), 339.

80. The oral argument for the case is available at http://www.oyez.org/cases/1970–1979/1976/1976_75_1153/argument/ (Chief Justice Burger's rebuke at 1:02:30).

81. See http://www.oyez.org/cases/1970–1979/1976/1976_75_1153/argument/ (the Rehnquist-Petro colloquy on this begins at 17:08).

82. David H. Rosenbloom and Rosemary O'Leary, *Public Administration and Law: A Practical Handbook for Public Administrators*, 2nd ed. (New York: Marcel Dekker, 1997), 200–201.

83. *Communications Workers of America et al. v. Beck et al.*, 487 U.S. 735 (1988).

84. Statement before the press, August 3, 1981, 10:45 a.m., OA 10520, David Gergen Files, Ronald Reagan Presidential Library, Simi Valley, Calif.

85. Sylvester Petro, "Public Sector Bargaining: An Assessment," *Government Union Review* 3:1 (Winter 1982), 28.

86. Interestingly, Pasco Bowman played a key role in the impeachment of President Bill Clinton. His court cleared the way for Special Prosecutor Ken Starr's open-ended investigation and prosecution of Clinton. See Joe Conason and Gene Lyons, *Hunting the President: The Ten-Year Campaign to Destroy Bill and Hillary Clinton* (New York: Thomas Dunne Books, 2000), 216–218.

87. Howard Dickman, *Industrial Democracy in America: Ideological Origins of National Labor Relations Policy* (LaSalle, Ill.: Open Court, 1987).

Chapter 12. Wal-Mart, John Tate, and Their Anti-Union America

1. Sam Walton, "Keeping Our Partnership Strong," *Wal-Mart World*, October 1989, 3.

2. Author's interview with Larry English, June 7, 2006, Diamond Head, Ark.

3. Gilbert Gall, *The Politics of Right to Work: The Labor Federations as Special Interests, 1943–1979* (Westport, Conn.: Greenwood Press, 1988); Martin Halpern, *Unions, Radicals, and Democratic Presidents: Seeking Social Change in the Twentieth Century* (Westport, Conn.: Praeger, 2003), 147–176, a chapter entitled "Arkansas and the Defeat of Labor Law Reform in 1978 and 1994."

4. David Brody, *Labor Embattled: History, Power, Rights* (Urbana: University of Illinois Press, 2005), 143.

5. James Brudney, "Neutrality Agreements and Card Check Recognition: Prospects for Changing Paradigms," *Iowa Law Review*, 90 (2005), 868–873.

6. Sanford Jacoby, *Modern Manors: Welfare Capitalism Since the New Deal* (Princeton: Princeton University Press, 1998), 203; Eisenhower-era NLRB member quoted in "Statement of Albert Cummings Beeson," *Hearings, National Labor Relations Board*, U.S. Senate Committee on Labor and Public Welfare, 83rd Cong., 2nd Sess., 22.

7. Alan Story, "Employer Speech, Union Representation Elections, and the First Amendment," *Berkeley Journal of Employment and Labor Law*, 16 (1995), 451–462.

8. Steve Jordon, "Anti-Union Attorney Took 'Golden Rule' to Wal-Mart," *Omaha World-Herald*, May 5, 1991, 1M; Bob Ortega, *In Sam We Trust: The Untold Story of Sam Walton and How Wal-Mart Is Devouring America* (New York: Random House, 1998), 87–88.

9. Jordon, "Anti-Union Attorney."

10. "My Name is John Tate," before Federal Communications Commission hearing, Omaha, 1962, in box 219, folder, Midwest Employer's Council, Inc. (hereafter MEC folder), Group Research Collection, Rare Book and Manuscript Library, Butler Library, Columbia University.

11. "Excerpts from Mid-West Employers Council Bulletins, February 19, 1963," in MEC folder.

12. *Midwest Employer's Council Bulletin*, February 19, 1960, in MEC folder.

13. United Press International news clipping, Nebraska AFL-CIO Convention, September 26, 1963, in MEC folder.

14. See generally Thomas Geoghegan, *Which Side Are You On? Trying to Be for Labor When It's Flat on Its Back* (New York: Farrar, Straus and Giroux, 1991); Paul Weiler, *Governing the Workplace: The Future of Labor and Employment Law* (Cambridge: Harvard University Press, 1990); Kate Bronfenbrenner, "Raw Power: Plant-Closing Threats and the Threat to Union Organizing," *Multinational Monitor* 21 (December 2000), 24–30.

15. Author's telephone interview with Duane Acklie, Lincoln, Nebraska, May 29, 2007.

16. Speech transcript, dated June 1, 1959, in MEC folder.

17. Speech transcript for W. F. Hoppe Manufacturing Company, 1961, in MEC folder.

18. Kim Phillips-Fein, "Business Conservatives on the Shop Floor: Anti-union Campaigns in the 1950s," *LABOR: Studies in Working-Class History of the Americas*, 7 (Spring 2010), 20, 25.

19. Wal-Mart Stores, Inc. and Retail Store Employees' Union, Local No. 655, affiliated with Retail Clerks International Association, Case 14-CA-6721, 201 NLRB, No. 35, 250–254.

20. John Tate, 1992 Wal-Mart managers meeting, reel 121, Wal-Mart Archive, Flagler Productions, Lenexa, Kansas; Jennifer Steinhauer, "William F. Farah Dies at 78; Led Family Clothing Business," *New York Times*, March 12, 1998, D19.

21. Ortega, *In Sam We Trust*, 89–90.

22. Sam Walton with John Huey, *Made in America: My Story* (New York: Bantam Books, 1992), 165.

23. Jacob Hacker, *The Great Risk Shift* (New York: Oxford University Press, 2006), 116–121.

24. Interview with Acklie.

25. Jacoby, *Modern Manors*, 108–109.

26. Ortega, *In Sam We Trust*, 349.

27. Debbie Campbell, "Wal-Mart Associates Receive Largest Company Contribution Ever!" *Wal-Mart World*, April 1990, 17.

28. "Still the Darling of Wall Street," *Discount Store News*, June 15, 1992, 137.

29. Campbell, "Wal-Mart Associates Receive Largest Company Contribution Ever!" 18.

30. Ortega, *In Sam We Trust*, 106; author's telephone interview with Ronald Heath, Teamster organizer, Little Rock, Ark., August 22, 2006.

31. Vance Trimble, *Sam Walton: The Inside Story of America's Richest Man* (New York: Dutton, 1990), 230.

32. Ortega, *In Sam We Trust*, 107.

33. Ibid., 106; author's interview with Heath.

34. Walton quoted in Trimble, *Sam Walton*, 230.

35. Author's interview with Joe Bare, Little Rock, Ark., June 5, 2006.

36. M. C. Associates, "Wal-Mart's Expansion in Missouri: Past Strategies, Future Plans," prepared for UFCW Local 88, St. Louis, July 1989, in files of Food and Allied Service Trades Department, AFL-CIO, Washington, D.C. Until 1983, Missouri had more Wal-Mart stores than any other state.

37. Erin Johansson, *Wal-Mart: Rolling Back Workers' Wages, Rights, and the American Dream*, (Washington, D.C.: American Rights at Work, 2006), 15–16.

38. Anthony Bianco, *The Bully of Bentonville: How the High Cost of Wal-Mart's Everyday Low Prices Is Hurting America* (New York: Doubleday, 2006), 130; author's telephone interview with Al Zack, Washington, D.C., August 24, 2005.

39. John Logan, "The Union Avoidance Industry in the United States," *British Journal of Industrial Relations*, 44 (December 2006), 653–654.

40. Kris Maher, "Union's New Foe: Consultants," *Wall Street Journal*, August 15, 2005, A1.

41. Rick Fantasia and Kim Voss, *Remaking the American Labor Movement* (Berkeley: University of California Press, 2004), 34–77.

42. Wal-Mart, *A Manager's Toolbox to Remaining Union Free* (Bentonville, Ark.: Wal-Mart Stores, 1997), on file at Food and Allied Service Trades Department, AFL-CIO, Washington, D.C.

43. Orson Mason, "Labor Relations and You at the Wal-Mart Distribution Center, #6022," September 1992, on file at Food and Allied Service Trades Department, AFL-CIO.

44. Meeting notes from Eddie Lindsey to Don Harris (March 24, 2000), located in unprocessed files of the Impact Fund, Berkeley, Calif.

45. Wal-Mart, "You've Picked a Great Place to Work" (Bentonville, Ark.: Wal-Mart Stores), video in author's possession.

46. Jacoby, *Modern Manors*, 111–113; Logan, "The Union Avoidance Industry," 664.

47. "1998 Grass Roots Survey"; "History of Grass Roots," January 29, 2001; e-mail note, Katherine Ali to Al Zack, April 4, 2003, all in Impact Fund, files.

48. Zack to Roger Doolittle, December 11, 2003; Laura Pope to Tom Coughlin, "Wal-Mart Stores Grass Roots Results," May 7, 2001, both in Impact Fund files.

49. Christopher Hayes, "Symbol of the System," *In These Times*, November 6, 2005.

50. Wal-Mart, *A Manager's Toolbox*.

51. Conrad B. MacKerron (As You Sow Foundation), et al., to H. Lee Scott, March 20, 2006, letter in author's possession.

52. Human Rights Watch, *Discounting Rights: Wal-Mart's Violation of US Workers' Right to Freedom of Association* (Washington, D.C.: Human Rights Watch, 2007), 92.

53. Ibid., 145–168; author's telephone interview with Tony Kuc, assistant manager at Kingman, Ariz., Wal-Mart, August 31, 2007; Wal-Mart Stores, Inc. and UFCW Local Union 99R, February 28, 2003, Case 28-CA-16832, NLRB.

54. Human Rights Watch, *Discounting Rights*, 154; Vicky Dodson, voice-mail transcripts, September 1, 5, 2000, Exhibit 50, Case 28-CA-16832, NLRB.

55. Wal-Mart Stores, Inc. and UFCW Local Union 99R, supplemental decision, March 30, 2007, Case 28-CA-16832.

56. Before the NLRB, Region 11, Wal-Mart Stores, Inc. and UFCW, Case No. 11-CA-19105–1, hearing transcript, February 3, 2003, 459–461. Williams later quit Wal-Mart to become a labor relations executive for Honeywell.

57. Human Rights Watch, *Discounting Rights*, 146, 151; interview with Kuc.

58. Kirk Williams, voice-mail transcript, September 6, 2000; Human Rights Watch, *Discounting Rights*, 153.

59. As reported in "U.S. Newswire," November 2, 2000.

60. Human Rights Watch, *Discounting Rights*, 147, 152.

61. Dodson and Williams, voice-mail transcripts, September 6, 13, 25, 28, and October 2, 3, 7, 9, 11, 2000. The labor team made eighty-four reports to Bentonville, all within less than two months.

62. Wal-Mart Stores, Inc. 2003 NLRB Lexis 86 (2003).

63. Human Rights Watch, *Discounting Rights*, 203.

64. A portion of this speech is reported in Brian Ross, Maddy Sauer, and Rhonda Schwartz, "Clinton Remained Silent as Wal-Mart Fought Unions," transcript, *ABC*

News, January 31, 2008, http://abcnews.go.com. A more complete version is found in the Wal-Mart Archive housed at Flagler Productions.

Chapter 13. "All Deals Are Off"

I would like to thank Harry Arthurs, David Brody, James Brudney, Paul Clark, Cynthia Estlund, Fred Feinstein, Douglas Fraser, Julius Getman, John Godard, William Gould, Richard Hyman, Sanford Jacoby, Thomas Kochan, Nelson Lichtenstein, Wilma Liebman, Ray Marshall, Sara Slinn, George Strauss, and Paula Voos for reading previous versions of this essay.

1. Melanie Trottman, "Showdown Looms over 'Card Check' Union Drives," *Wall Street Journal,* November 29, 2008, A9.

2. John Logan, "Labor's Last Stand in National Politics? The Campaign for Striker Replacement Legislation, 1990–1994," in Bruce Kaufman and David Lewin, eds., *Advances in Industrial and Labor Relations,* 13 (Oxford: Elsevier JAI Press, 2004), 197–256.

3. John Logan, "The Clinton Administration and Labor Law: Was Comprehensive Reform Ever A Realistic Possibility?" *Journal of Labor Research* 28 (2007), 609–628; Robert Reich, *Locked in the Cabinet* (New York: Random House, 1998).

4. United States Department of Labor, "Brown and Reich Announce Worker-Management Commission," news release, March 24, 1993.

5. *Daily Labor Report,* "Task of Dunlop Panel to Meld Interests of Business, Labor," November 28, 1994, C-1.

6. David Silberman, Memo to Lane Kirkland, Thomas Donahue, James Baker, Charles McDonald and Laurence Gold, RE: Dunlop Commission Meeting, May 24, 1993, unprocessed, Legal Department, AFL-CIO Collection, George Meany Memorial Archives, National Labor College, Silver Spring, Md. Unless otherwise stated, all manuscript sources are from this collection.

7. John T. Dunlop, "Comments on S.245 and H.R.743: Teamwork for Employees and Managers Act," February 14, 1995.

8. On this point, see Nelson Lichtenstein, "Labor and the New Congress: A Strategy for Winning," *Dissent* (Spring 2007), 64–70.

9. Robert M. McGlotten, director, Department of Legislation, to members of Congress, July 18, 1994.

10. *Daily Labor Report,* "Task of Dunlop Panel," C-1.

11. Ron Carey, general president, International Brotherhood of Teamsters, to William H. Wynn, president, United Food and Commercial Workers, December 16, 1992.

12. John J. Sweeney, international president, Service Employees International Union, to Rich Trumka, AFL-CIO Labor Law Reform Committee, December 23, 1992.

13. Morris M. Kleiner, "What Will It Take? Establishing the Economic Costs to Management of Noncompliance with the NLRA," in Sheldon Friedman et al., eds.,

Restoring the Promise of American Labor Law (Ithaca: Cornell University Press, 1994), 137–146.

14. Unfair employer practices had increased in number from 9,067 per year in 1960 to 24,075 in 1990. During the same thirty-year period, union organizing activity had declined significantly. For a conservative critique of Weiler, see Robert J. LaLonde and Bernard D. Meltzer, "Hard Times for Unions: Another Look at the Significance of Employer Illegalities," *University of Chicago Law Review* 58 (Summer 1991), 953–1014.

15. Sweeney to Trumka, December 23, 1992.

16. *Daily Labor Report*, "AFL-CIO, Employers Spar over Reform of Labor Laws Before Dunlop Commission," September 9, 1994, C1.

17. Morris Kleiner, "Intensity of Management Resistance: Understanding the Decline of Unionization in the Private Sector," *Journal of Labor Research* 22 (Summer 2001), 519–540.

18. James Brudney, "Judicial Hostility Toward Labor Unions? Applying the Social Background Model to a Celebrated Concern," *Ohio State Law Journal* 60 (1999), 1675–1789.

19. Barry T. Hirsch and Edward Schumacher, "Private Sector Union Density and the Wage Premium: Past, Present, and Future," *Journal of Labor Research* 22 (Summer 2001), 433–457; Richard Freeman, "The Effect of Union Wage Differential on Management Opposition and Union Organizing Success," *American Economic Review* 78 (May 1986), 92–96; Richard Freeman and Morris Kleiner, "Employer Behavior in the Face of Union Organizing Drives," *Industrial and Labor Relations Review* 43:4 (April 1990), 351–365.

20. Sanford Jacoby, "American Exceptionalism Revisited: The Importance of Management," in Sanford Jacoby, ed., *Masters to Managers: Historical and Comparative Perspectives on American Employers* (New York: Columbia University Press, 1991); Robert J. Flanagan, "Macroeconomic Performance and Collective Bargaining: An International Perspective," *Journal of Economic Literature* 37 (September 1999), 1150–1175.

21. John Logan, "The Union Avoidance Industry in the United States," *British Journal of Industrial Relations* 44:4 (2006), 651–675; Bruce Kaufman and Paula Stephan, "The Role of Management Attorneys in Union Organizing Campaigns," *Journal of Labor Research* 16 (Fall 1995), 439–454.

22. Freeman and Kleiner, "Employer Behavior."

23. Sanford Jacoby, "Employee Representation and Corporate Governance: A Missing Link," *University of Pennsylvania Journal of Labor and Employment Law* 3:3 (2001), 449–489.

24. John Logan, "Consultants, Lawyers and the Union Free Movement in the United States Since the 1970s," *Industrial Relations Journal* 33:3 (2002), 197–214; John Logan, "Lifting the Veil on Anti-Union Campaigns: Employer and Consultant Reporting Under the LMRDA, 1959–2001," in Bruce Kaufman and David Lewin, eds., *Advances in Industrial and Labor Relations* 15 (Oxford: Elsevier JAI Press 2007), 295–

332; Samuel Estreicher, "Employee Voice in Competitive Markets," *American Prospect* 14 (Summer 1993), 48–57.

25. Statement of David M. Silberman, director, AFL-CIO Task Force on Labor Law, before the Commission on the Future of Worker-Management Relations, August 10, 1994; Thomas Kochan, "The Future of British Unions: A Perspective from the U.S.," in Howard Gospel and Stephen Wood, eds., *The Future of British Unions* (London: Routledge, 2003); George Strauss, "Is the New Deal System Collapsing? With What Might It Be Replaced?" *Industrial Relations* 34 (1995), 329–349.

26. Paula Voos and Lawrence Mishel, eds., *Unions and Economic Competitiveness* (Armonk, N.Y.:M.E. Sharpe, 1992); Richard Freeman, "Do Unions Make Enterprises Insolvent?" *Industrial and Labor Relations Review* 52 (July 1999), 510–527.

27. Statement of Silberman, August 10, 1994; AFL-CIO, *The New American Workplace: A Labor Perspective* (Washington, D.C.: AFL-CIO, 1994); Cynthia Estlund, "The Ossification of American Labor Law," *Columbia Law Review* 102 (2002), 1527–1612.

28. Statement of Richard Besinger, executive director, AFL-CIO Organizing Institute, before the Commission on the Future of Worker-Management Relations, August 10, 1994.

29. Commission on the Future of Worker-Management Relations, *Fact Finding Report Issued by the Commission on the Future of Worker-Management Relations*, June 2, 1994, Washington, D.C.; "A Soothing Report on Labor Relations," editorial, *New York Times*, June 7, 1994, 22.

30. Louis Uchitelle, "A Call for Easing Labor-Management Tension," *New York Times*, May 30, 1994, 33; *Daily Labor Report*, "Business Reaction to Dunlop Report Ranges from Mild Skepticism to Praise," June 3, 1994, AA-6.

31. Thomas Gibbons, "Labor Laws Should Reflect Reality," *Chicago Tribune*, June 30, 1994.

32. Steve Early, "Worker Abuse Is Documented; Now, Action," *Los Angeles Times*, June 14, 1994, 7.

33. Kirk Victor, "Try, Try Again," *National Journal*, July 9, 1994, 1624–1625.

34. Sweeney to Trumka; David P. Koppelman, International Union of Operating Engineers, to Lawrence J. Cohen, general counsel, Building and Construction Trades Department, AFL-CIO, May 17, 1993.

35. *Daily Labor Report*, "AFL-CIO, Employers Spar," C1; Joe Ward, "Worker-Management Panel Gets Earful in Louisville," *Louisville Courier-Journal*, September 23, 1993; *Daily Labor Report*, "Need for Ongoing Bargaining, Employee Training Stressed During Atlanta Hearing by Dunlop Panel," January 12, 1994, A-8; Kenneth L. Coss, international president, United Rubber Workers International Union, to Elmer Chatak, president, Industrial Union Department, AFL-CIO, December 10, 1992.

36. Statement of Andrew M. Kramer, appearing on behalf of "The Management Lawyers Working Group," before the Commission for the Future of Worker-Management Relations, September 8, 1994.

37. Electromation, Inc., 309 NLRB 990 (1992), enforced, 35 F.3d 1148 (7th Cir. 1994); 311 NLRB 893 (1993); *Daily Labor Report*, "*Electromation* Creates Risks for Employers Who Set Up Employee Participation Groups," May 26, 1993, AA-1.

38. Eileen Applebaum and Rose Batt, *The New American Workplace* (Ithaca: Cornell University Press, 1994), 152; Richard Freeman and Joel Rogers, *What Workers Want* (Ithaca: Cornell University Press, 1999); *Daily Labor Report*, "Dunlop Commission Told of Connection Between Participation, Competitiveness," June 22, 1993, C1.

39. Richard Freeman and Cheri Ostroff, *The Anatomy of Employee Involvement and Its Effects on Firms and Workers*, National Bureau of Economic Research Working Paper No. 8059, December 2000.

40. Hearing of the Dunlop Commission, September 8, 1994.

41. *Daily Labor Report*, "AFL-CIO, Employers Spar," C1; statement of Daniel V. Yager, assistant general counsel for Labor Policy Association, appearing on behalf of "The Working Group," before the Commission for the Future of Worker-Management Relations, January 19, 1994.

42. Testimony of David M. Silberman, director, AFL-CIO Task Force on Labor Law, before the Senate Committee on Labor and Human Resources on S. 295, February 9, 1995.

43. Statement of Silberman, August 10, 1994.

44. Freeman and Rogers, *What Workers Want*.

45. Testimony of Silberman, February 9, 1995. In support of 8(a)(2) reform, see Samuel Estreicher, "Employee Involvement and the 'Company Union' Prohibition: The Case for Partial Repeal of Section 8(a)(2) of the NLRA," *New York University Law Review* 69 (1994), 125.

46. Testimony of Silberman, February 9, 1995.

47. *Daily Labor Report*, "Need for Change to Labor Law Debated Before Dunlop Commission," December 16, 1994, A-15; *Daily Labor Report*, "Testimony on Employee Committees Highlights Dunlop Commission Hearing," January 6, 1994, A-12.

48. Statement of Howard V. Knicely before the Commission on the Future of Worker-Management Relations on behalf of the Labor Policy Association, September 8, 1994; statement of Steven M. Darien, vice president, human resources, Merck & Company, Inc. for the Labor Policy Association before the Commission on the Future of Worker-Management Relations, August 10, 1994.

49. Statement of Harold Coxson before the Industrial Relations Research Association, Washington, D.C. Chapter, Issues Forum, "The U.S. System of Workplace Representation: Is it Broken? How Should We Fix It?" November 10, 1993.

50. *Daily Labor Report*, "Academics Call for Consistent National Policy on Labor, Rather Than Strict Labor Law Reform," October 27, 1993, C-3.

51. Statement of the U.S. Chamber of Commerce by William A. Stone before the Commission on the Future of Worker-Management Relations, December 15, 1993.

52. Statement of National Federation of Independent Business on "Small Businesses and the Work Place," before the Commission on the Future of Worker-Management Relations, December 15, 1993; *Daily Labor Report*, "Need for Change in Labor Law Debated Before Dunlop Commission," December 16, 1993, A-15.

53. Logan, "Labor's Last Stand."

54. *Daily Labor Report*, "Dunlop Commission Findings Document Need for Comprehensive Reform, AFL-CIO Says," June 3, 2003, AA-4; J. Peter Nixon, Department of Public Policy, Memo to John J. Sweeney, Service Employees International Union, RE: Meeting of the Staff Group of the Collective Bargaining Forum, September 2, 1992.

55. Nelson Lichtenstein, *The Retail Revolution: How Wal-Mart Created a Brave New World of Business* (New York: Metropolitan Books, 2009); Bethany Morten, *To Serve God and Wal-Mart: The Making of Christian Free Enterprise* (Cambridge: Harvard University Press, 2009).

56. *Daily Labor Report*, "Task of Dunlop Panel," C-1.

57. Francis T. Coleman, executive director/counsel, Voice for the American Workplace, to LABNET Conference Participants (n.d.); *Voice for the American Workplace*, 1:2 (March 1994), 6.

58. *Daily Labor Report*, "Impact of Labor Law on Organizing Debated Before Labor-Management Panel," February 25, 1994, A-7.

59. A few academic studies have stressed declining employee desire for unionization, rather than heightened employer resistance, as a principal cause of union decline. See Henry Farber and Alan Krueger, "Union Membership in the United States: The Decline Continues," in Bruce Kaufman and Morris Kleiner, eds., *Employee Representation: Alternatives and Future Directions* (Industrial Relations Research Association, 1993); Henry Farber and Bruce Western, "Accounting for the Decline of Unions in the Private Sector," *Journal of Labor Research* 22 (Summer 2001), 459–485.

60. Statement of Edward B. Miller, counsel, Seyfarth, Shaw, Fairweather and Geraldson, before the Commission on the Future of Worker-Management Relations, September 8, 1994.

61. Statement of Joe Ivey, 1993 president, Associated Builders and Contractors, before the Commission on the Future of Worker-Management Relations, speaking for the merit shop, January 5, 1994.

62. Statement of Clifford J. Ehrlich, senior vice president, human resources, Marriott International, before the Commission for the Future of Worker/Management Relations, February 24, 1994; *Daily Labor Report*, "Impact of Labor Law," A-7.

63. *Daily Labor Report*, "Impact of Labor Law," A-7; *Daily Labor Report*, "Academics Call for Consistent National Labor Policy," C-3.

64. "Statement of William J. Kilberg," *Employee Relations Law Journal* 20:1 (Summer 1994), 17–28.

65. One exception was privately owned public spaces, such as shopping malls and public parking lots. Here, the commission recommended the reversal of the Supreme

Court's *Lechmere* decision (139 LRRM 2225). Commission on the Future of Worker-Management Relations, *Report and Recommendations*, January 1995, Washington, D.C., 23.

66. Kenneth Swinnerton and Howard Wial, "Is Job Stability Declining in the U.S. Economy?" *Industrial and Labor Relations Review* 48 (1995), 293–304.

67. Frank Swoboda, "Panel Urges Labor Law Changes," *Washington Post*, January 10, 1995.

68. "Dead on Arrival," *Industry Week*, February 6, 1995, 56.

69. "LPA Reacts to Dunlop Commission Report," Labor Policy Association, news release, January 9, 1995.

70. *Daily Labor Report*, "Labor, Business Both Critical of Dunlop Commission Report," January 10, 1995; Robert Verdisco and Morrison Cain, "Dunlop Report Holds Few Surprises," *Discount Merchandiser*, February 1995.

71. *Daily Labor Report*, "Labor, Business Both Critical."

72. *Daily Labor Report*, "Dunlop Panel Urges Clarification of Sec. 8(a)(2), Expedited Elections," January 10, 1995, AA1.

73. *Daily Labor Report*, "Labor, Business Both Critical."

74. Douglas Dority, international president, United Food and Commercial Workers, to Paul Allaire, chairman and CEO, Xerox Corporation, December 28, 1994; Dunlop, "Comments on S.245 and H.R.743."

75. Thomas Kochan, professor of management, Massachusetts Institute of Technology, letter to the editor, *Regulation: The Cato Review of Business and Government* 18:2 (1995).

Chapter 14. Is Democracy in the Cards?

1. Victor Kirk, Will Englund, and Ashley Johnson, "Where Obama Might Say 'No': Labor," *National Journal*, December 20, 2008, www.nationaljournal.com, accessed December 22, 2008.

2. This process is frequently referred to as "card check" or "majority sign-up."

3. It is important to note that the proposed bill does not eliminate the NLRB-regulated secret ballot election as a route to union certification; it simply allows workers to choose if they would like to use majority sign-up instead.

4. Most important for present purposes, in its decision in *Dana Corporation*, 351 NLRB 451 (2007), the NLRB modified the usual "recognition bar" that prohibits a decertification petition or rival union recognition petition for a "reasonable time" after a union is certified. The modified "recognition bar" that applies to cases of voluntary recognition of a labor organization does not bar a decertification petition or a petition by a rival union filed within forty-five days of the unit employees' receiving notice of the voluntary recognition. In fact, it requires employers to post notices in the workplace informing employees of their right to decertify.

5. Roger C. Hartley, "The Framework of Democracy in Union Government," *Catholic University Law Review* 13 (1982); Craig Becker, "Democracy in the Work-

place: Union Representation Elections and Federal Labor Law," *Minnesota Law Review* 77 (1993); Nelson Lichtenstein and Howell John Harris, eds., *Industrial Democracy in America: The Ambiguous Promise*, Woodrow Wilson Center Series (Washington, D.C. and Cambridge: Woodrow Wilson Center Press and Cambridge University Press, 1993); Joseph A. McCartin, *Labor's Great War: The Struggle for Industrial Democracy and the Origins of Modern American Labor Relations, 1912–21* (Chapel Hill: University of North Carolina Press, 1997); Reuel Schiller, "Group Rights to Individual Liberties: Post-War Labor Law, Liberalism, and the Waning of Union Strength," *Berkeley Journal of Employment and Labor Law* 20 (1999).

6. Paul Weiler, "Promises to Keep: Securing Workers' Rights to Self Organize under the NLRA," *Harvard Law Review* 96 (1983); Becker, "Democracy in the Workplace"; Gordon Lafer, "What's More Democratic Than a Secret Ballot? The Case for Majority Sign-Up," *Working USA: The Journal of Labor and Society* 11 (2008); David Cingranelli, "International Elections Standards and NLRB Representation Elections," in *Justice on the Job: Perspectives on the Erosion of Collective Bargaining in the United States*, ed. Richard Block et al. (Kalamazoo, Mich.: W. E. Upjohn Institute, 2006).

7. Gordon Lafer, "Free and Fair? How Labor Law Fails U.S. Democratic Election Standards," *American Rights* (2005), http://www.americanrightsatwork.org/, accessed June 20, 2010.

8. A selection of the group's advertisements is available at http://www.unionfacts.-com/ads/laborElections2.cfm.

9. These ads can be viewed at www.myprivate.com. National Public Radio also provides descriptions and links to these ads as part of its *"Secret Money" Project Blog* at http://www.npr.org/blogs/secretmoney/outside_groups/employee_freedom_action_commit.

10. George McGovern, op-ed., "My Party Should Respect Secret Union Ballots," *Wall Street Journal*, August 8, 2008.

11. Qtd. in Brendan Sasso, "McGovern Joins Business Groups' Push to Defeat Labor-Backed 'Card Check' Bill," *The Hill Online*, 2008, http://thehill.com/business—lobby/mcgovern-joins-business-groups-push-to-defeat-labor-backed-card-check-bill-2008-10-07.html, accessed December 12, 2008.

12. This advertisement is available at http://www.myprivateballot.com/.

13. The advertisement can be viewed at the website of Americans for Job Security, http://www.savejobs.org/mediacenter.php.

14. The op-ed can be accessed at Representative Boehner's leadership website: http://republicanleader.house.gov/news/DocumentSingle.aspx?DocumentID = 110818.

15. Peter H. Stone, "Epic Battle Taking Shape over 'Card-Check,'" *National Journal*, November 22, 2008b, www.national journal.com, accessed November 23, 2008.

16. Qtd. in Steven Greenhouse, "After Push for Obama, Unions Seek New Rules," *New York Times*, November 9, 2008.

17. Qtd. in ibid.

18. A transcript of the speech is available at *Politico*, http://www.politico.com/livepulse/0110/Trumka_warns_Dems_not_to_take_workers_for_granted.html. An online video of the speech is available at the National Press Club website, http://press.org/.

19. Qtd. in "Labor Group Counters Anti-union TV Ads," *Northwest Labor Press*, September 19, 2008.

20. The full interview is available at Bloggingheads TV, http://bloggingheads.tv/diavlogs/16661?in = 07:25&out = 12:04.

21. Robert Nozick, *The Nature of Rationality* (Princeton: Princeton University Press, 1993). For purposes of my argument, I will treat "democracy" as a principle; though others may argue it is a concept, the differences are superficial insofar as they relate to the point I wish to make.

22. Ibid., 6.

23. The way in which I refer to the "principle(s) of democracy" may seem to imply that I believe there is some fixed definition or meaning to the term. In fact, I do not. I actually doubt that there is any consensus regarding precisely what the concept of democracy entails. In the next section, I outline the concerns I have with the way in which opponents of the Employee Free Choice Act use the principle and offer some alternatives.

24. John Cowley, "Uses and Abuses of the Secret Ballot in the American Age of Reform," in *The Hidden History of the Secret Ballot*, ed. Roman Bertrand, Jean-Louis Briquet, and Peter Pels (Bloomington: Indiana University Press, 2006).

25. McCartin, *Labor's Great War*.

26. David Brody, *Labor Embattled: History, Power, Rights* (Urbana: University of Illinois Press, 2005), 99–109 and 149–156; Becker, "Democracy in the Workplace."

27. The cases in which the NLRB adopted this new standard are Cudahy Packing Co. 13 NLRB 526 (1939), a case in which two unions were competing to represent workers, and Armour & Co. 13. NLRB 567 (1939), a case that extended the standard to situations where only one union sought certification. Becker, "Democracy in the Workplace," 501–515, provides a detailed account of the evolution of the election standard, as does Brody, *Labor Embattled*, 99–109.

28. Qtd. in Becker, "Democracy in the Workplace," 512.

29. Brody, *Labor Embattled*, 99–109 and 149–156.

30. See Becker, "Democracy in the Workplace," 528–531, for the legislative history.

31. Weiler, "Promises to Keep," 1812–1814.

32. Referenda and citizen initiatives are exceptions.

33. Becker, "Democracy in the Workplace," 533.

34. Martin Levitt, *Confessions of a Union Buster* (New York: Random House, 1993), provides accounts of employers' use of delay tactics in certification proceedings.

35. American Tube Bending Co. 44 NLRB 121, 133–134 (1942).

36. In *NLRB v. Virginia Electric & Power Co.* (1941), the Supreme Court had ruled—prior to the Taft-Hartley Amendments—that *noncoercive* employer speech was protected by the First Amendment and therefore could not be judged to violate the Wagner Act. Whether this changed NLRB policy with regard to employer speech is questionable (see Becker, "Democracy in the Workplace," n. 218).

37. General Shoe Corp. 77 NLRB 124 (1948).

38. For a detailed account of the evolution of the doctrine, see Shawn Larson Bright, "Free Speech and the NLRB's Laboratory Conditions Doctrine," *New York University Law Review* 112 (2002), who argues that the standard unfairly restricts employer speech in violation of the First Amendment and against congressional intent. For opposing views, see Kate Andrias, "A Robust Public Debate: Realizing Free Speech in Workplace Representation Elections," *Yale Law Review* 112 (2002), 2415; Alan Story, "Employer Speech, Union Representation Elections, and the First Amendment," *Berkeley Journal of Employment and. Labor Law* 16 (1995).

39. See Becker, "Democracy in the Workplace," 557–561, for an outline of relevant cases.

40. Qtd. in Story, "Employer Speech," 361. The case, *Thomas v. Collins*, 323 U.S. 516 (1945), was actually brought to challenge the conviction of a union organizer who made a speech encouraging workers to organize without registering as a union organizer in the state. The case challenges the Texas state law that required union organizers to register as a violation of First Amendment speech rights. The decision was a victory for the union organizer, but at the same time language in the decision implied employer speech in union certification elections had First Amendment protection.

41. Qtd. in Andrias, "A Robust Public Debate," 2435.

42. *National Labor Relations Board v. Gissel Packing Co., Inc.,* U.S. (1969).

43. In response to the power inequity, Becker suggests a return to the view that union representations elections are matters of workers' self-organization, not contests between unions and employers. Thus, he advocates the denial of employers' "party" status in proceedings related to the certification process so that they cannot use these proceedings to delay and disrupt the election process. See Becker, "Democracy in the Workplace."

44. Ibid., 535.

45. Lafer, "What's More Democratic Than a Secret Ballot?"

46. Qtd. in Amy Guttman and Dennis Thompson, *Democracy and Disagreement* (Cambridge: Harvard University Press, 1996), 114.

47. Ian Shapiro, *The State of Democratic Theory* (Princeton: Princeton University Press, 2003), 1.

48. John Dewey, *The Public and Its Problems* (1927; rpt., Athens, Ohio: Swallow Press, 1954), 143.

49. Bernard Manin, *The Principles of Representative Government* (Cambridge: Cambridge University Press, 1997) 191; Nadia Urbanati, *Representative Government: Principles and Genealogy* (Chicago: University of Chicago Press, 2006).

50. James Johnson, "Political Parties and Deliberative Democracy?" in *Handbook of Party Politics*, ed. William J. Crotty and Richard Katz (New York: Sage, 2006), 49.

51. James Madison, Alexander Hamilton, and John Jay, *The Federalist Papers*, ed. Isaac Kramnick (1788; rpt., New York: Penguin Books, 1987), 126.

52. Dewey, *The Public and Its Problems*, 207.

53. See, for example, Manin, *The Principles of Representative Government*. See also Urbanati, *Representative Government*.

54. Cowley, "Uses and Abuses of the Secret Ballot." The term *secret ballot* in the United States actually refers largely to what is deemed the Australian ballot. This means not only that votes are cast in private at neutral polling places but also that ballots are printed at public expense.

55. Ibid. See also Andreas Teuber, "Elections of Yore," *New York Times*, November 4, 1980.

56. John Stuart Mill, *Considerations on Representative Government* (1861; rpt., Amherst, N.Y.: Prometheus Books, 1991), 211.

57. Thomas Schelling, *The Strategy of Conflict* (1960; rpt., Cambridge: Harvard University Press, 1980), 19.

58. I use the term *threat*, although employers—with assistance from their consultants—are unlikely to explicitly make threats, as they are "unfair labor practices" prohibited by the NLRB. What they do make are carefully couched predictions that from an employee's position are indistinguishable from threats; thus I use the term *threat* without qualification in this section.

59. For detailed accounts of employer tactics, see Kate Bronfenbrenner, "The Role of Union Strategies in NLRB Certification Elections," *Industrial and Labor Relations Review* 50:2 (1997): 195–212; Kate Bronfenbrenner, "Uneasy Terrain: The Impact of Capital Mobility on Workers, Wages, and Union Organizing," for the U.S. Trade Deficit Review Commission, 2000; Kate Bronfenbrenner, "No Holds Barred: The Intensification of Employer Opposition to Organizing," Economic Policy Institute Briefing Paper No. 235, May 20, 2009; Adrienne E. Eaton and Jill Kriesky, "NLRB Elections vs. Card Check Campaigns: Results of a Worker Survey," *Industrial and Labor Relations Review* 62 (2008); Adrienne E. Eaton and Jill Kriesky, "Union Organizing Under Neutrality and Card Check Agreements," *Industrial and Labor Relations Review* 55 (2001); Chirag Mehta and Nik Theodore, "Undermining the Right to Organize: Employer Behavior During Union Representation Campaigns," report for American Rights at Work, 2005, http://araw.org/resources/studies.cfm; John Logan, "Consultants, Lawyers, and the 'Union Free' Movement in the USA Since the 1970's," *Industrial Relations Journal* 33 (2002); Levitt, *Confessions of a Union Buster*.

60. The latest figures are from Bronfenbrenner, "No Holds Barred." Earlier data documents employer threats to close plants at 52 percent (Bronfenbrenner and Hickey, "Changing to Organize: A National Assessment of Union Organizing Strategies." In *Rebuilding Labor: Organizing and Organizers in the New Union Movement*, ed. R. Milkman and K. Voss (Ithaca, N.Y.: Cornell University Press, [2004]); 50 percent

(Bronfenbrenner, "Role of Union Strategies"); 49 percent (Mehta and Theodore, "Undermining the Right to Organize"); and 29 percent (Bronfenbrenner, "Employer Behavior in Certification Elections and First-Contract Campaigns: Implications for Labor Law Reform"). In *Restoring the Promise of American Labor Law*, ed. Sheldon Friedman et al. (Ithaca, N.Y.: ILR Press [1994]).

61. This is not an exhaustive list of union avoidance strategies; Logan, "Consultants, Lawyers," and Levitt, *Confessions of a Union Buster*, provide comprehensive accounts.

62. The number of campaigns in which employers suggested they would improve working conditions range from 46 percent (Bronfenbrenner, "No Holds Barred") to 59 percent (Mehta and Theodore, "Undermining the Right to Organize"). Other studies generate similar findings: 48 percent (Bronfenbrenner and Hickey, "Changing to Organize"); 64 percent (Bronfenbrenner, "Role of Union Strategies"); and 56 percent (Bronfenbrenner, "Employer Behavior in Certification Elections").

63. See Bonfrenbrenner, "Uneasy Terrain" and "No Holds Barred"; Mehta and Theodore, "Undermining the Right to Organize."

64. While dismissal threats are leveled at individuals, they are quite plausibly characterized as group threats. The purpose of firing key organizers is to dampen the general enthusiasm for the union. As it is unpredictable whether, and indeed which, employees involved in organizing the union may be fired, the credible possibility of losing one's job would deter many workers from becoming union organizers. While dismissal for union organizing is unlawful, the route to reinstatement for workers illegally fired is a long process administered by the NLRB. The maximum compensation workers can claim is back pay less any wages they have earned in the interim. This would be increased if the Employee Free Choice Act passes. However, the current sanctions for dismissing workers for union organizing are insufficient to deter employers resistant to unions. As Paul Weiler points out, even if the compensation for the individual who was illegally fired for union organizing were adequate, this would in no way repair the damage inflicted on the group of workers trying to form a union as the chilling effect of the firing erodes support generally ("Promises to Keep," 1769).

65. Bronfenbrenner, "No Holds Barred," reports 5 percent of discharged organizers were reinstated before the election. Earlier studies documented 3 percent (Bronfenbrenner and Hickey, "Changing to Organize"); 11 percent (Bronfrenbrenner, "Role of Union Strategies"); and 12 percent (Bronfenbrenner, "Employer Behavior in Certification Elections").

66. The percentage of campaigns in which employers use this tactic has varied across studies from 77 percent (Bronfenbrenner, "No Hold Barred") to 91 percent (Mehta and Theodore, "Undermining the Right to Organize"). Other studies generate similar findings: 78 percent (Bronfenbrenner and Hickey, "Changing to Organize"); 82 percent (Bronfenbrenner, "Role of Union Strategies"); and 79 percent (Bronfenbrenner, "Employer Behavior in Certification Elections").

67. The Landrum-Griffin Act mandated that unions hold regular secret ballot elections for some union representatives, primarily on the local level. However, in many unions, higher level officials are elected by delegates who have been elected by members. Thus they are one step removed from the accountability of the rank and file. It is debatable whether these requirements and practices are sufficient to allow union members to control the union and ensure accountability.

68. Lafer, "What's More Democratic Than a Secret Ballot?" 96. This vast inequity in reported intimidation cannot be explained by the lower incidence of majority sign-up campaigns, although the disparity may be somewhat mitigated by this fact.

69. Eaton and Kriesky, "NLRB Elections vs. Card Check Campaigns," 22.

70. Jim Bohman, "The Coming of Age of Deliberative Democracy," *Journal of Political Philosophy* 6 (2002); Jane Mansbridge et al., "The Place of Self-Interest and the Role of Power in Deliberative Democracy," *Journal of Political Philosophy* 18 (2010).

71. Mansbridge et al., "The Place of Self-Interest," 66.

72. See Jon Elster, "Deliberation and Constitution Making," in *Deliberative Democracy*, ed. Jon Elster (Cambridge: Cambridge University Press, 1998); Simone Chambers, "Behind Closed Doors: Publicity, Secrecy, and the Quality of Deliberation," *Journal of Political Philosophy* 12 (2004).

73. For a full discussion of the current legal framework concerning captive audience meetings, see Elizabeth J. Masson, "'Captive Audience' Meetings in Union Organizing Campaigns: Free Speech or Unfair Advantage?" *Hastings Law Journal* 56: (2004). For a more complete accounting of the regulation governing communications in representation campaigns, see Andrias, "Robust Public Debate"; from an opposing perspective, see Larson-Bright, "Free Speech." Lafer, "Free and Fair?" provides an account of how speech rights in union certification elections differ from those in American political elections.

74. Eaton and Kriesky, "NLRB Elections vs. Card Check Campaigns," and "Union Organizing."

Contributors

Kyle Bruce is a Senior Lecturer in Management at the Graduate School of Management, Macquarie University, Australia. He has published on the historiography of scientific management and human relations, institutional theory in economics, organization studies, and international business, U.S. interwar business history, the history of U.S. economic and management thought, and evolutionary economics, strategy, and the theory of the firm.

Andrew Wender Cohen is an associate professor of history at Syracuse University's Maxwell School of Citizenship and Public Affairs. He is currently completing a book entitled, *Contraband: Smuggling and the Birth of the American Century*. Cohen's first book was *The Racketeer's Progress: Chicago and the Struggle for the Modern American Economy, 1900–1940* (2004, paperback 2010).

Tami J. Friedman is an associate professor of history at Brock University in St. Catharines, Ontario. Her article "Exploiting the North-South Differential: Corporate Power, Southern Politics, and the Decline of Organized Labor After World War II" received the 2009 Organization of American Historians Binkley-Stephenson Award. She is completing a book on the causes and consequences of postwar capital migration in the U.S. carpet industry.

Alexander Gourse is a Ph.D. candidate in the history department at Northwestern University. He is writing a dissertation about how the emergence of public interest lawyers as major actors in California politics influenced the Reagan administration's attempts to reform the legal system.

Sophia Z. Lee is an assistant professor at the University of Pennsylvania Law School. She has written about administrative agencies' role in shaping constitutional law; civil rights and labor advocates' challenges to workplace discrimination during the early Cold War; and conservative legal movements in the post–New Deal era. She is currently completing a history of the workplace Constitution from the 1930s to the 1980s.

Nelson Lichtenstein is the MacArthur Foundation Chair in History and director of the Center for the Study of Work, Labor, and Democracy at the University of California, Santa Barbara. He is the author of *Labor's War at Home: The CIO in World War II*, *Walter Reuther: The Most Dangerous Man in Detroit*, *State of the Union: A Century of American Labor*, and *The Retail Revolution: How Wal-Mart Created a Brave New World of Business*.

John Logan is an associate professor and the director of labor studies at San Francisco State University. He is an expert on the anti-union industry and anti-union legislation in the United States, and comparative labor issues, particularly how multinational companies treat employees and unions differently in the U.S. compared to European countries.

Joseph A. McCartin is an associate professor of history and executive director of the Kalmanovitz Initiative for Labor and the Working Poor at Georgetown University. He is the author of *Labor's Great War: The Struggle for Industrial Democracy and the Origins of Modern American Labor Relations*, and, most recently, *Collision Course: Ronald Reagan, the Air Traffic Controllers, and the Strike That Changed America*.

Christopher Nehls received his Ph.D. in U.S. history from the University of Virginia in 2007. He has held a number of teaching positions, most recently at Providence College. He lives in Washington, D.C.

Chris Nyland is a Professor of International Business at Monash University, Australia. This revisionist scholar of the historiography of scientific management has also explored how economic, social, and business phenomena associated with globalization have impacted on human security and how local, national, and global agents seek to optimize the level of well-being experienced by individuals confronted by increased market openness.

Susan Orr is an assistant professor of political science at the College at Brockport, SUNY. Her research focuses on how ideas about democracy shape and constrain the formation and operation of American labor unions and, in turn, how American unions influence the nation's democracy.

Michael Pierce is an associate professor of History at the University of Arkansas and the author of *Striking with the Ballot: Ohio Labor and the Populist Party*. His essays have appeared in *Labor History, Agricultural History*, the *Arkansas Historical Quarterly* and various edited volumes. He serves as associate editor of the *Arkansas Historical Quarterly*.

Reuel Schiller is a Professor of Law at the University of California, Hastings College of the Law. He has written numerous articles on twentieth-century American legal history, with a particular focus on the history of administrative law, and of labor and employment law. He is currently writing a book, entitled *Forging Rivals: Race, Class, and the Fate of Postwar Liberalism* that will be published by Cambridge University Press.

Elizabeth Tandy Shermer has published widely on the intersecting histories of labor, business, capitalism, and conservatism, topics covered in her first book, *Creating the Sunbelt: Phoenix and the Political Economy of Metropolitan Growth*. She was the Paul Mellon Fellow of American History at the University of Cambridge and is now an assistant professor of history at Loyola University Chicago.

Jean-Christian Vinel teaches twentieth-century labor and political history at the Université Paris-Diderot (Paris 7). He is at work on a book on the history of the legal construction of workers, tentatively entitled *Travails of the Worker: The Social and Political History of the "Employee" in America, 1892–2006*.

David Witwer is an associate professor of History and American Studies at Penn State Harrisburg. He is the author of *Corruption and Reform in the Teamsters Union* (2003) and *Shadow of the Racketeer: Scandal in Organized Labor* (2009). Currently he is a resident fellow at the Institute of Arts and Humanities at Penn State University.

Index

National War Labor Board (NWLB), 81, 116, 119
Nebraska, 32, 164, 166, 256–57, 261
Nevada, 117, 127; right-to-work battle in, 115, 122, 123, 125–26, 128, 130, 352–53n33
New Deal, 29–30, 69, 81, 84, 118, 169–70, 184–85
New Mexico, 115, 117, 118; right-to-work election in, 122–24, 127–29
Newsweek, 207–10
New York City, 32, 245
New York Conservative Party, 235, 239
New York Mirror, 210
New York state, 235; and capital flight, 83, 90, 92
New York Times, 179, 199, 222, 283, 300
New York University, 230–31
Nixon, Jim, 177–79
NLRB elections, 205, 257, 266–67, 291, 303; employers' intervention in, 262–63, 266, 305, 316–17; secret ballot in, 297–300, 302–4, 308, 310, 311, 313–17, 319; Taft-Hartley Act and, 303, 305; unions' dissatisfaction with, 284, 297; unions' loss of most, 291, 294, 297; at Wal-Mart, 262–64
NLRB v. Gissel Packing Co. (1969), 307–8
North American Free Trade Agreement (NAFTA), 16, 24, 25
Nozick, Robert, 302

Oakland General Strike (1946), 118
Obama, Barack, 1, 251, 300, 308; and Employee Free Choice Act, 296
O'Connor, Ellen, 43–45, 55
Oklahoma, 167, 170
Open shop, 53–54, 91, 119. *See also* right-to-work campaigns
Organized Labor and Production (Cooke and Murray), 49, 71, 73
Ortega, Bob, 263
Owsley, Alvin, 28

Pacific Research Institute, 8
Page, Leonard, 265–66
Palmer, Kyle, 143–44
PATCO strike (1981), 204, 250–51, 262
Pegler, Westbrook, 4, 105, 229; on union corruption, 125, 214, 215, 217–20
Pennsylvania, 19, 245, 264

Pension plans, 81, 204, 260–61
Percy, Charles, 198
Permanent replacement workers, 277, 289
Permanent Subcommittee on Investigation (PSI), 211–12, 217, 222
Person, Harlow, 49–52, 55, 63
Petro, Sylvester, 204, 226–27, 231–34, 241, 250–51; background of, 228–29; on "compulsory unionism," 204, 229, 232, 234, 236–39, 244, 249, 250; influences on, 229–30, 234–36, 382n12; influence wielded by, 239–40, 243–48, 250; on NLRB, 183, 226, 238; on public-sector unionism, 204, 241–51; on strikes, 234, 236–38, 240
Phares, W. A., 30–31
Phillips, Kevin, 135
Phillips-Fein, Kim, 4, 231, 258–59
Phoenix, Ariz., 117–19, 124, 132
Poll tax, 100, 101, 104–8, 112
Popper, Karl, 234
Portland Oregonian, 216, 217, 223
Potts, Herbert L. "Jack," 88–89
Pound, Roscoe, 229, 373n39
Powell, Lewis, 247
Pozusek, Edward, 207; construction site of, 207, 217–19, 221, 224
Pray, W. A., 124
Private Soldiers and Sailors' Legion (World War Veterans), 32
Professional Air Traffic Controllers' Organization. *See* PATCO strike
Profit-sharing plans, 258, 260–62
Progressive Era reforms, 169, 184, 230
Progressivism, 184, 235; American Legion and, 28–29, 34; Taylorists and, 45
Property rights, 233, 239
"Prophecy doctrine," 255
Proposition 18 (California, 1958), 142, 145–49; black voters and, 134, 139–41, 149–59, 360n84; defeat of, 135, 144, 158; impetus for, 142–43; party politics and, 135, 142–45, 159
Protectionism, 16–24; recent negative connotations of, 11, 15–16, 24–25
Public sector unions, 3, 240, 245, 295; Congress and: *see* National Public Employee Relations Act; National Right to Work Committee and, 171, 241–43, 245, 248; strikes by, 245, 247; Supreme Court

Acknowledgments

This book had its origins at a University of California, Santa Barbara conference held in January 2009. Sponsored by the UCSB Center for the Study of Work, Labor, and Democracy, the conference was occasioned by the possibility of labor law reform during the Obama administration as well as by the intense opposition which was already well mobilized against the unions and the legislation they sought. Among the participants were dozens of scholars who looked at these issues from both an historical and contemporary vantage point as well as from such disciplinary perspectives as law, political science, sociology, history, business administration, and public policy.

Financial support for the conference came from the UCLA Institute for Labor and Employment, the College of Arts and Sciences, Department of History, Hull Chair of Feminist Studies, and the Interdisciplinary Humanities Center at UCSB, and the University of Pennsylvania Press.

Among the participants were John Borsos, David Brody, Jennifer Brooks, Kyle Bruce, Edward Canedo, Shannon Clark, Andrew Cohen, Patricia Cooper, Jefferson Cowie, Anthony De Stafanis, Melvyn Dubofsky, Steve Early, Fred Feinstein, Catherine Fisk, Tami Friedman, Mary Furner, Alexander Gourse, Todd Holmes, Michael Honey, Sanford Jacoby, Dolores Janiewski, Gordon Lafer, Nelson Lichtenstein, Lizzie Lamoree, Sophia Lee, John Logan, Jennifer Luff, Jeffry Manuel, Joseph McCartin, Christopher Nehls, Alice O'Connor, Susan Orr, Michael Pierce, Lisa Phillips, Jonathan Rees, Larry Richards, Reuel Schiller, Elizabeth Shermer, Judith Stein, Chris Tilly, Jean-Christian Vinel, David Witwer, and Clyde Woods.

In addition we want to extend thanks to Bruce Laurie, who offered us guidance in turning a collection of essays into a much more coherent book, and to Robert Lockhart of the University of Pennsylvania Press, whose enthusiasm for this project never flagged. Copyeditor Robert Milks and production editor Noreen O'Connor-Abel helped get the manuscript in final form.